Mirion Malle is also the author of *The League of Super Feminists*

Entire contents copyright © 2021, 2022 Mirion Malle. Translation copyright © 2021, 2022 Aleshia Jensen and Bronwyn Haslam. All rights reserved. No part of this book (except small portions for review purposes) may be reproduced in any form without written permission from Mirion Malle or Drawn & Quarterly. Originally published by © 2020 éditions La ville brûle (France)—lavillebrule.com through BOOKSAGENT (France)—www.booksagent.fr.

drawnandquarterly.com

ISBN 978-1-77046-461-2 | First edition: October 2021; Second edition: October 2022 | Printed in China | 10 9 8 7 6 5 4 3 2

Cataloguing data available from Library and Archives Canada

Published in the USA by Drawn & Quarterly, a client publisher of Farrar, Straus and Giroux; published in Canada by Drawn & Quarterly, a client publisher of Raincoast Books; published in the United Kingdom by Drawn & Quarterly, a client publisher of Publishers Group UK

Drawn & Quarterly acknowledges the support of the Government of Canada and the Canada Council for the Arts for our publishing program, and the National Translation Program for Book Publishing, an initiative of the Roadmap for Canada's Official Languages 2013–2019: Education, Immigration, Communities, for our translation activities.

Canada

Drawn & Quarterly reconnaît l'aide financière du gouvernement du Québec par l'entremise de la Société de développement des entreprises culturelles (SODEC) pour nos activités d'édition. Gouvernement du Québec—Programme de crédit d'impôt pour l'édition de livres—Gestion SODEC.

MIRION MALLE

this is how i disappear

Translated by Aleshia Jensen
and Bronwyn Haslam

Drawn & Quarterly

A bad dream.
To the person in the bell jar,
blank and stopped as a dead baby,
the world itself is the bad dream.
A bad dream.
I remembered everything.

—Sylvia Plath, *The Bell Jar*

Hm.

The first time I felt
like I wanted to die, I
was probably, like, twelve?
But that time doesn't
really count.

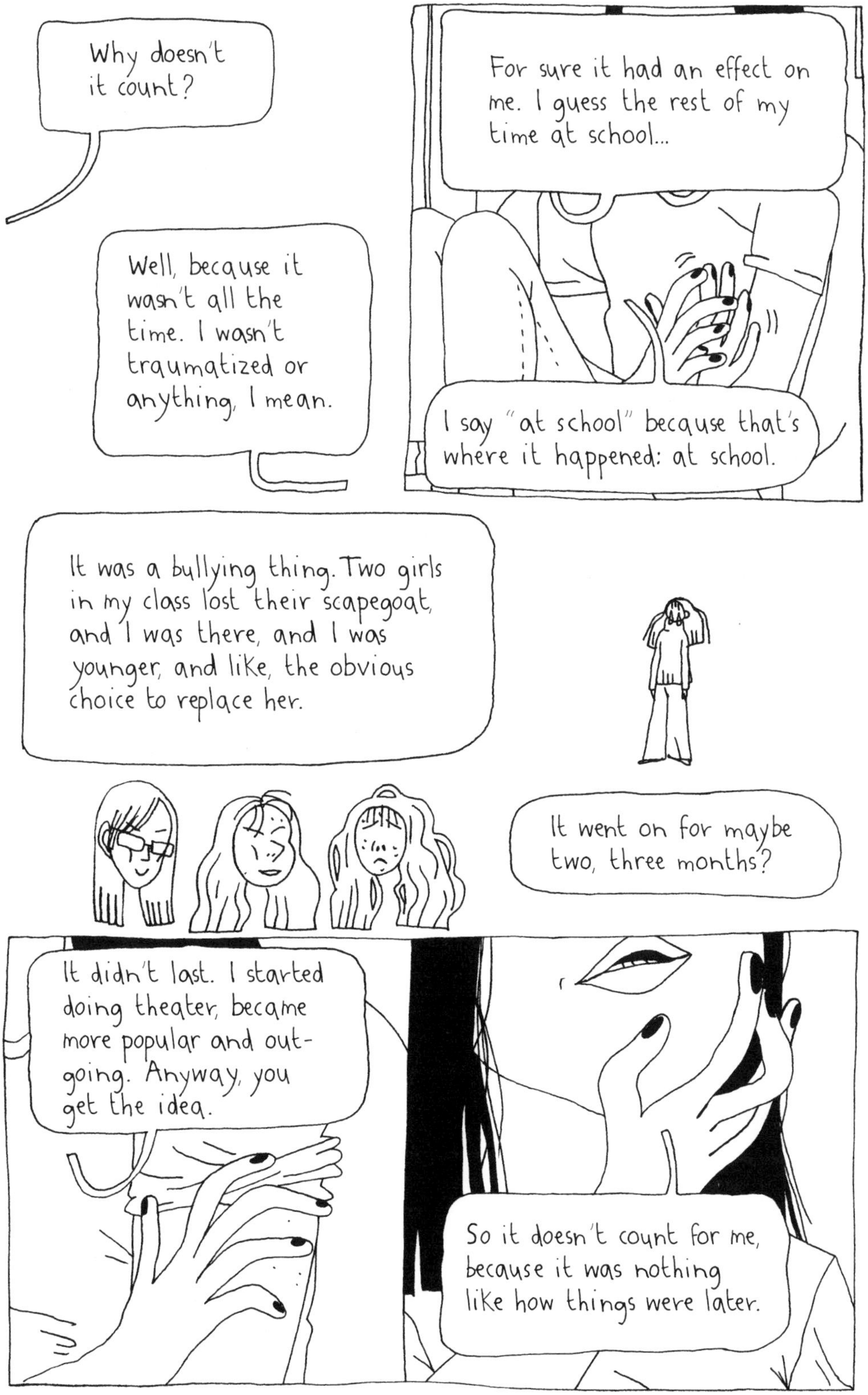
Why doesn't it count?
Well, because it wasn't all the time. I wasn't traumatized or anything, I mean.
For sure it had an effect on me. I guess the rest of my time at school...
I say "at school" because that's where it happened: at school.
It was a bullying thing. Two girls in my class lost their scapegoat, and I was there, and I was younger, and like, the obvious choice to replace her.
It went on for maybe two, three months?
It didn't last. I started doing theater, became more popular and outgoing. Anyway, you get the idea.
So it doesn't count for me, because it was nothing like how things were later.

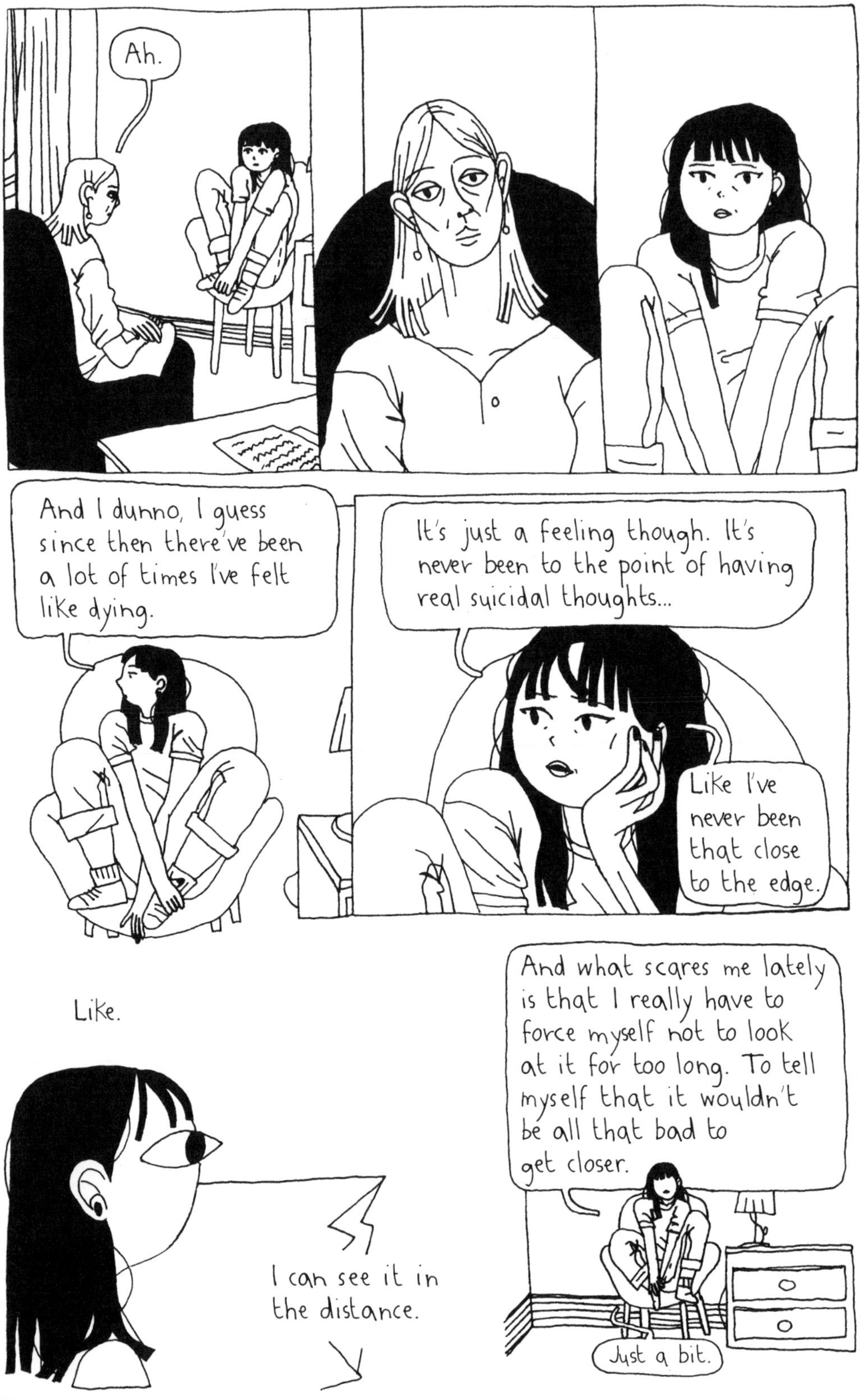
Ah.
And I dunno, I guess since then there've been a lot of times I've felt like dying.
It's just a feeling though. It's never been to the point of having real suicidal thoughts...
Like I've never been that close to the edge.
Like.
I can see it in the distance.
And what scares me lately is that I really have to force myself not to look at it for too long. To tell myself that it wouldn't be all that bad to get closer.
Just a bit.

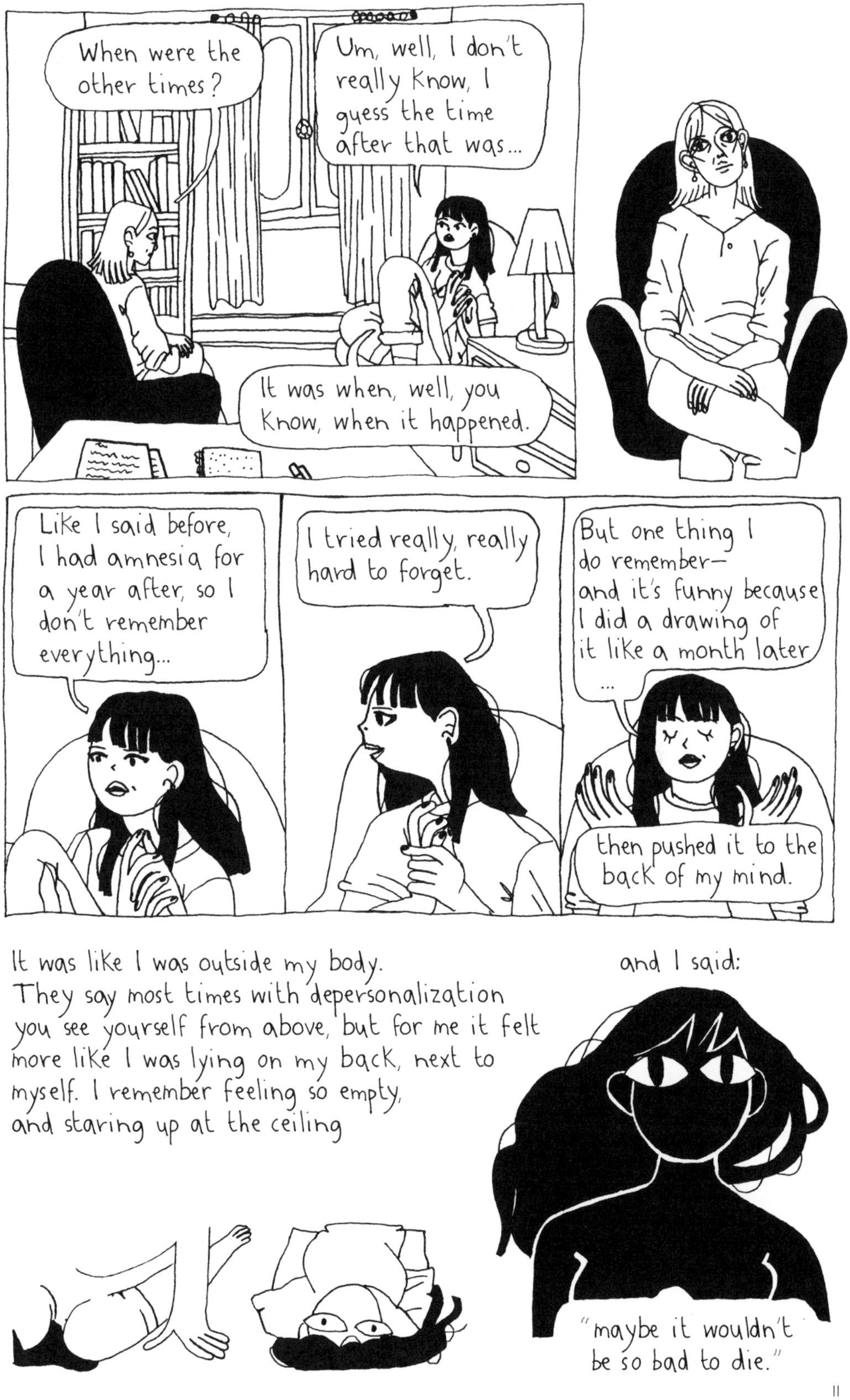
When were the other times?
Um, well, I don't really know, I guess the time after that was...
It was when, well, you know, when it happened.
Like I said before, I had amnesia for a year after, so I don't remember everything...
I tried really, really hard to forget.
But one thing I do remember— and it's funny because I did a drawing of it like a month later ...
then pushed it to the back of my mind.
It was like I was outside my body. They say most times with depersonalization you see yourself from above, but for me it felt more like I was lying on my back, next to myself. I remember feeling so empty, and staring up at the ceiling
and I said:
"maybe it wouldn't be so bad to die."

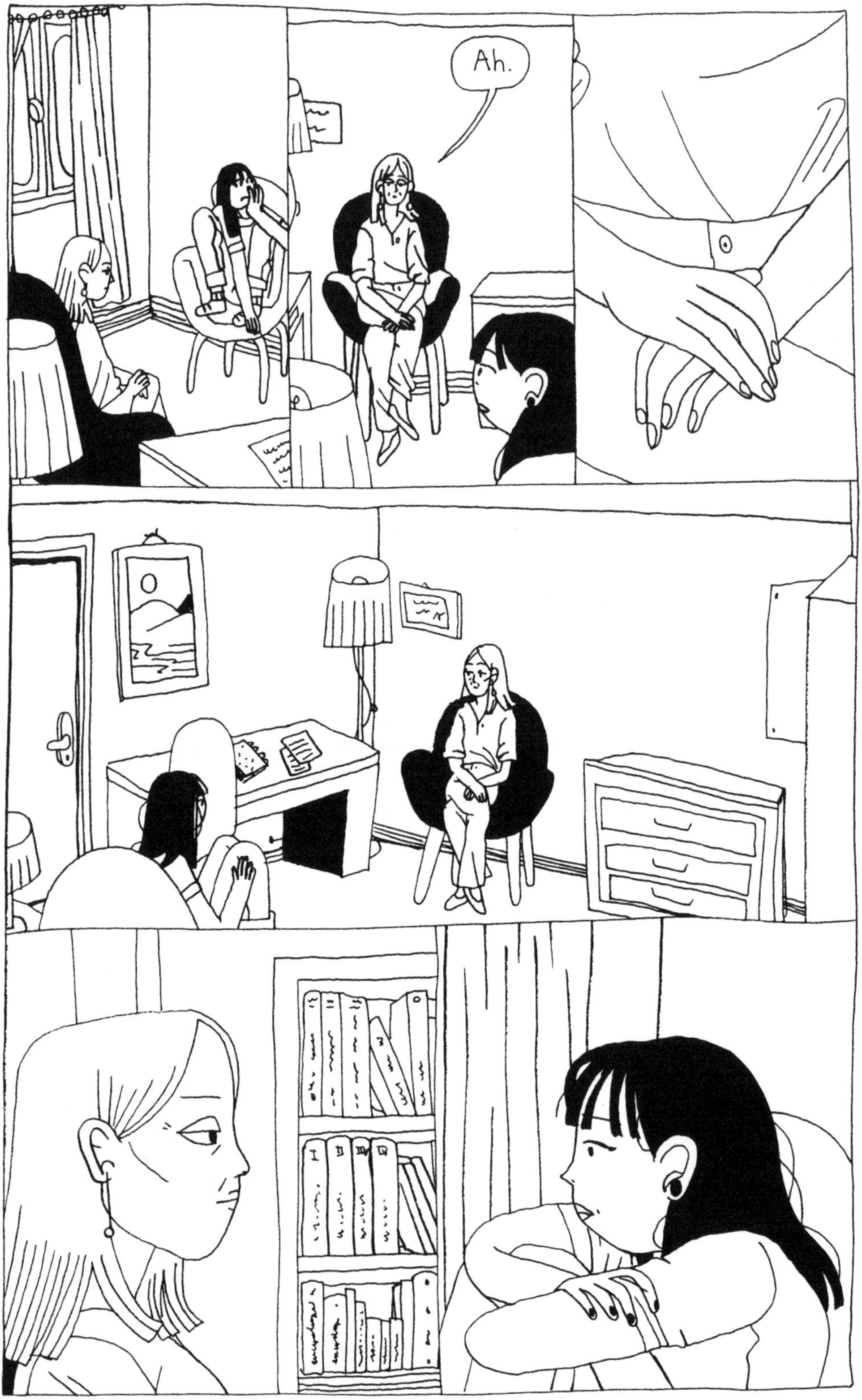
Ah.

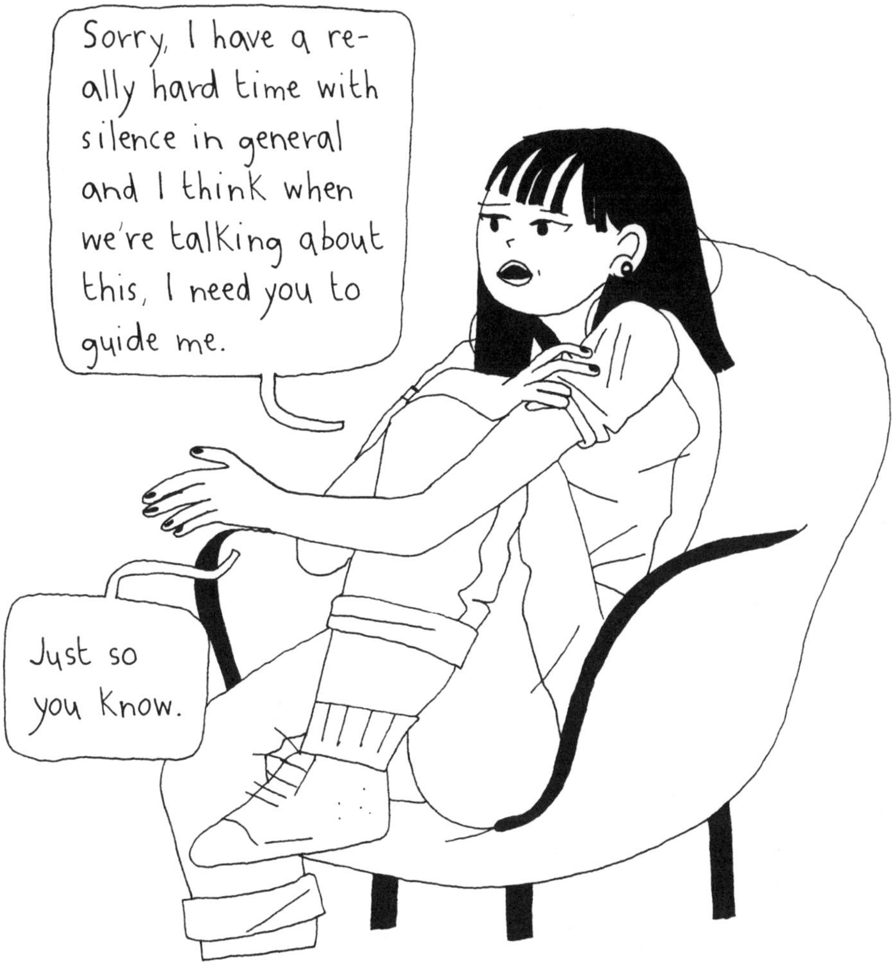
Sorry, I have a really hard time with silence in general and I think when we're talking about this, I need you to guide me.
Just so you know.

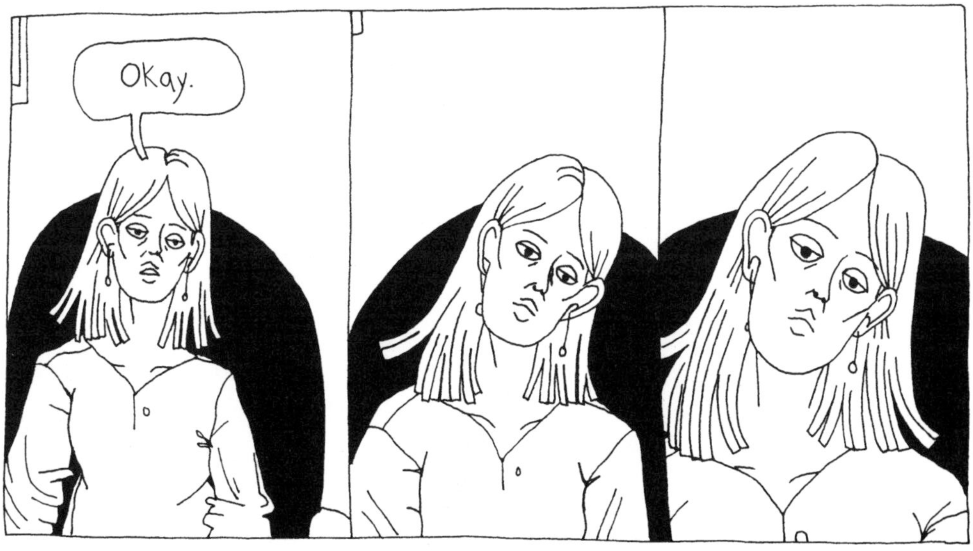
Okay.

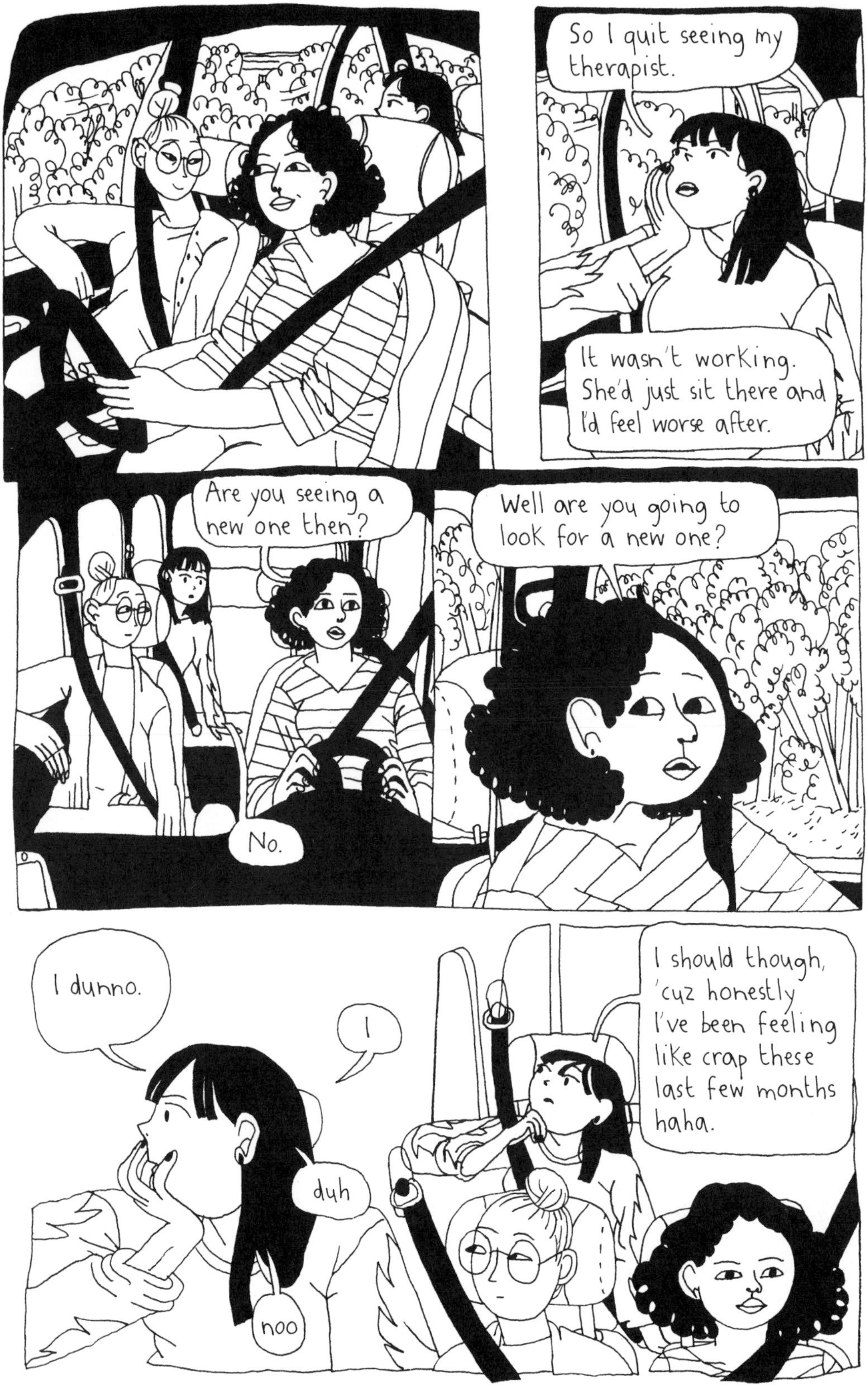
So I quit seeing my therapist.
It wasn't working. She'd just sit there and I'd feel worse after.
Are you seeing a new one then?
No.
Well are you going to look for a new one?
I dunno.
I
duh
noo
I should though, 'cuz honestly I've been feeling like crap these last few months haha.

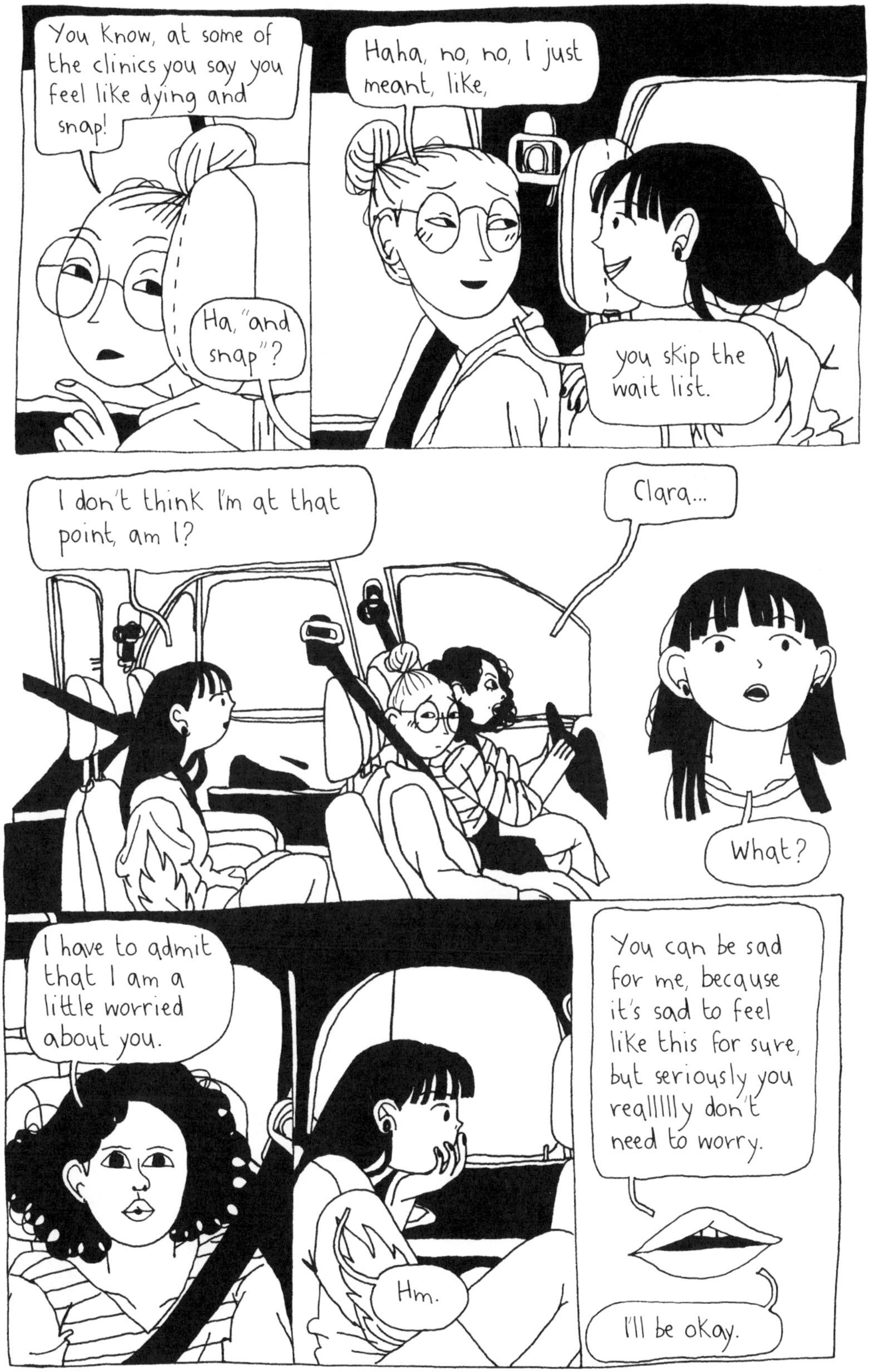
You Know, at some of the clinics you say you feel like dying and snap!
Ha, "and snap"?
Haha, no, no, I just meant, like,
you skip the wait list.
I don't think I'm at that point, am I?
Clara...
What?
I have to admit that I am a little worried about you.
Hm.
You can be sad for me, because it's sad to feel like this for sure, but seriously you reallllly don't need to worry.
I'll be okay.

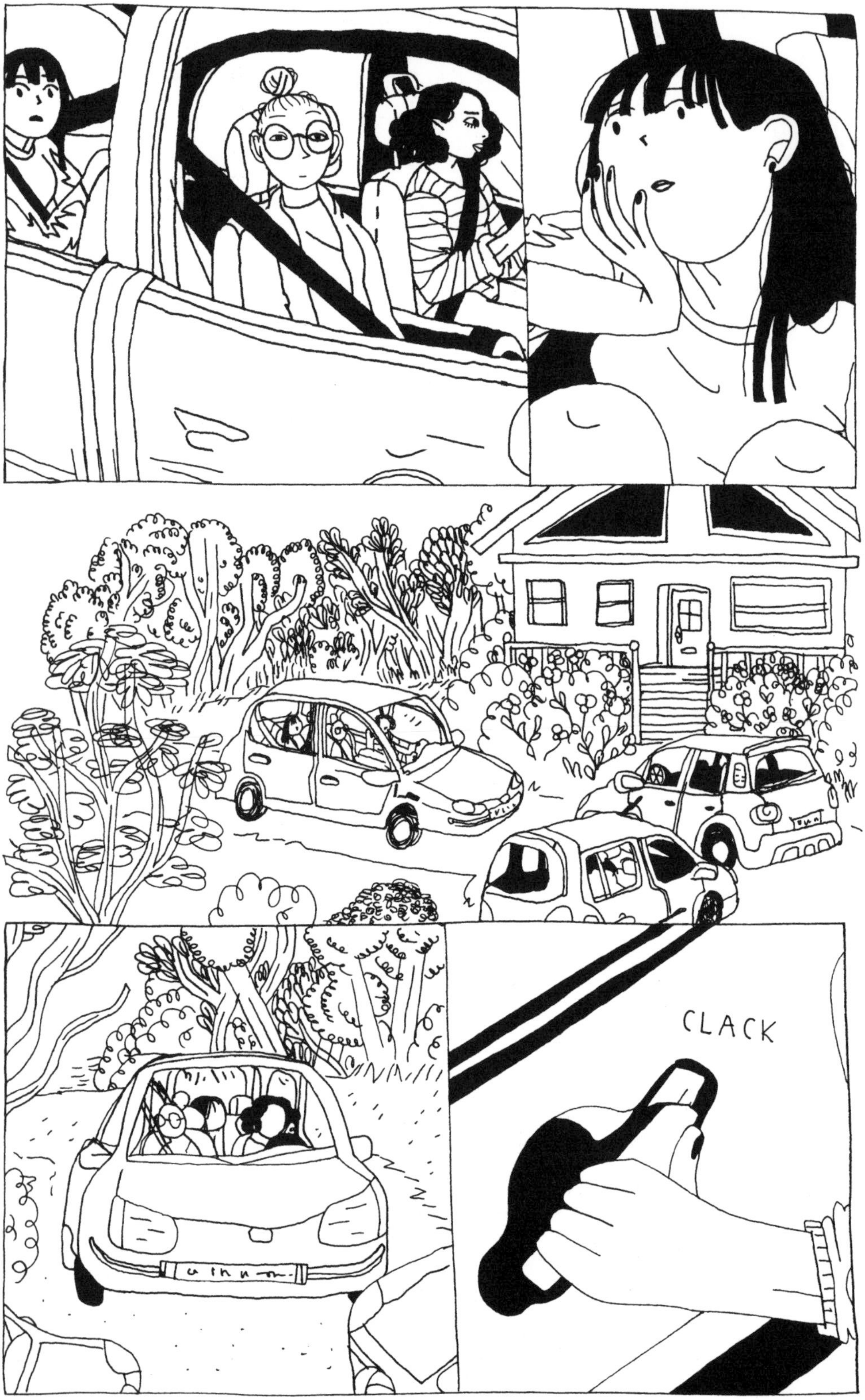
CLACK

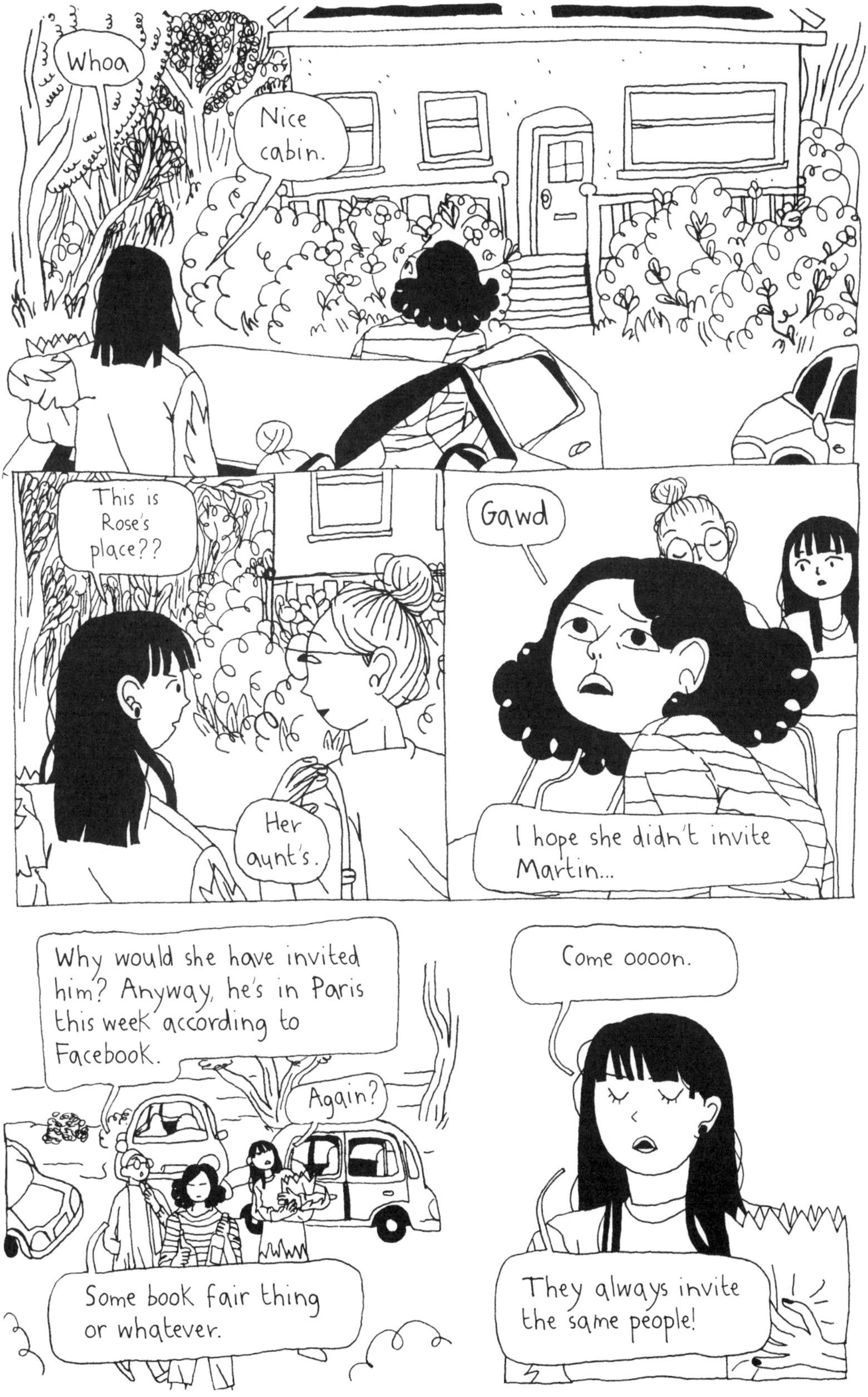
Whoa
Nice cabin.
This is Rose's place??
Her aunt's.
Gawd
I hope she didn't invite Martin...
Why would she have invited him? Anyway, he's in Paris this week according to Facebook.
Again?
Some book fair thing or whatever.
Come oooon.
They always invite the same people!

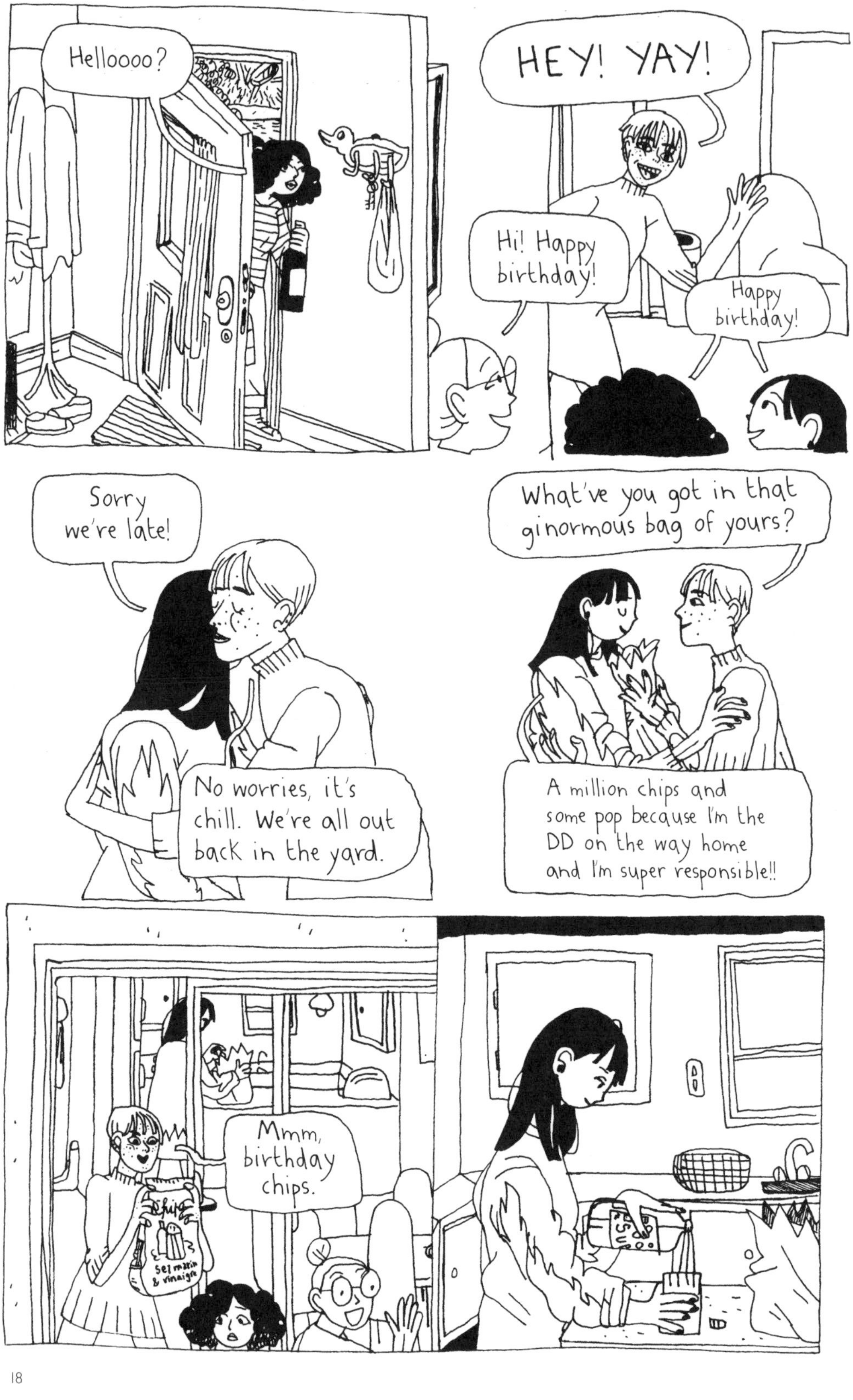
Helloooo?
HEY! YAY!
Hi! Happy birthday!
Happy birthday!
Sorry we're late!
No worries, it's chill. We're all out back in the yard.
What've you got in that ginormous bag of yours?
A million chips and some pop because I'm the DD on the way home and I'm super responsible!!
Mmm, birthday chips.
sel marin & vinaigre

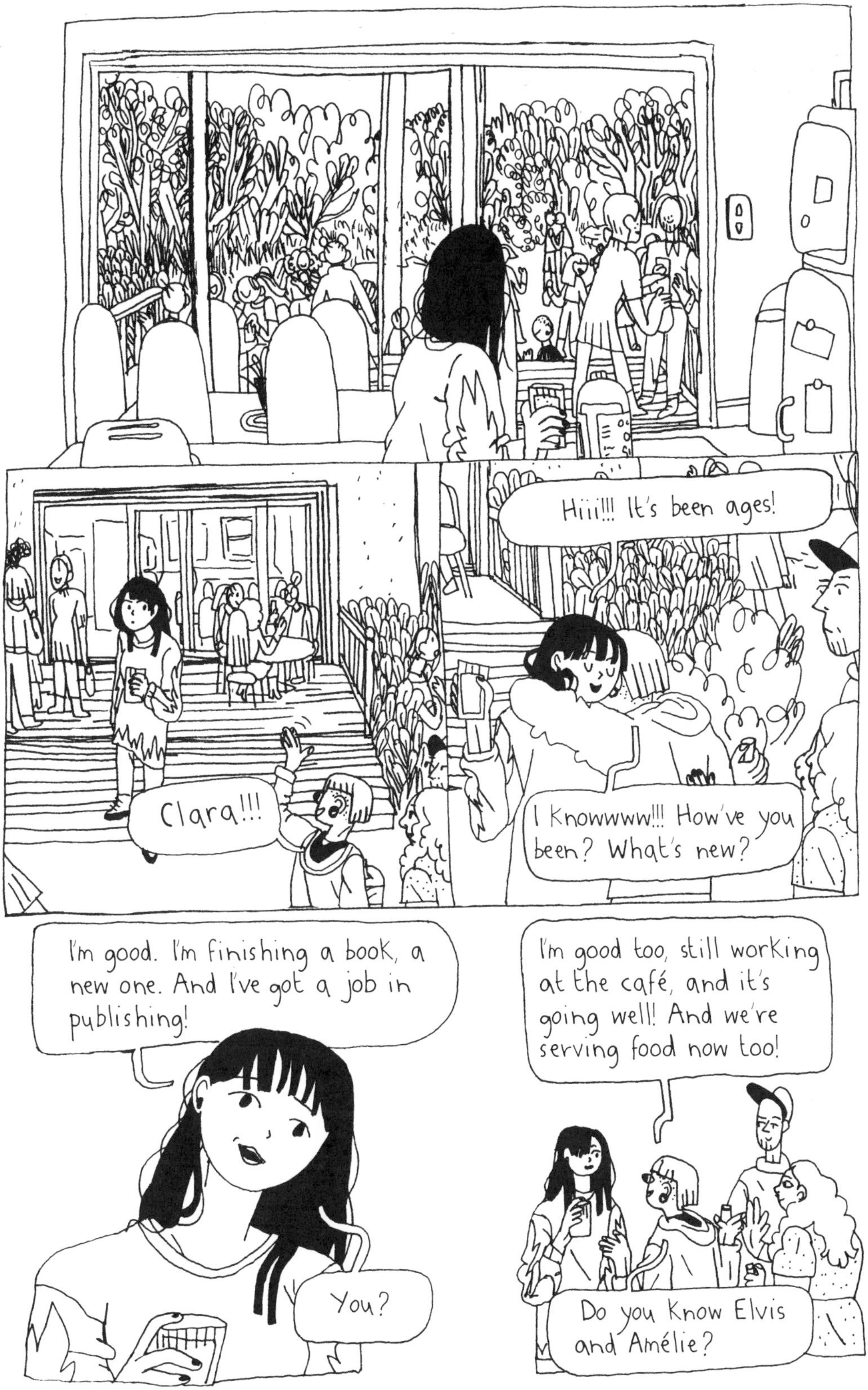
Clara!!!
Hiii!!! It's been ages!
I Knowwww!!! How've you been? What's new?
I'm good. I'm finishing a book, a new one. And I've got a job in publishing!
You?
I'm good too, still working at the café, and it's going well! And we're serving food now too!
Do you Know Elvis and Amélie?

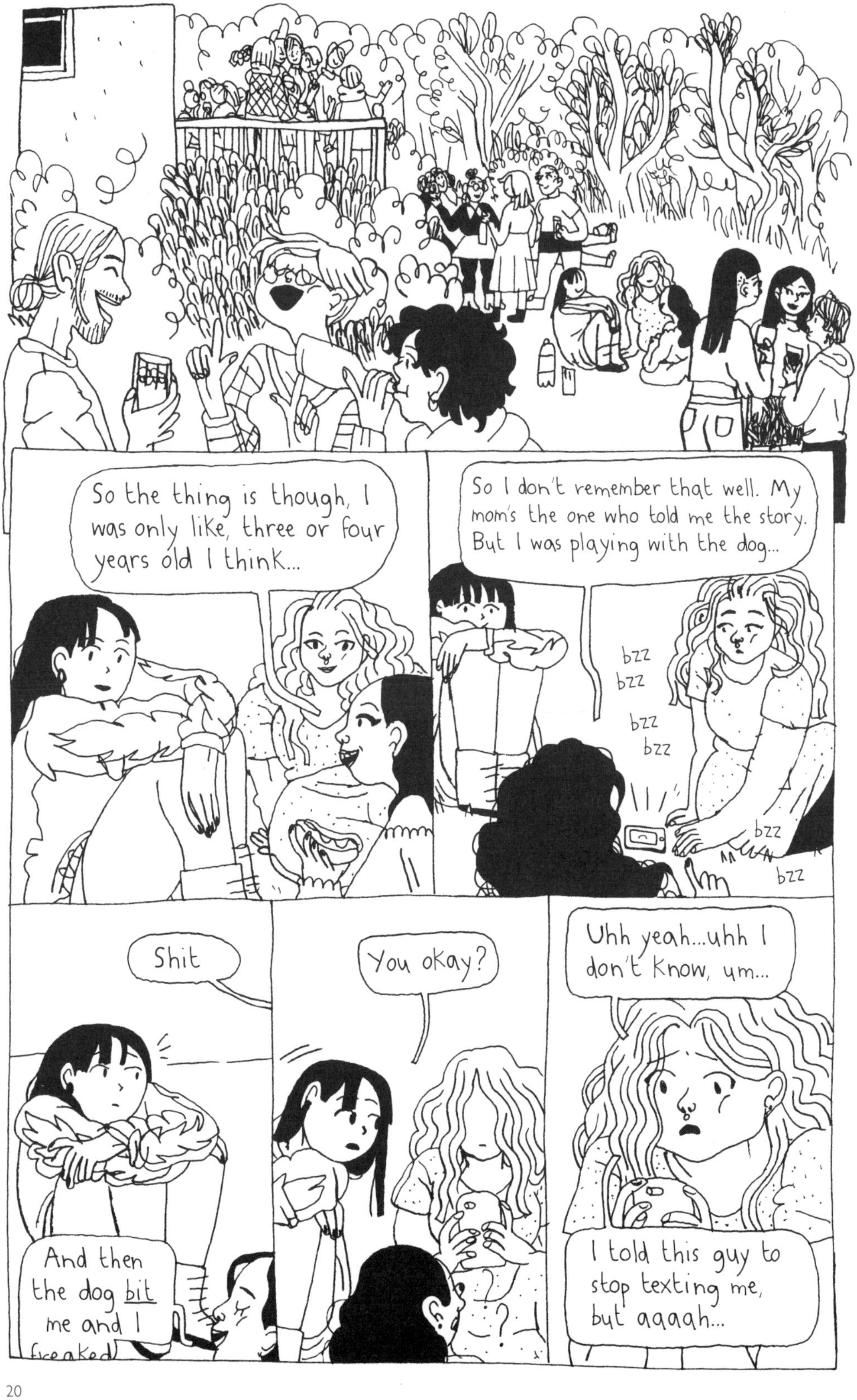
So the thing is though, I was only like, three or four years old I think...
So I don't remember that well. My mom's the one who told me the story. But I was playing with the dog...
bzz
bzz
bzz
bzz
bzz
bzz
Shit
You okay?
Uhh yeah...uhh I don't know, um...
And then the dog bit me and I freaked
I told this guy to stop texting me, but aaaah...

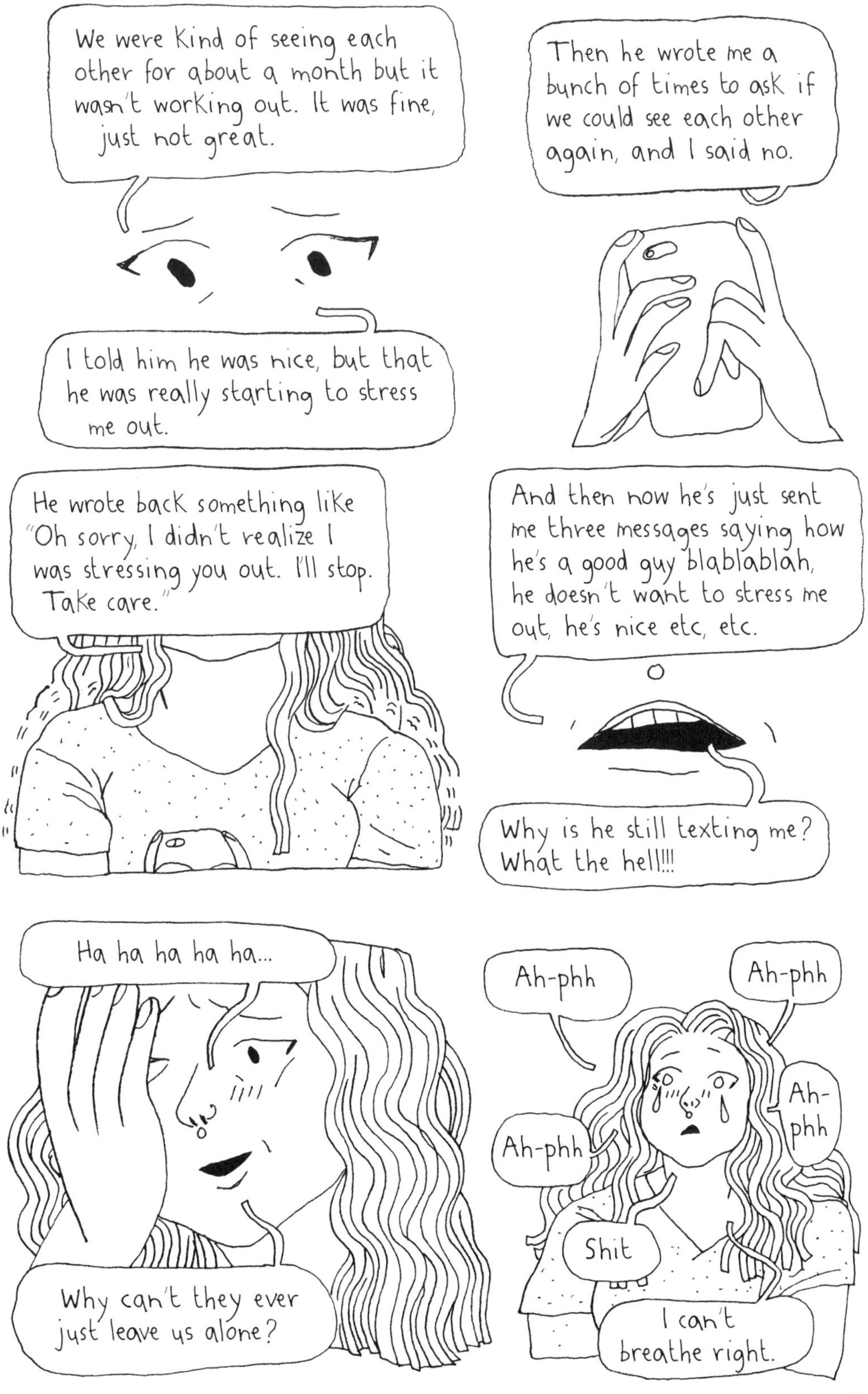
We were kind of seeing each other for about a month but it wasn't working out. It was fine, just not great.
I told him he was nice, but that he was really starting to stress me out.
Then he wrote me a bunch of times to ask if we could see each other again, and I said no.
He wrote back something like "Oh sorry, I didn't realize I was stressing you out. I'll stop. Take care."
And then now he's just sent me three messages saying how he's a good guy blablablah, he doesn't want to stress me out, he's nice etc, etc.
Why is he still texting me? What the hell!!!
Ha ha ha ha ha...
Why can't they ever just leave us alone?
Ah-phh
Ah-phh
Ah-phh
Ah-phh
Shit
I can't breathe right.

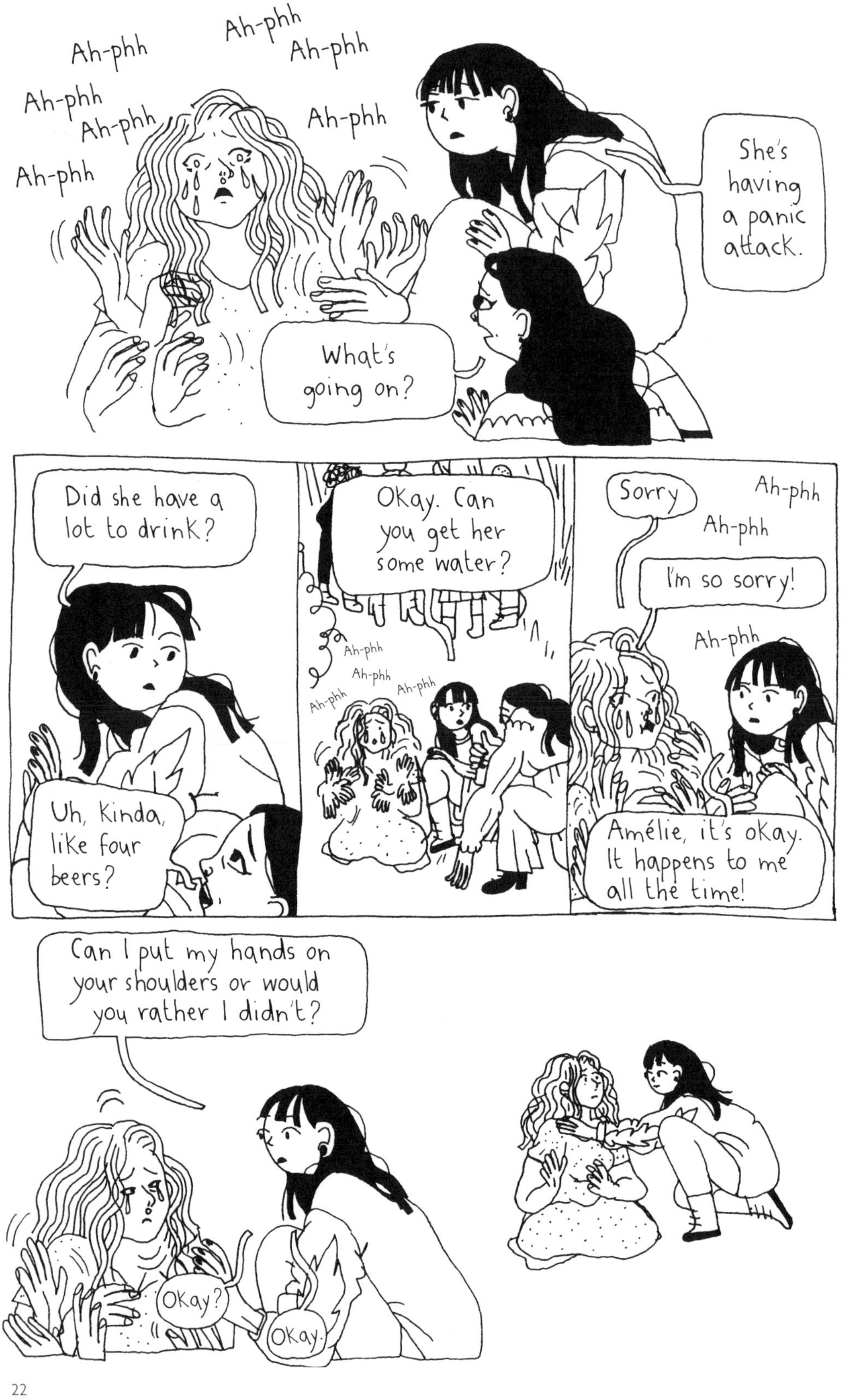
Ah-phh
Ah-phh
Ah-phh
Ah-phh
Ah-phh
Ah-phh
Ah-phh
She's having a panic attack.
What's going on?
Did she have a lot to drink?
Uh, kinda, like four beers?
Okay. Can you get her some water?
Ah-phh
Ah-phh
Ah-phh
Ah-phh
Sorry
Ah-phh
Ah-phh
I'm so sorry!
Ah-phh
Amélie, it's okay. It happens to me all the time!
Can I put my hands on your shoulders or would you rather I didn't?
Okay?
Okay.

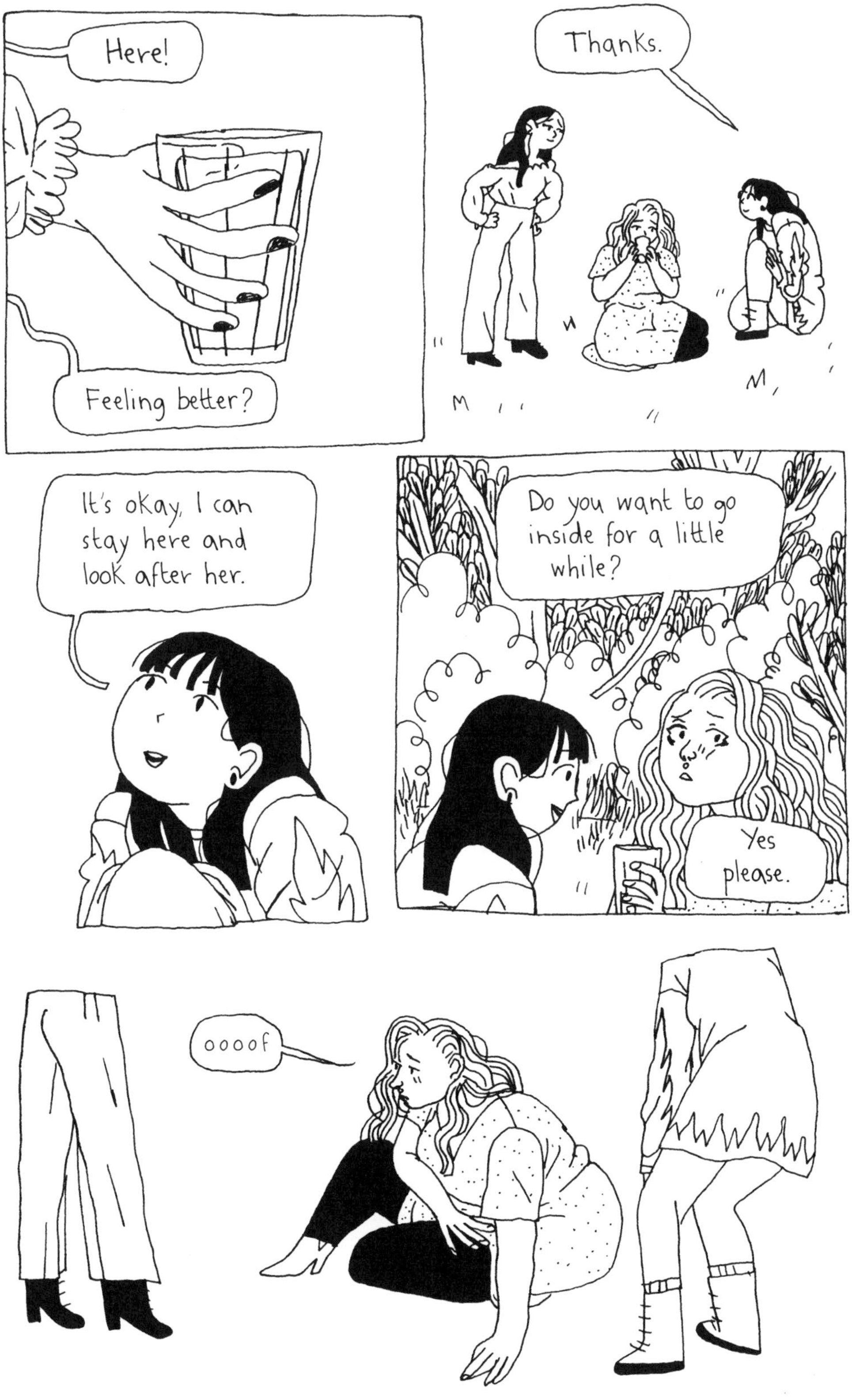
Here!
Feeling better?
Thanks.
It's okay, I can stay here and look after her.
Do you want to go inside for a little while?
Yes please.
ooooF

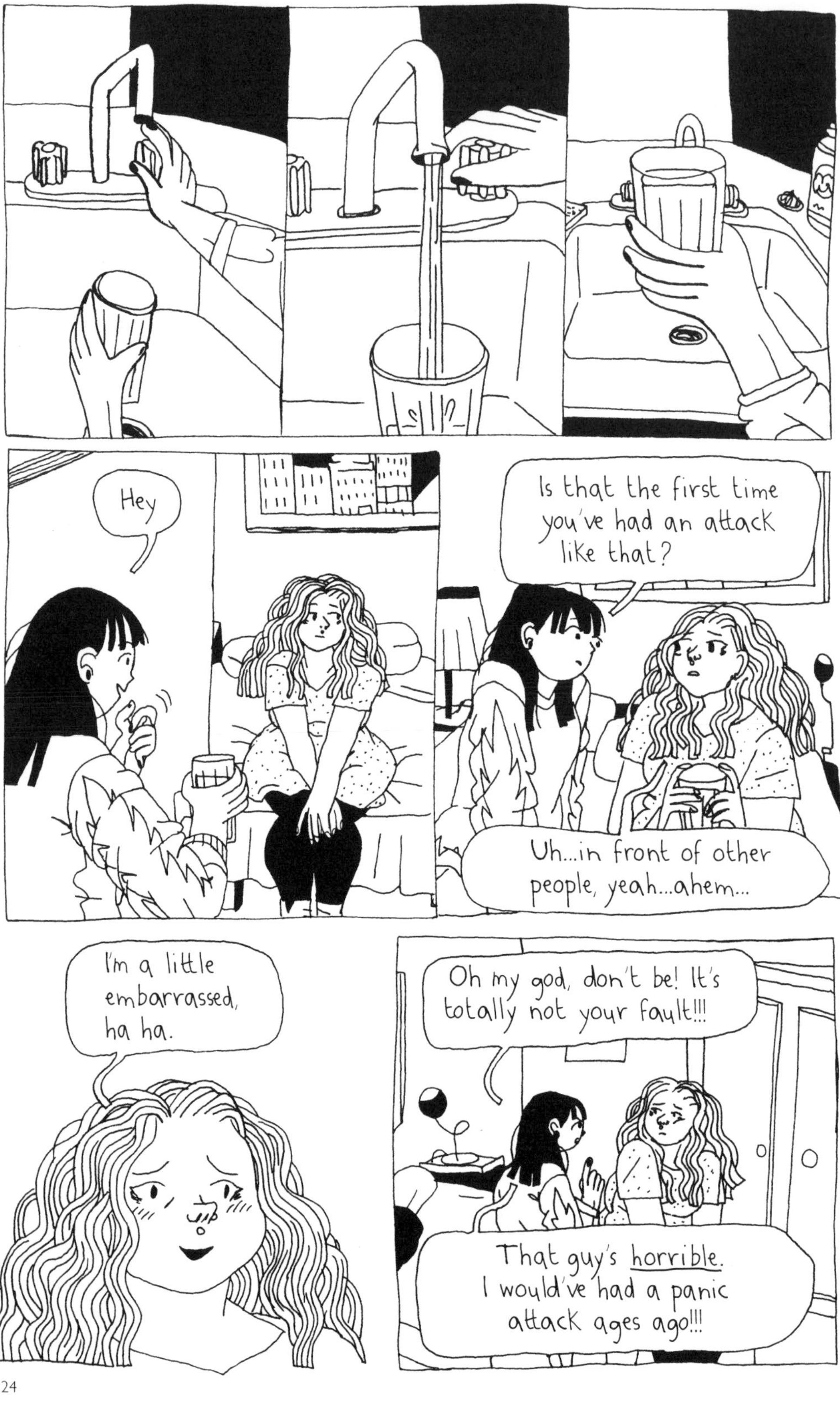
Hey
Is that the first time you've had an attack like that?
Uh...in front of other people, yeah...ahem...
I'm a little embarrassed, ha ha.
Oh my god, don't be! It's totally not your fault!!!
That guy's horrible. I would've had a panic attack ages ago!!!

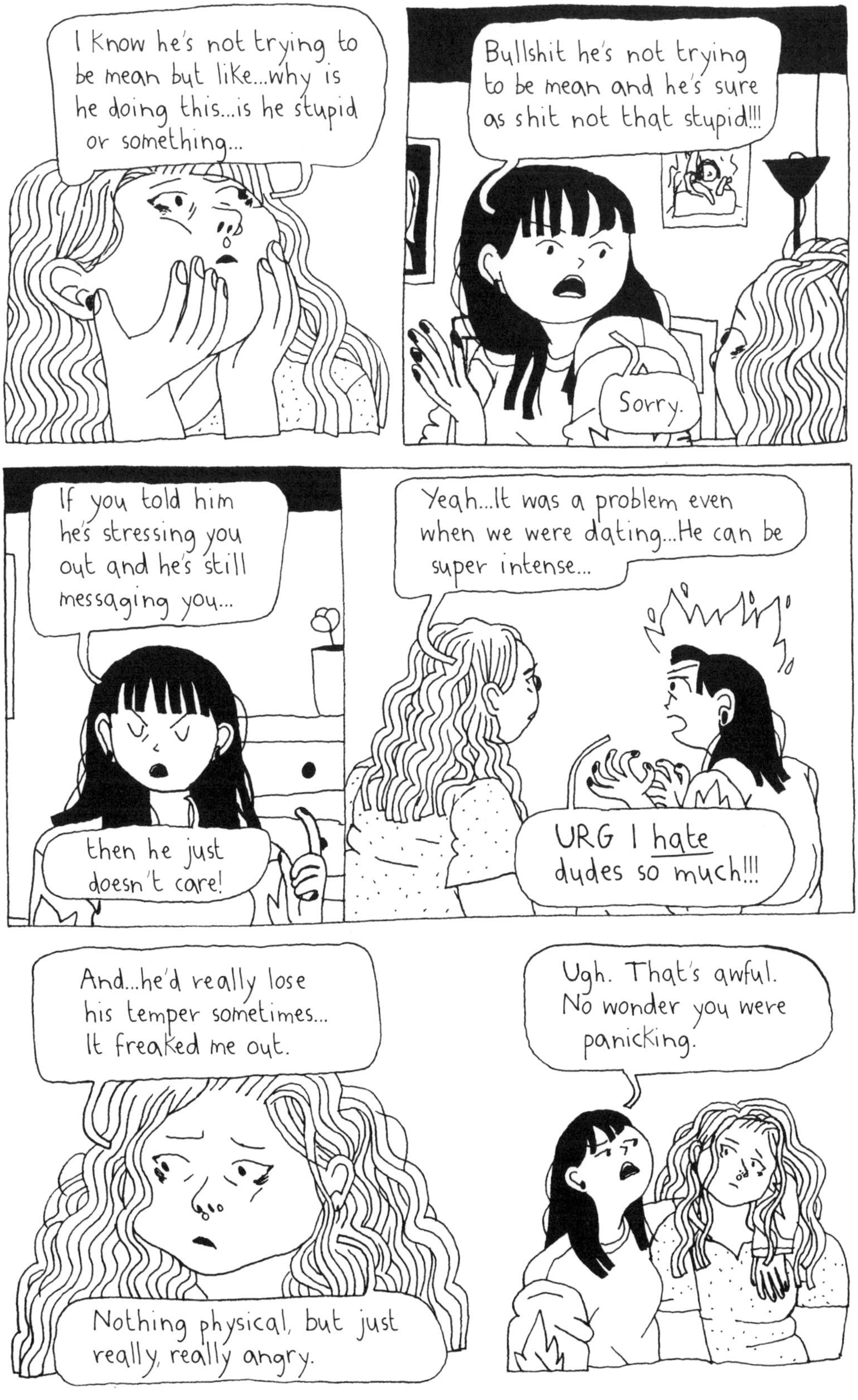
I Know he's not trying to be mean but like...why is he doing this...is he stupid or something...
Bullshit he's not trying to be mean and he's sure as shit not that stupid!!!
Sorry.
If you told him he's stressing you out and he's still messaging you...
then he just doesn't care!
Yeah...It was a problem even when we were dating...He can be super intense...
URG I hate dudes so much!!!
And...he'd really lose his temper sometimes... It freaked me out.
Nothing physical, but just really, really angry.
Ugh. That's awful. No wonder you were panicking.

Ack! I must seem totally nuts right now.

Heyyyy!!! Don't say stuff like that.

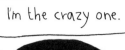
I'm the crazy one.

But it's okay.

What do you mean?

Bahhh most days I don't really want to be alive.

I tried seeing a therapist for a bit but she was useless.

And like, when I talk to my friends...I dunno, it's weird.

They don't really get it. It scares them.

It was the same with my ex. I broke up with her because it wasn't helping things.

She used to yell at me every time I had a panic attack haha.

Yikes.

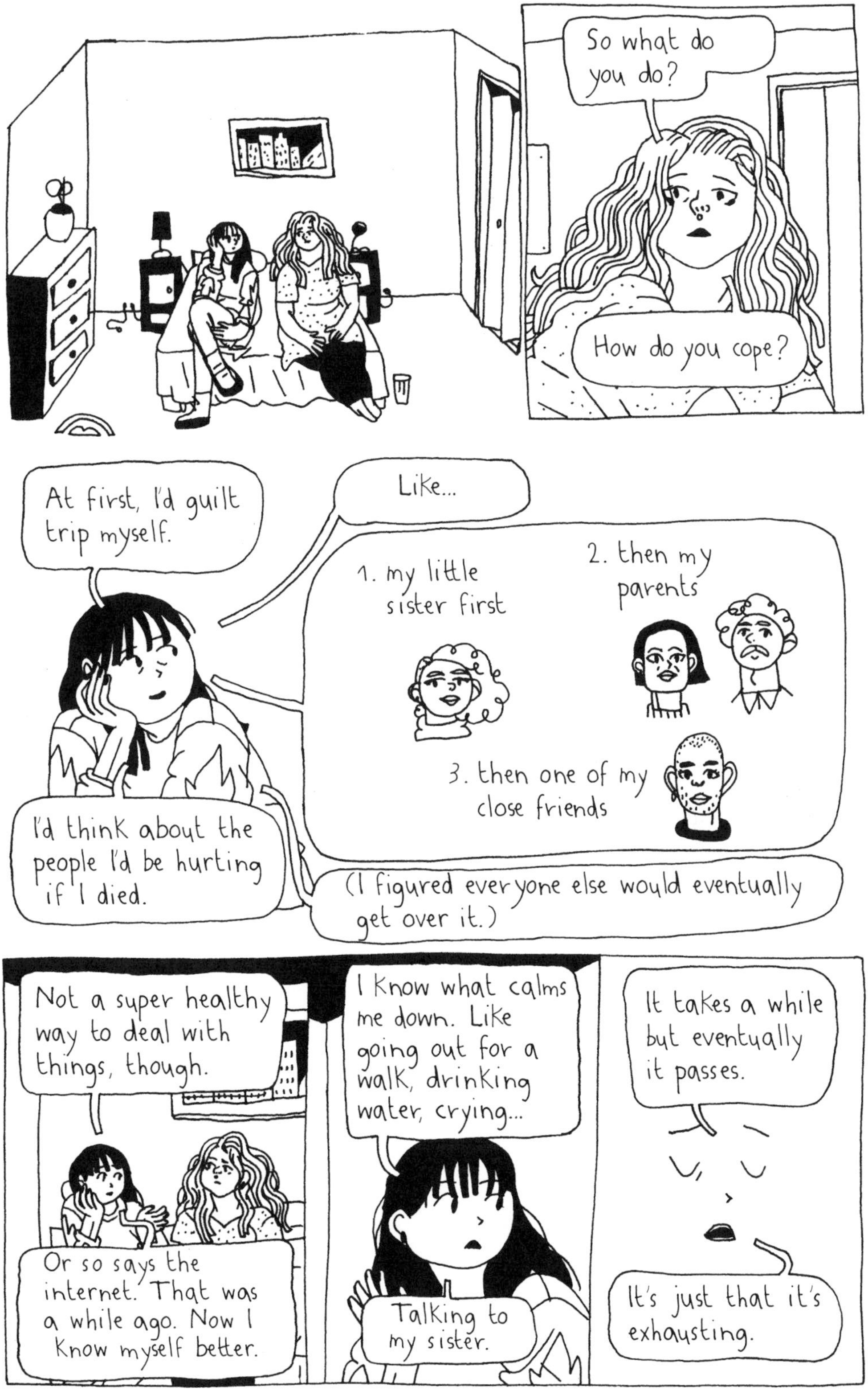
So what do you do?
How do you cope?
At first, I'd guilt trip myself.
Like...
1. my little sister first
2. then my parents
3. then one of my close friends
I'd think about the people I'd be hurting if I died.
(I figured everyone else would eventually get over it.)
Not a super healthy way to deal with things, though.
Or so says the internet. That was a while ago. Now I know myself better.
I know what calms me down. Like going out for a walk, drinking water, crying...
Talking to my sister.
It takes a while but eventually it passes.
It's just that it's exhausting.

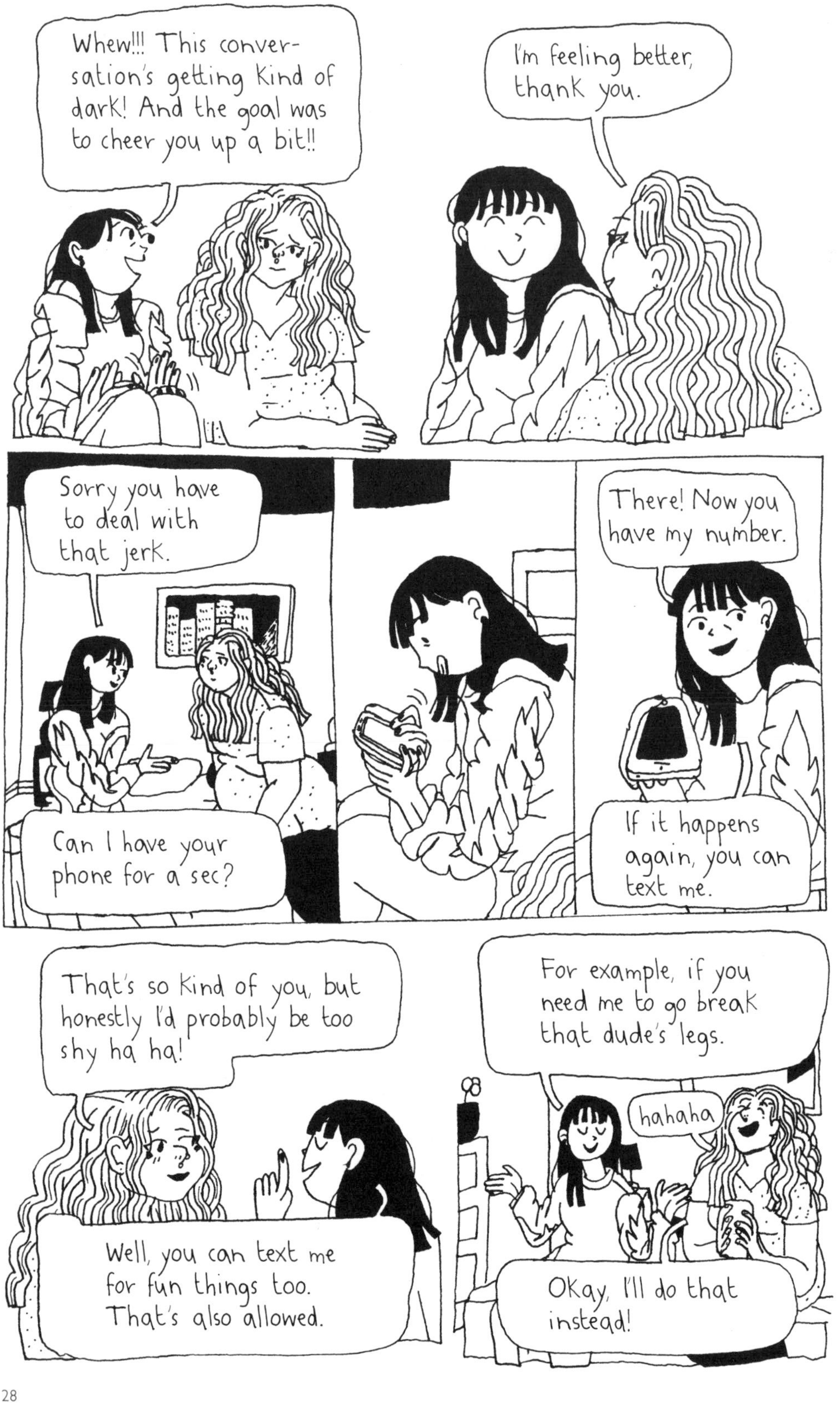

Whew!!! This conversation's getting kind of dark! And the goal was to cheer you up a bit!!
I'm feeling better, thank you.
Sorry you have to deal with that jerk.
Can I have your phone for a sec?
There! Now you have my number.
If it happens again, you can text me.
That's so kind of you, but honestly I'd probably be too shy ha ha!
Well, you can text me for fun things too. That's also allowed.
For example, if you need me to go break that dude's legs.
hahaha
Okay, I'll do that instead!

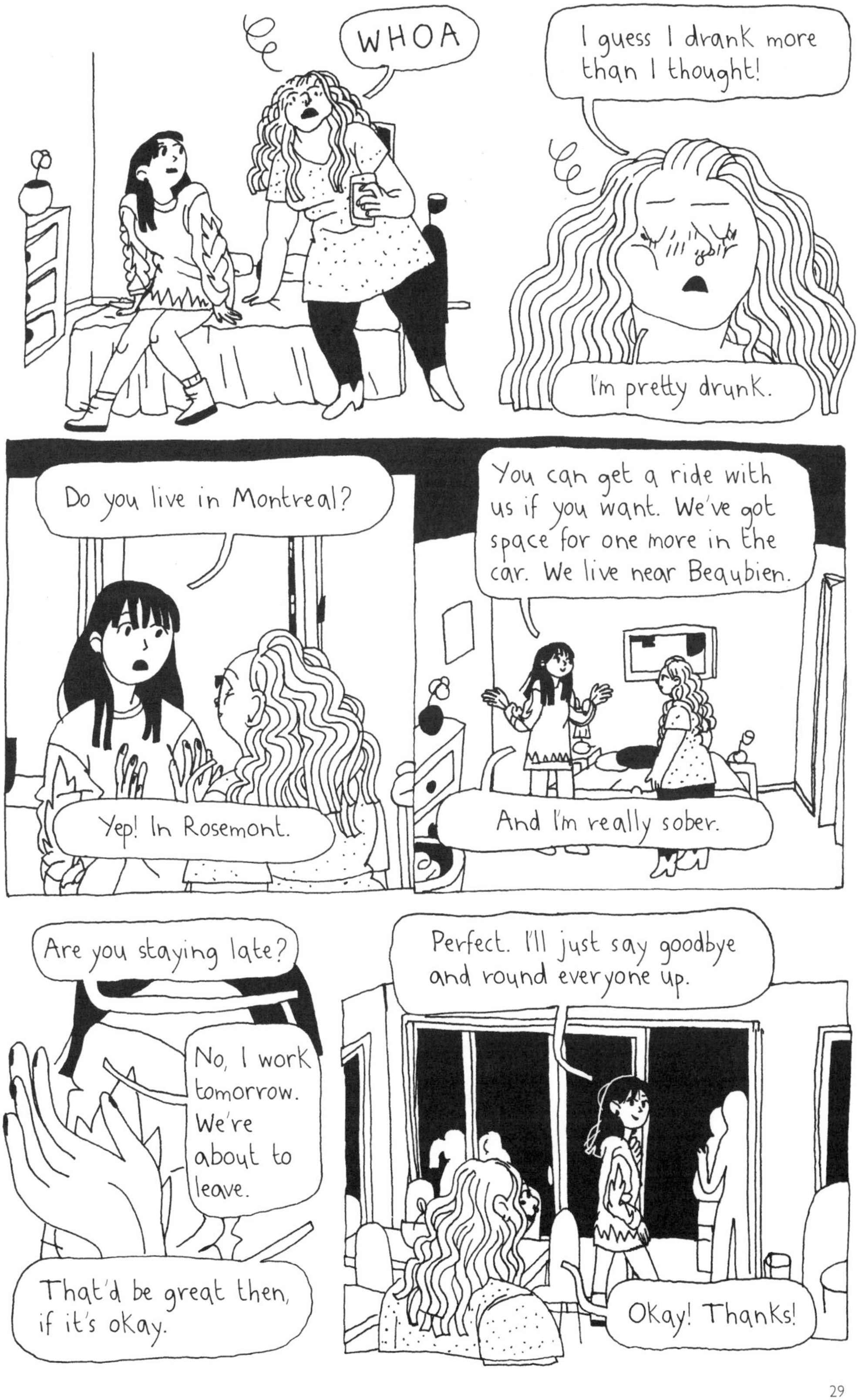
WHOA
I guess I drank more than I thought!
I'm pretty drunk.
Do you live in Montreal?
Yep! In Rosemont.
You can get a ride with us if you want. We've got space for one more in the car. We live near Beaubien.
And I'm really sober.
Are you staying late?
No, I work tomorrow. We're about to leave.
That'd be great then, if it's okay.
Perfect. I'll just say goodbye and round everyone up.
Okay! Thanks!

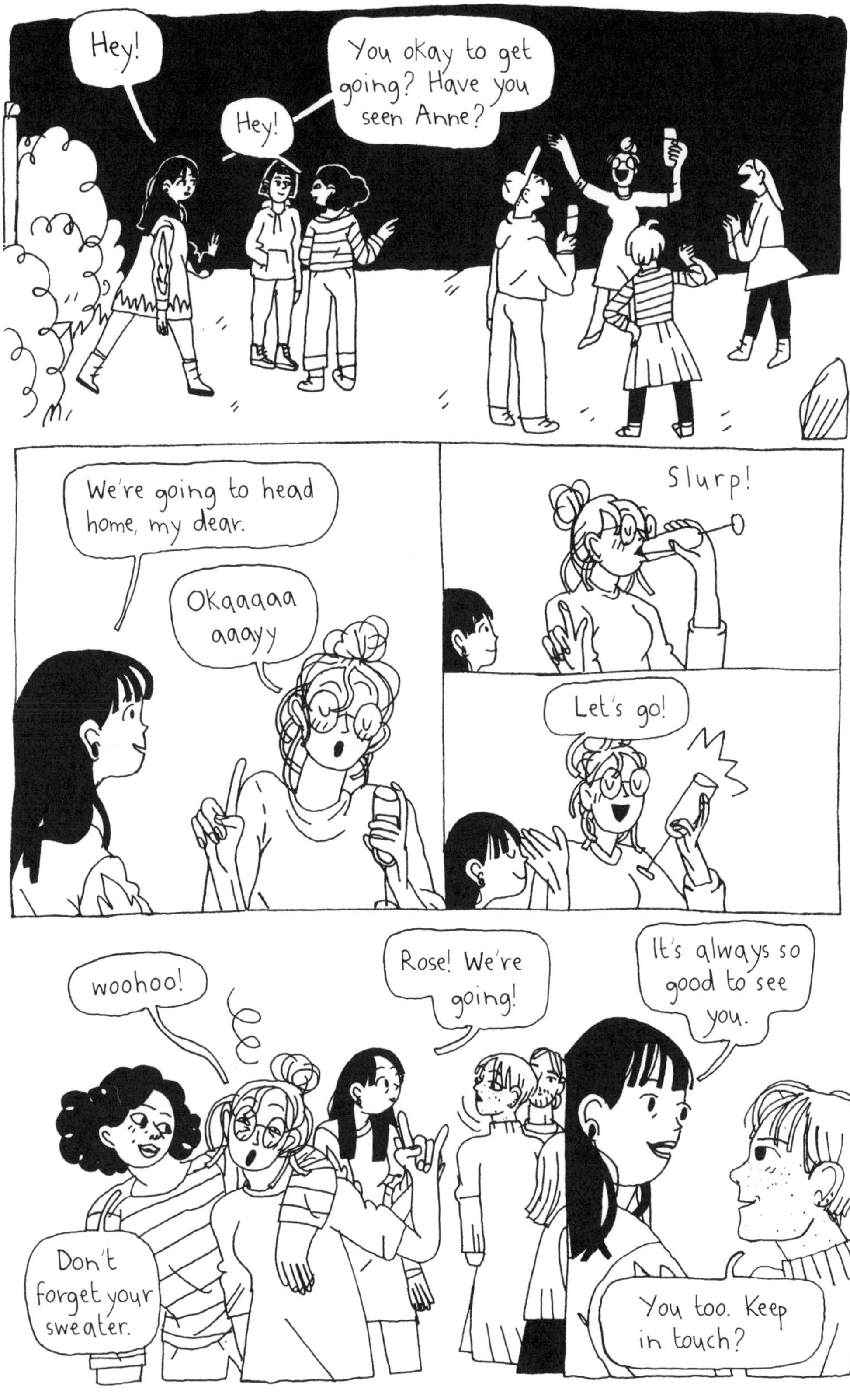
Hey!
Hey!
You okay to get going? Have you seen Anne?
We're going to head home, my dear.
Okaaaaa aaayy
Slurp!
Let's go!
woohoo!
Rose! We're going!
It's always so good to see you.
Don't forget your sweater.
You too. Keep in touch?

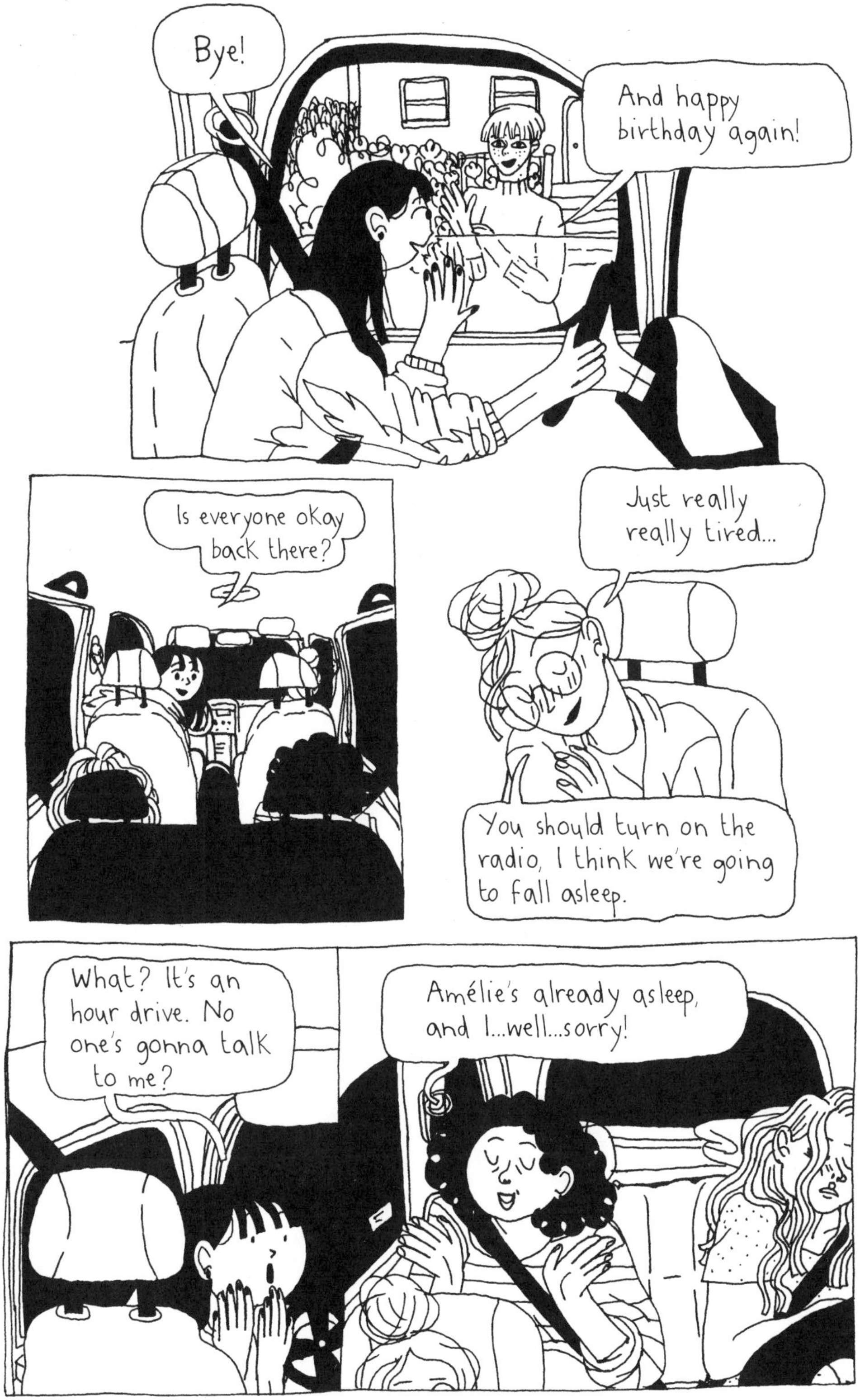
Bye!
And happy birthday again!
Is everyone okay back there?
Just really really tired...
You should turn on the radio, I think we're going to fall asleep.
What? It's an hour drive. No one's gonna talk to me?
Amélie's already asleep, and I...well...sorry!

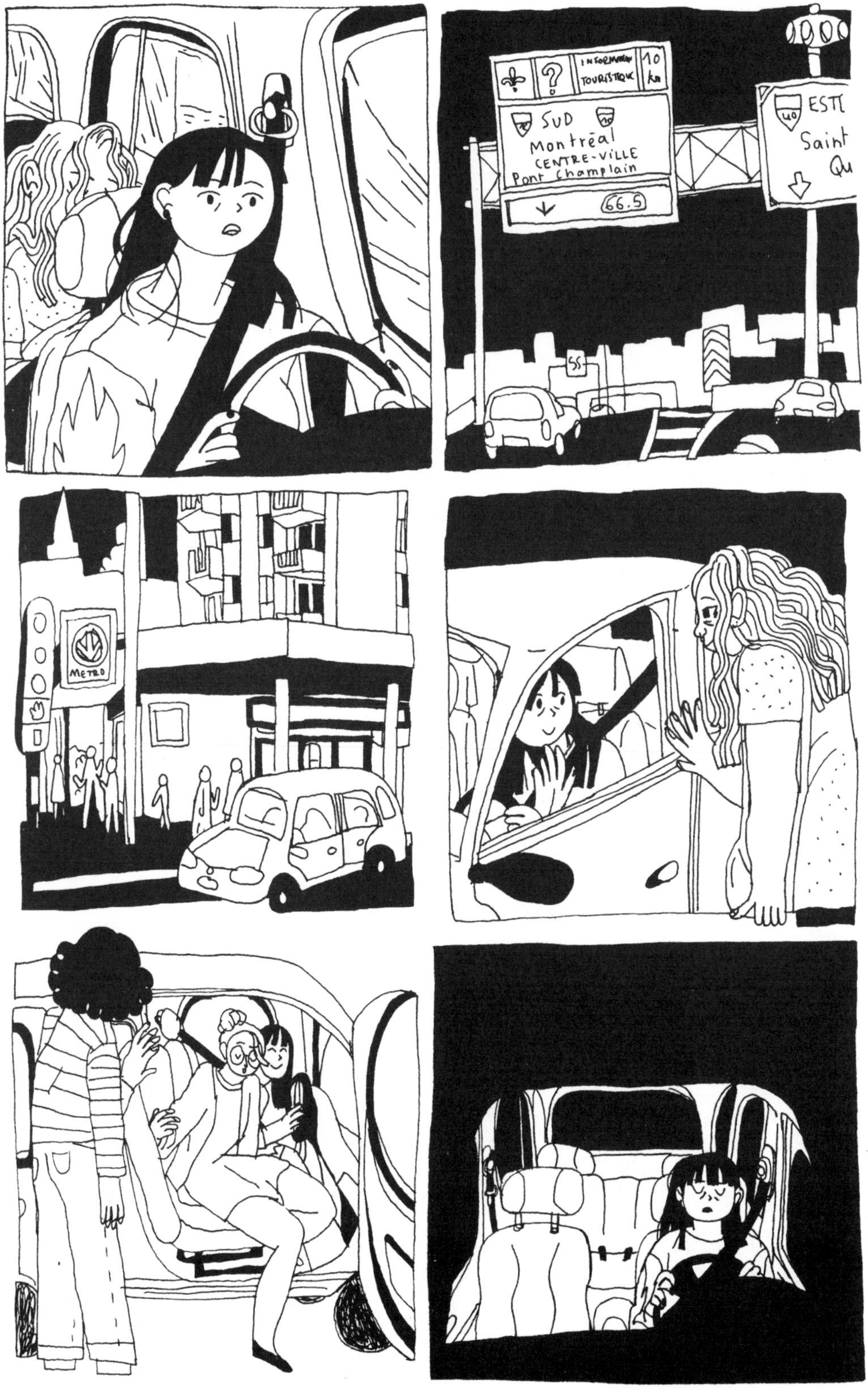
TOURISTIQUE
10 km
SUD
Montréal
CENTRE-VILLE
Pont Champlain
66.5
Saint
METRO

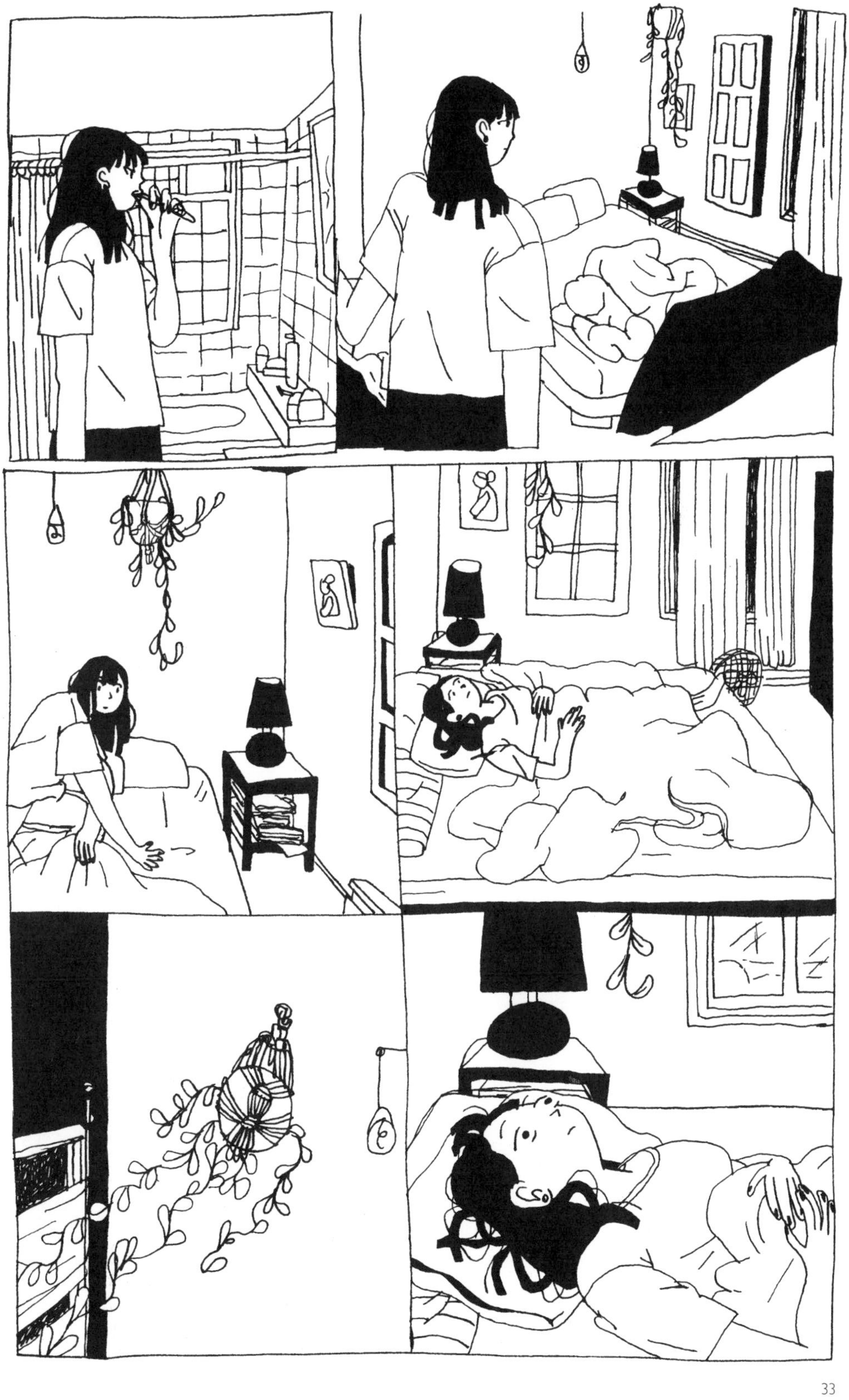

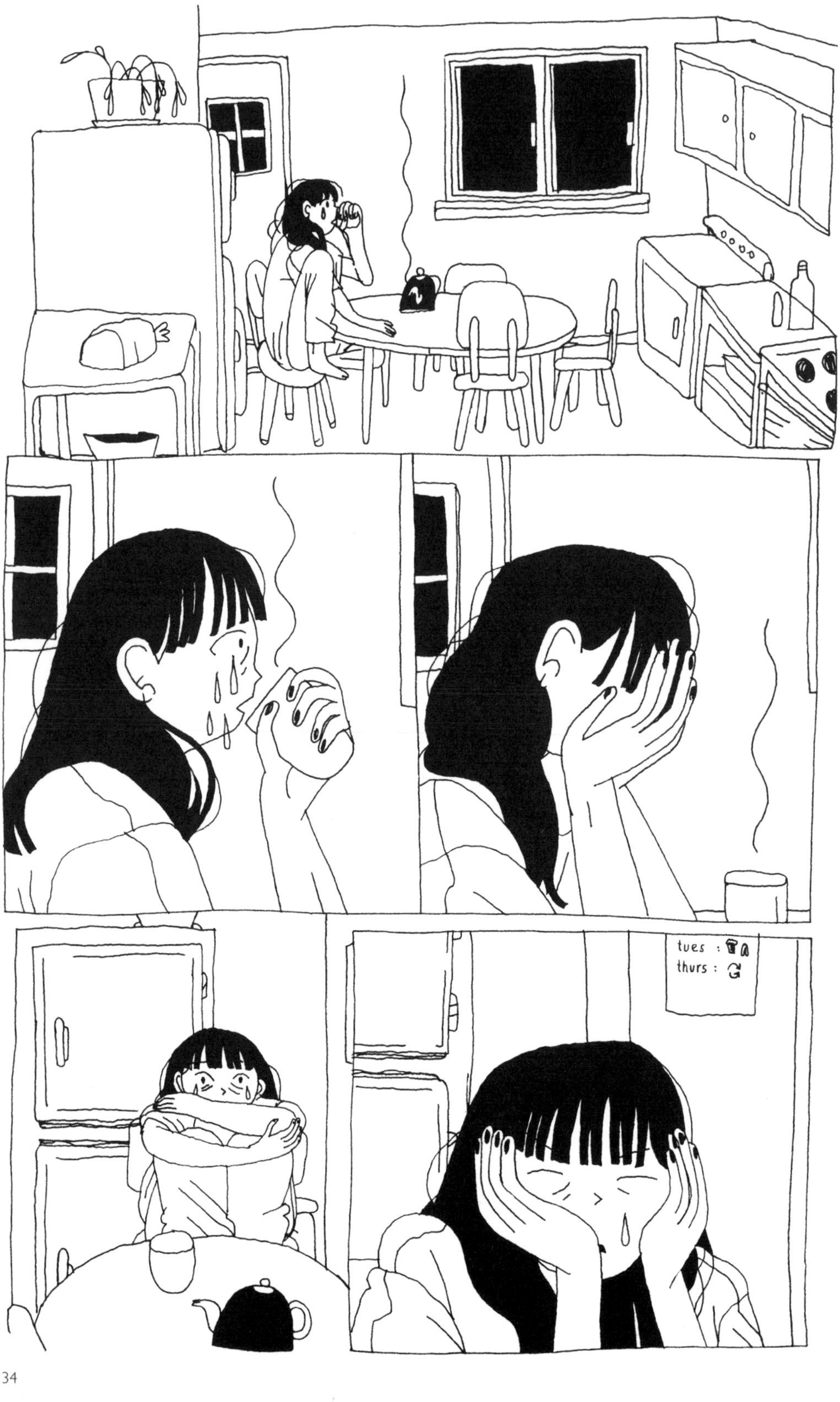
tues :
thurs :

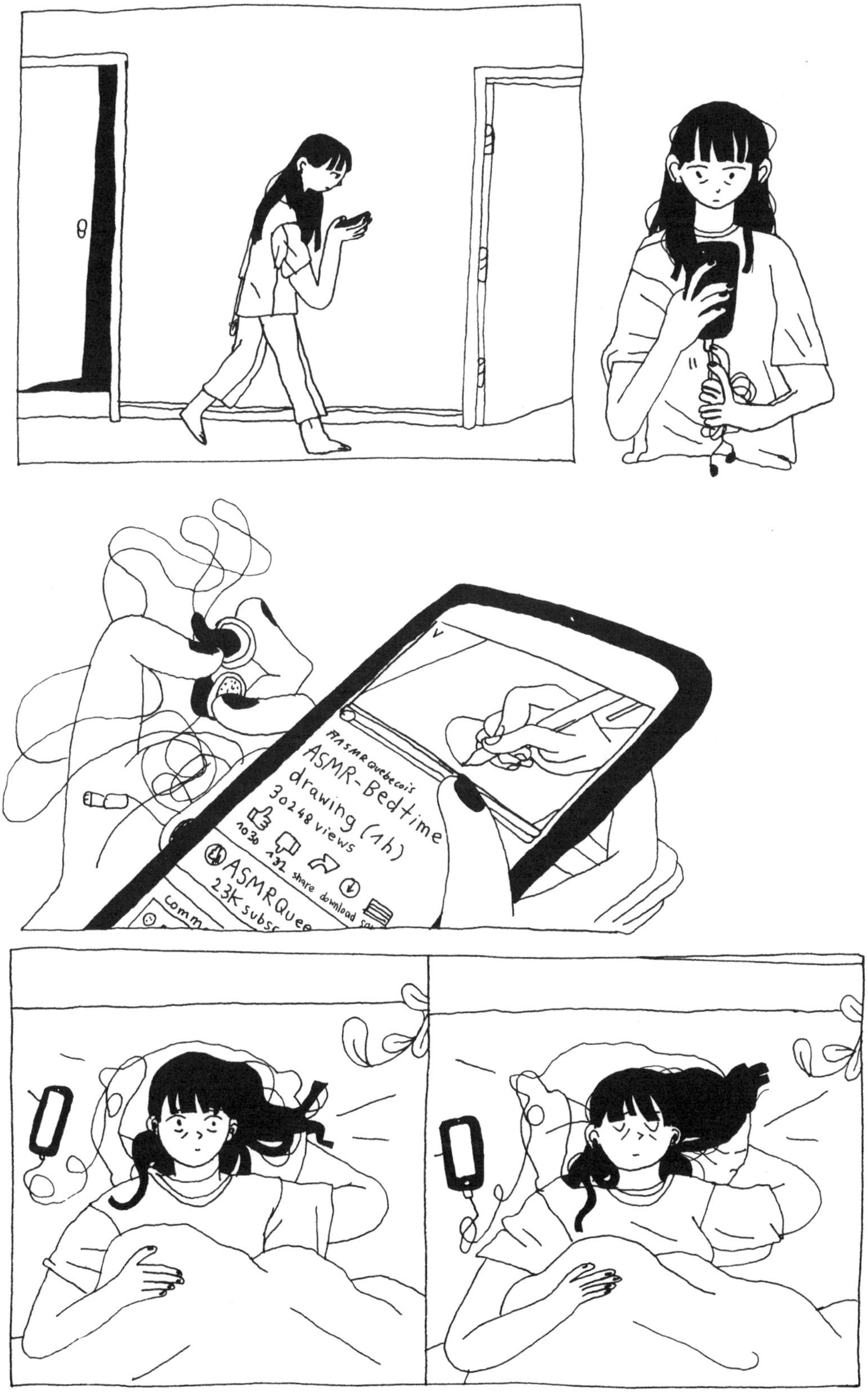
ASMRQuebecois
ASMR-Bedtime drawing (1h)
30248 views
1030
132
share
download

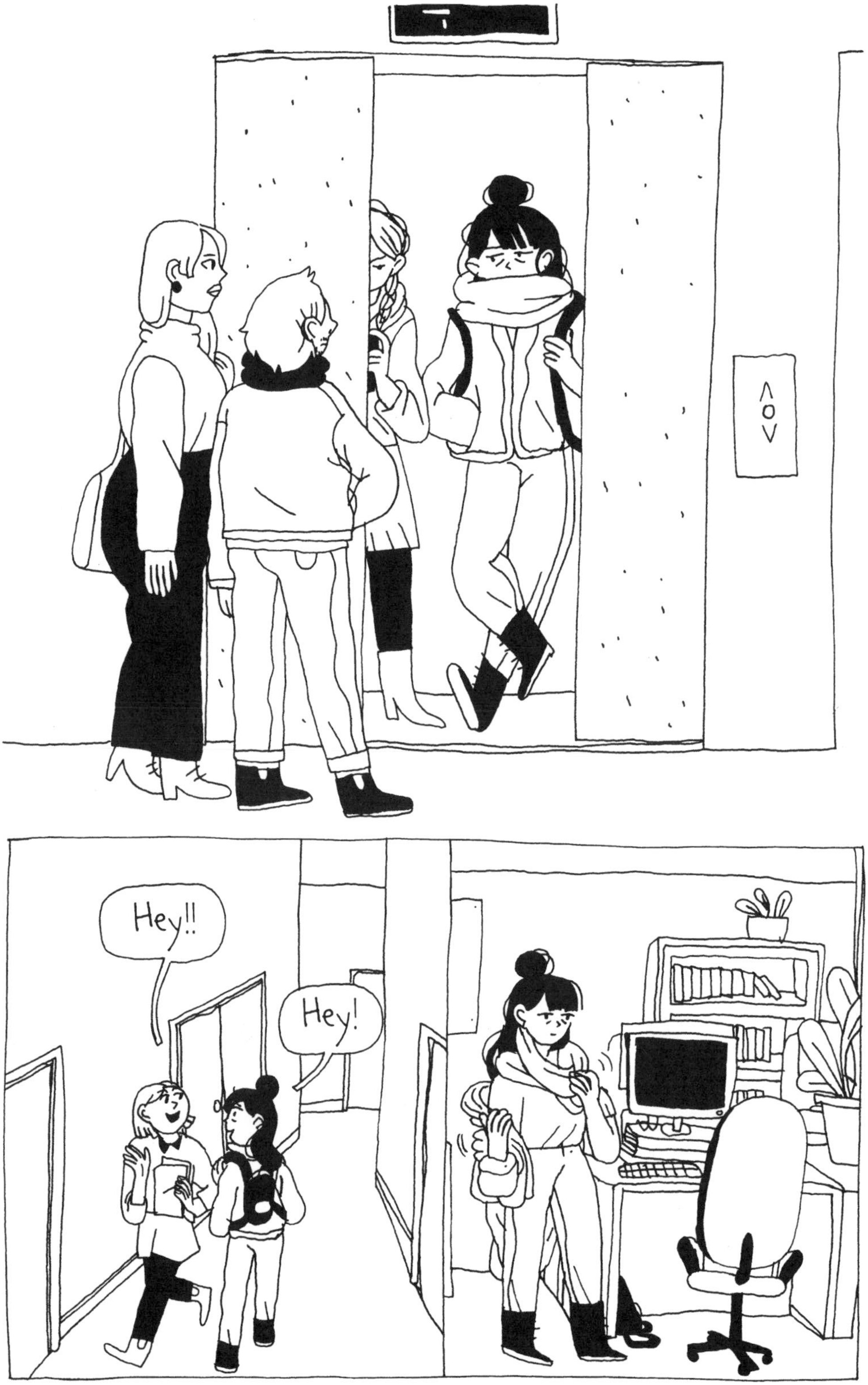
Hey!!
Hey!

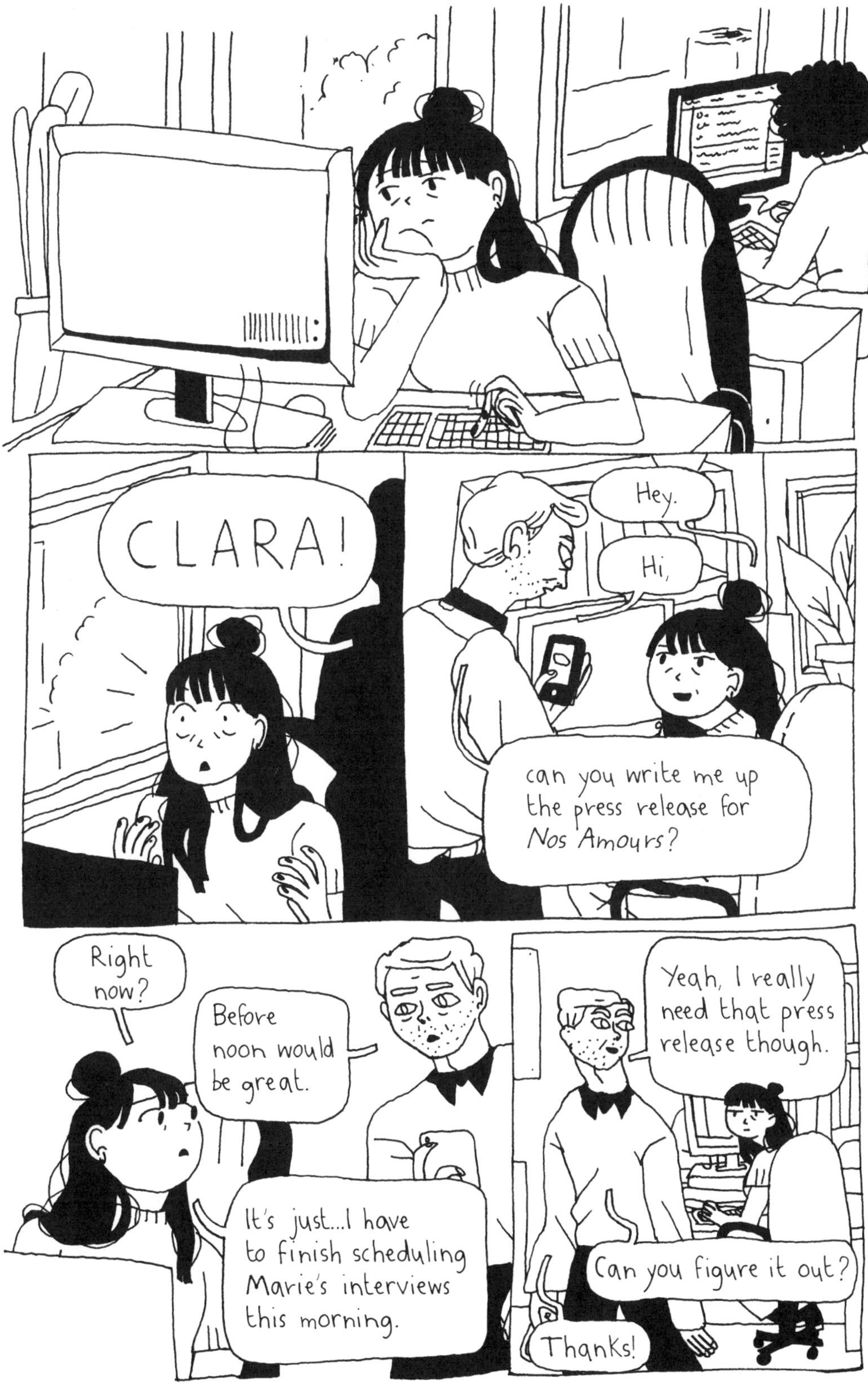
CLARA!
Hey.
Hi,
can you write me up the press release for *Nos Amours*?
Right now?
Before noon would be great.
It's just...I have to finish scheduling Marie's interviews this morning.
Yeah, I really need that press release though.
Can you figure it out?
Thanks!

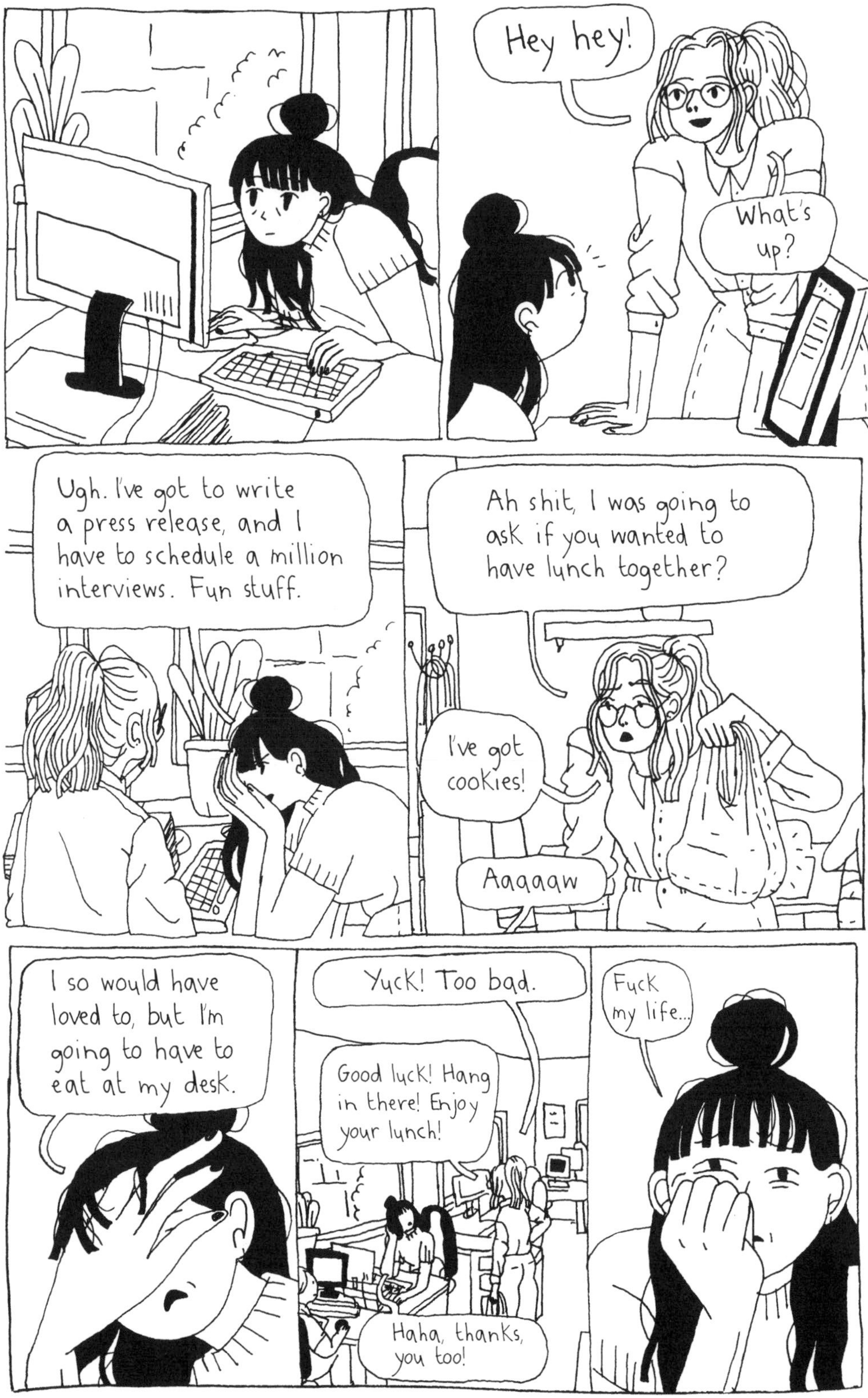
Hey hey!
What's up?
Ugh. I've got to write a press release, and I have to schedule a million interviews. Fun stuff.
Ah shit, I was going to ask if you wanted to have lunch together?
I've got cookies!
Aaaaaw
I so would have loved to, but I'm going to have to eat at my desk.
Yuck! Too bad.
Good luck! Hang in there! Enjoy your lunch!
Haha, thanks, you too!
Fuck my life...

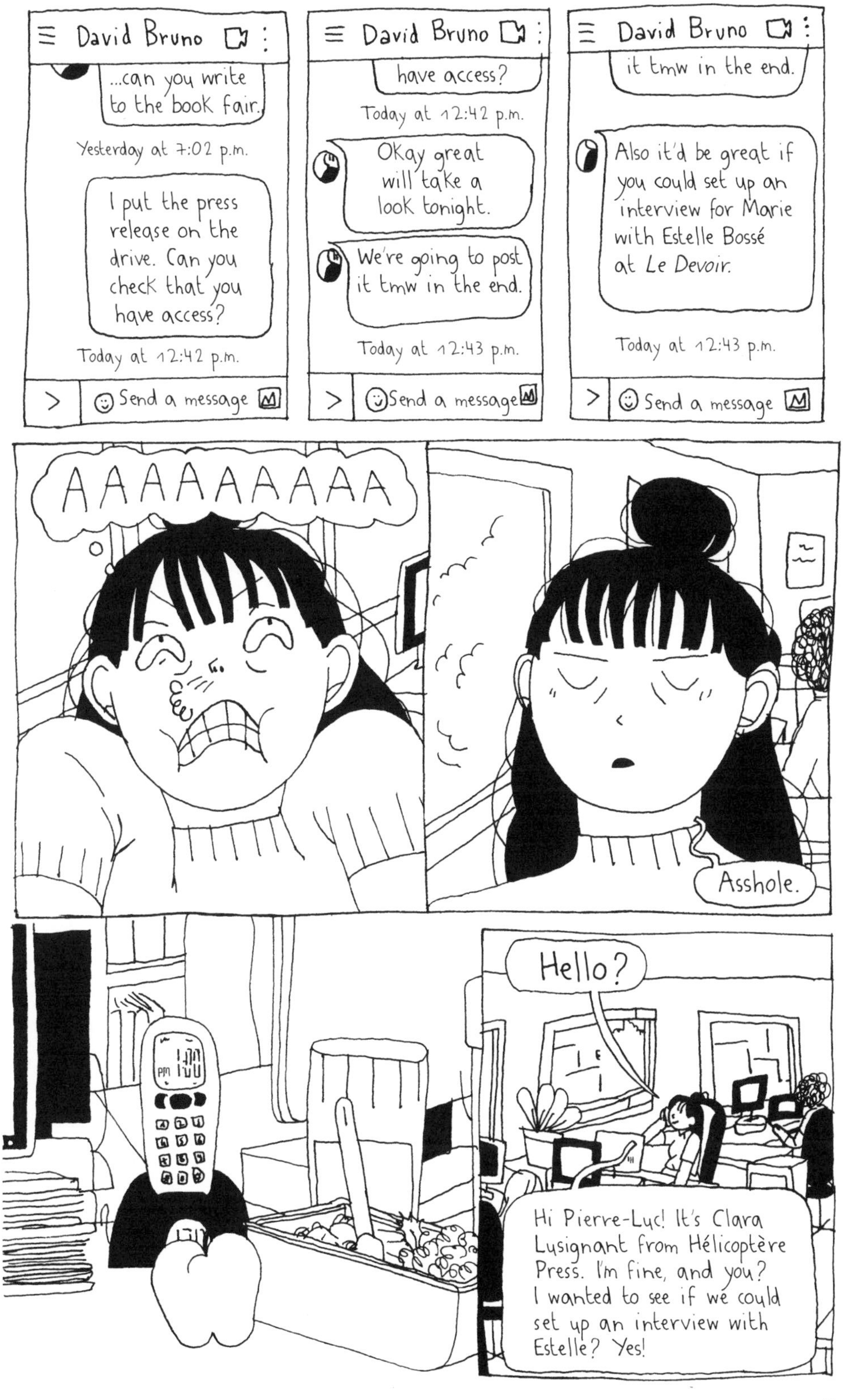

David Bruno
...can you write to the book fair.
Yesterday at 7:02 p.m.
I put the press release on the drive. Can you check that you have access?
Today at 12:42 p.m.
Send a message
David Bruno
have access?
Today at 12:42 p.m.
Okay great will take a look tonight.
We're going to post it tmw in the end.
Today at 12:43 p.m.
Send a message
David Bruno
it tmw in the end.
Also it'd be great if you could set up an interview for Marie with Estelle Bossé at *Le Devoir*.
Today at 12:43 p.m.
Send a message
AAAAAAAAA
Asshole.
Hello?
Hi Pierre-Luc! It's Clara Lusignant from Hélicoptère Press. I'm fine, and you? I wanted to see if we could set up an interview with Estelle? Yes!

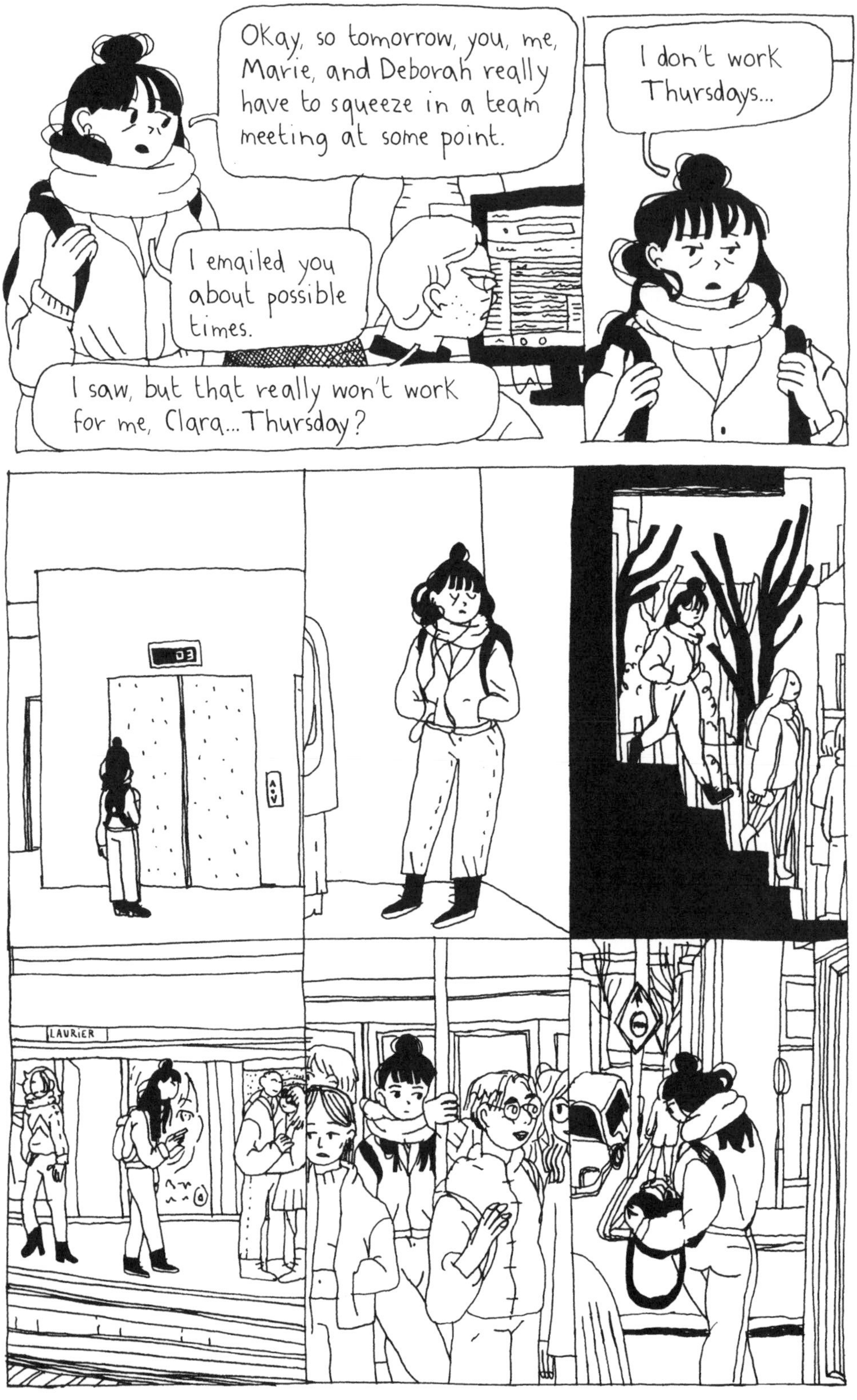
Okay, so tomorrow, you, me, Marie, and Deborah really have to squeeze in a team meeting at some point.
I emailed you about possible times.
I saw, but that really won't work for me, Clara... Thursday?
I don't work Thursdays...
LAURIER

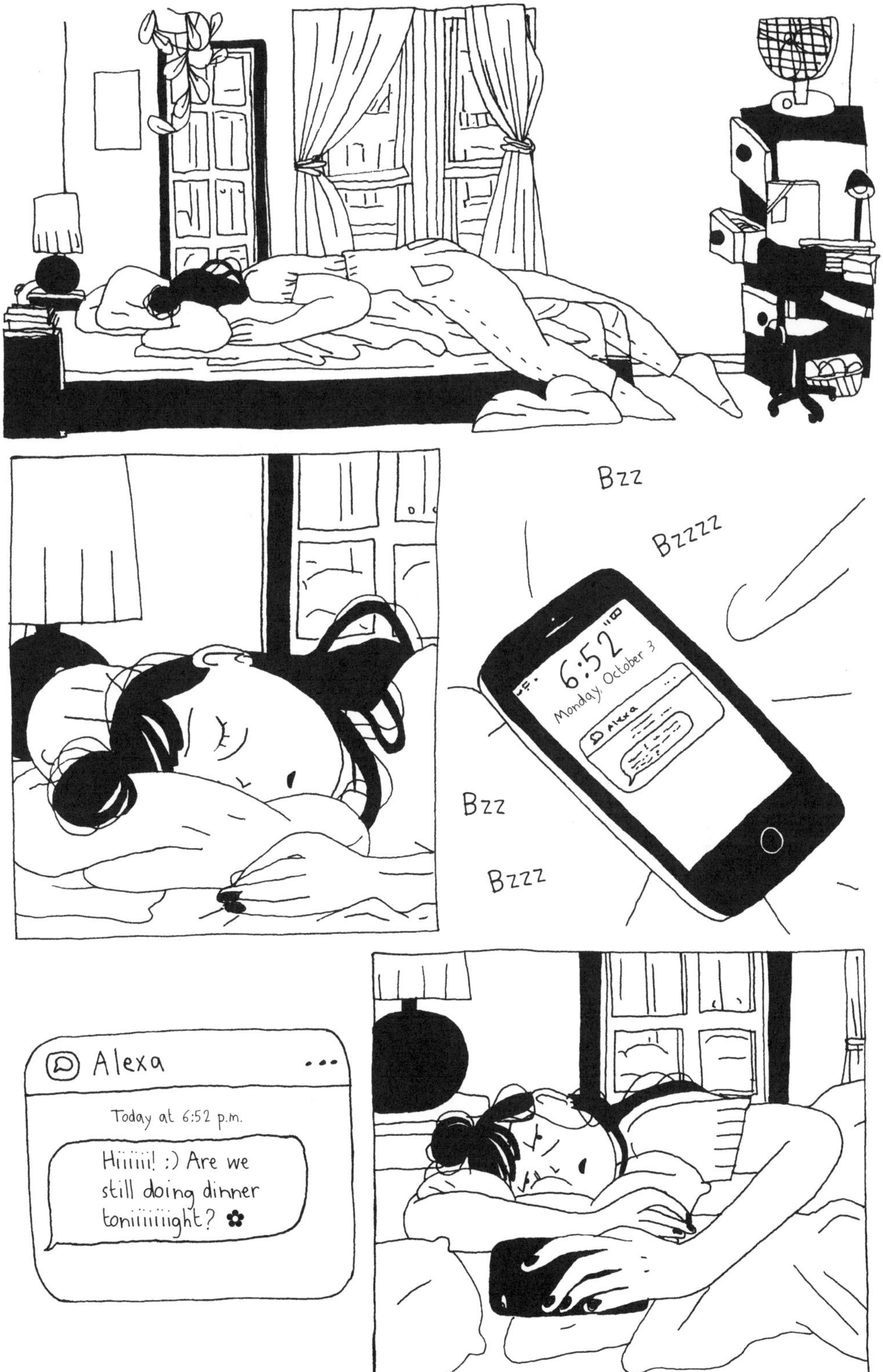
Bzz
Bzzzz
6:52
Monday, October 3
Alexa
Bzz
Bzzz
Alexa
Today at 6:52 p.m.
Hiiiiii! :) Are we still doing dinner toniiiiiiight? ✿

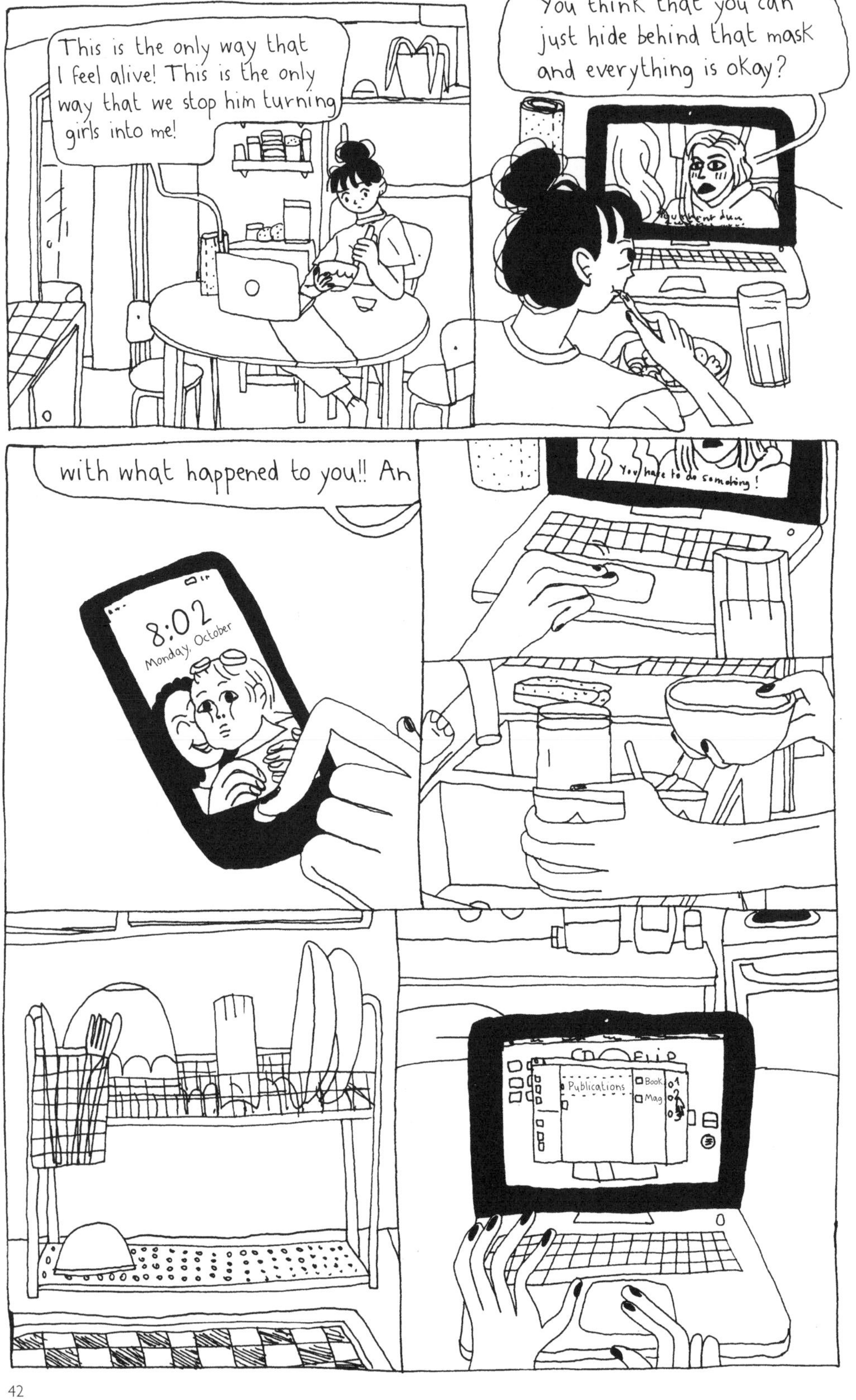
This is the only way that I feel alive! This is the only way that we stop him turning girls into me!
You think that you can just hide behind that mask and everything is okay?
with what happened to you!! An
8:02
Monday, October
You have to do something !
Publications
Book
Mag

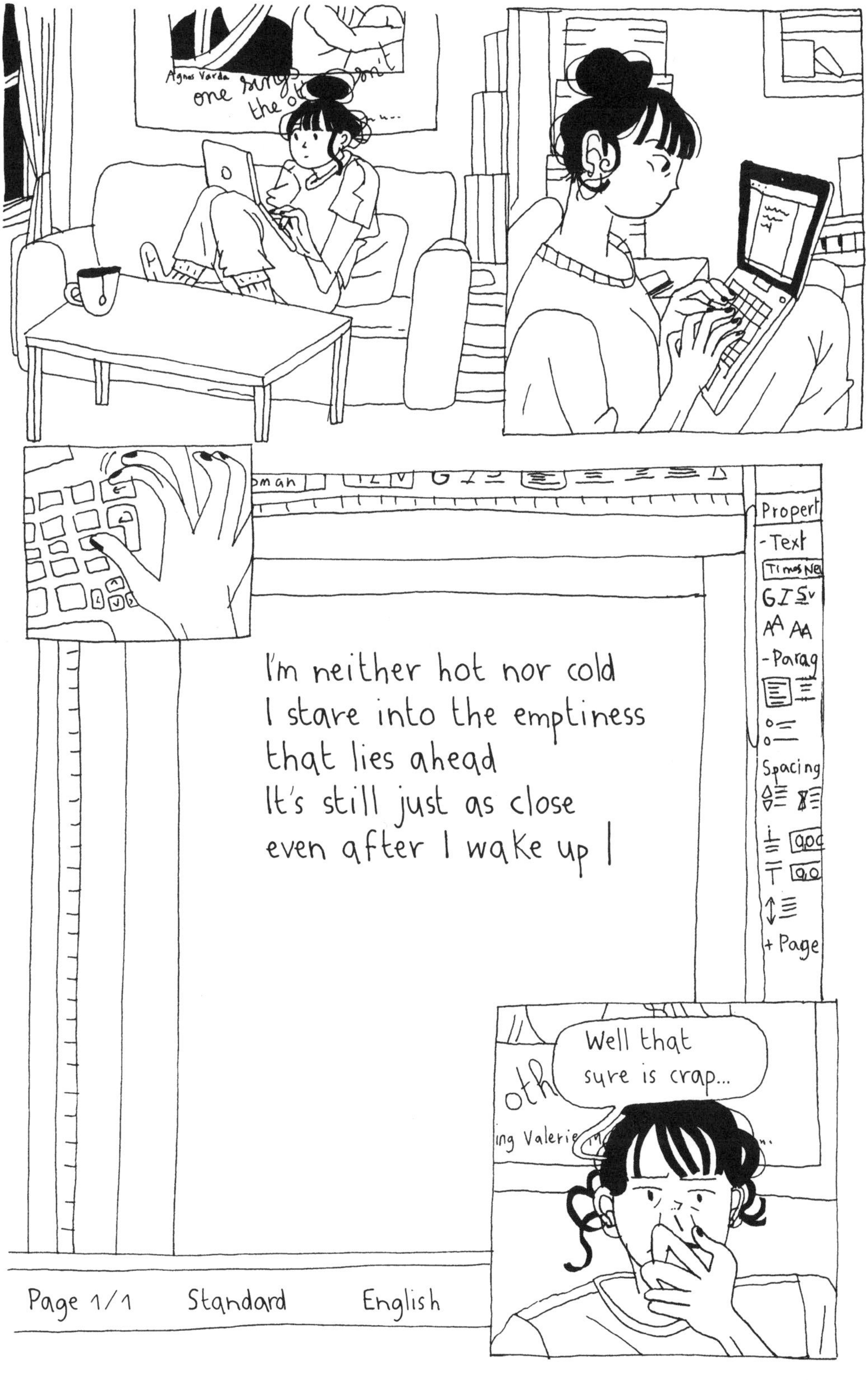
Agnes Varda
-Text
Spacing
+ Page
I'm neither hot nor cold
I stare into the emptiness
that lies ahead
It's still just as close
even after I wake up |
Page 1/1 Standard English
Well that sure is crap...

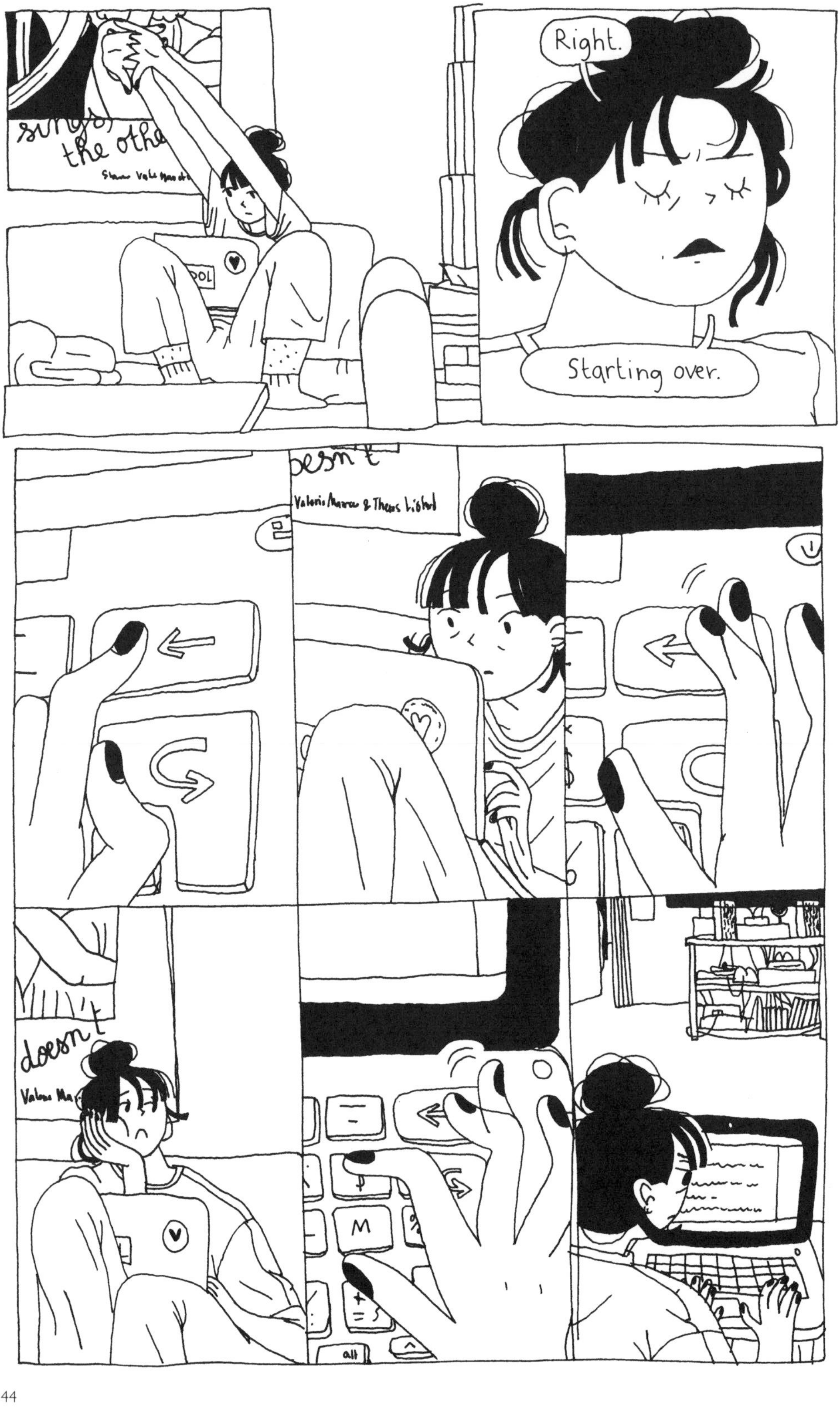
Right.
Starting over.
doesn't

Sometimes I think about
how you used to
hold me against you
and I'd think,
you must love me
just a little.
But in the end (I was wrong)

I'm still holding back
tears
trying not to let them go
because they're better than
this void

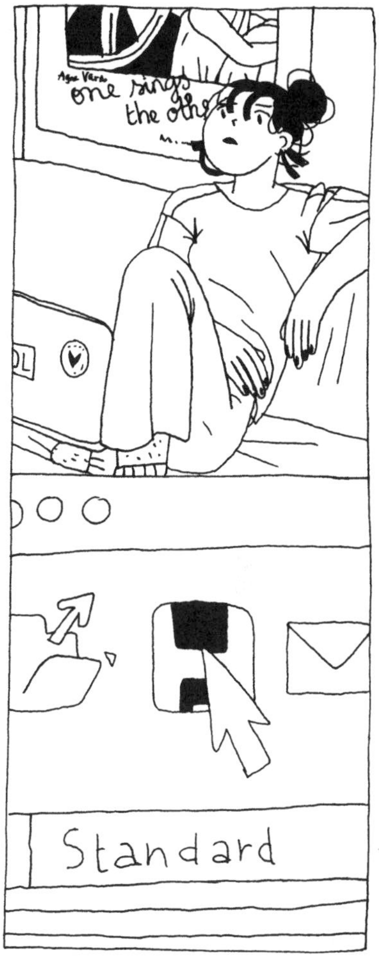
Standard

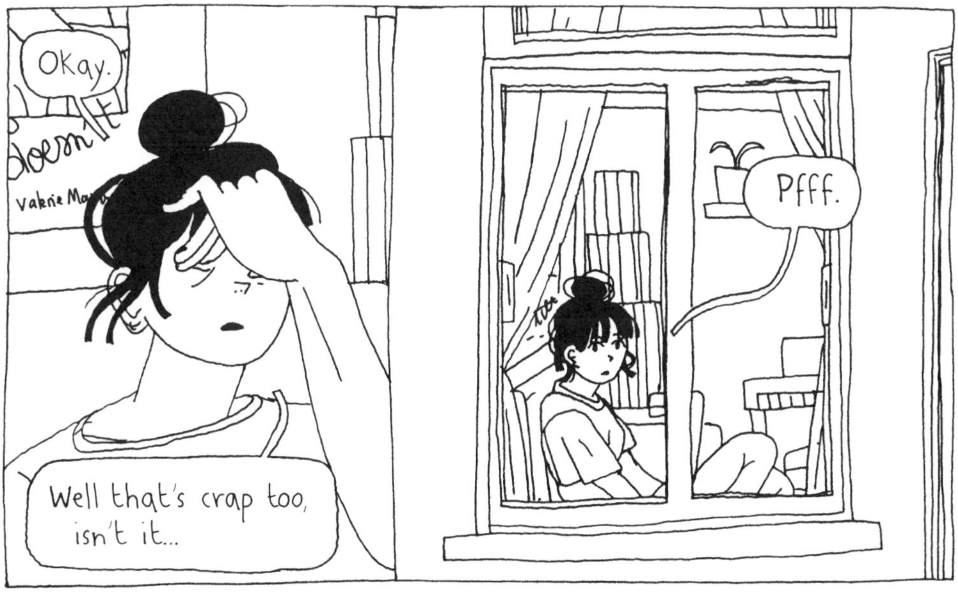
Okay.
Well that's crap too, isn't it...
Pfff.

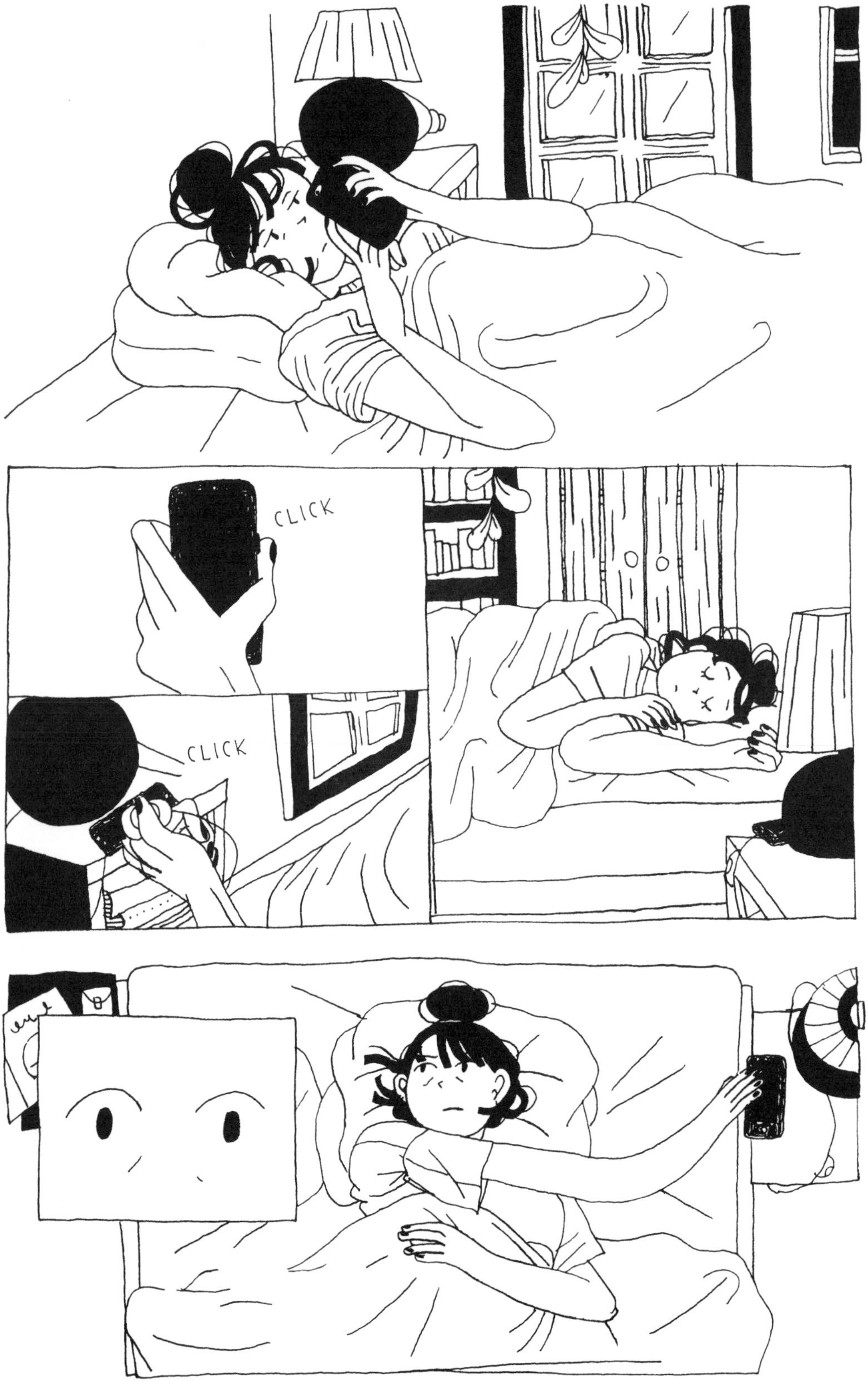
CLICK
CLICK

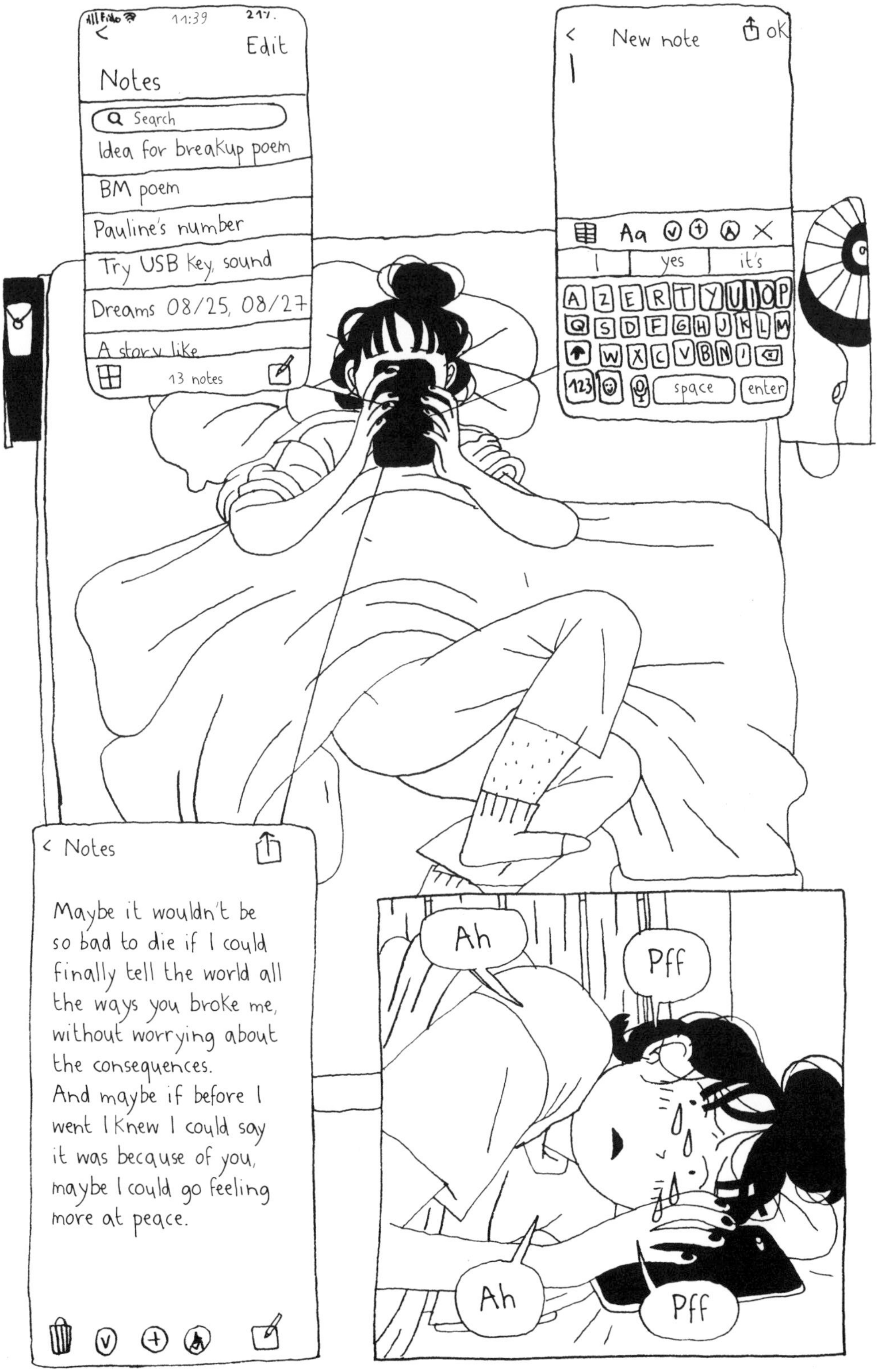
11:39
Edit
Notes
Search
Idea for breakup poem
BM poem
Pauline's number
Try USB key, sound
Dreams 08/25, 08/27
A story like
13 notes
New note
ok
Aa
I
yes
it's
AZERTYUIOP
QSDFGHJKLM
WXCVBN
123
space
enter
Notes
Maybe it wouldn't be so bad to die if I could finally tell the world all the ways you broke me, without worrying about the consequences.
And maybe if before I went I knew I could say it was because of you, maybe I could go feeling more at peace.
Ah
Pff
Ah
Pff

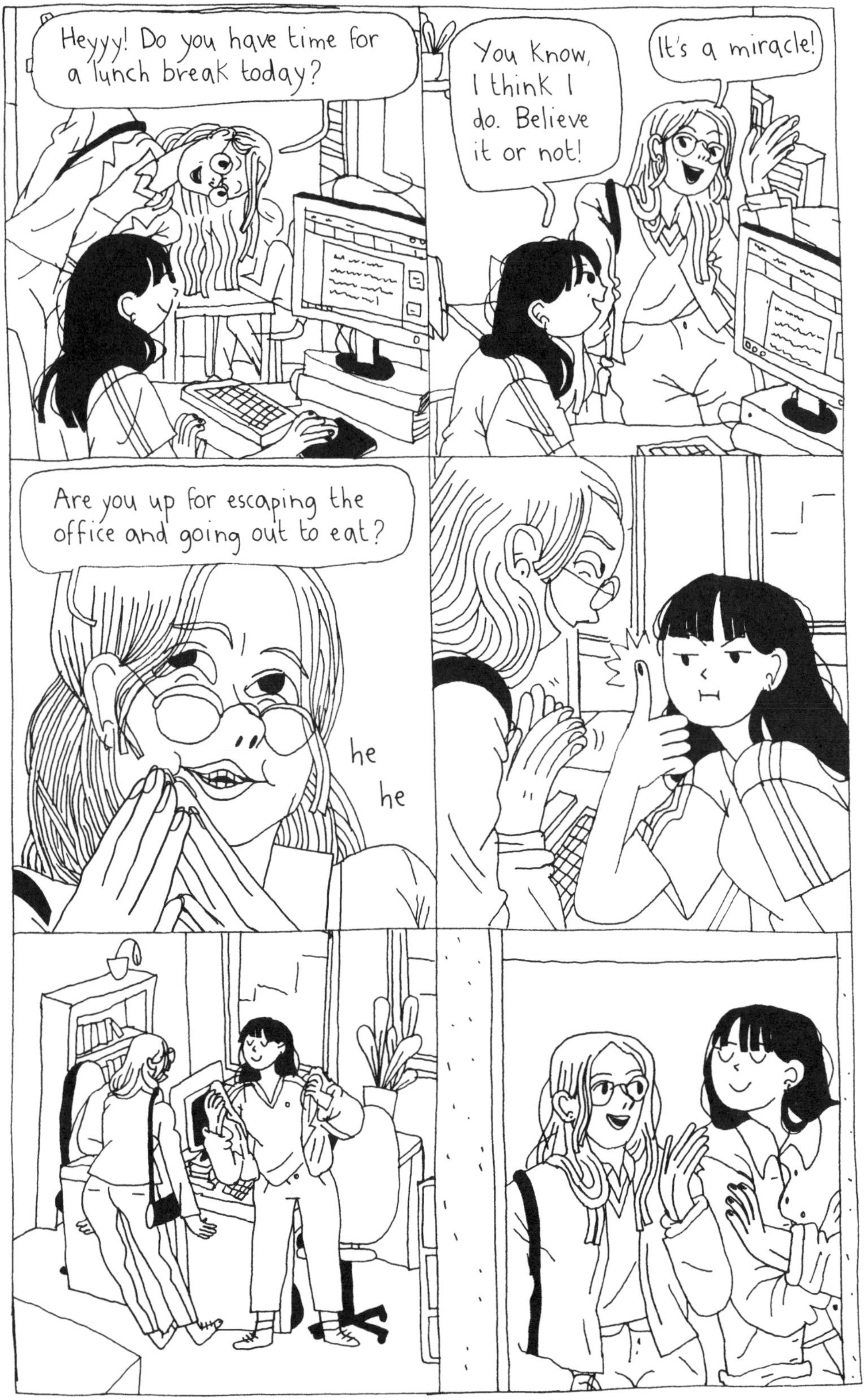
Heyyy! Do you have time for a lunch break today?
You know, I think I do. Believe it or not!
It's a miracle!
Are you up for escaping the office and going out to eat?
he
he

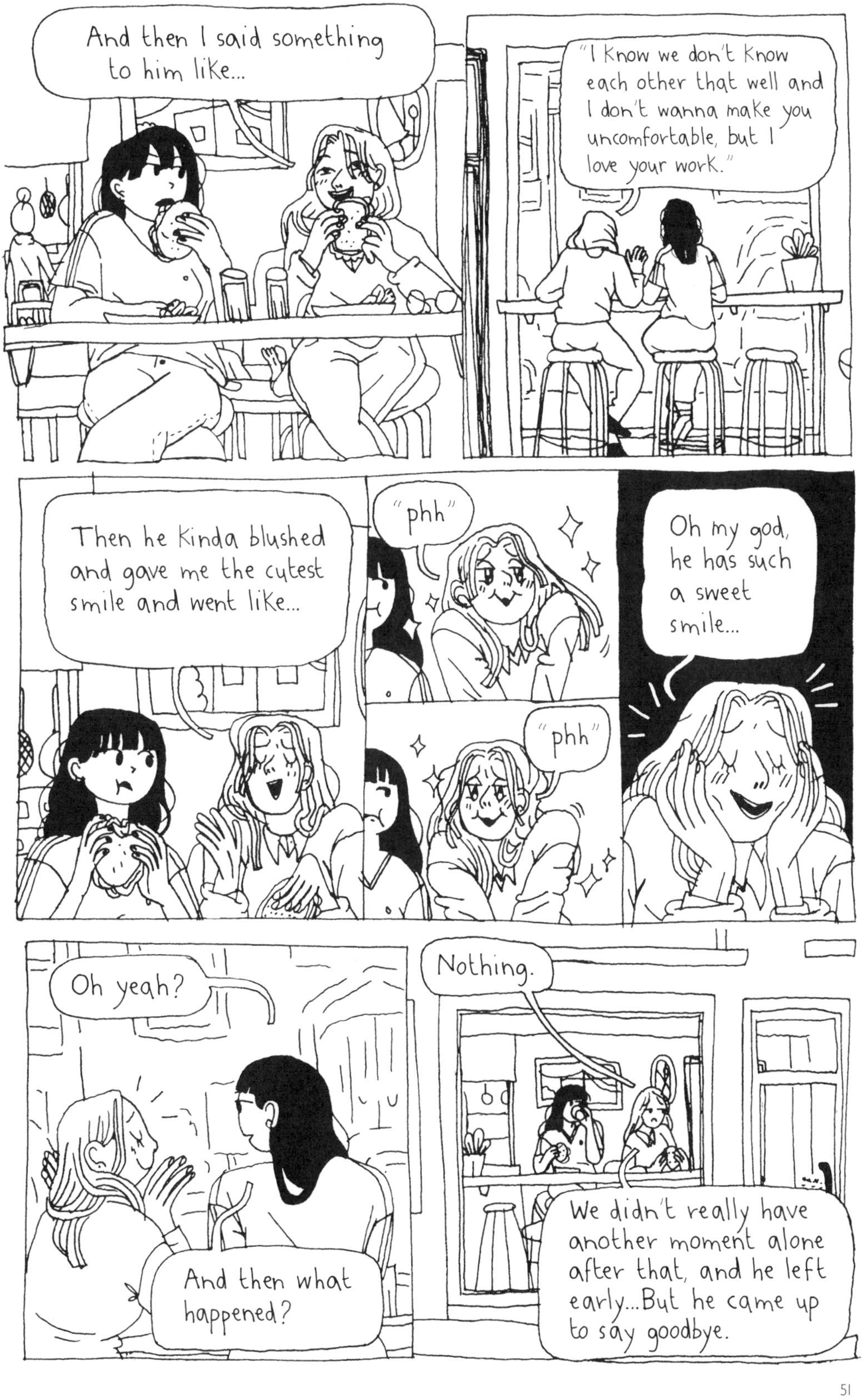
And then I said something to him like...
"I know we don't know each other that well and I don't wanna make you uncomfortable, but I love your work."
Then he kinda blushed and gave me the cutest smile and went like...
"phh"
"phh"
Oh my god, he has such a sweet smile...
Oh yeah?
And then what happened?
Nothing.
We didn't really have another moment alone after that, and he left early...But he came up to say goodbye.

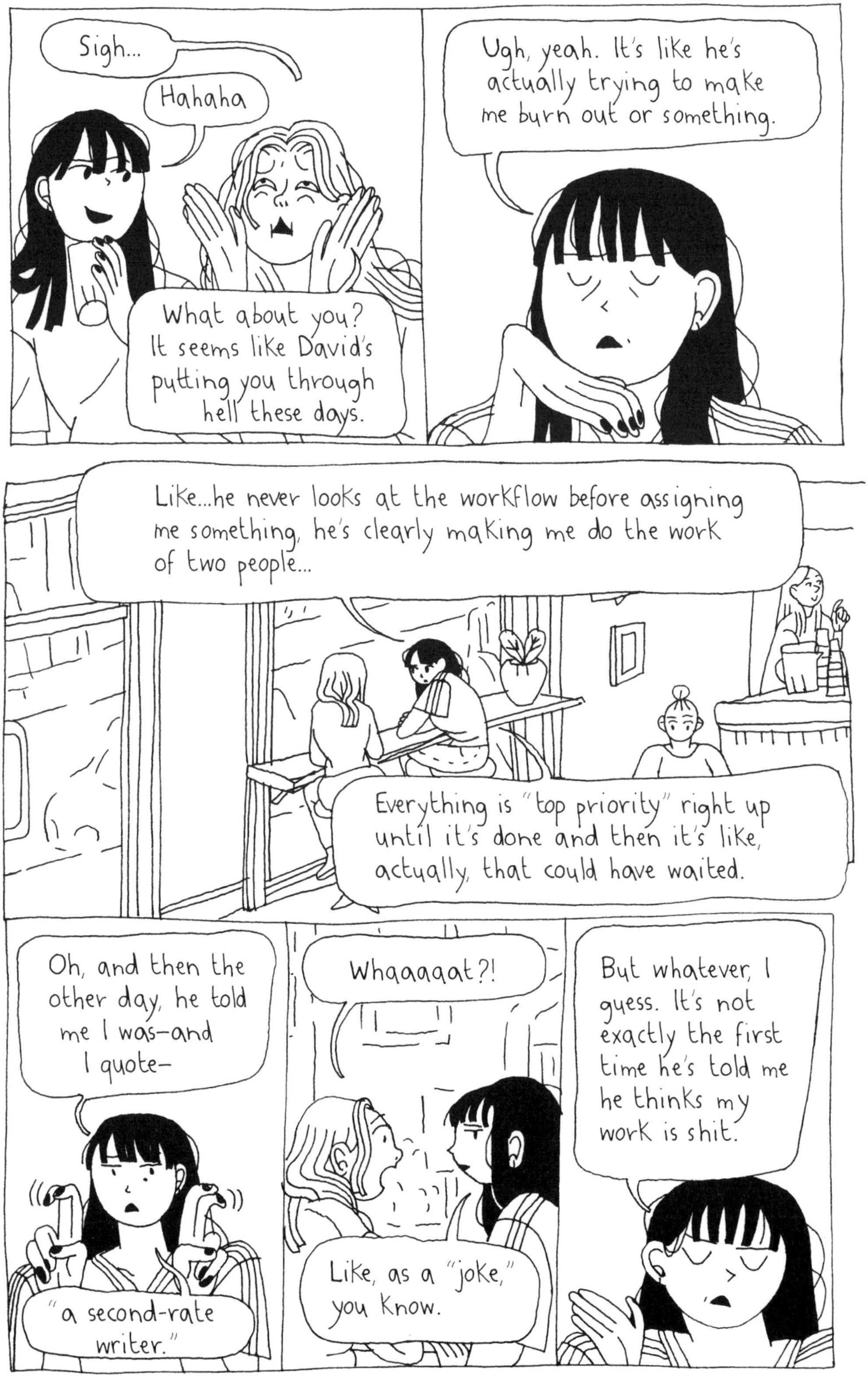
Sigh...
Hahaha
What about you? It seems like David's putting you through hell these days.
Ugh, yeah. It's like he's actually trying to make me burn out or something.
Like...he never looks at the workflow before assigning me something, he's clearly making me do the work of two people...
Everything is "top priority" right up until it's done and then it's like, actually, that could have waited.
Oh, and then the other day, he told me I was—and I quote—
"a second-rate writer."
Whaaaaat?!
Like, as a "joke," you know.
But whatever, I guess. It's not exactly the first time he's told me he thinks my work is shit.

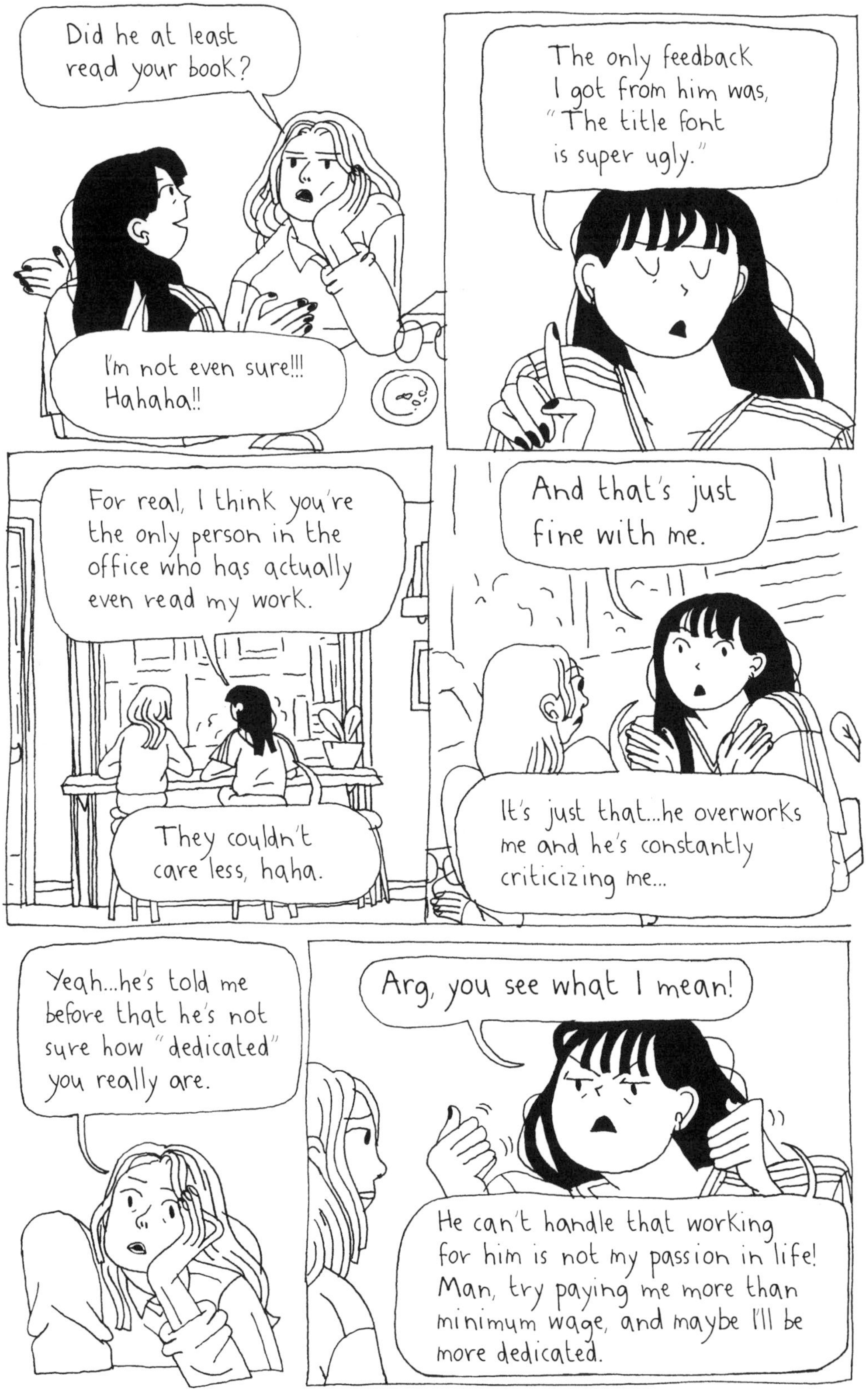

Did he at least read your book?
I'm not even sure!!! Hahaha!!
The only feedback I got from him was, "The title font is super ugly."
For real, I think you're the only person in the office who has actually even read my work.
They couldn't care less, haha.
And that's just fine with me.
It's just that...he overworks me and he's constantly criticizing me...
Yeah...he's told me before that he's not sure how "dedicated" you really are.
Arg, you see what I mean!
He can't handle that working for him is not my passion in life! Man, try paying me more than minimum wage, and maybe I'll be more dedicated.

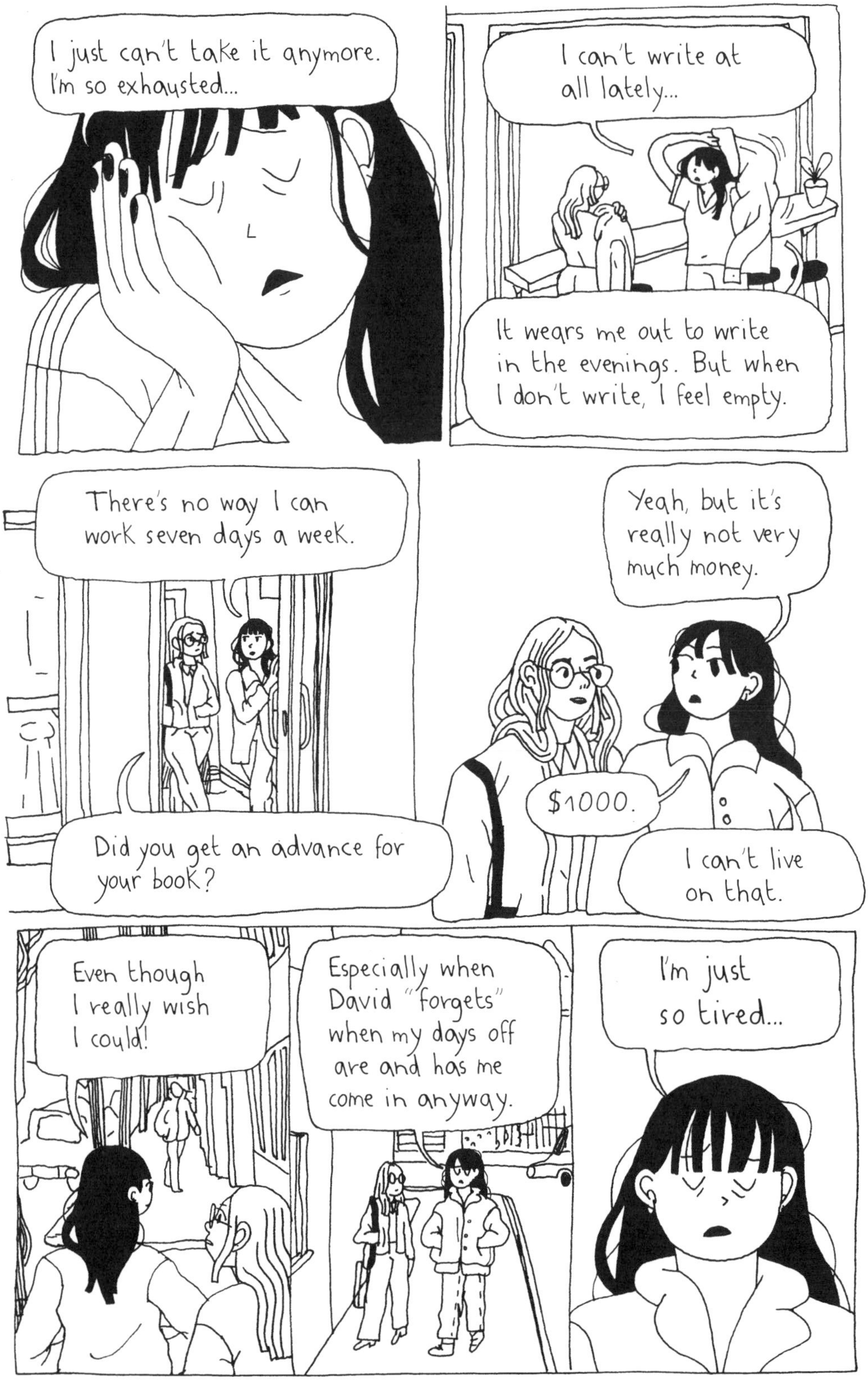
I just can't take it anymore. I'm so exhausted...
I can't write at all lately...
It wears me out to write in the evenings. But when I don't write, I feel empty.
There's no way I can work seven days a week.
Did you get an advance for your book?
Yeah, but it's really not very much money.
$1000.
I can't live on that.
Even though I really wish I could!
Especially when David "forgets" when my days off are and has me come in anyway.
I'm just so tired...

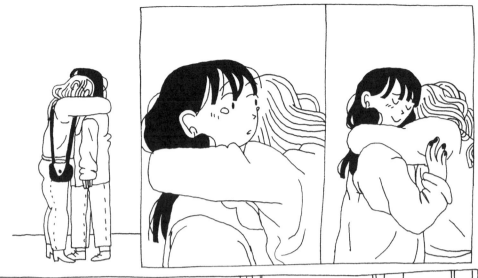

®RV Roxane Vallée - Bleue Publishing ↰↰
Tues, 2 Oct 2019
: to me ⌄

Hi Clara!

Just checking in to see how the book is going. Any chance you would be able to send me a chunk (maybe 30%?) in January? It would help us to start working on marketing details...Let me Know!! <3

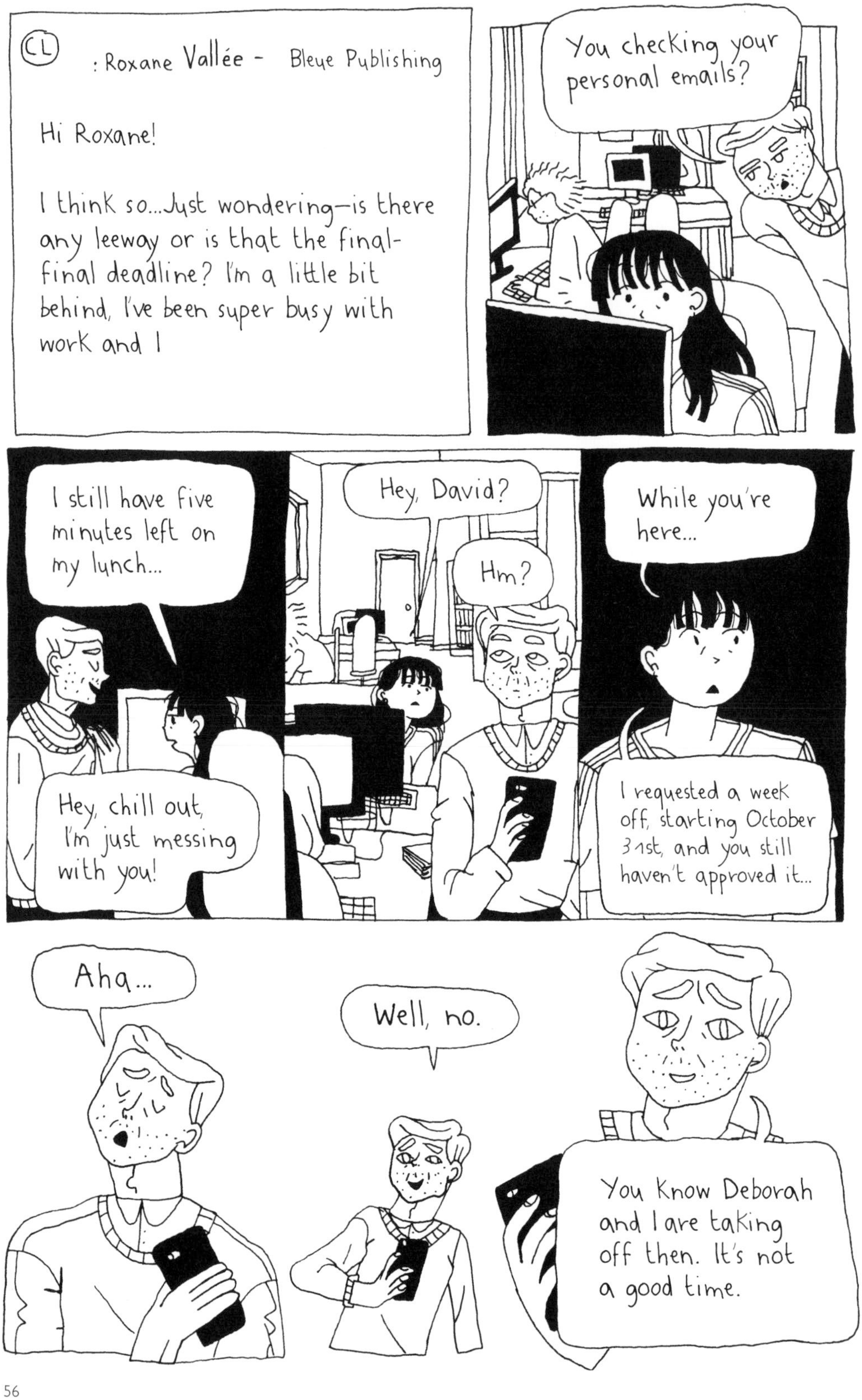
CL : Roxane Vallée - Bleue Publishing
Hi Roxane!
I think so...Just wondering—is there any leeway or is that the final-final deadline? I'm a little bit behind, I've been super busy with work and I
You checking your personal emails?
I still have five minutes left on my lunch...
Hey, chill out, I'm just messing with you!
Hey, David?
Hm?
While you're here...
I requested a week off, starting October 31st, and you still haven't approved it...
Aha...
Well, no.
You know Deborah and I are taking off then. It's not a good time.

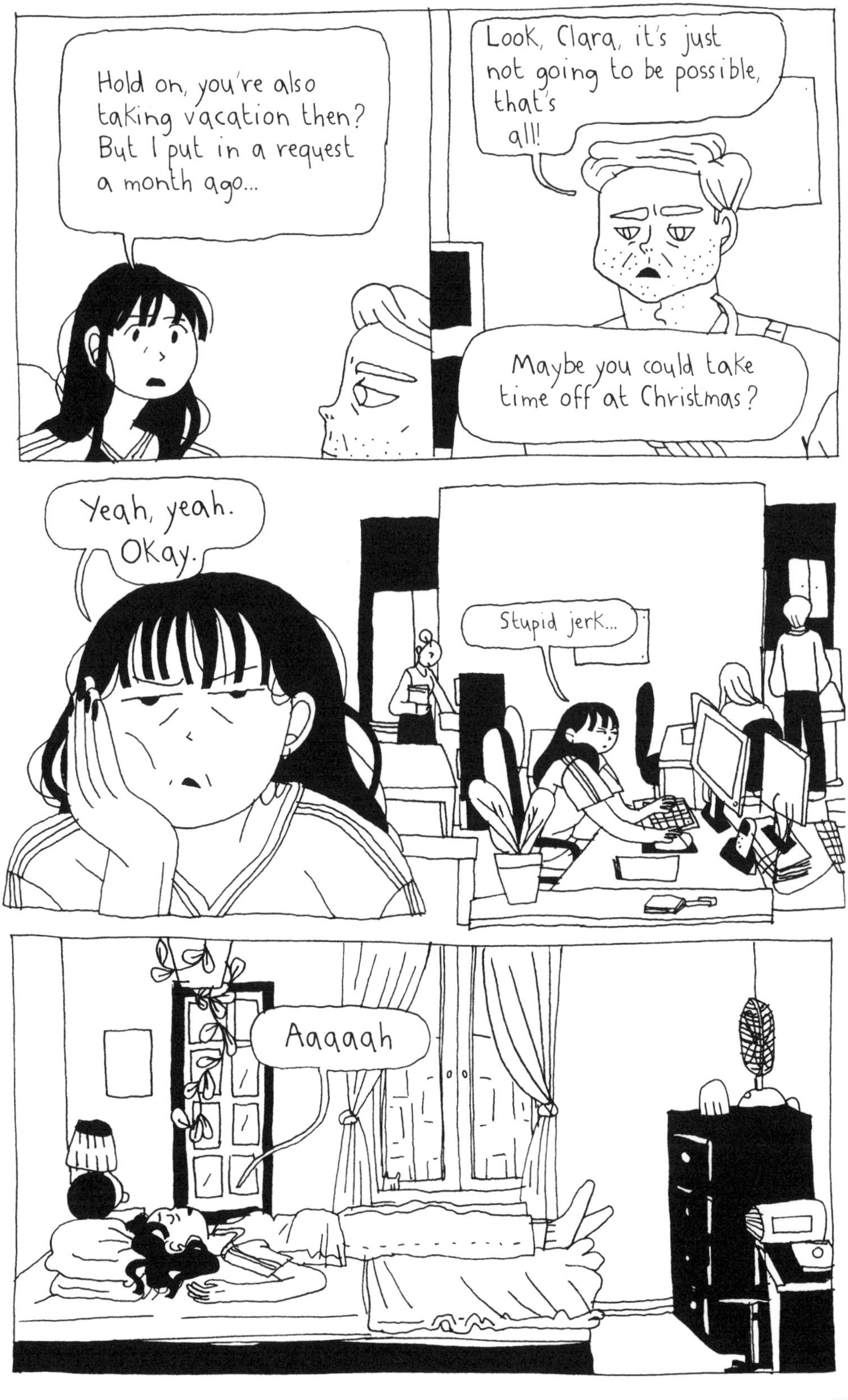
Hold on, you're also taking vacation then? But I put in a request a month ago...
Look, Clara, it's just not going to be possible, that's all!
Maybe you could take time off at Christmas?
Yeah, yeah. Okay.
Stupid jerk...
Aaaaah

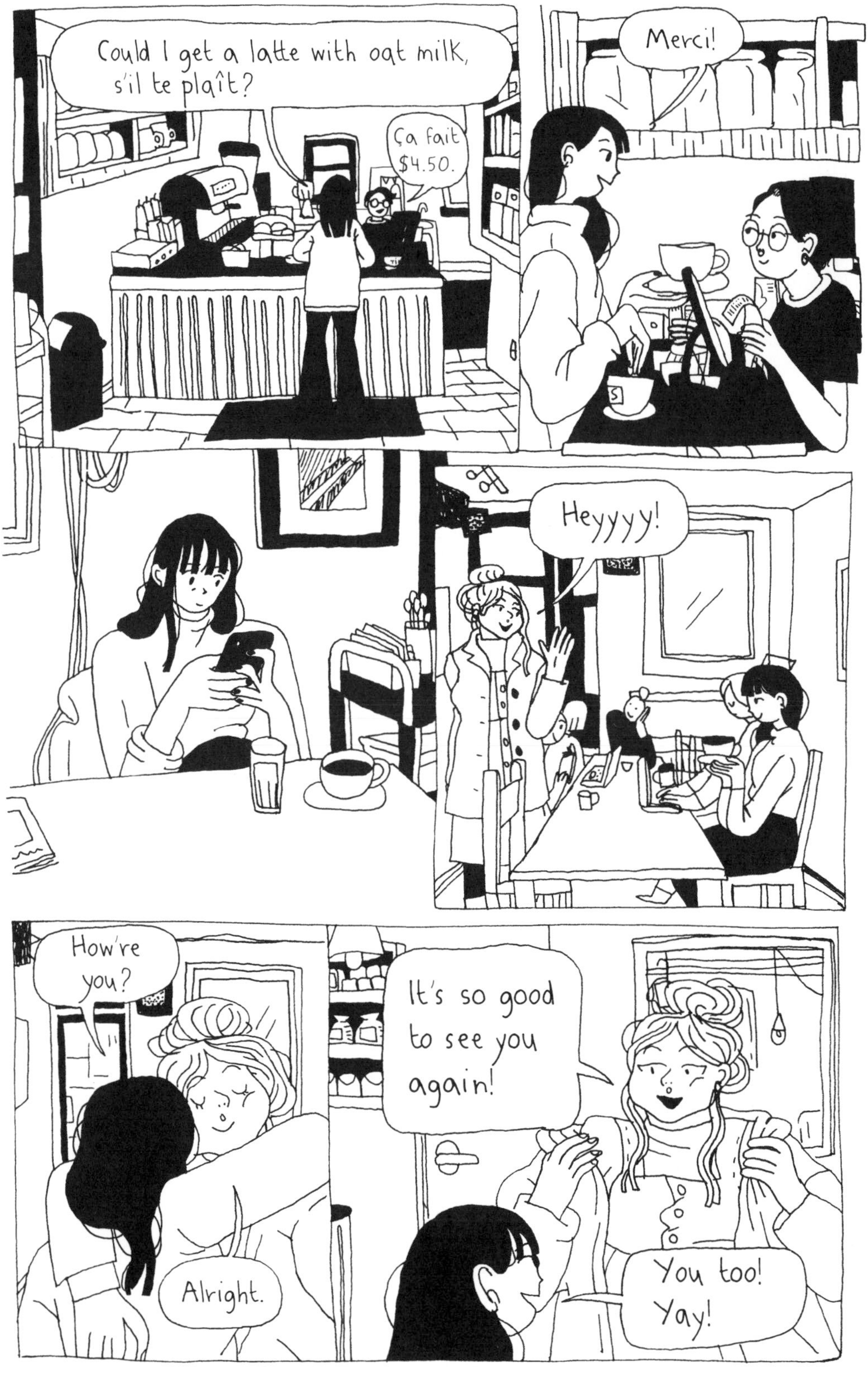
Could I get a latte with oat milk, s'il te plaît?
Ça fait $4.50.
Merci!
Heyyyy!
How're you?
Alright.
It's so good to see you again!
You too! Yay!

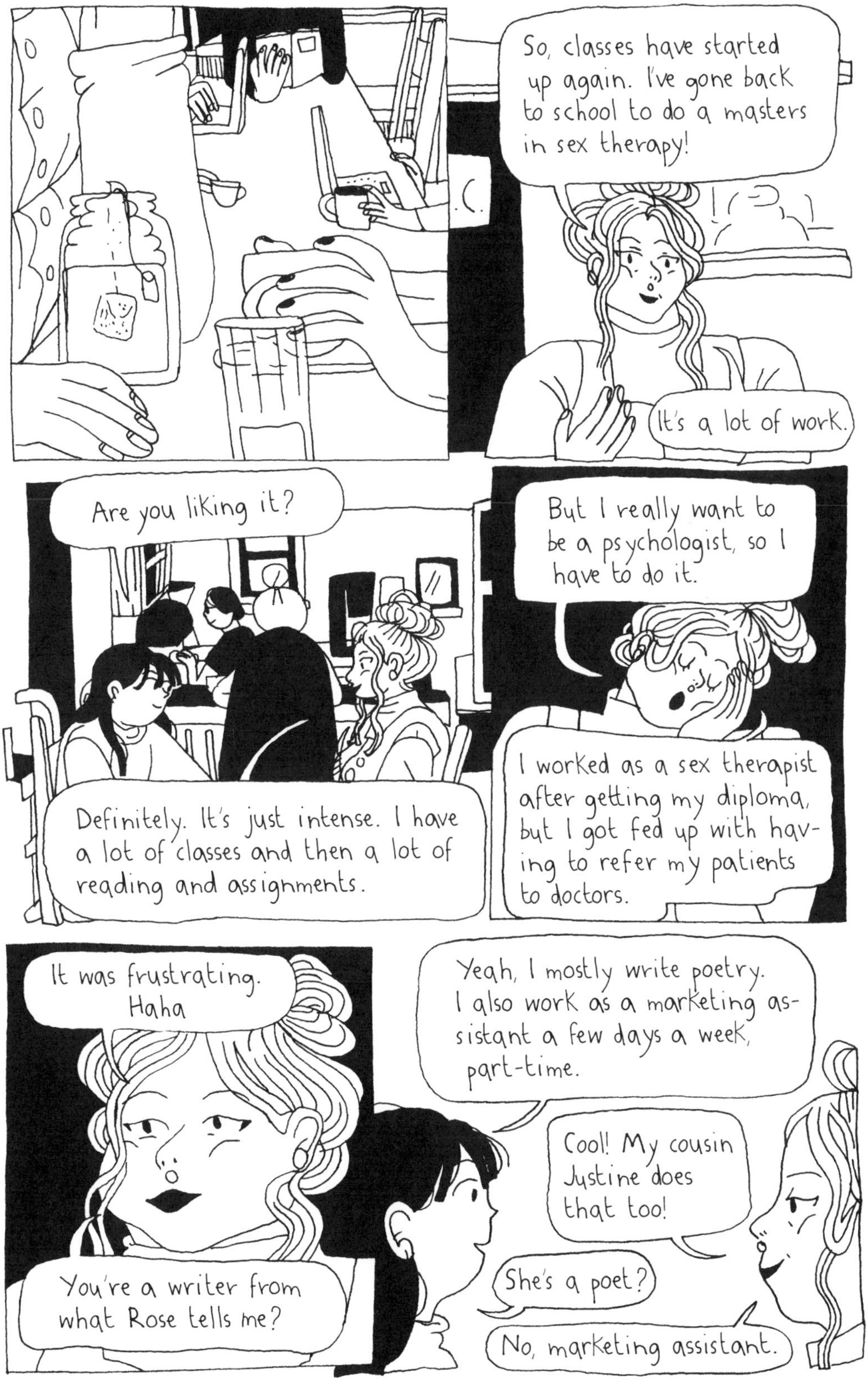
So, classes have started up again. I've gone back to school to do a masters in sex therapy!
It's a lot of work.
Are you liking it?
Definitely. It's just intense. I have a lot of classes and then a lot of reading and assignments.
But I really want to be a psychologist, so I have to do it.
I worked as a sex therapist after getting my diploma, but I got fed up with having to refer my patients to doctors.
It was frustrating. Haha
You're a writer from what Rose tells me?
Yeah, I mostly write poetry. I also work as a marketing assistant a few days a week, part-time.
Cool! My cousin Justine does that too!
She's a poet?
No, marketing assistant.

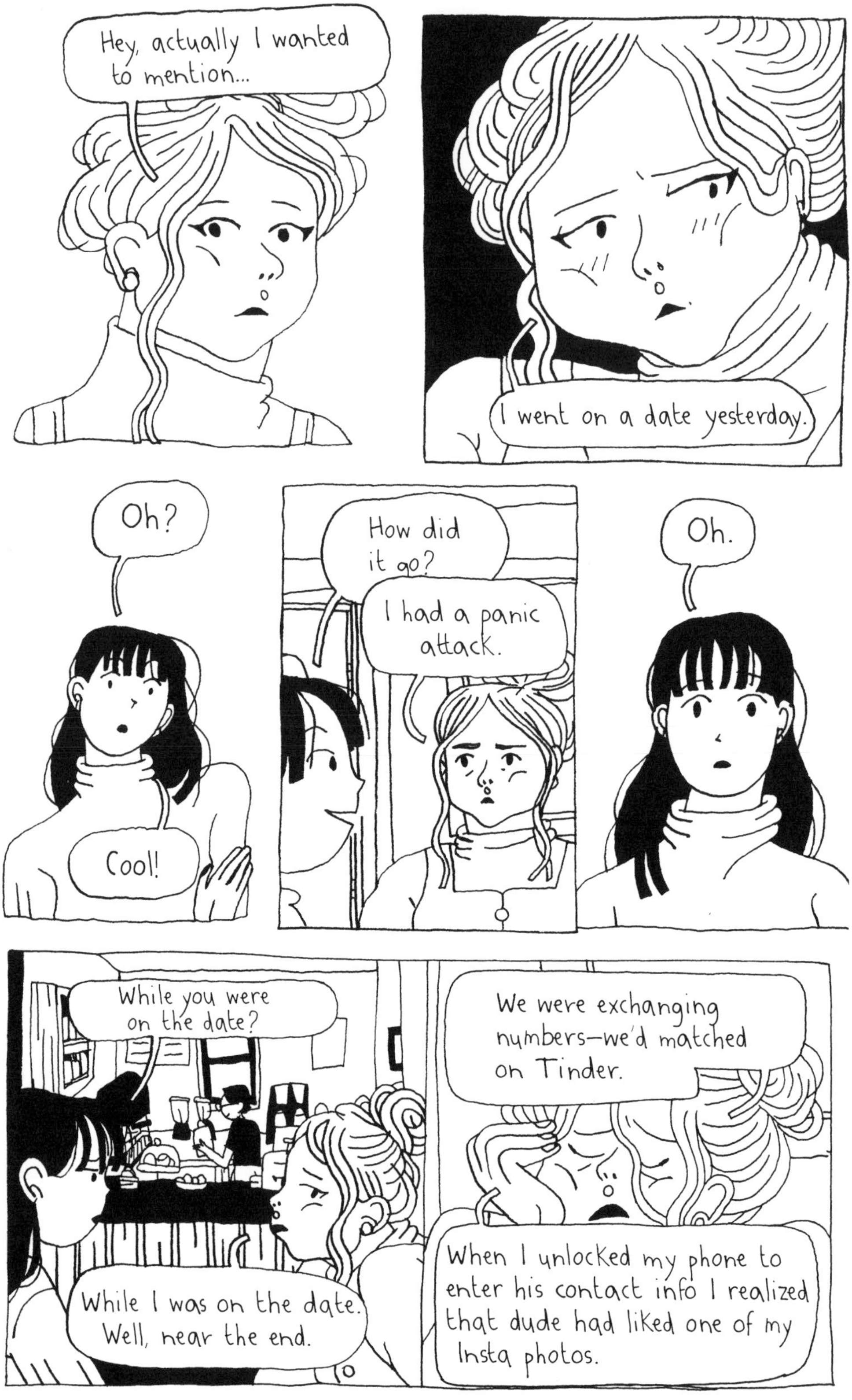

Hey, actually I wanted to mention...
I went on a date yesterday.
Oh?
Cool!
How did it go?
I had a panic attack.
Oh.
While you were on the date?
While I was on the date. Well, near the end.
We were exchanging numbers—we'd matched on Tinder.
When I unlocked my phone to enter his contact info I realized that dude had liked one of my Insta photos.

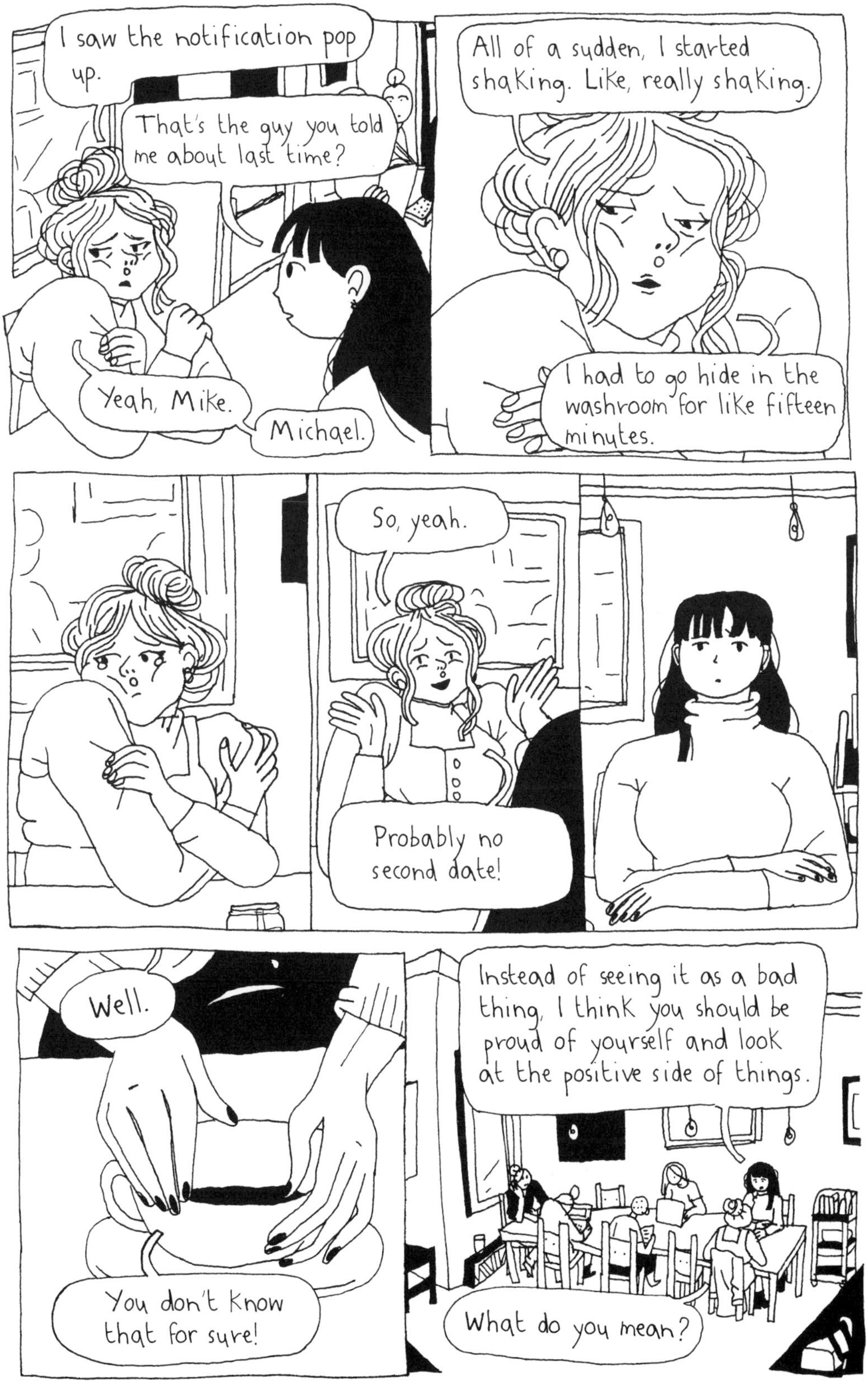
I saw the notification pop up.
That's the guy you told me about last time?
Yeah, Mike.
Michael.
All of a sudden, I started shaking. Like, really shaking.
I had to go hide in the washroom for like fifteen minutes.
So, yeah.
Probably no second date!
Well.
You don't know that for sure!
Instead of seeing it as a bad thing, I think you should be proud of yourself and look at the positive side of things.
What do you mean?

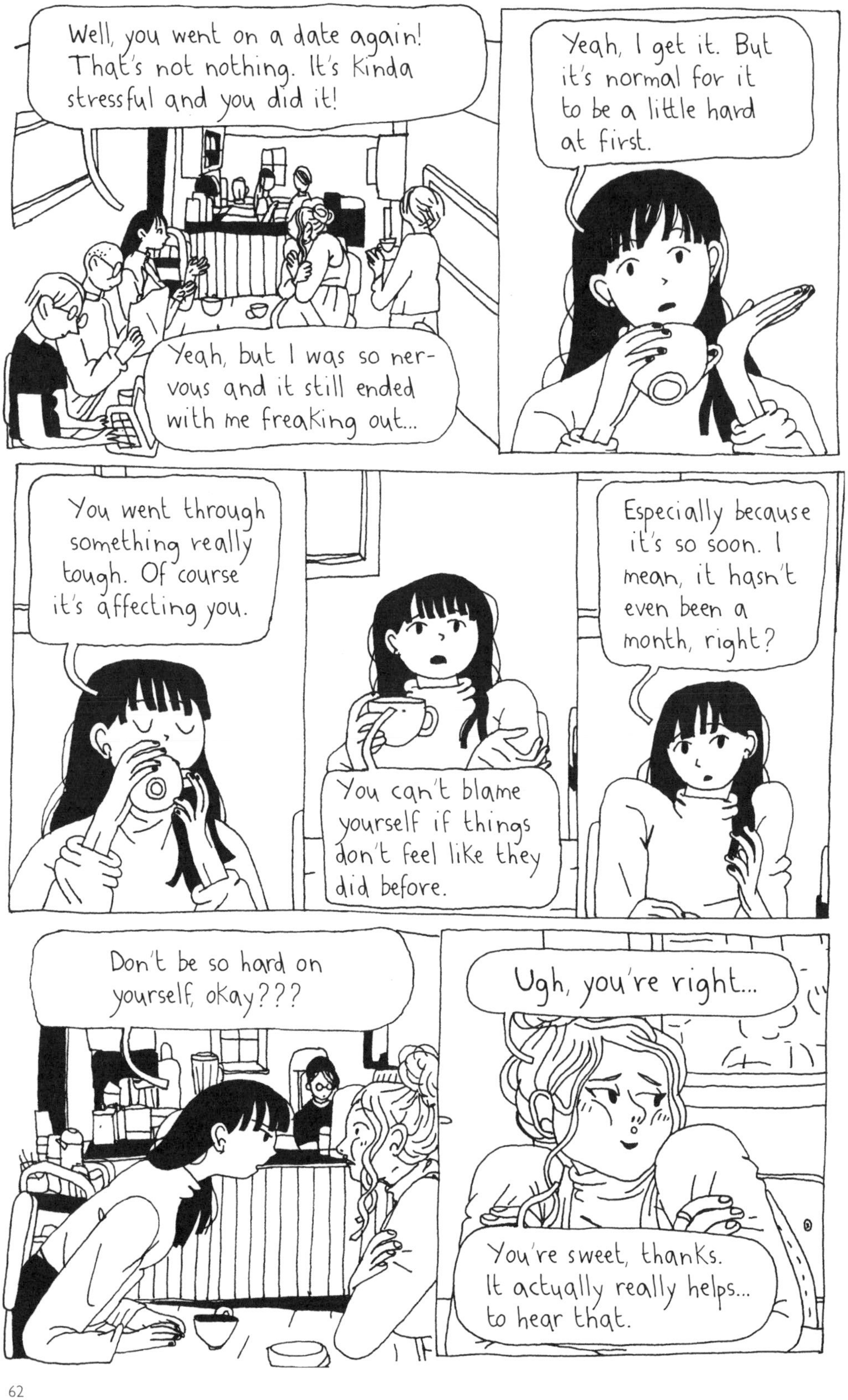
Well, you went on a date again! That's not nothing. It's kinda stressful and you did it!
Yeah, but I was so nervous and it still ended with me freaking out...
Yeah, I get it. But it's normal for it to be a little hard at first.
You went through something really tough. Of course it's affecting you.
You can't blame yourself if things don't feel like they did before.
Especially because it's so soon. I mean, it hasn't even been a month, right?
Don't be so hard on yourself, okay???
Ugh, you're right...
You're sweet, thanks. It actually really helps... to hear that.

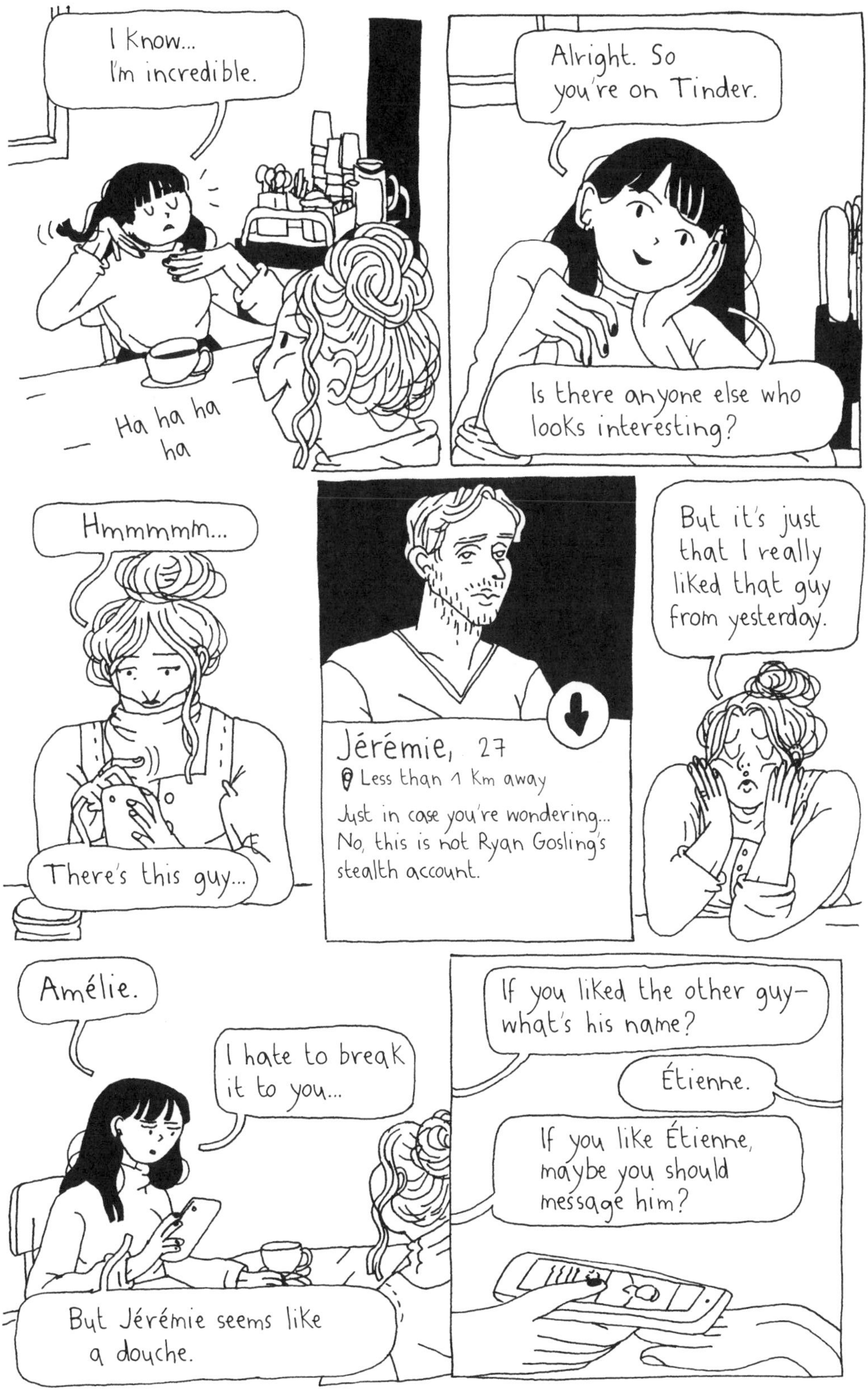
I know... I'm incredible.
Ha ha ha ha
Alright. So you're on Tinder.
Is there anyone else who looks interesting?
Hmmmmm...
There's this guy...
Jérémie, 27
Less than 1 Km away
Just in case you're wondering... No, this is not Ryan Gosling's stealth account.
But it's just that I really liked that guy from yesterday.
Amélie.
I hate to break it to you...
But Jérémie seems like a douche.
If you liked the other guy- what's his name?
Étienne.
If you like Étienne, maybe you should message him?

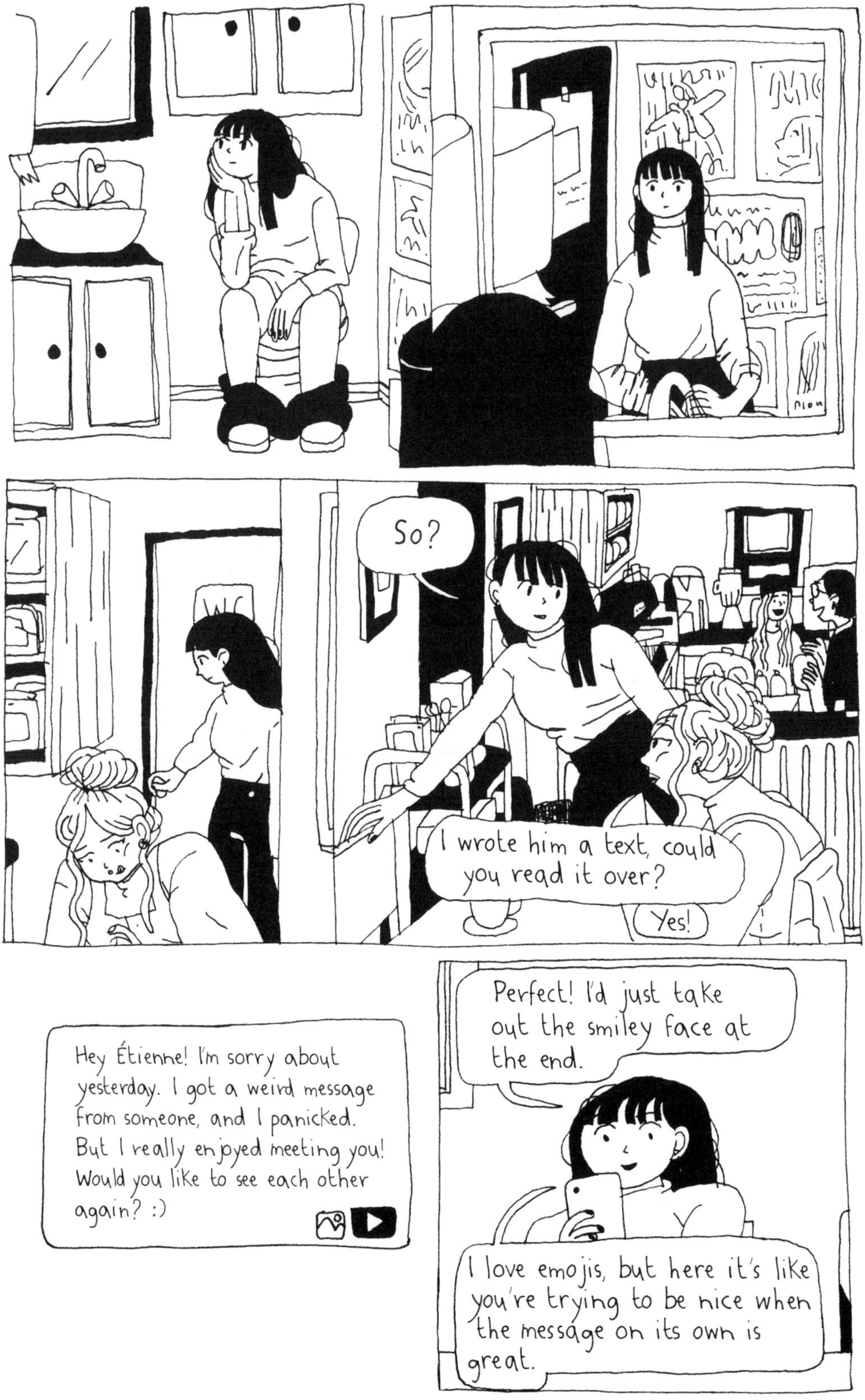
So?
I wrote him a text, could you read it over?
Yes!
Hey Étienne! I'm sorry about yesterday. I got a weird message from someone, and I panicked. But I really enjoyed meeting you! Would you like to see each other again? :)
Perfect! I'd just take out the smiley face at the end.
I love emojis, but here it's like you're trying to be nice when the message on its own is great.

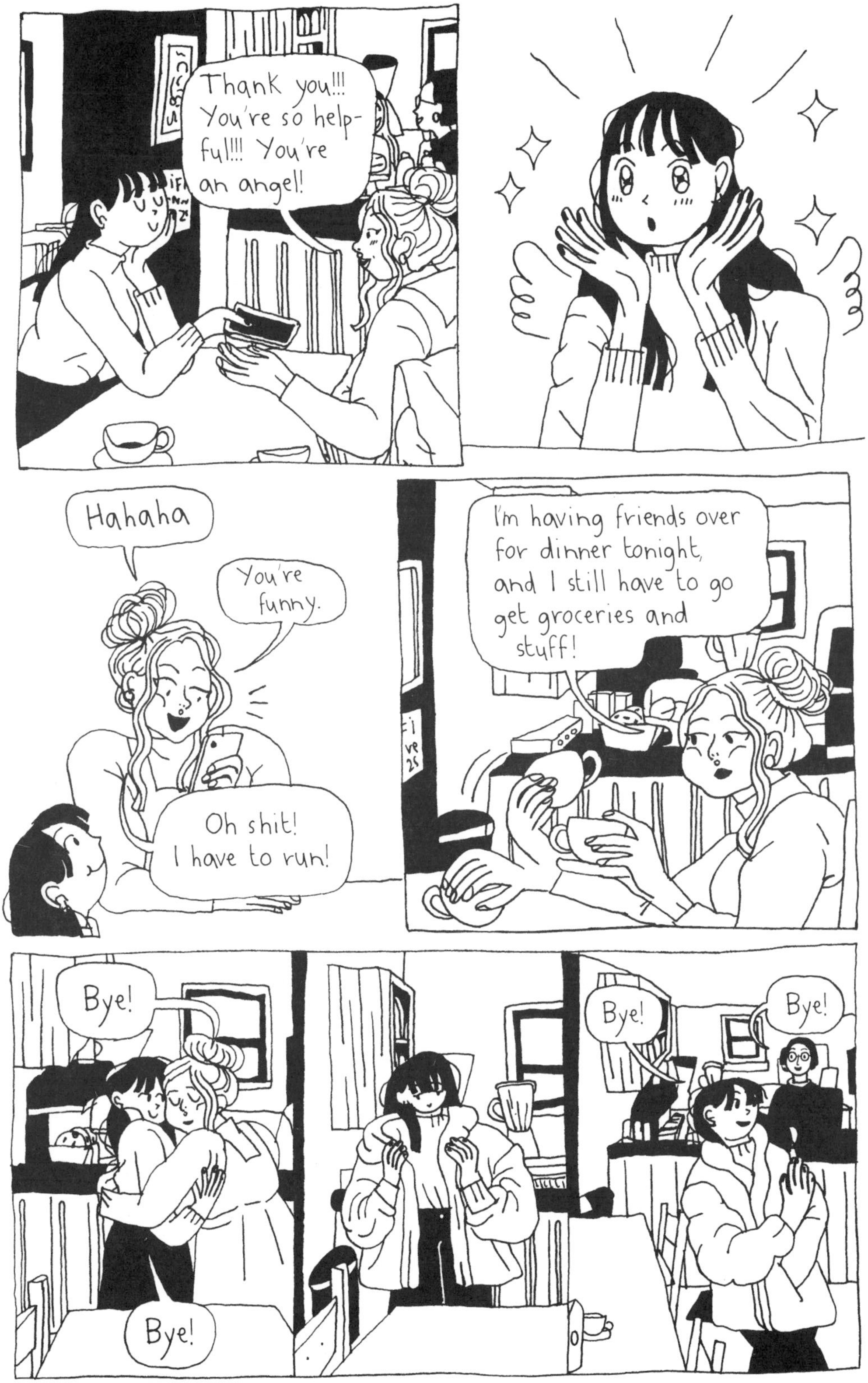
Thank you!!! You're so help-ful!!! You're an angel!
Hahaha
You're funny.
Oh shit! I have to run!
I'm having friends over for dinner tonight, and I still have to go get groceries and stuff!
Bye!
Bye!
Bye!
Bye!

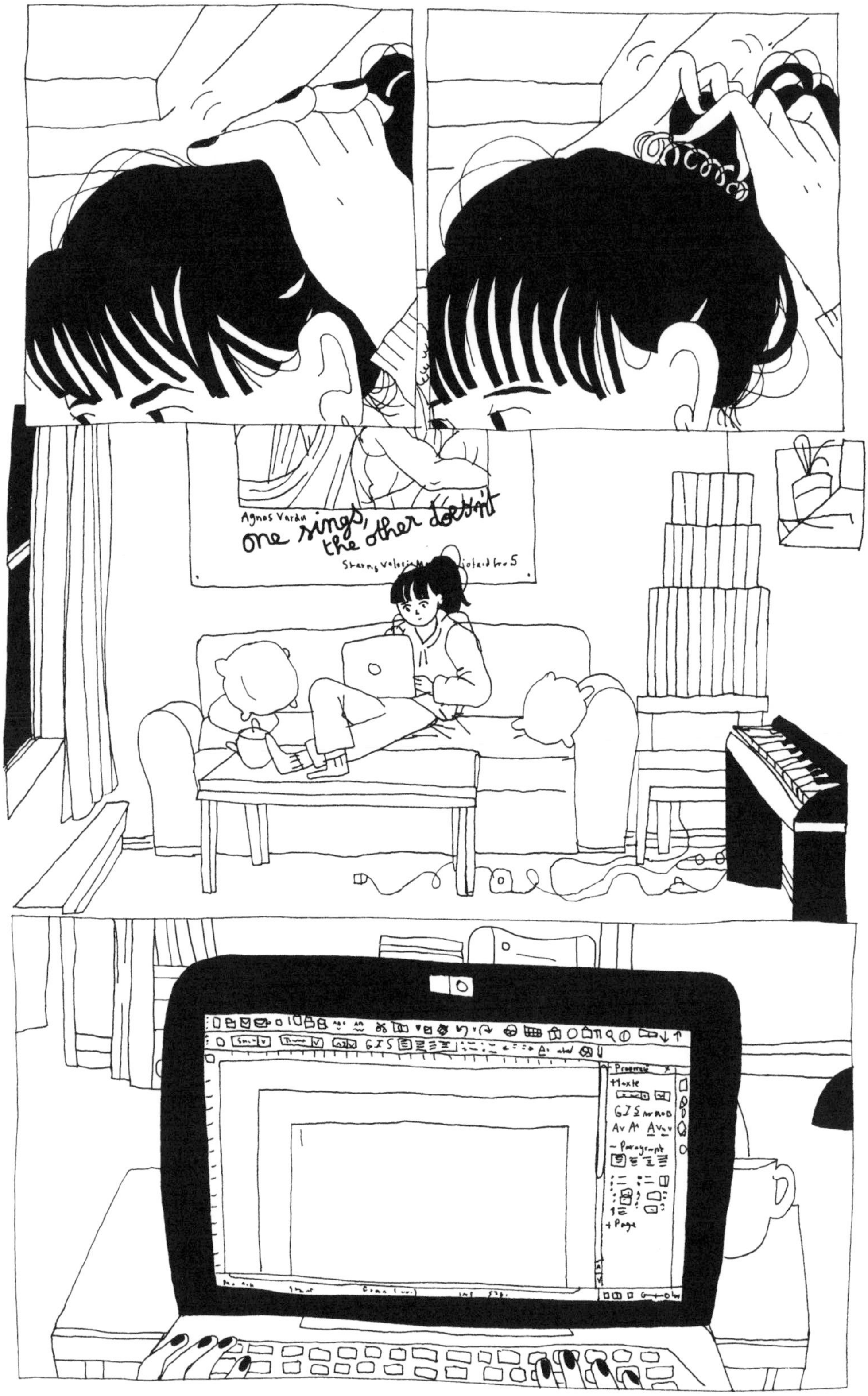
Agnes Varda
one sings, the other doesn't

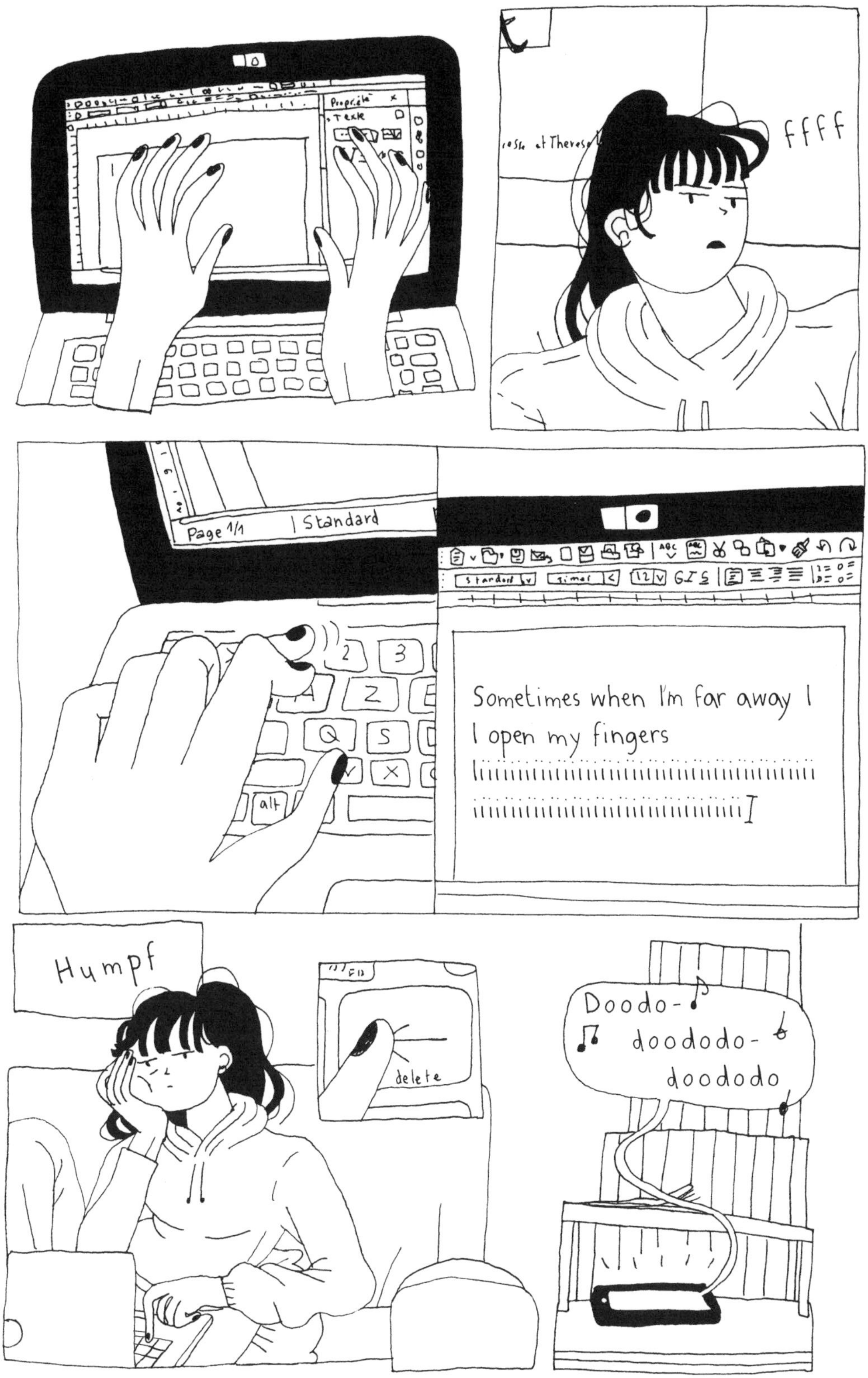
ffff
Page 1/1
Standard
Sometimes when I'm far away I
I open my fingers
Humpf
delete
Doodo-
doododo-
doododo

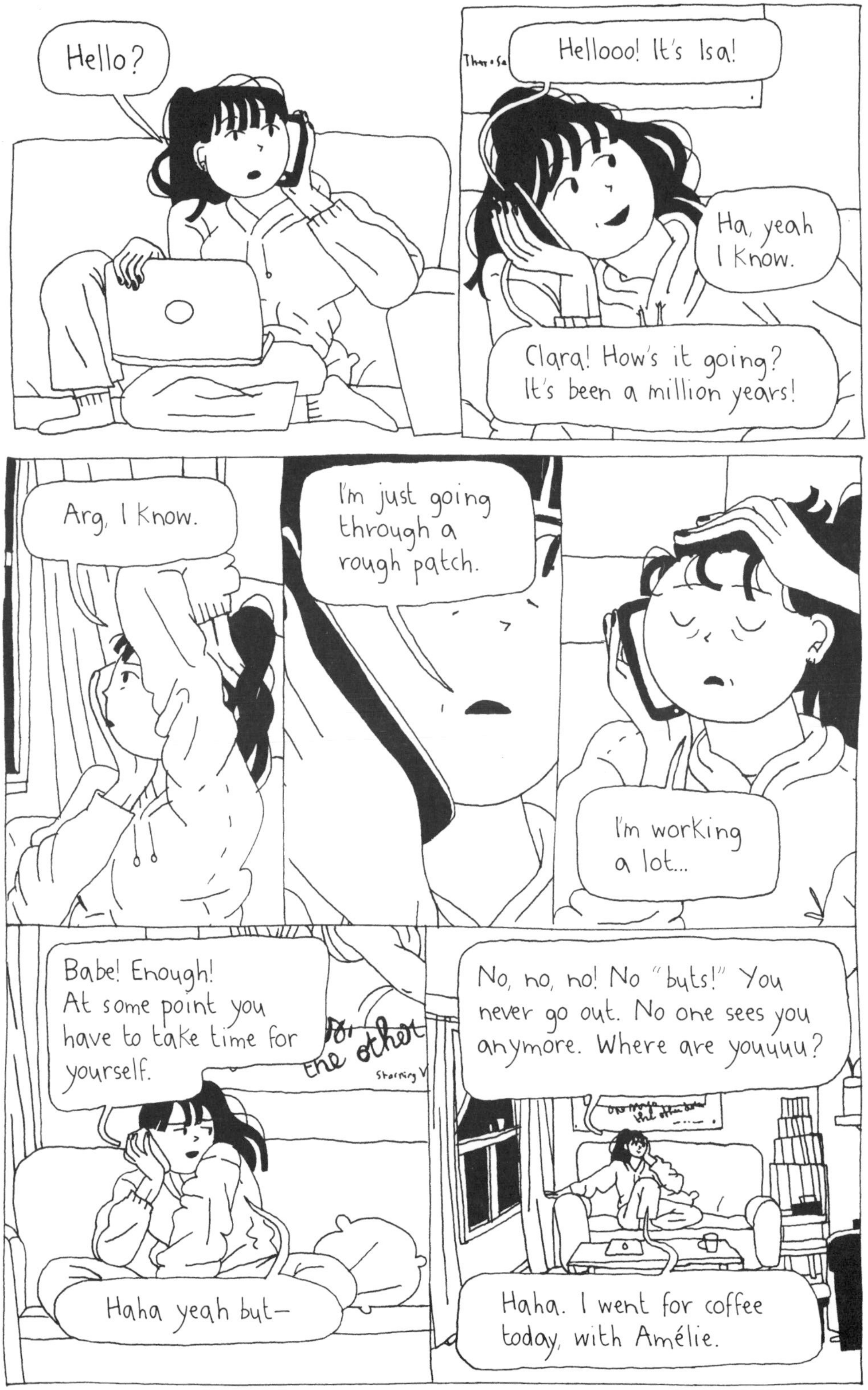
Hello?
Hellooo! It's Isa!
Ha, yeah I know.
Clara! How's it going? It's been a million years!
Arg, I know.
I'm just going through a rough patch.
I'm working a lot...
Babe! Enough! At some point you have to take time for yourself.
Haha yeah but–
No, no, no! No "buts!" You never go out. No one sees you anymore. Where are youuuu?
Haha. I went for coffee today, with Amélie.

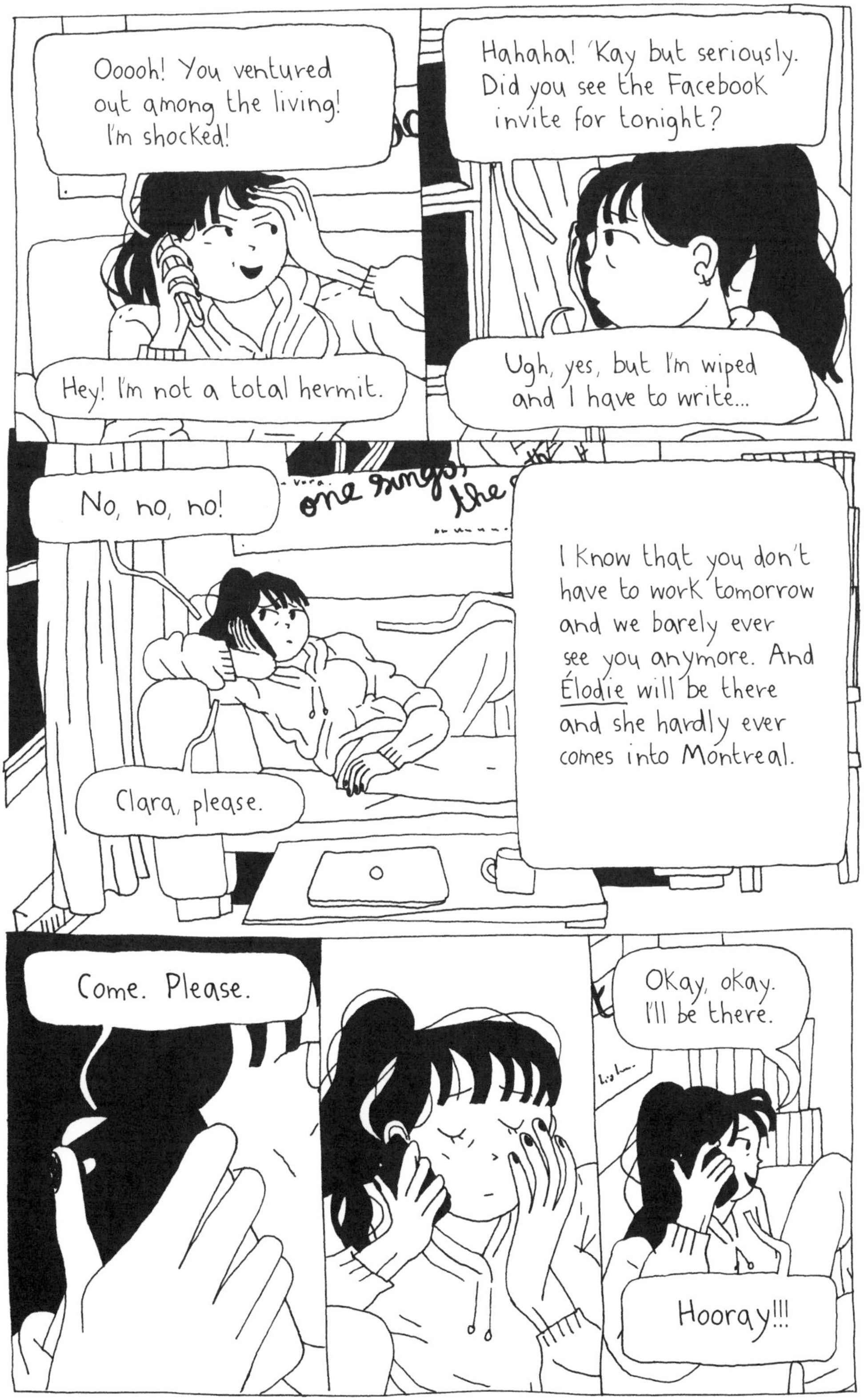
Ooooh! You ventured out among the living! I'm shocked!
Hey! I'm not a total hermit.
Hahaha! 'Kay but seriously. Did you see the Facebook invite for tonight?
Ugh, yes, but I'm wiped and I have to write...
No, no, no!
one sings, the
Clara, please.
I know that you don't have to work tomorrow and we barely ever see you anymore. And Élodie will be there and she hardly ever comes into Montreal.
Come. Please.
Okay, okay. I'll be there.
Hooray!!!

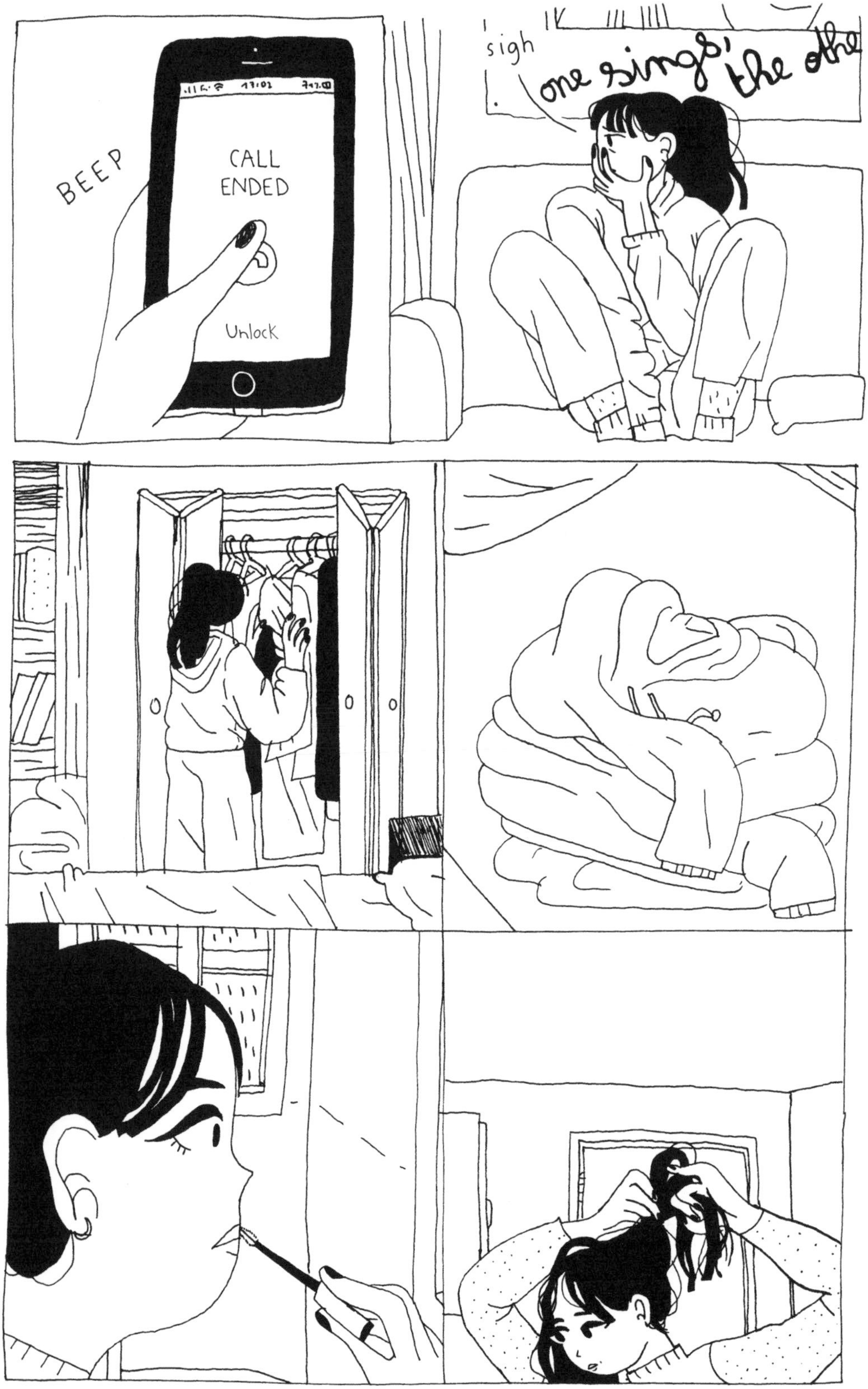
BEEP
CALL
ENDED
Unlock
sigh
one sings, the othe

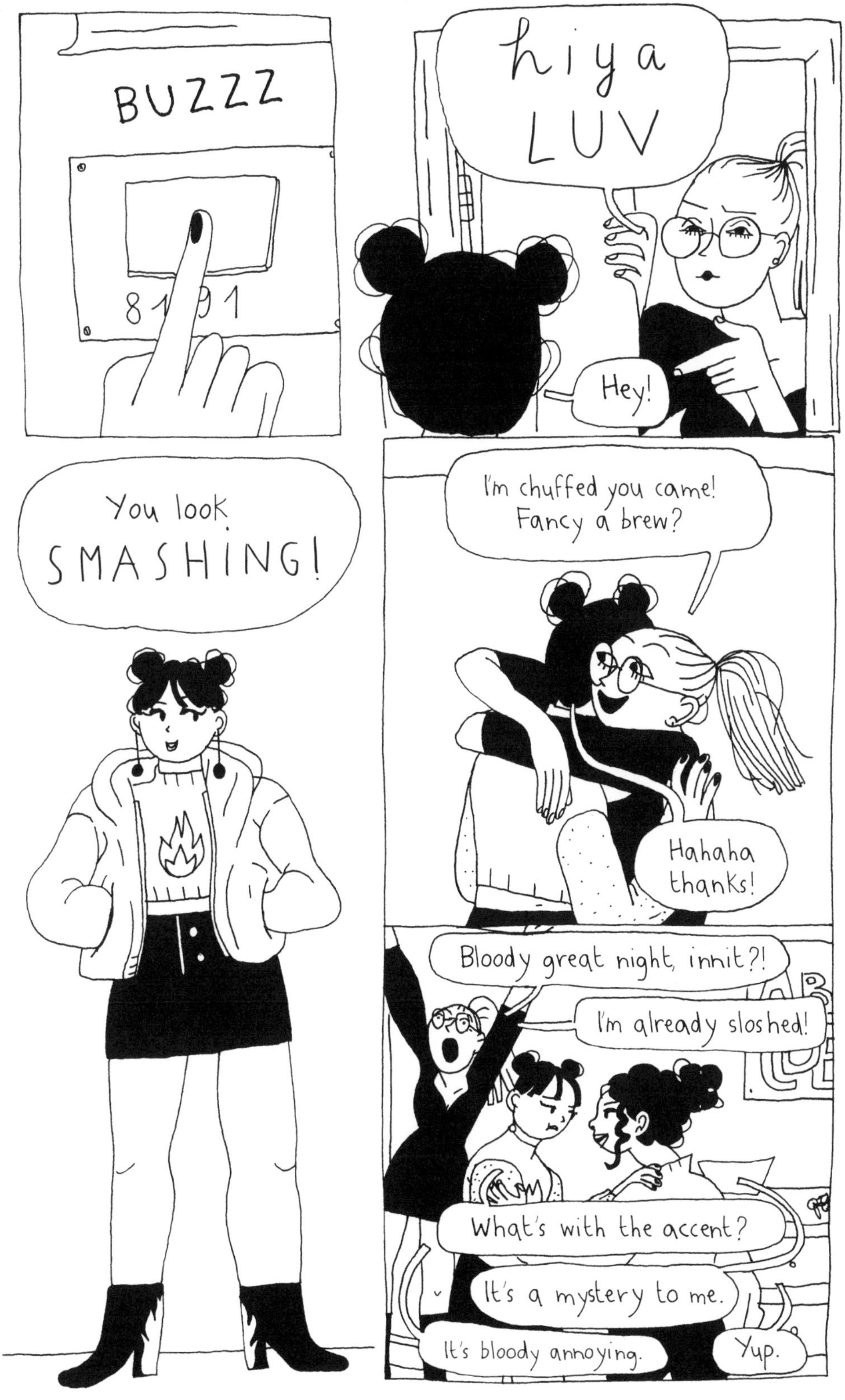
BUZZZ
8191
hiya LUV
Hey!
You look SMASHING!
I'm chuffed you came! Fancy a brew?
Hahaha thanks!
Bloody great night, innit?!
I'm already sloshed!
What's with the accent?
It's a mystery to me.
It's bloody annoying.
Yup.

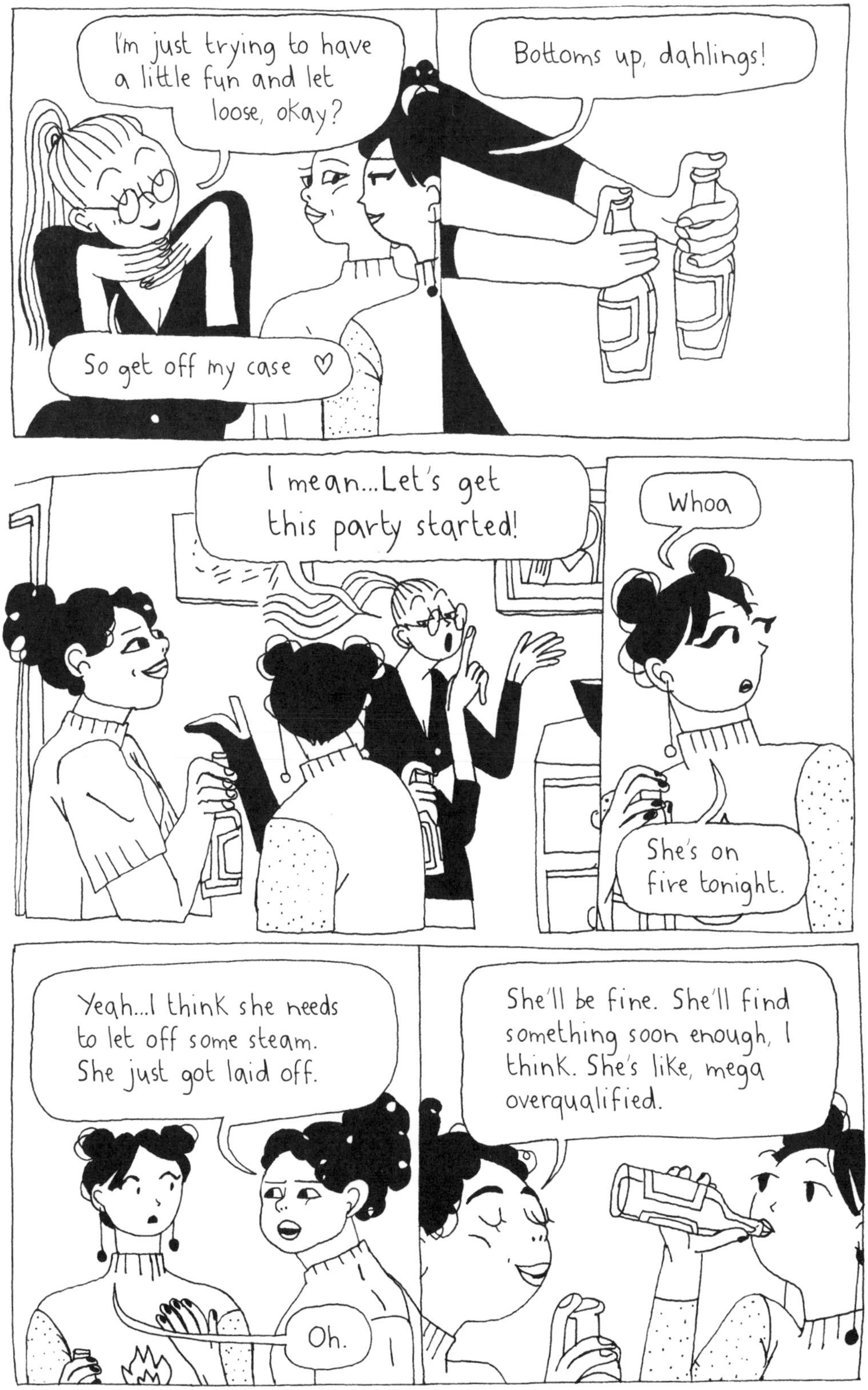
I'm just trying to have a little fun and let loose, okay?
So get off my case ♡
Bottoms up, dahlings!
I mean...Let's get this party started!
Whoa
She's on fire tonight.
Yeah...I think she needs to let off some steam. She just got laid off.
Oh.
She'll be fine. She'll find something soon enough, I think. She's like, mega overqualified.

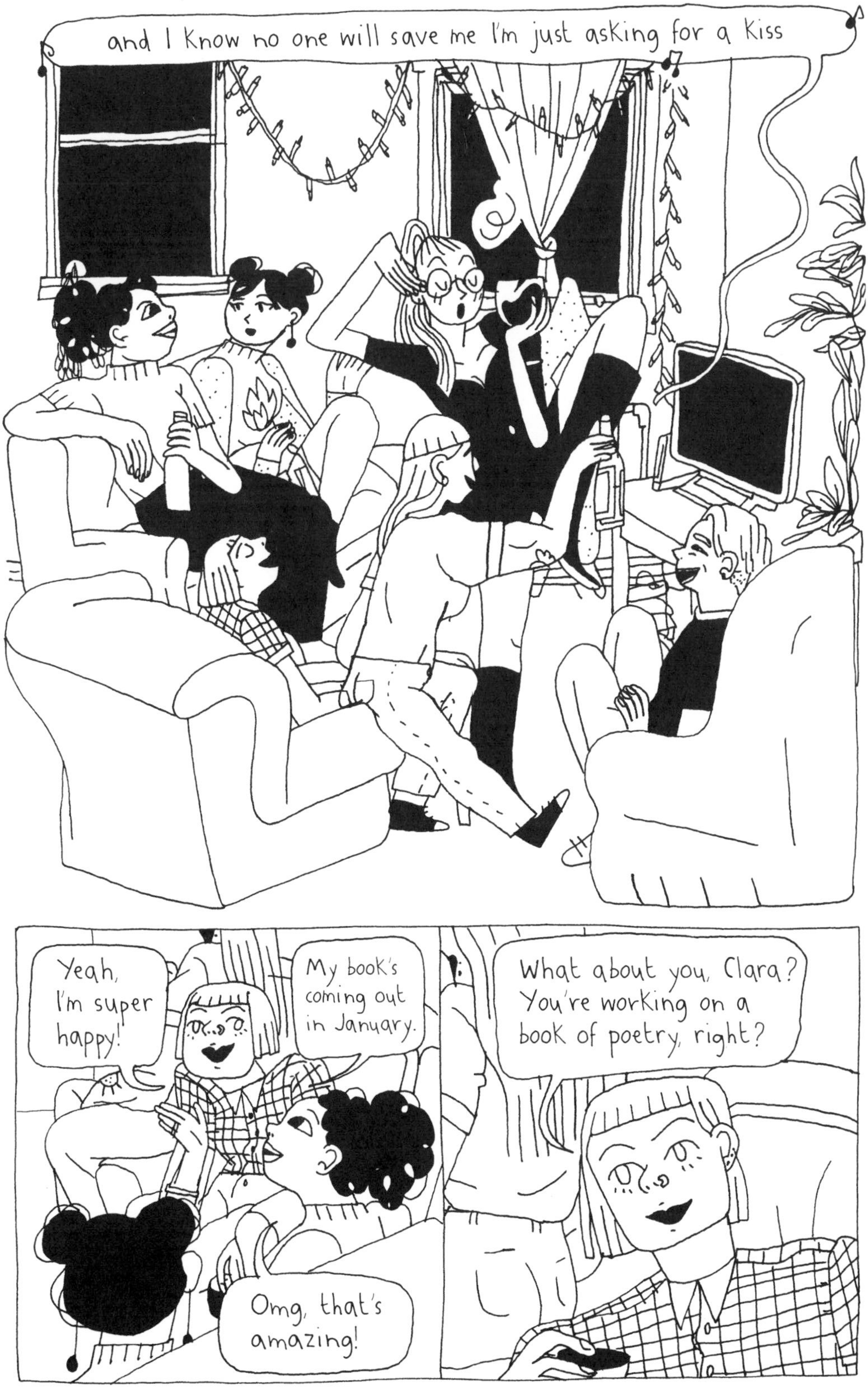
and I know no one will save me I'm just asking for a kiss
Yeah, I'm super happy!
My book's coming out in January.
Omg, that's amazing!
What about you, Clara? You're working on a book of poetry, right?

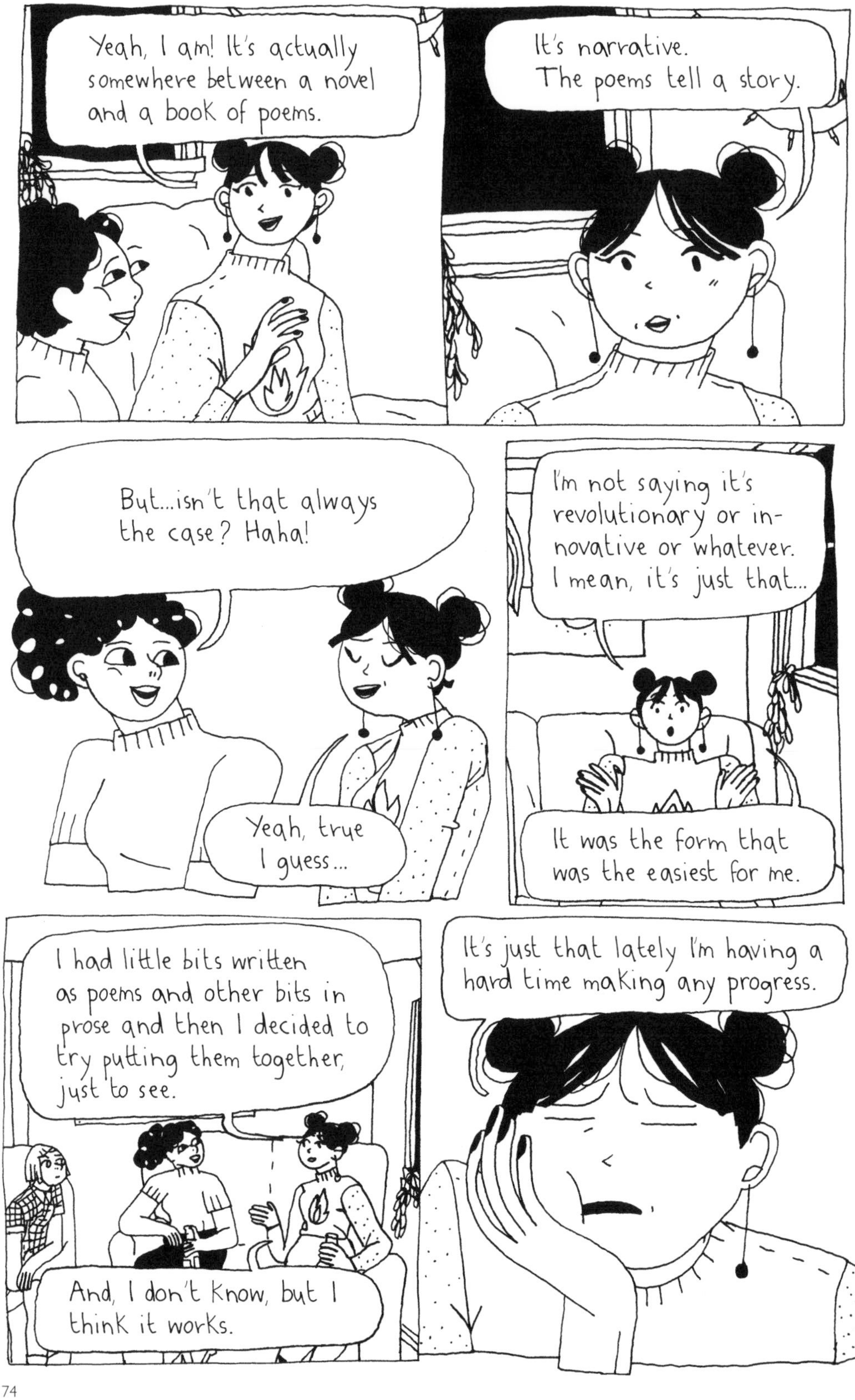
Yeah, I am! It's actually somewhere between a novel and a book of poems.
It's narrative. The poems tell a story.
But...isn't that always the case? Haha!
Yeah, true I guess...
I'm not saying it's revolutionary or innovative or whatever. I mean, it's just that...
It was the form that was the easiest for me.
I had little bits written as poems and other bits in prose and then I decided to try putting them together, just to see.
And, I don't know, but I think it works.
It's just that lately I'm having a hard time making any progress.

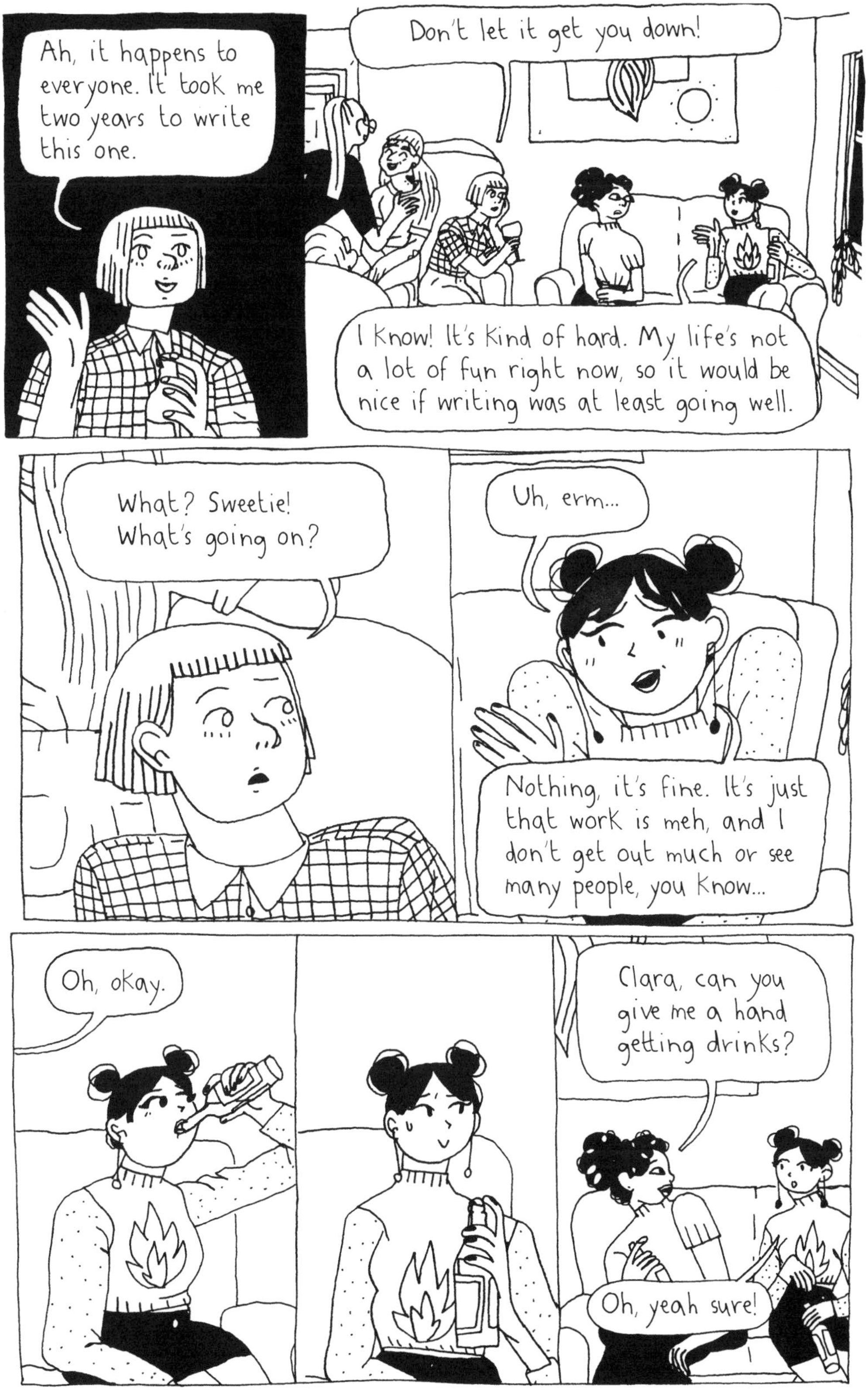
Ah, it happens to everyone. It took me two years to write this one.
Don't let it get you down!
I know! It's kind of hard. My life's not a lot of fun right now, so it would be nice if writing was at least going well.
What? Sweetie! What's going on?
Uh, erm...
Nothing, it's fine. It's just that work is meh, and I don't get out much or see many people, you know...
Oh, okay.
Clara, can you give me a hand getting drinks?
Oh, yeah sure!

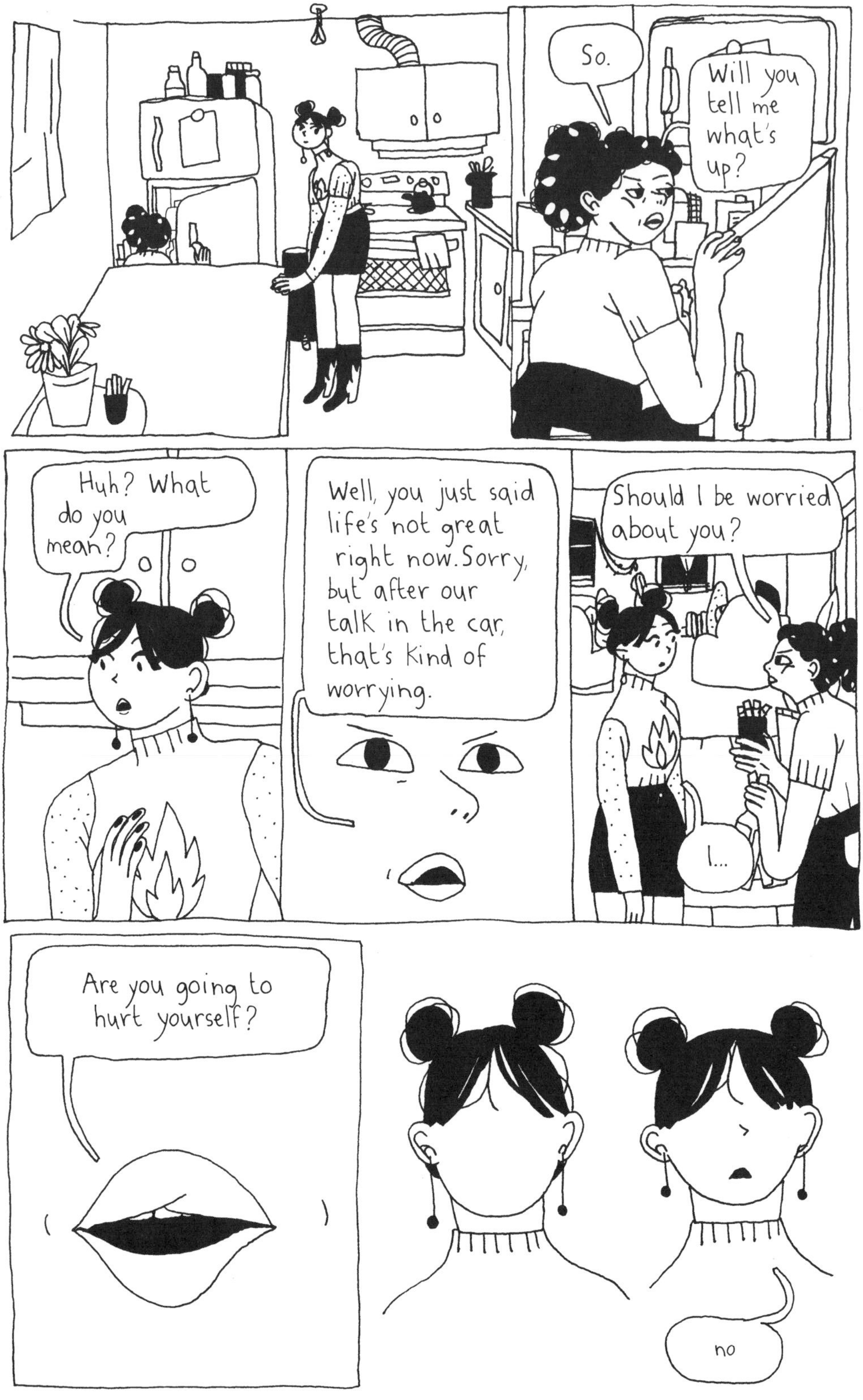
So.
Will you tell me what's up?
Huh? What do you mean?
Well, you just said life's not great right now. Sorry, but after our talk in the car, that's kind of worrying.
Should I be worried about you?
I...
Are you going to hurt yourself?
no

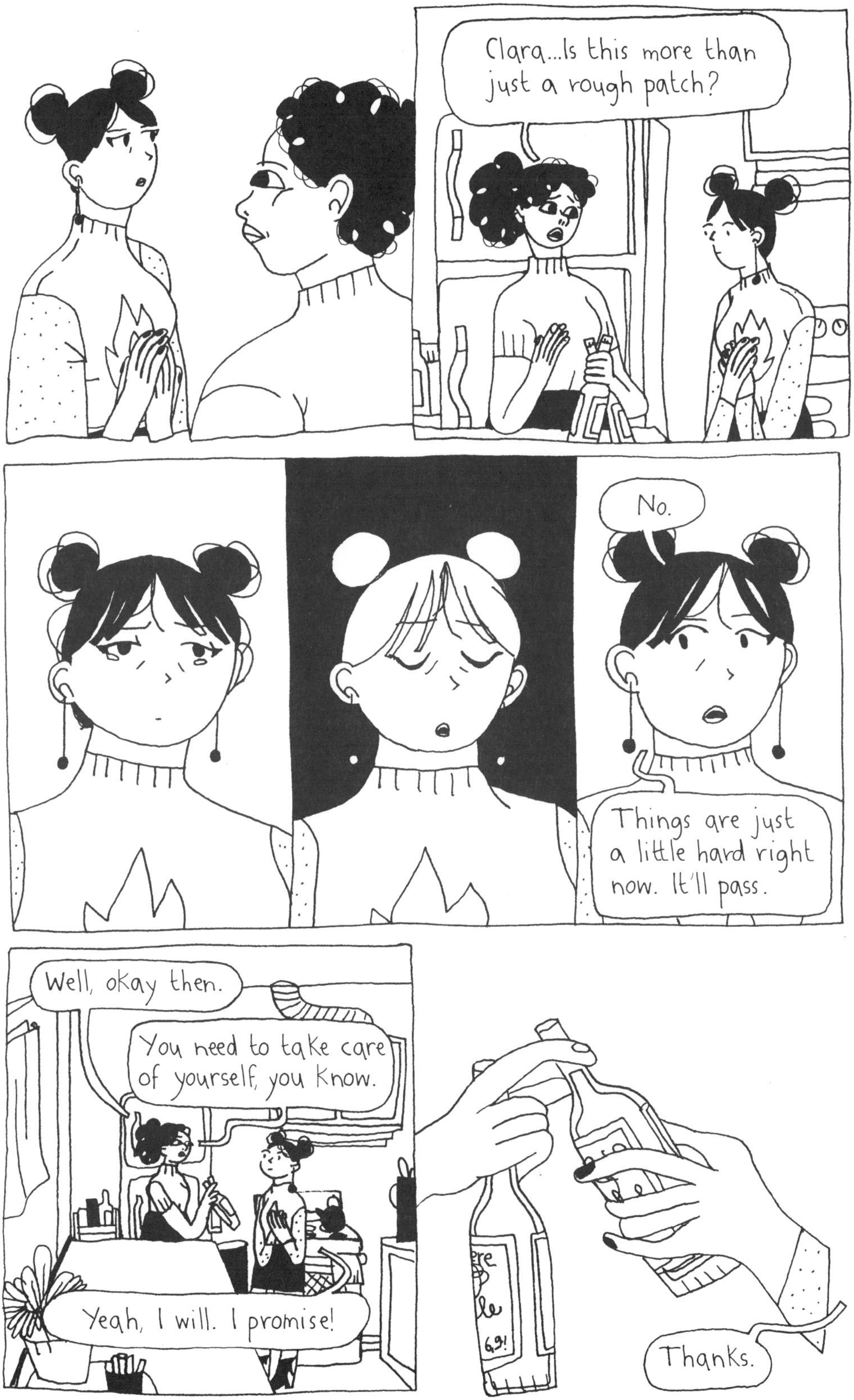
Clara...Is this more than just a rough patch?
No.
Things are just a little hard right now. It'll pass.
Well, okay then.
You need to take care of yourself, you know.
Yeah, I will. I promise!
Thanks.

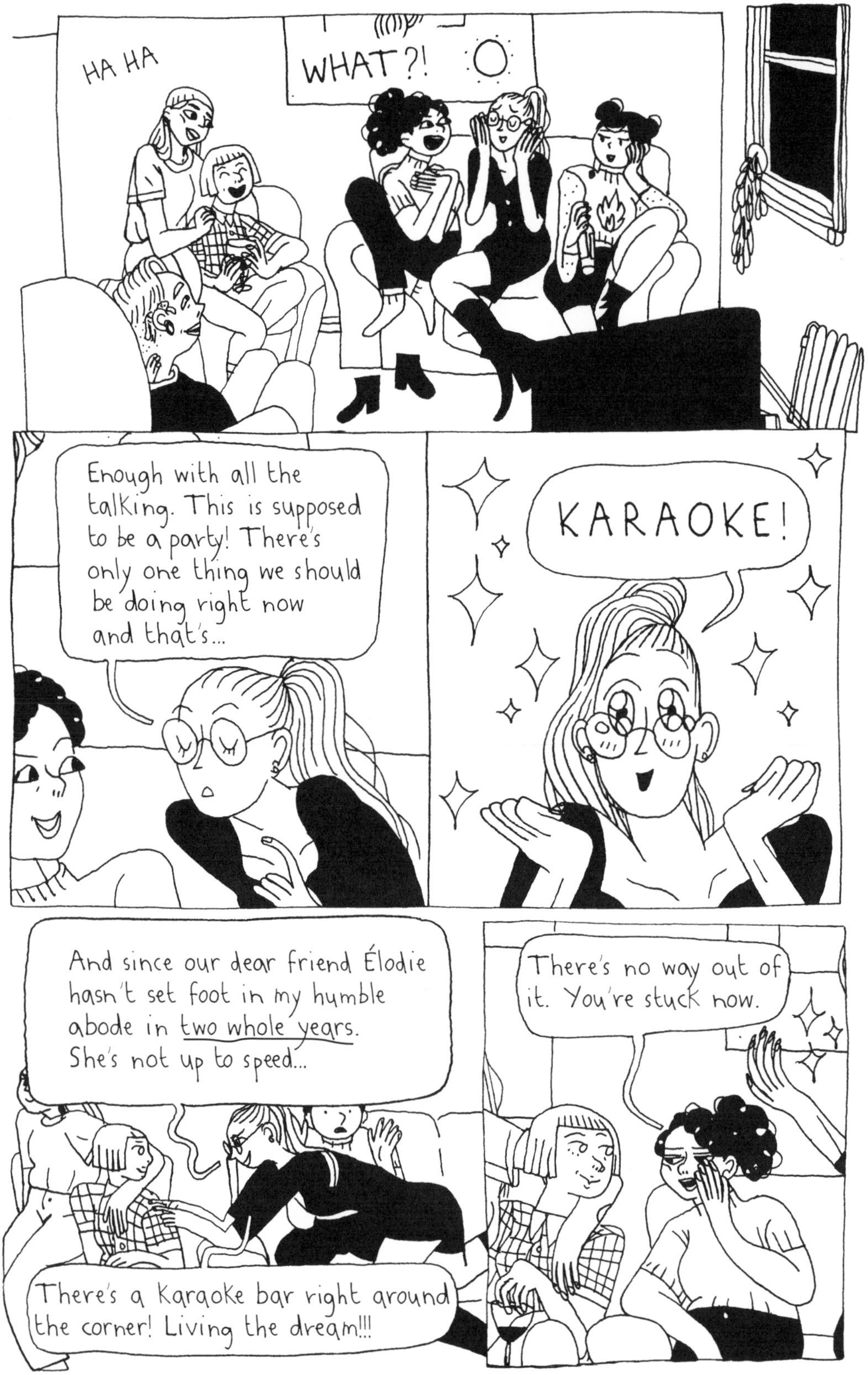

HA HA
WHAT?!
Enough with all the talking. This is supposed to be a party! There's only one thing we should be doing right now and that's...
KARAOKE!
And since our dear friend Élodie hasn't set foot in my humble abode in two whole years. She's not up to speed...
There's a karaoke bar right around the corner! Living the dream!!!
There's no way out of it. You're stuck now.

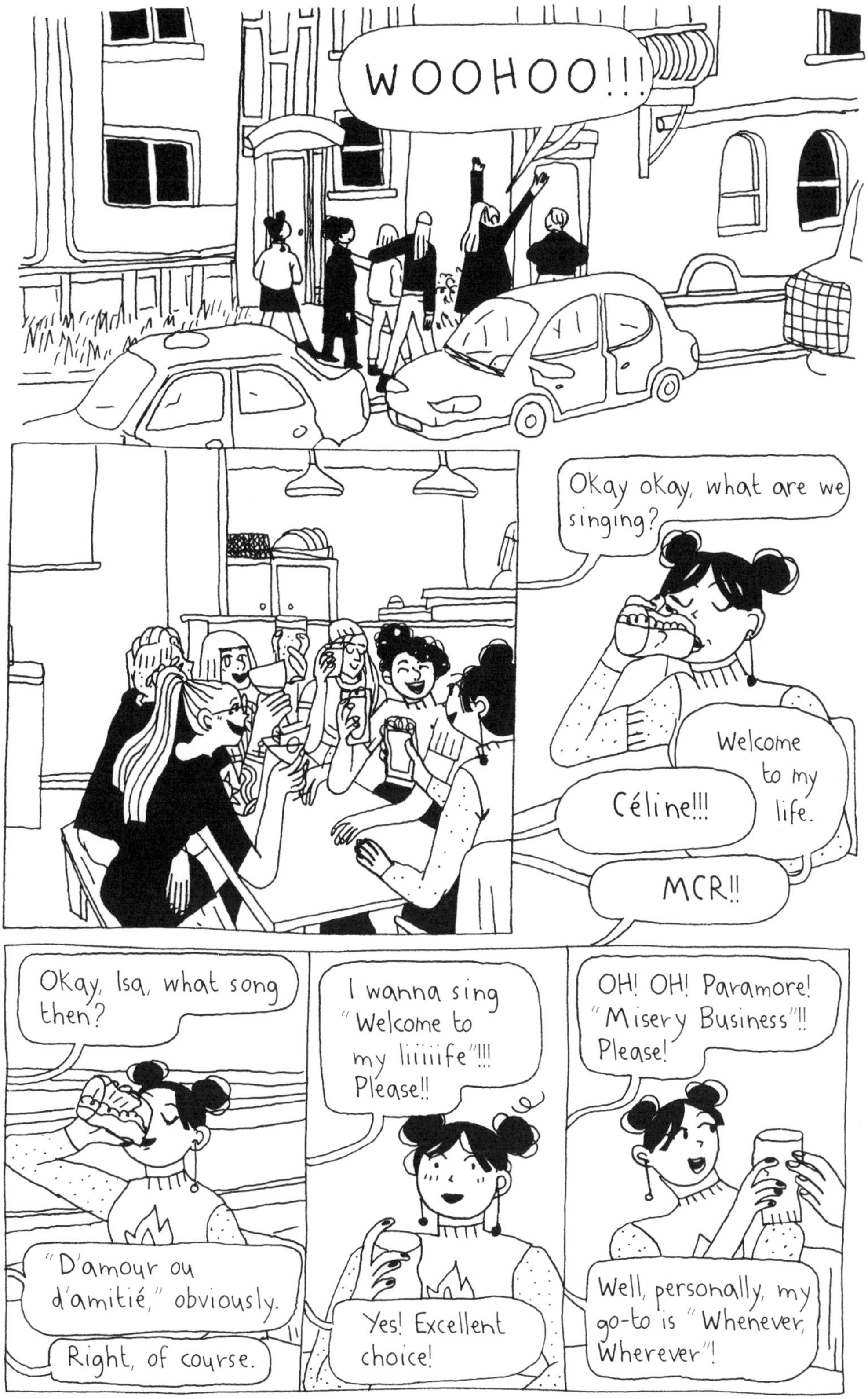
WOOHOO!!!
Okay okay, what are we singing?
Welcome to my life.
Céline!!!
MCR!!
Okay, Isa, what song then?
"D'amour ou d'amitié," obviously.
Right, of course.
I wanna sing "Welcome to my liiiiife"!!! Please!!
Yes! Excellent choice!
OH! OH! Paramore! "Misery Business"!! Please!
Well, personally, my go-to is "Whenever, Wherever"!

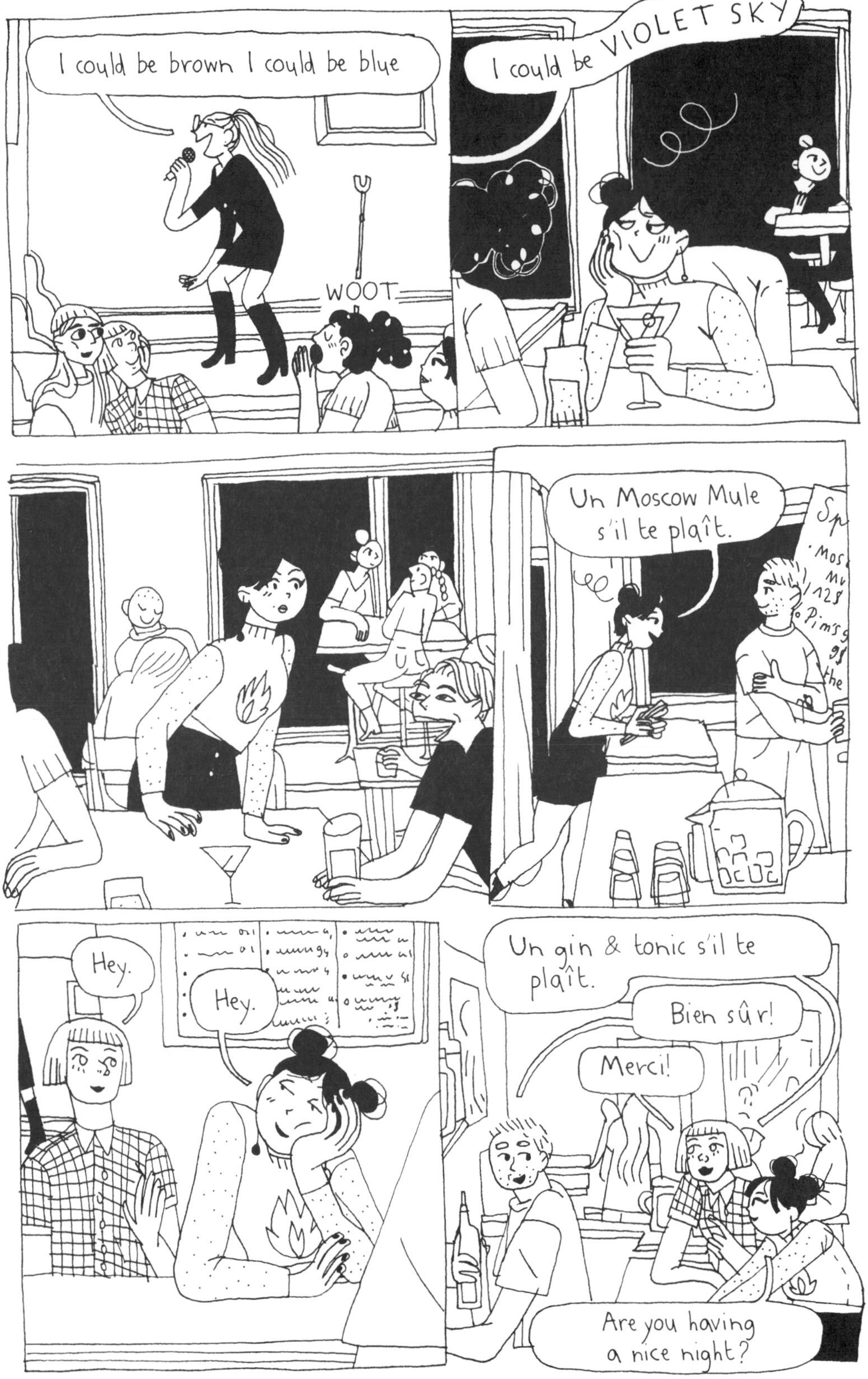
I could be brown I could be blue
WOOT
I could be VIOLET SKY
Un Moscow Mule s'il te plaît.
Hey.
Hey.
Un gin & tonic s'il te plaît.
Bien sûr!
Merci!
Are you having a nice night?

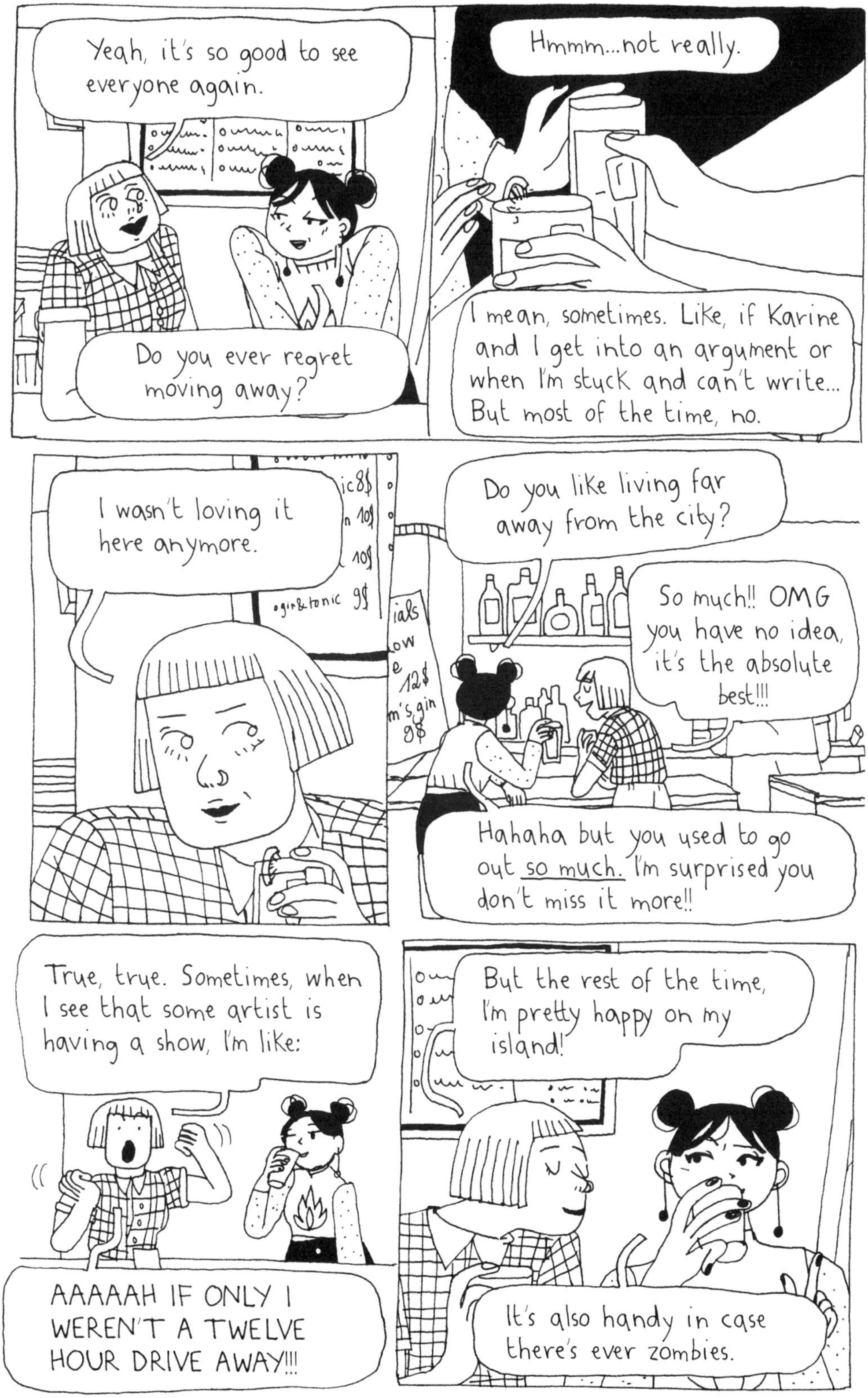
Yeah, it's so good to see everyone again.
Do you ever regret moving away?
Hmmm...not really.
I mean, sometimes. Like, if Karine and I get into an argument or when I'm stuck and can't write... But most of the time, no.
I wasn't loving it here anymore.
Do you like living far away from the city?
So much!! OMG you have no idea, it's the absolute best!!!
Hahaha but you used to go out so much. I'm surprised you don't miss it more!!
True, true. Sometimes, when I see that some artist is having a show, I'm like:
AAAAAH IF ONLY I WEREN'T A TWELVE HOUR DRIVE AWAY!!!
But the rest of the time, I'm pretty happy on my island!
It's also handy in case there's ever zombies.

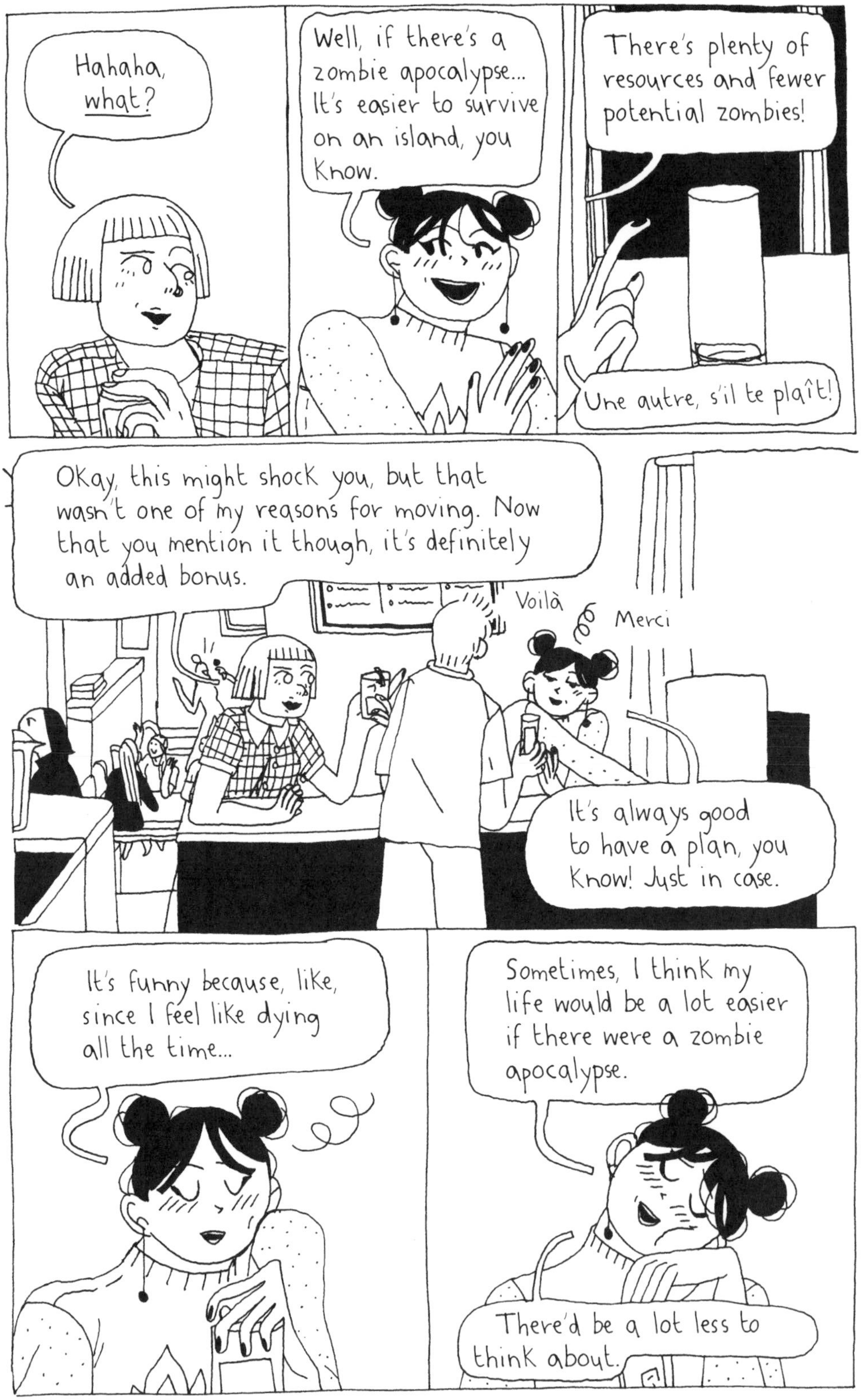
Hahaha, what?
Well, if there's a zombie apocalypse... It's easier to survive on an island, you Know.
There's plenty of resources and fewer potential zombies!
Une autre, s'il te plaît!
Okay, this might shock you, but that wasn't one of my reasons for moving. Now that you mention it though, it's definitely an added bonus.
Voilà
Merci
It's always good to have a plan, you Know! Just in case.
It's funny because, like, since I feel like dying all the time...
Sometimes, I think my life would be a lot easier if there were a zombie apocalypse.
There'd be a lot less to think about.

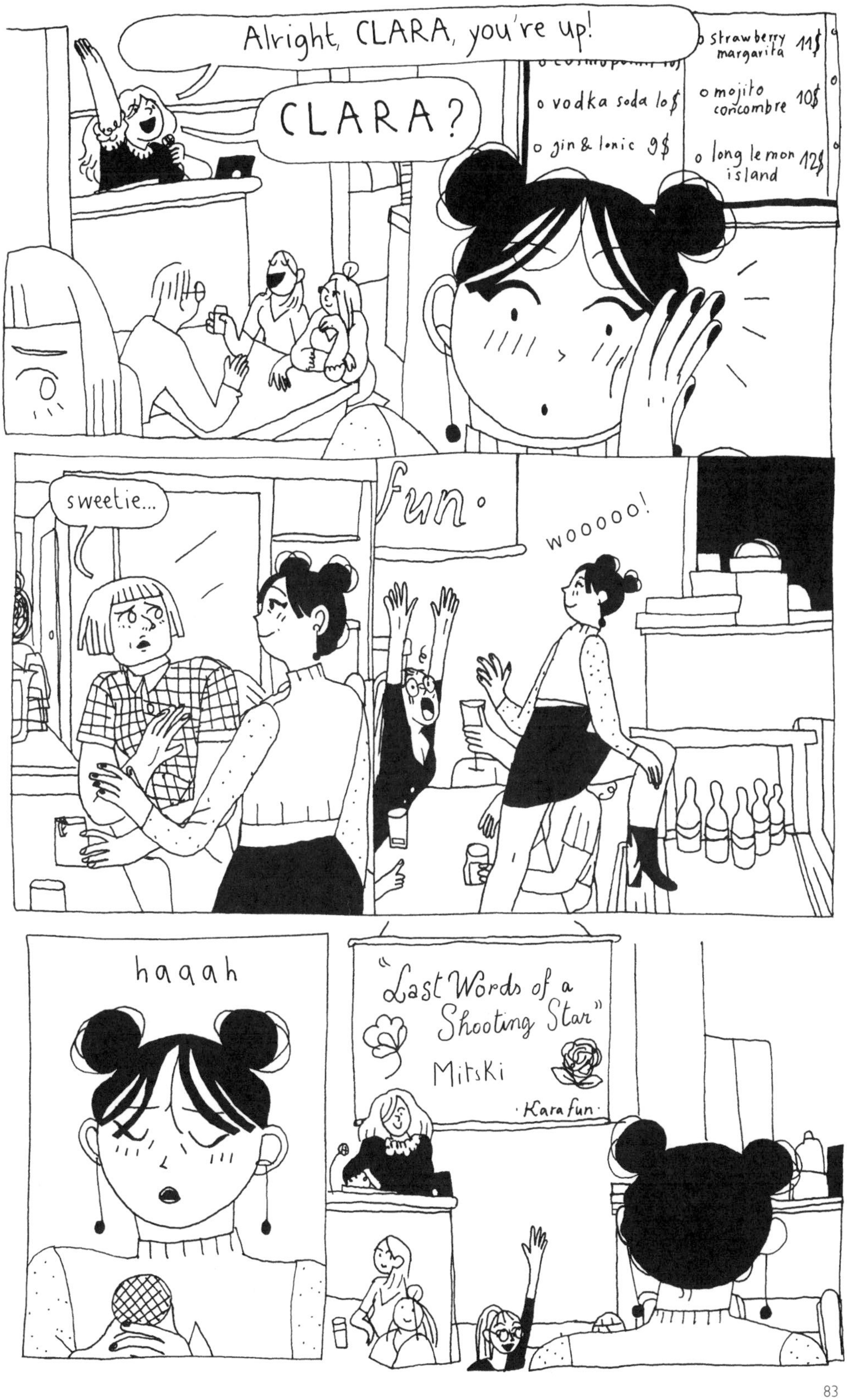

Alright, CLARA, you're up!
CLARA?
o vodka soda 10$
o gin & tonic 9$
o strawberry margarita 11$
o mojito concombre 10$
o long lemon island 12$
sweetie...
fun
wooooo!
haaah
"Last Words of a Shooting Star"
Mitski
Karafun

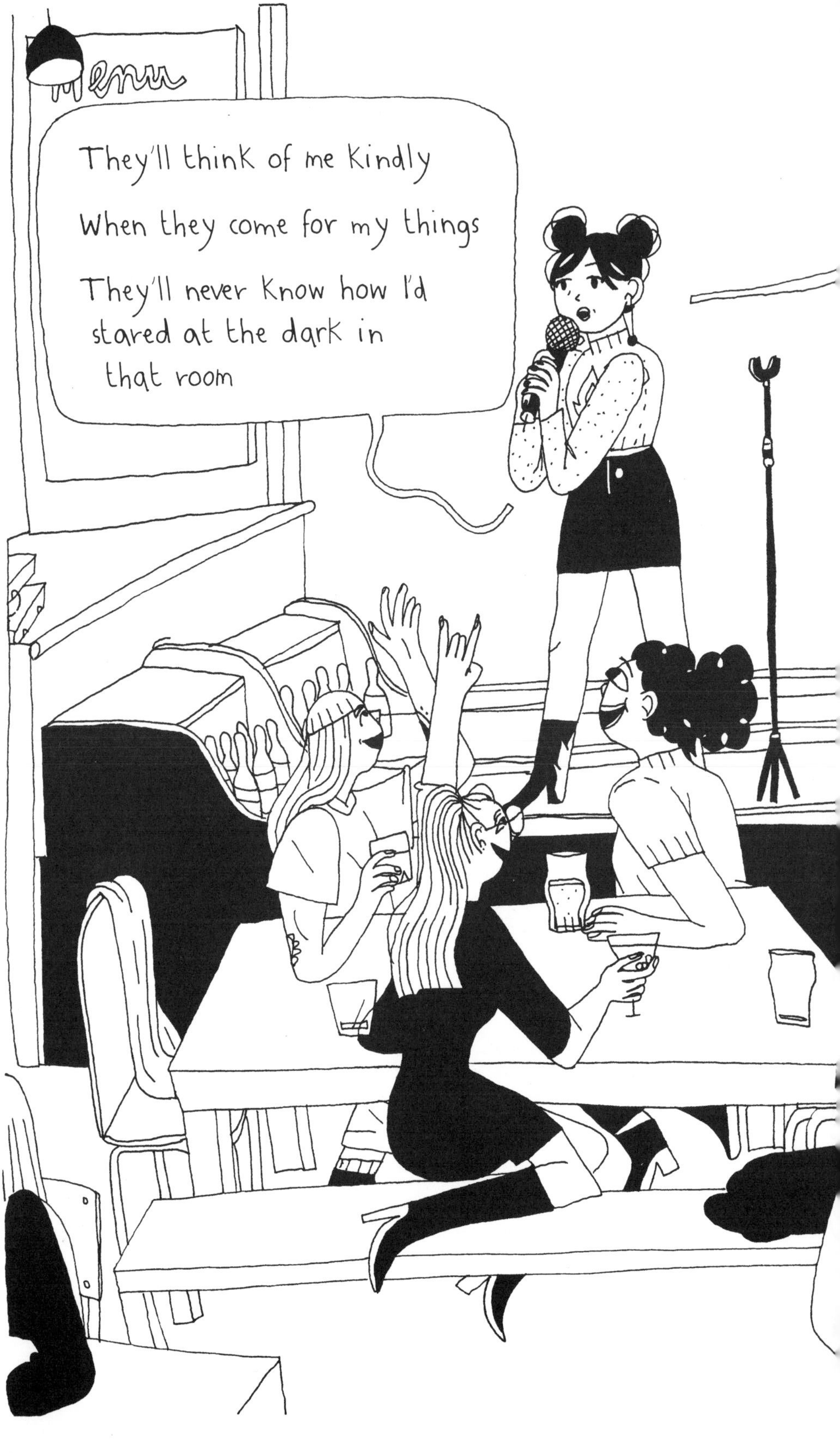
Menu
They'll think of me kindly
When they come for my things
They'll never know how I'd stared at the dark in that room

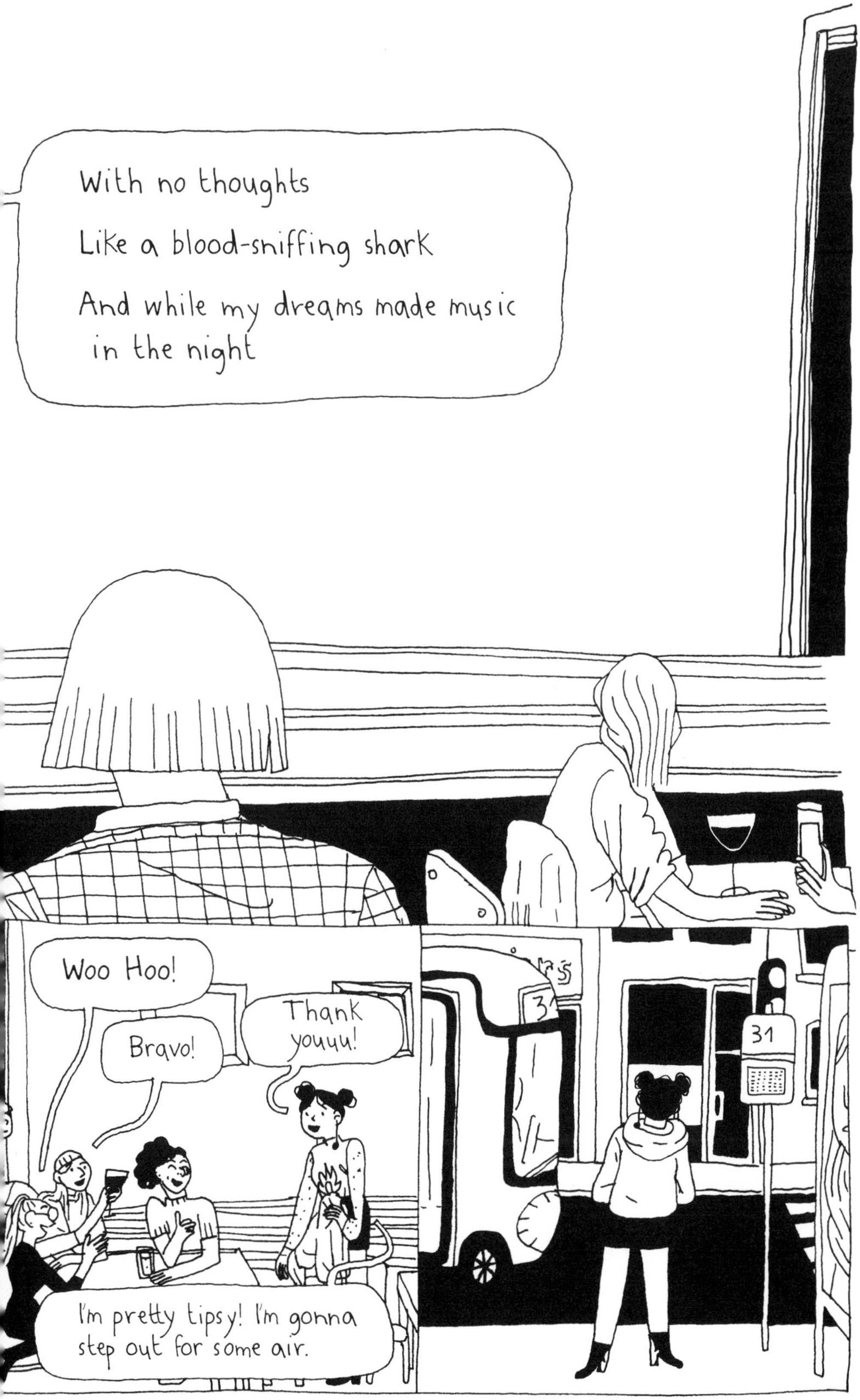
With no thoughts
Like a blood-sniffing shark
And while my dreams made music in the night
Woo Hoo!
Bravo!
Thank youuu!
I'm pretty tipsy! I'm gonna step out for some air.
31

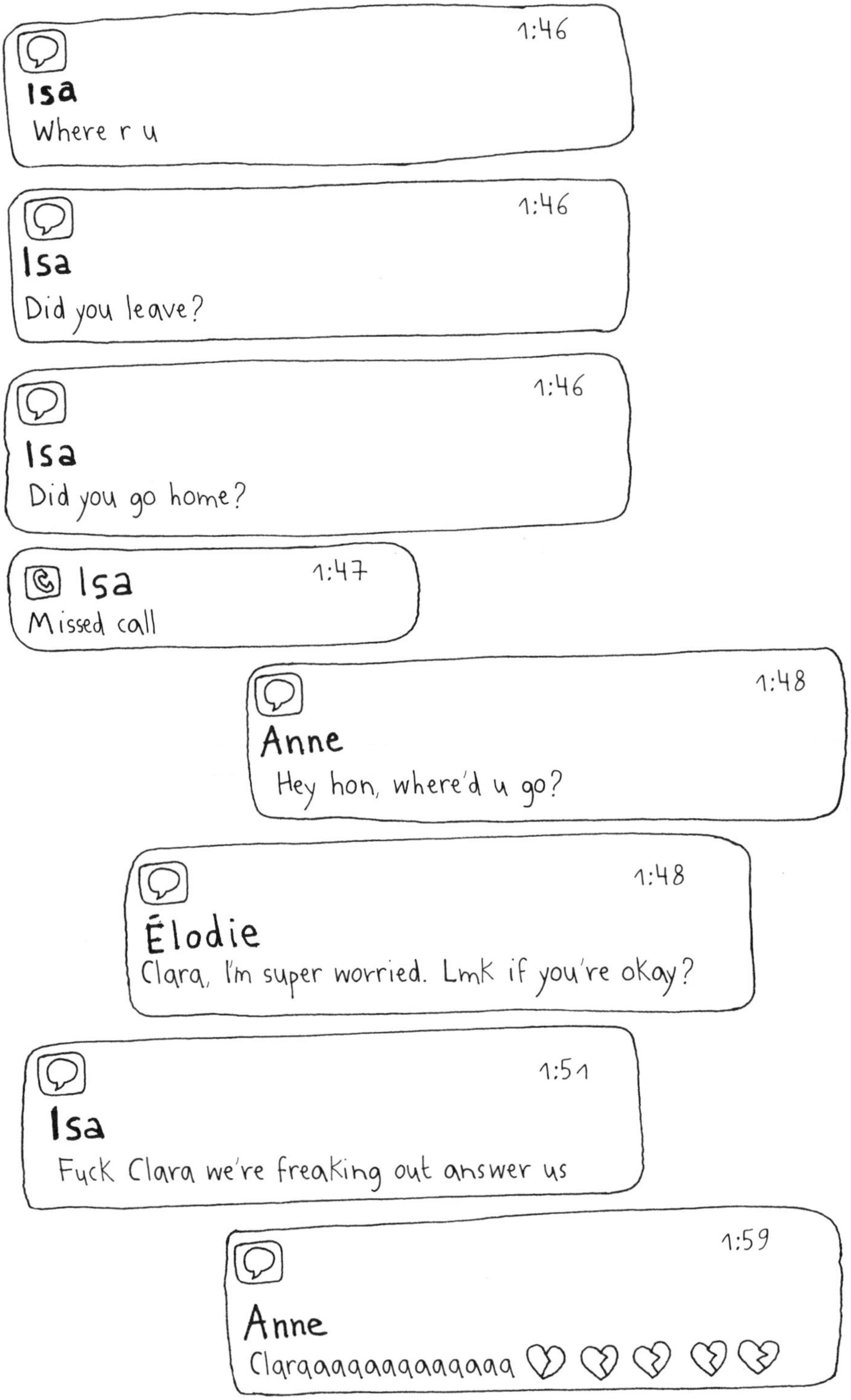
1:46
Isa
Where r u
1:46
Isa
Did you leave?
1:46
Isa
Did you go home?
Isa
1:47
Missed call
1:48
Anne
Hey hon, where'd u go?
1:48
Élodie
Clara, I'm super worried. Lmk if you're okay?
1:51
Isa
Fuck Clara we're freaking out answer us
1:59
Anne
Claraaaaaaaaaaaaa

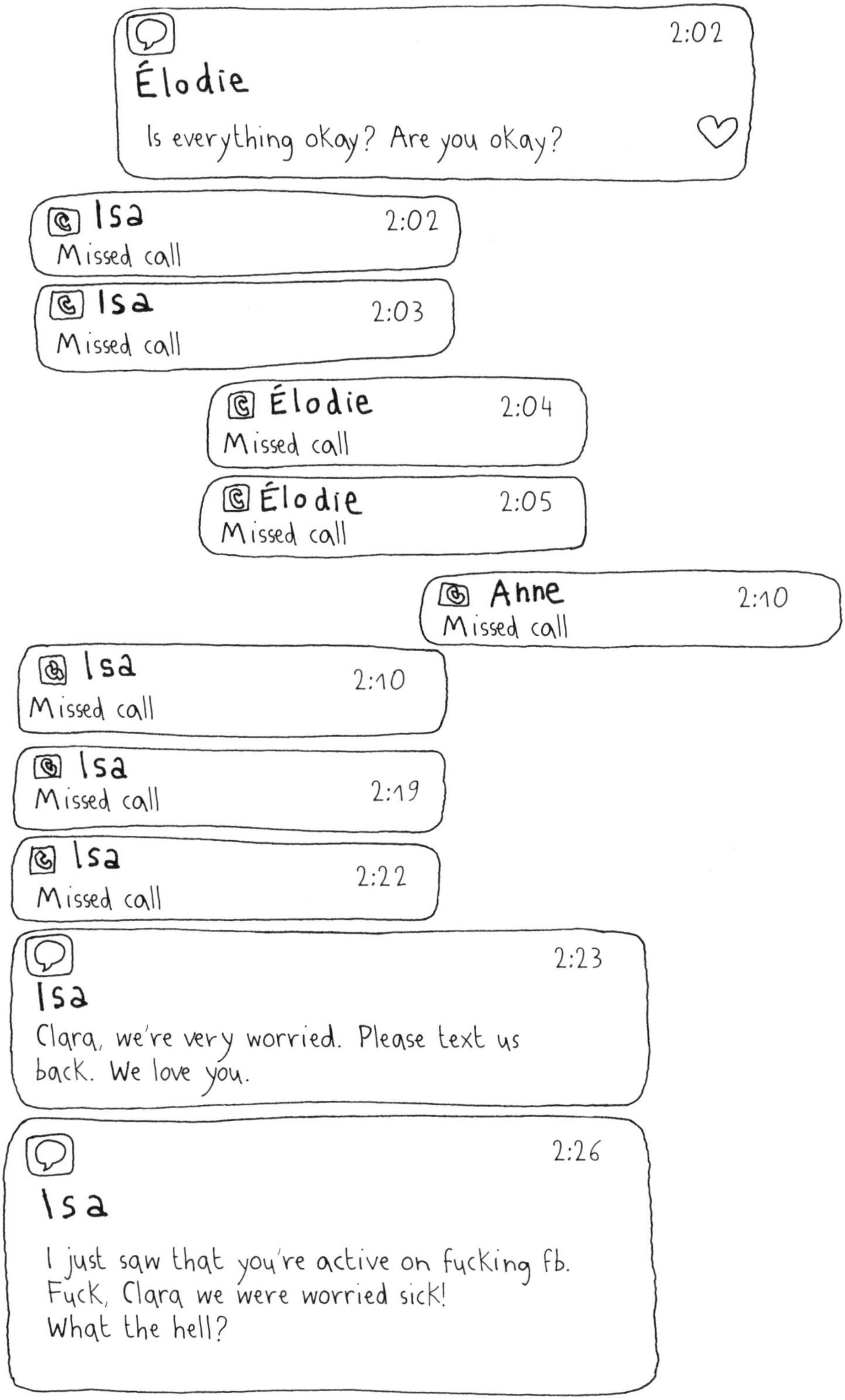
2:02
Élodie
Is everything okay? Are you okay?
Isa 2:02
Missed call
Isa 2:03
Missed call
Élodie 2:04
Missed call
Élodie 2:05
Missed call
Anne 2:10
Missed call
Isa 2:10
Missed call
Isa 2:19
Missed call
Isa 2:22
Missed call
2:23
Isa
Clara, we're very worried. Please text us back. We love you.
2:26
Isa
I just saw that you're active on fucking fb.
Fuck, Clara we were worried sick!
What the hell?

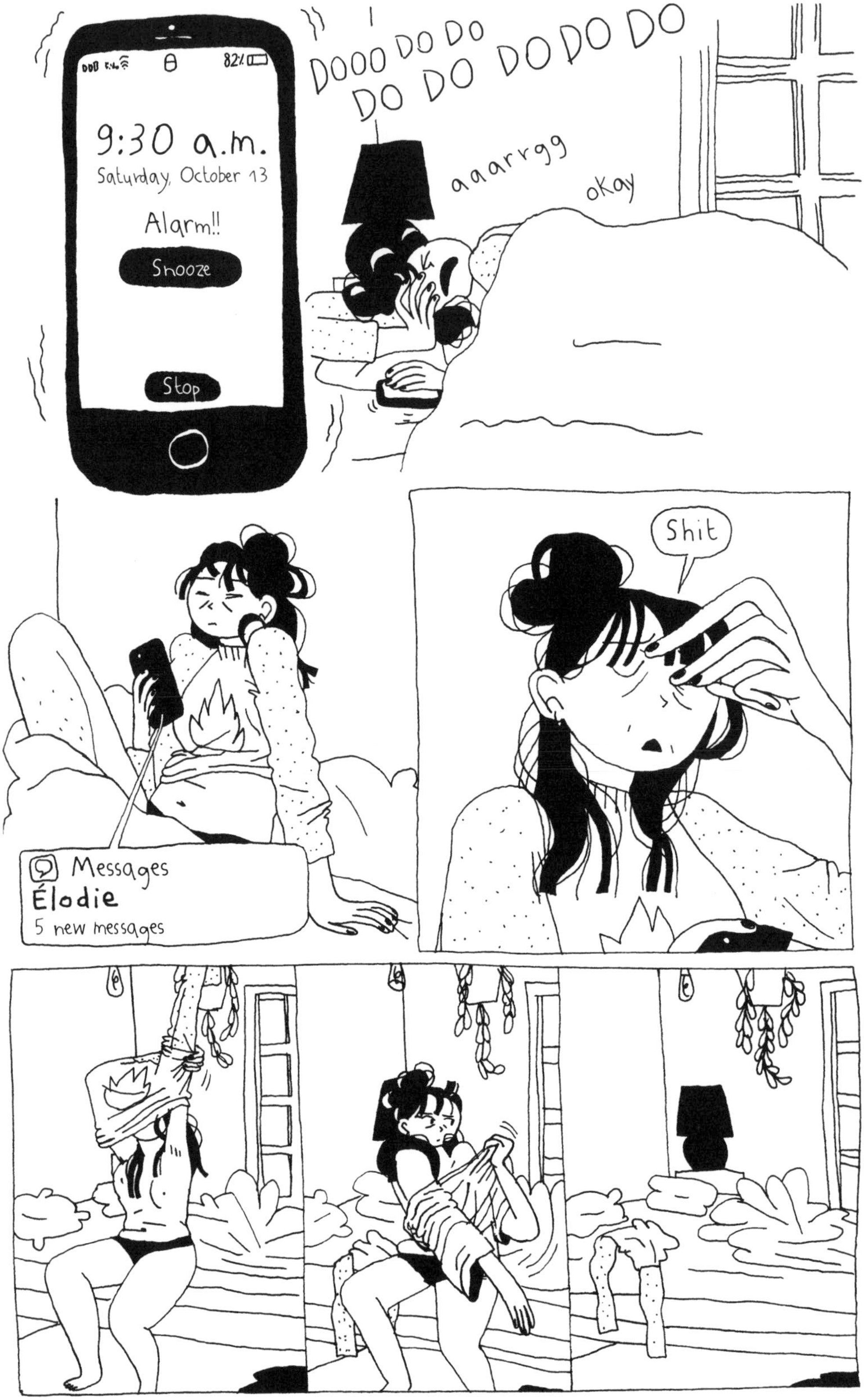
82%
9:30 a.m.
Saturday, October 13
Alarm!!
Snooze
Stop
DOOO DO DO
DO DO DO DO DO DO
aaarrgg
okay
Messages
Élodie
5 new messages
Shit

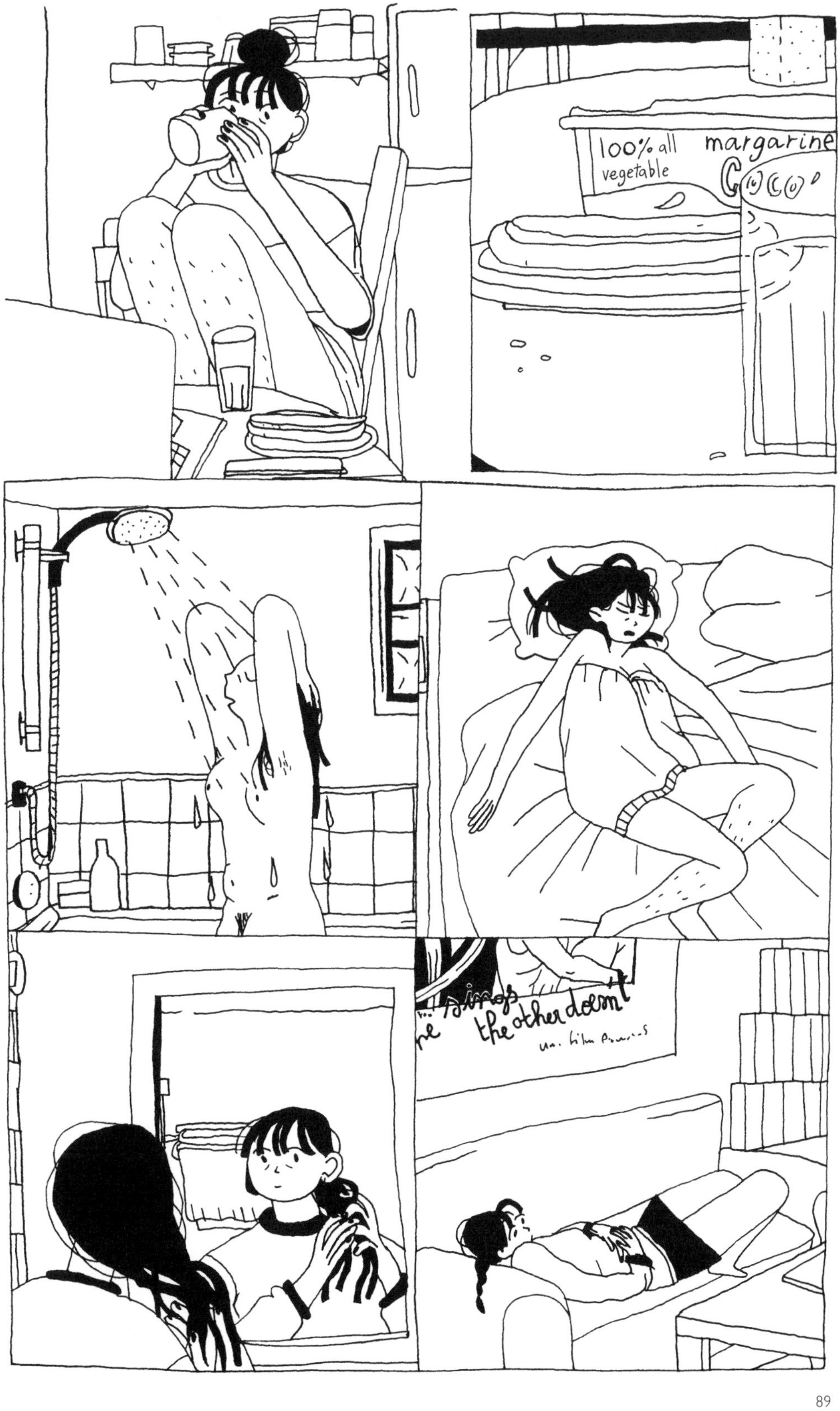
100% all
vegetable
margarine
sings
the other doesn't

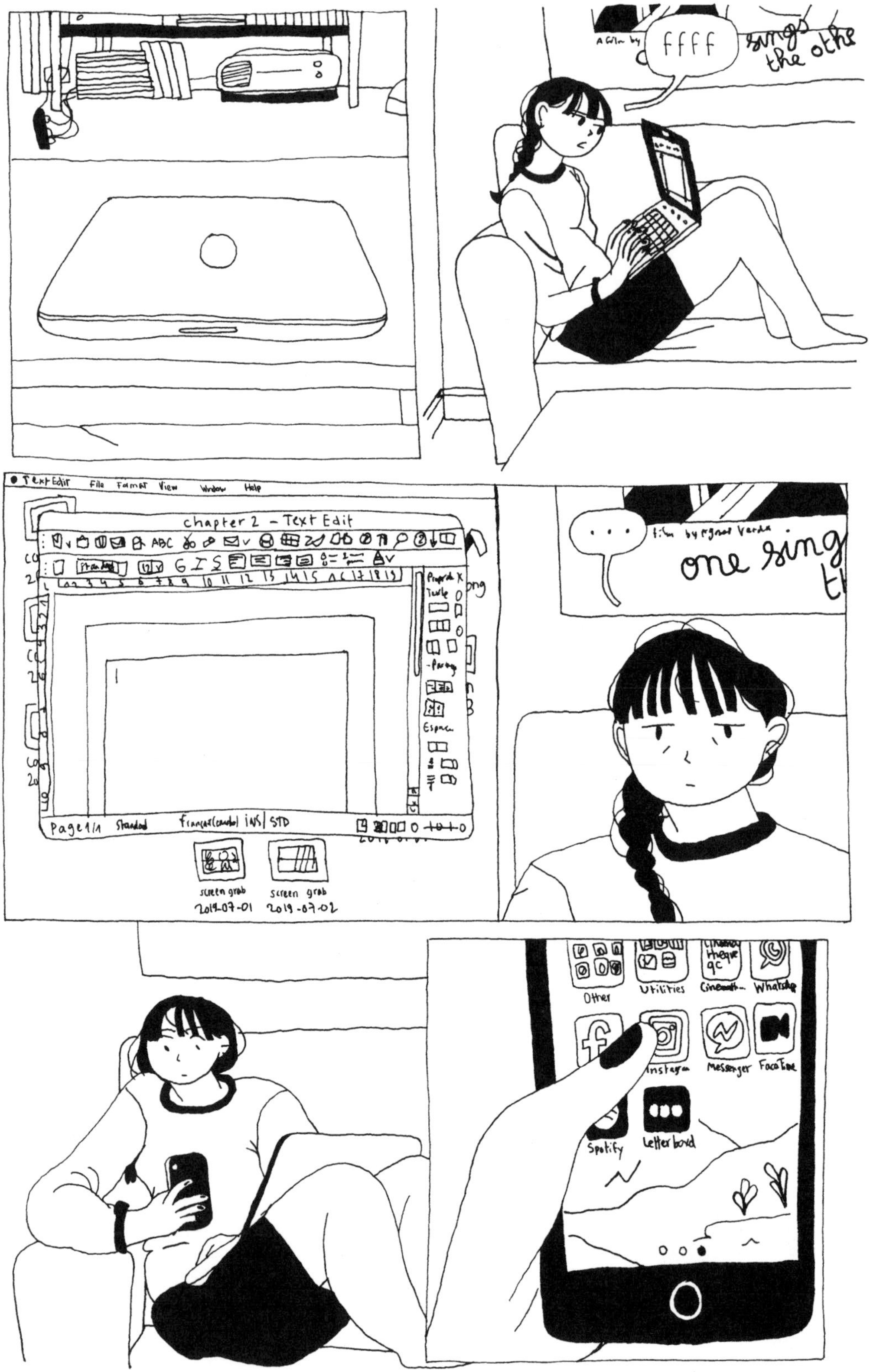
ffff
TextEdit File Format View Window Help
chapter 2 - Text Edit
Page 1/1 Standard
screen grab 2019-07-01
screen grab 2019-07-02
. . .
Other
Utilities
Whatsapp
Instagram
Messenger
FaceTime
Spotify
Letterboxd

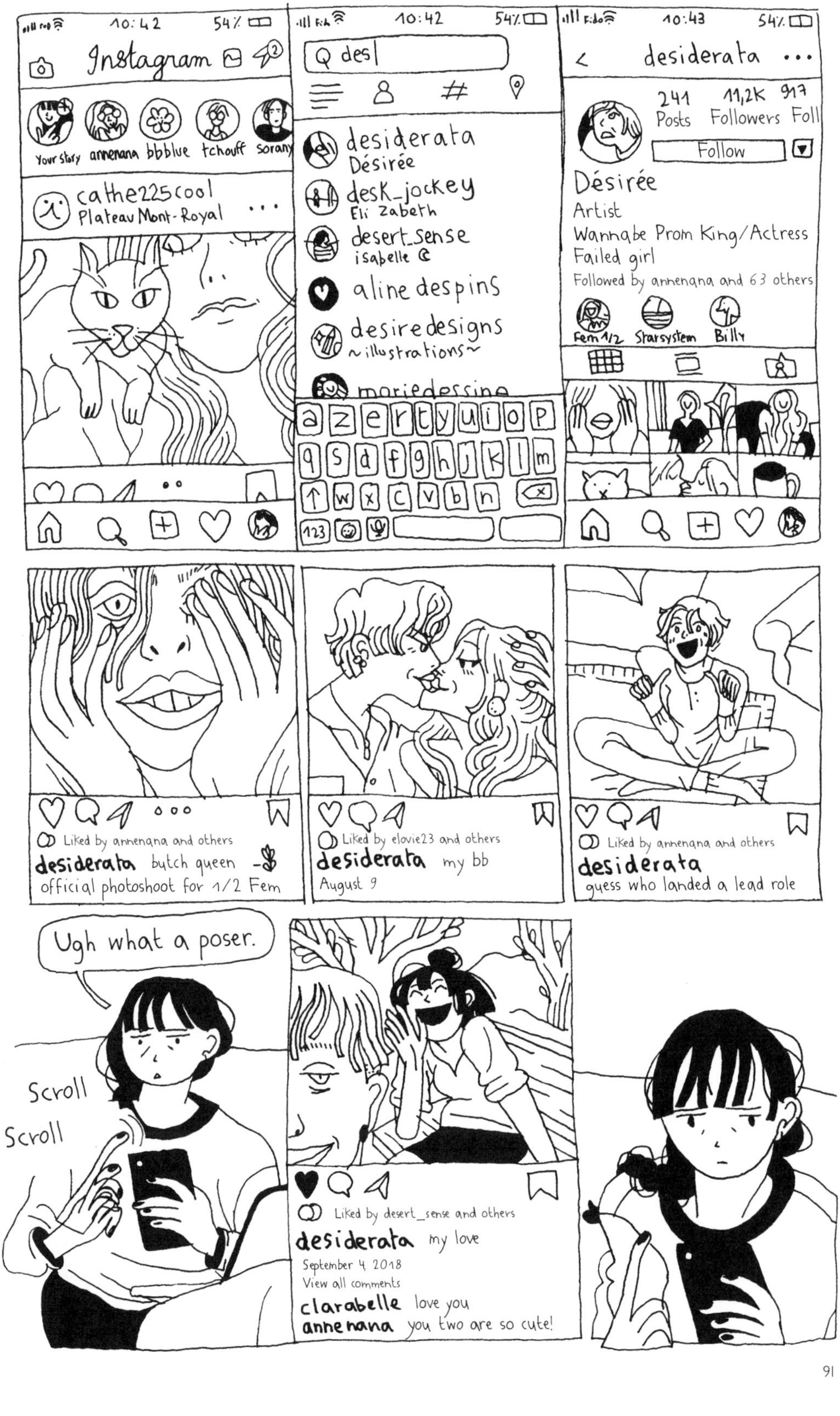
10:42
54%
Instagram
Your story
annenana
bbblue
tchouff
sorany
cathe225cool
Plateau Mont-Royal
10:42
54%
Q desl
desiderata
Désirée
desk_jockey
Eli Zabeth
desert_sense
isabelle
aline despins
desiredesigns
~illustrations~
mariedessine
a z e r t y u i o p
q s d f g h j k l m
w x c v b n
123
10:43
54%
desiderata
241 Posts
11,2K Followers
917
Follow
Désirée
Artist
Wannabe Prom King/Actress
Failed girl
Followed by annenana and 63 others
Fem 1/2
Starsystem
Billy
Liked by annenana and others
desiderata butch queen
official photoshoot for 1/2 Fem
Liked by elovie23 and others
desiderata my bb
August 9
Liked by annenana and others
desiderata
guess who landed a lead role
Ugh what a poser.
Scroll
Scroll
Liked by desert_sense and others
desiderata my love
September 4 2018
View all comments
clarabelle love you
annenana you two are so cute!

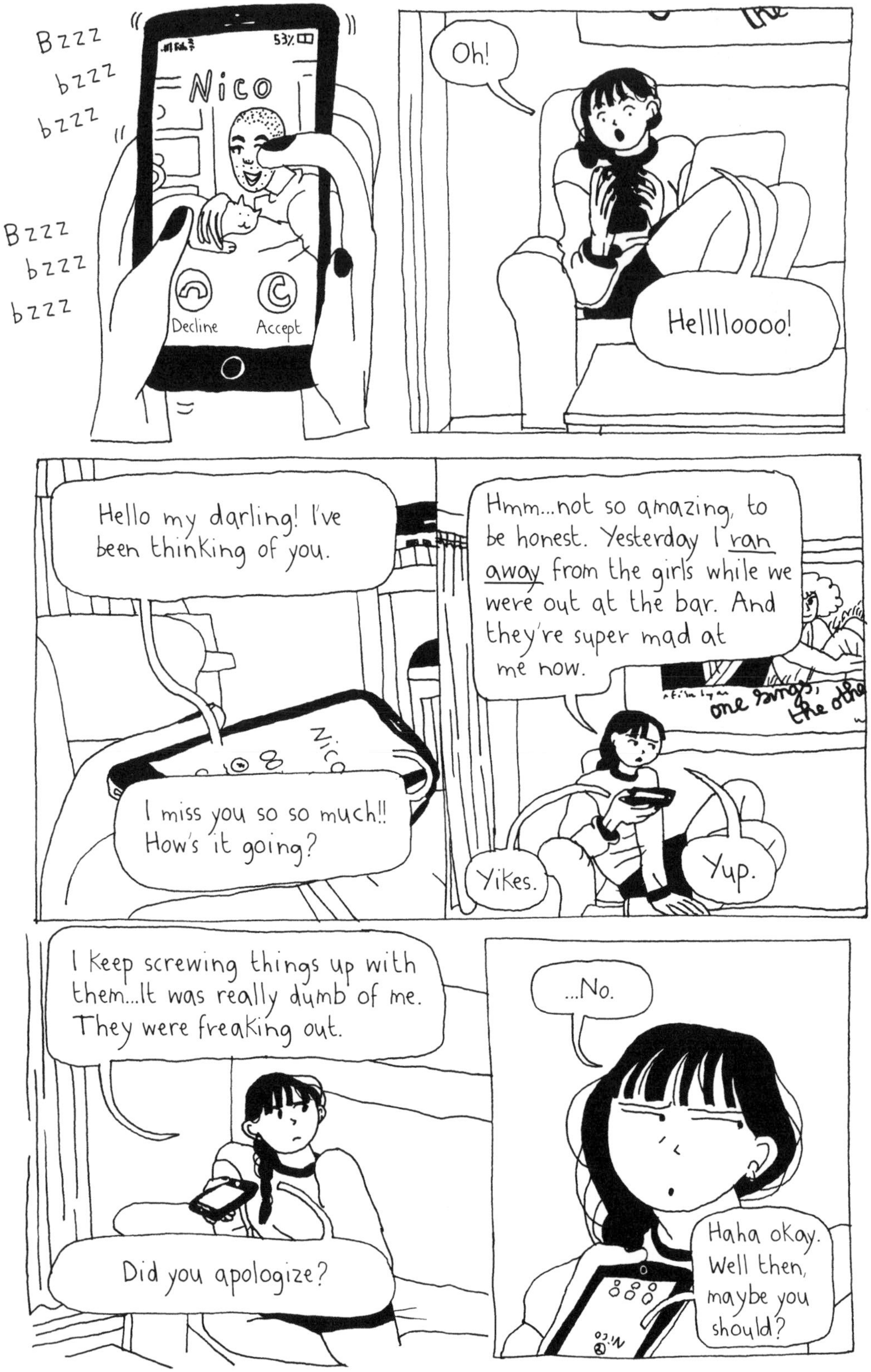
Bzzz
bzzz
bzzz
Nico
53%
Bzzz
bzzz
bzzz
Decline
Accept
Oh!
Hellllloooo!
Hello my darling! I've been thinking of you.
I miss you so so much!! How's it going?
Hmm...not so amazing, to be honest. Yesterday I ran away from the girls while we were out at the bar. And they're super mad at me now.
Yikes.
Yup.
I keep screwing things up with them...It was really dumb of me. They were freaking out.
Did you apologize?
...No.
Haha okay. Well then, maybe you should?

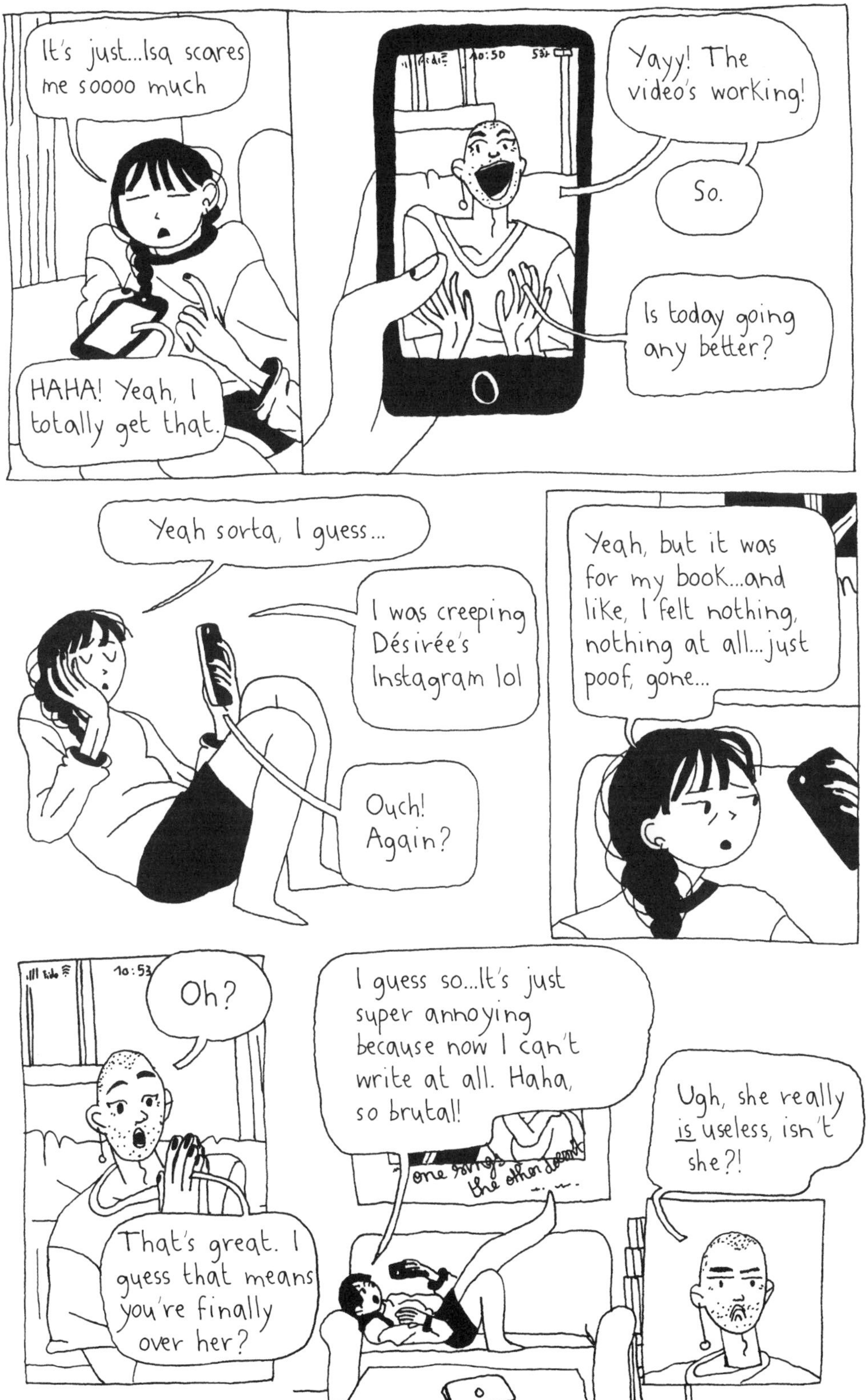

It's just...Isa scares me soooo much
HAHA! Yeah, I totally get that.
Yayy! The video's working!
So.
Is today going any better?
Yeah sorta, I guess...
I was creeping Désirée's Instagram lol
Ouch! Again?
Yeah, but it was for my book...and like, I felt nothing, nothing at all...just poof, gone...
Oh?
That's great. I guess that means you're finally over her?
I guess so...It's just super annoying because now I can't write at all. Haha, so brutal!
Ugh, she really is useless, isn't she?!

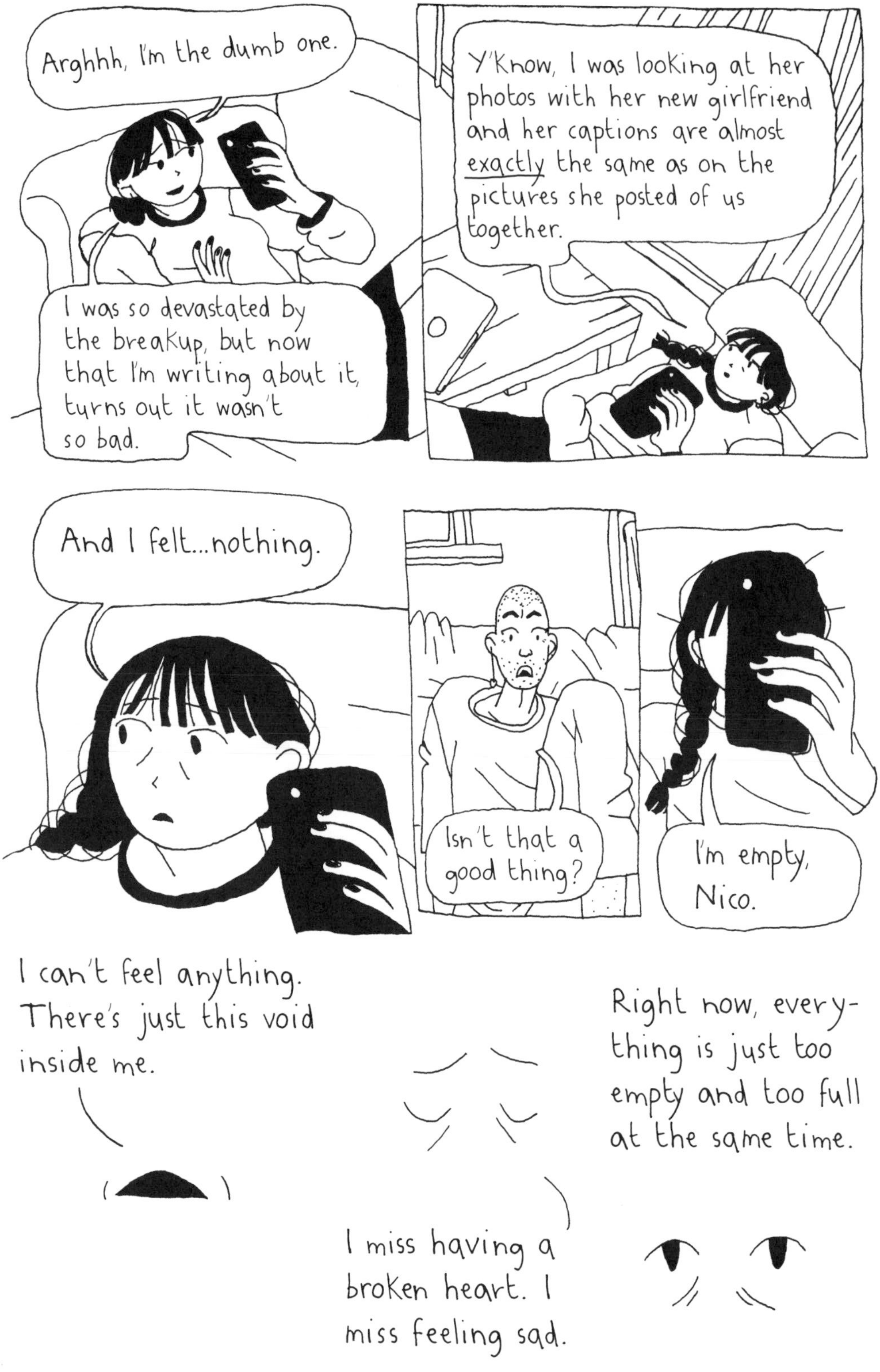
Arghhh, I'm the dumb one.
I was so devastated by the breakup, but now that I'm writing about it, turns out it wasn't so bad.
Y'Know, I was looking at her photos with her new girlfriend and her captions are almost exactly the same as on the pictures she posted of us together.
And I felt...nothing.
Isn't that a good thing?
I'm empty, Nico.
I can't feel anything. There's just this void inside me.
Right now, everything is just too empty and too full at the same time.
I miss having a broken heart. I miss feeling sad.

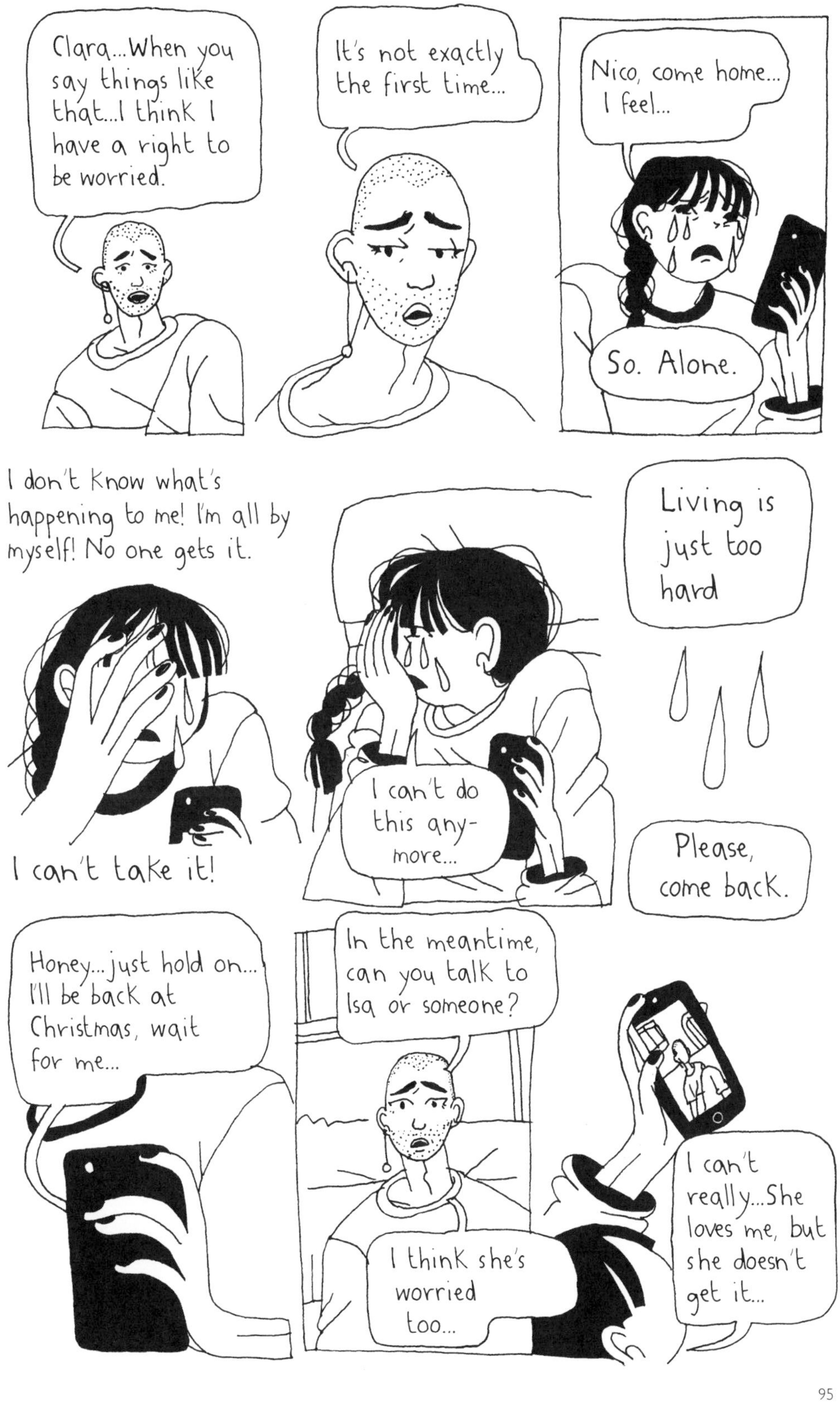
Clara...When you say things like that...I think I have a right to be worried.
It's not exactly the first time...
Nico, come home... I feel...
So. Alone.
I don't know what's happening to me! I'm all by myself! No one gets it.
I can't take it!
I can't do this any-more...
Living is just too hard
Please, come back.
Honey...just hold on... I'll be back at Christmas, wait for me...
In the meantime, can you talk to Isa or someone?
I think she's worried too...
I can't really...She loves me, but she doesn't get it...

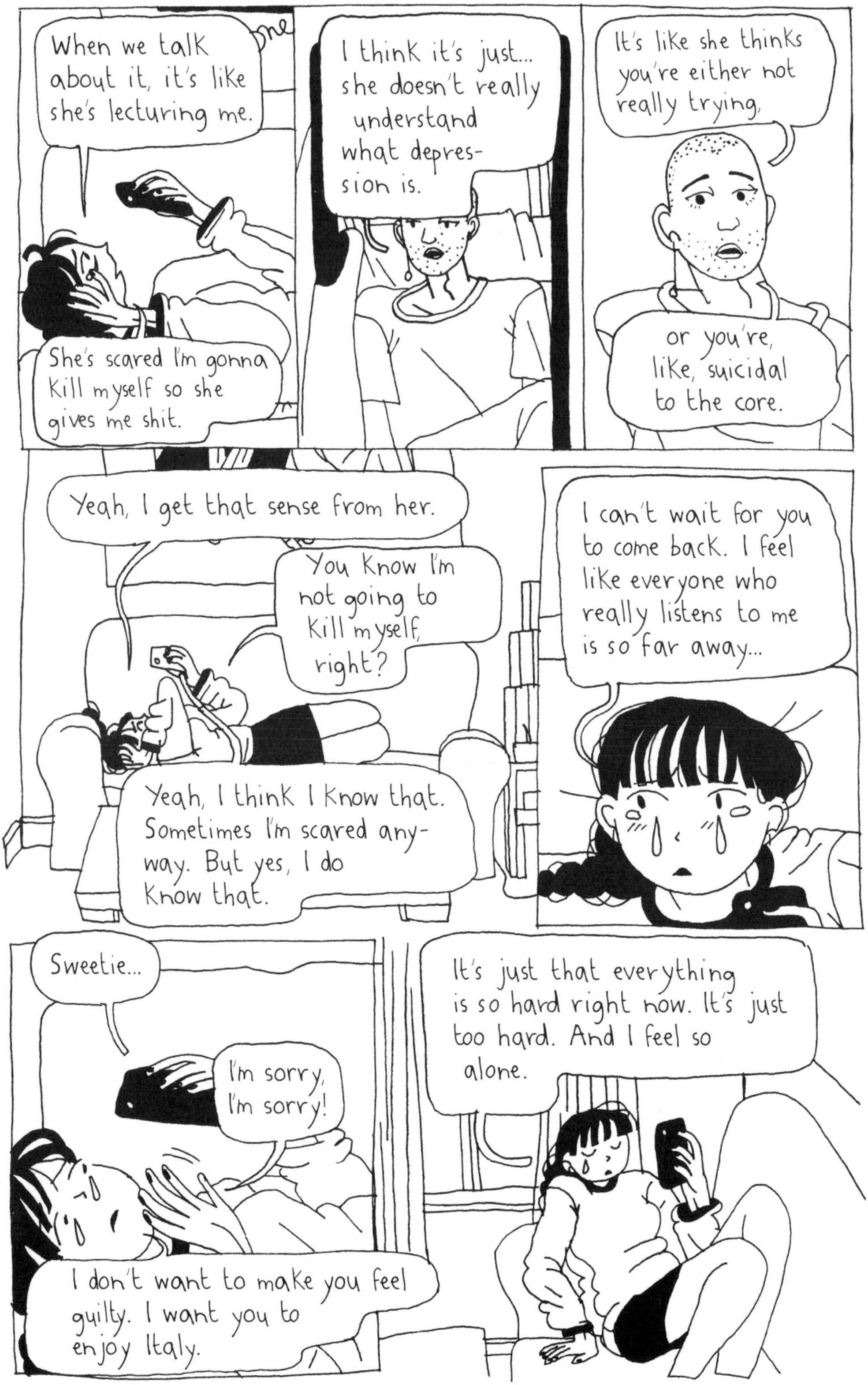
When we talk about it, it's like she's lecturing me.
She's scared I'm gonna kill myself so she gives me shit.
I think it's just... she doesn't really understand what depression is.
It's like she thinks you're either not really trying,
or you're, like, suicidal to the core.
Yeah, I get that sense from her.
You know I'm not going to kill myself, right?
Yeah, I think I know that. Sometimes I'm scared anyway. But yes, I do know that.
I can't wait for you to come back. I feel like everyone who really listens to me is so far away...
Sweetie...
I'm sorry, I'm sorry!
I don't want to make you feel guilty. I want you to enjoy Italy.
It's just that everything is so hard right now. It's just too hard. And I feel so alone.

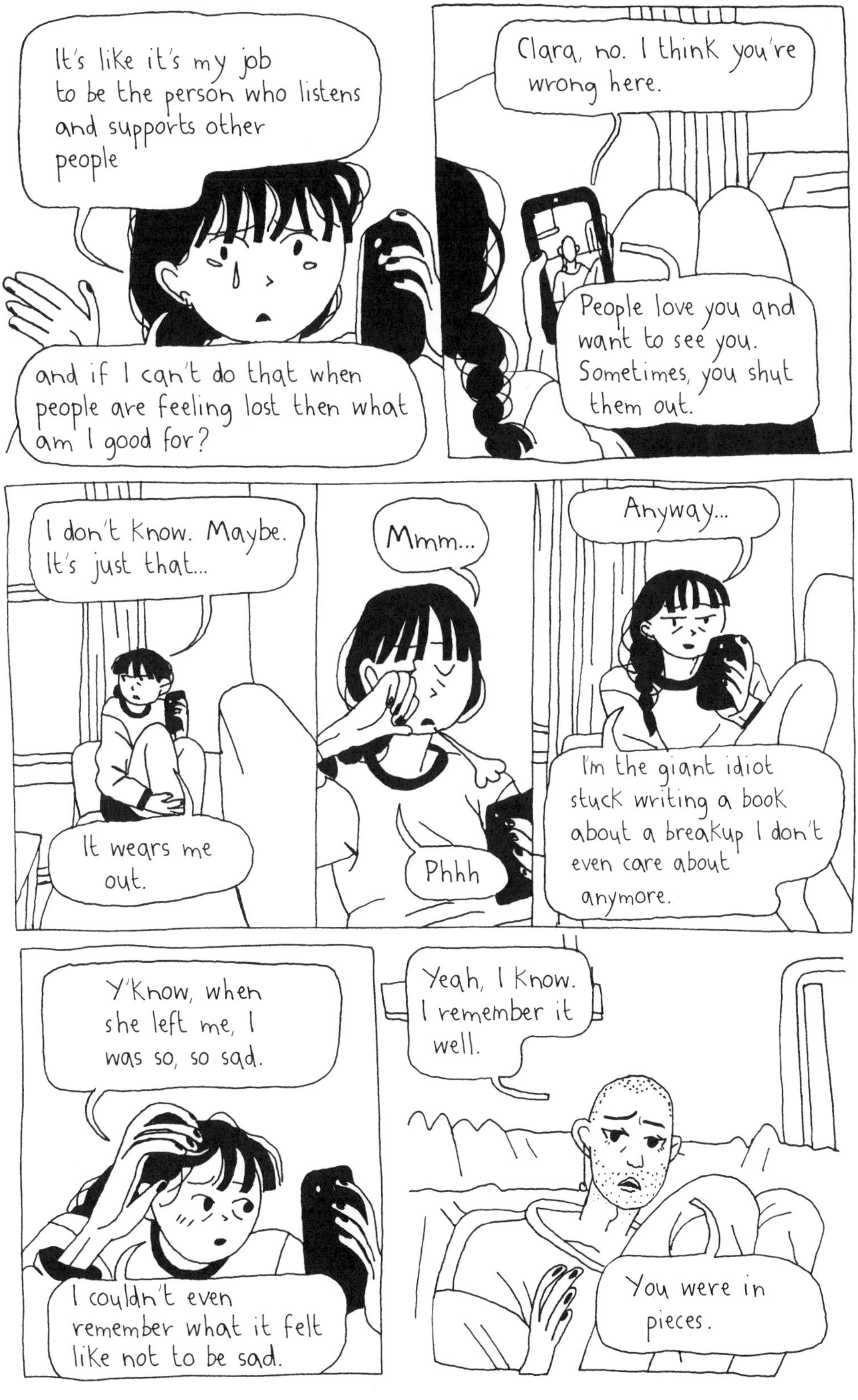
It's like it's my job to be the person who listens and supports other people
and if I can't do that when people are feeling lost then what am I good for?
Clara, no. I think you're wrong here.
People love you and want to see you. Sometimes, you shut them out.
I don't know. Maybe. It's just that...
It wears me out.
Mmm...
Phhh
Anyway...
I'm the giant idiot stuck writing a book about a breakup I don't even care about anymore.
Y'know, when she left me, I was so, so sad.
I couldn't even remember what it felt like not to be sad.
Yeah, I know. I remember it well.
You were in pieces.

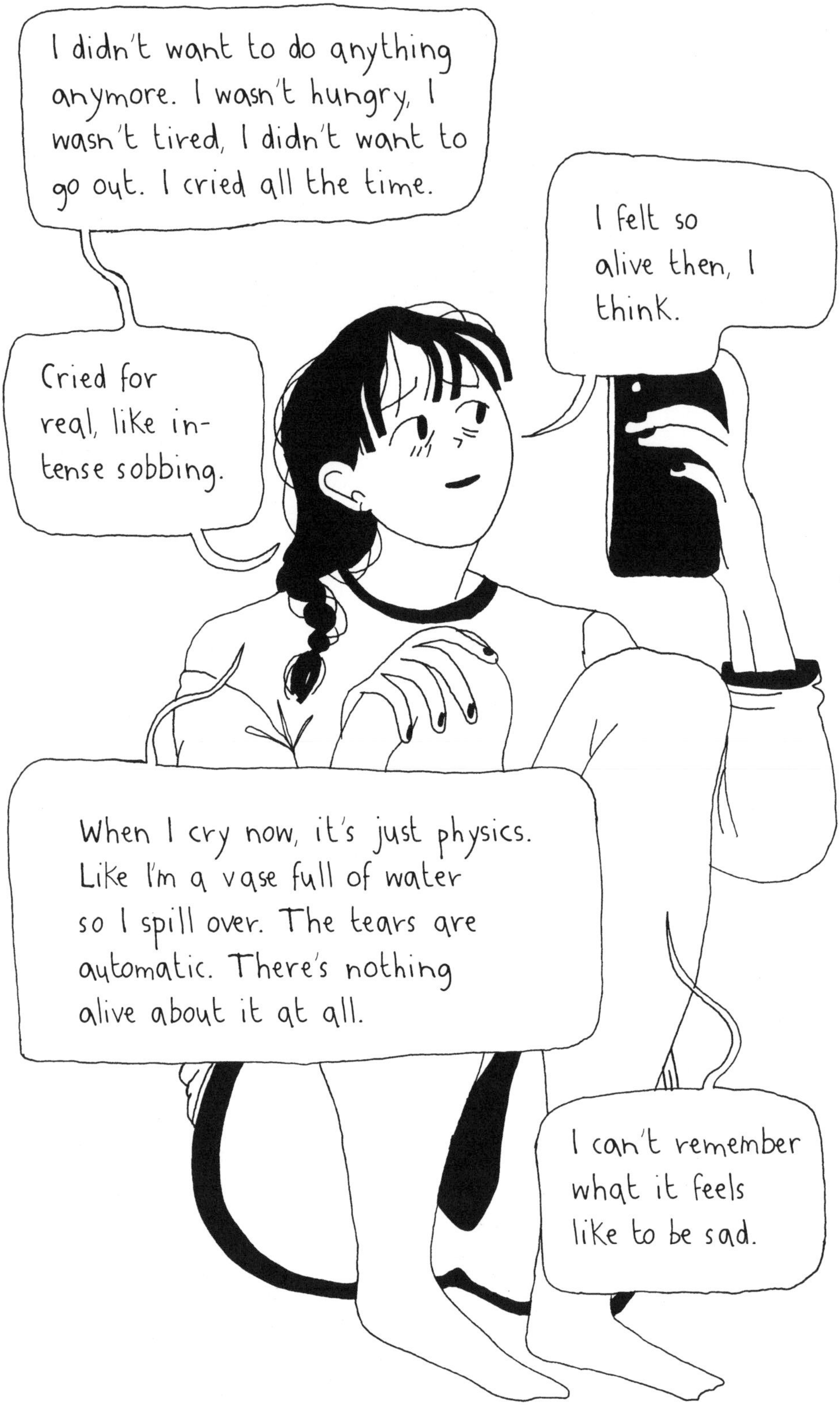
I didn't want to do anything anymore. I wasn't hungry, I wasn't tired, I didn't want to go out. I cried all the time.
Cried for real, like in-tense sobbing.
I felt so alive then, I think.
When I cry now, it's just physics. Like I'm a vase full of water so I spill over. The tears are automatic. There's nothing alive about it at all.
I can't remember what it feels like to be sad.

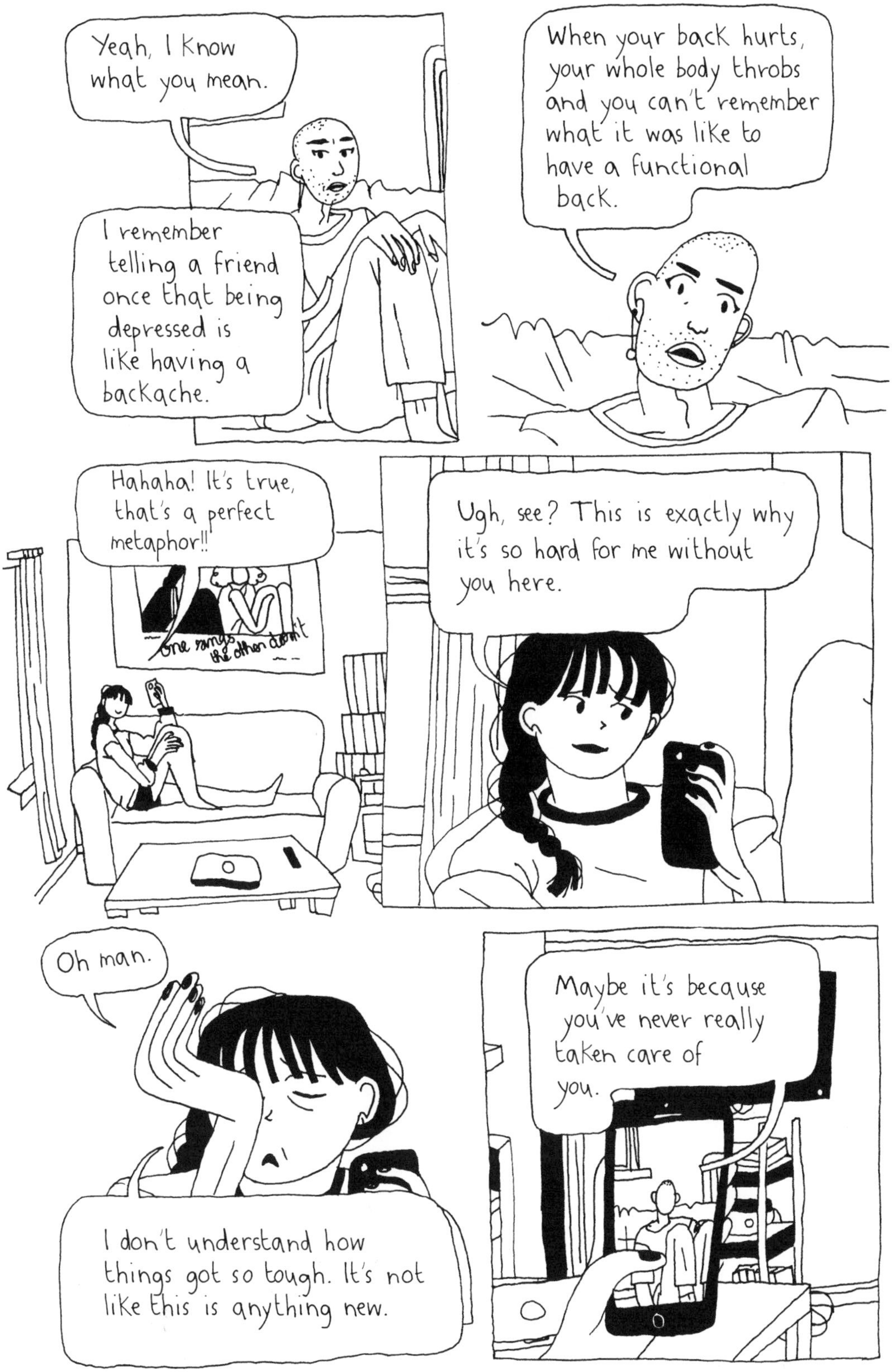
Yeah, I know what you mean.
I remember telling a friend once that being depressed is like having a backache.
When your back hurts, your whole body throbs and you can't remember what it was like to have a functional back.
Hahaha! It's true, that's a perfect metaphor!!
one sings the other doesn't
Ugh, see? This is exactly why it's so hard for me without you here.
Oh man.
I don't understand how things got so tough. It's not like this is anything new.
Maybe it's because you've never really taken care of you.

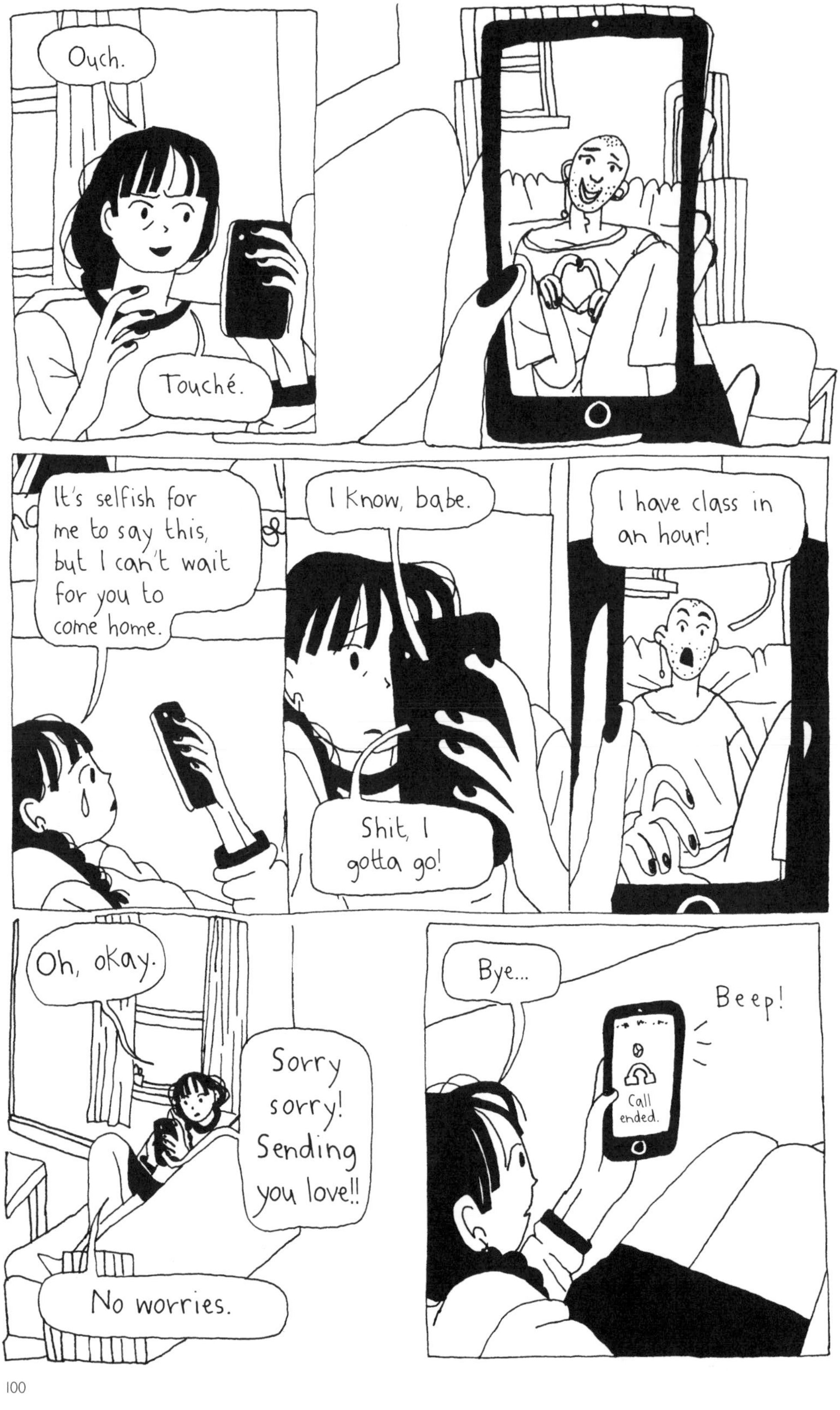

Ouch.
Touché.
It's selfish for me to say this, but I can't wait for you to come home.
I Know, babe.
Shit, I gotta go!
I have class in an hour!
Oh, okay.
Sorry sorry! Sending you love!!
No worries.
Bye...
Beep!
Call ended.

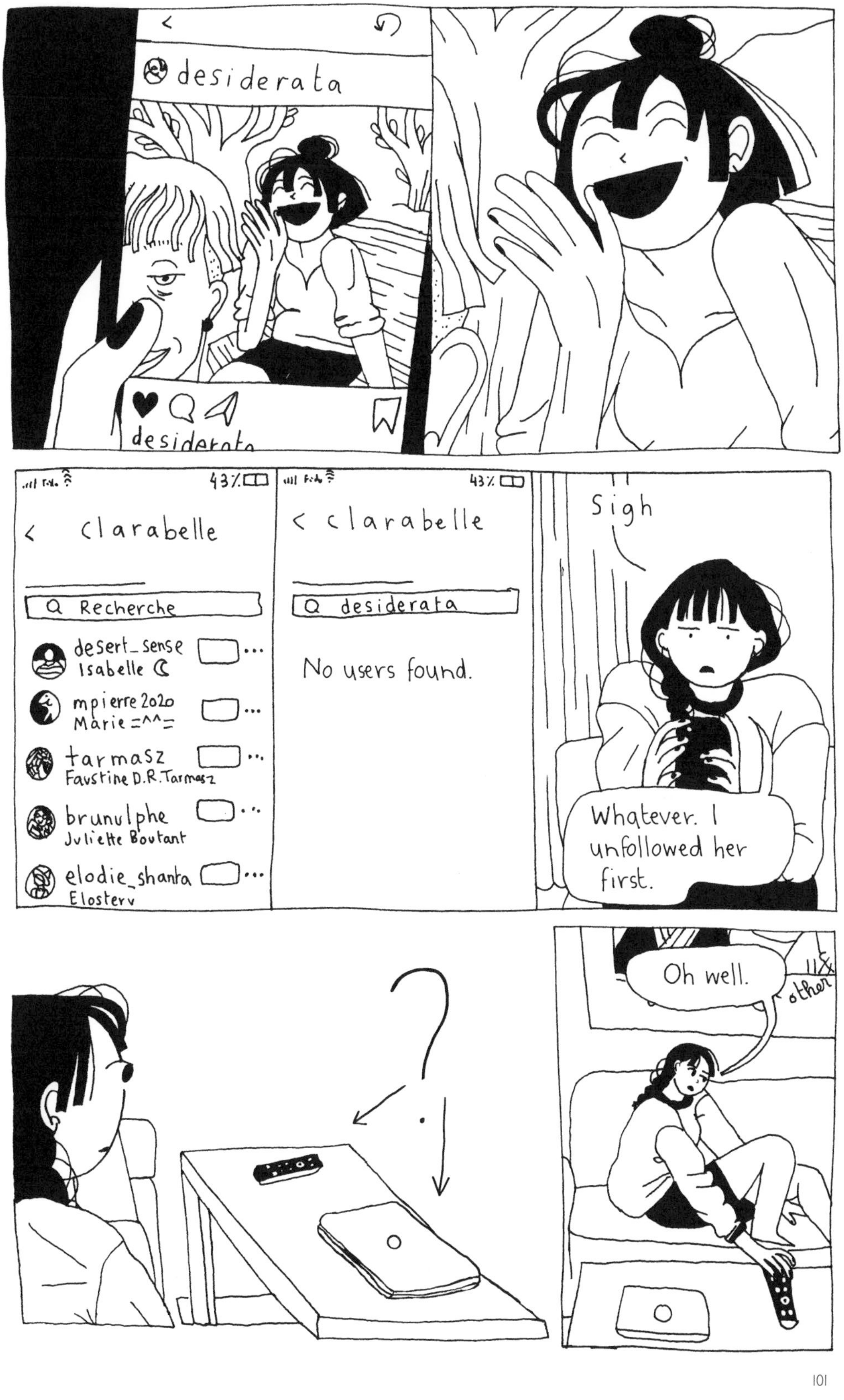
desiderata
desiderata
clarabelle
Recherche
desert_sense
Isabelle
mpierre2020
Marie =^^=
tarmasz
Faustine D.R.Tarmasz
brunulphe
Juliette Boutant
elodie_shanta
Elosterv
clarabelle
desiderata
No users found.
Sigh
Whatever. I unfollowed her first.
?
Oh well.
other

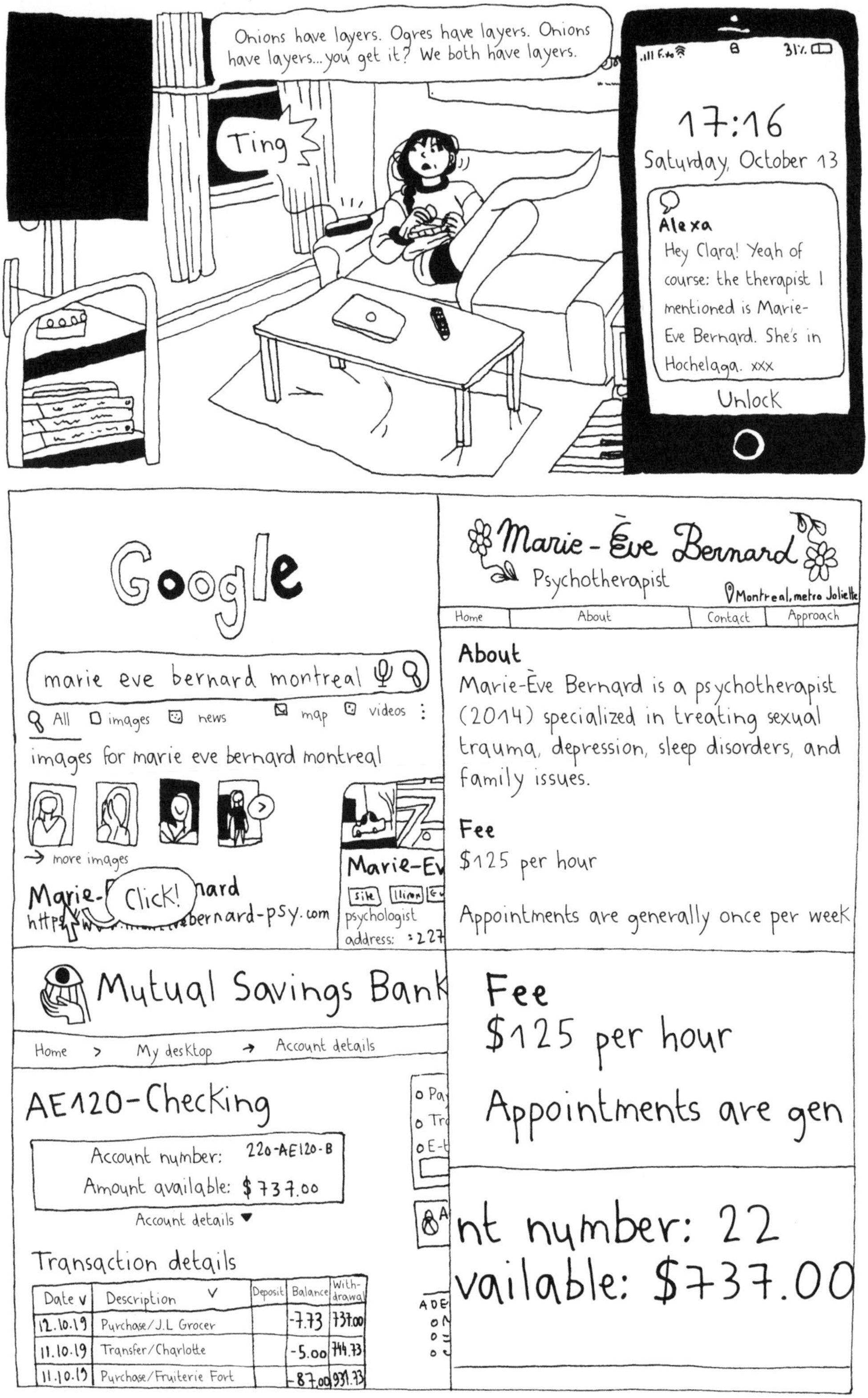

Onions have layers. Ogres have layers. Onions have layers... you get it? We both have layers.
Ting
31%
17:16
Saturday, October 13
Alexa
Hey Clara! Yeah of course: the therapist I mentioned is Marie-Eve Bernard. She's in Hochelaga. xxx
Unlock
Google
marie eve bernard montreal
All
images
news
map
videos
images for marie eve bernard montreal
more images
Click!
psychologist
address:
Marie-Ève Bernard
Psychotherapist
Montreal, metro Joliette
Home
About
Contact
Approach
About
Marie-Ève Bernard is a psychotherapist (2014) specialized in treating sexual trauma, depression, sleep disorders, and family issues.
Fee
$125 per hour
Appointments are generally once per week
Mutual Savings Bank
Home > My desktop → Account details
AE120-Checking
Account number: 220-AE120-B
Amount available: $737.00
Account details
Transaction details
Date
Description
Deposit
Balance
Withdrawal
12.10.19 Purchase/J.L Grocer -7.73 737.00
11.10.19 Transfer/Charlotte -5.00 744.73
11.10.19 Purchase/Fruiterie Fort -87.00 931.73
Fee
$125 per hour
Appointments are gen
nt number: 22
vailable: $737.00

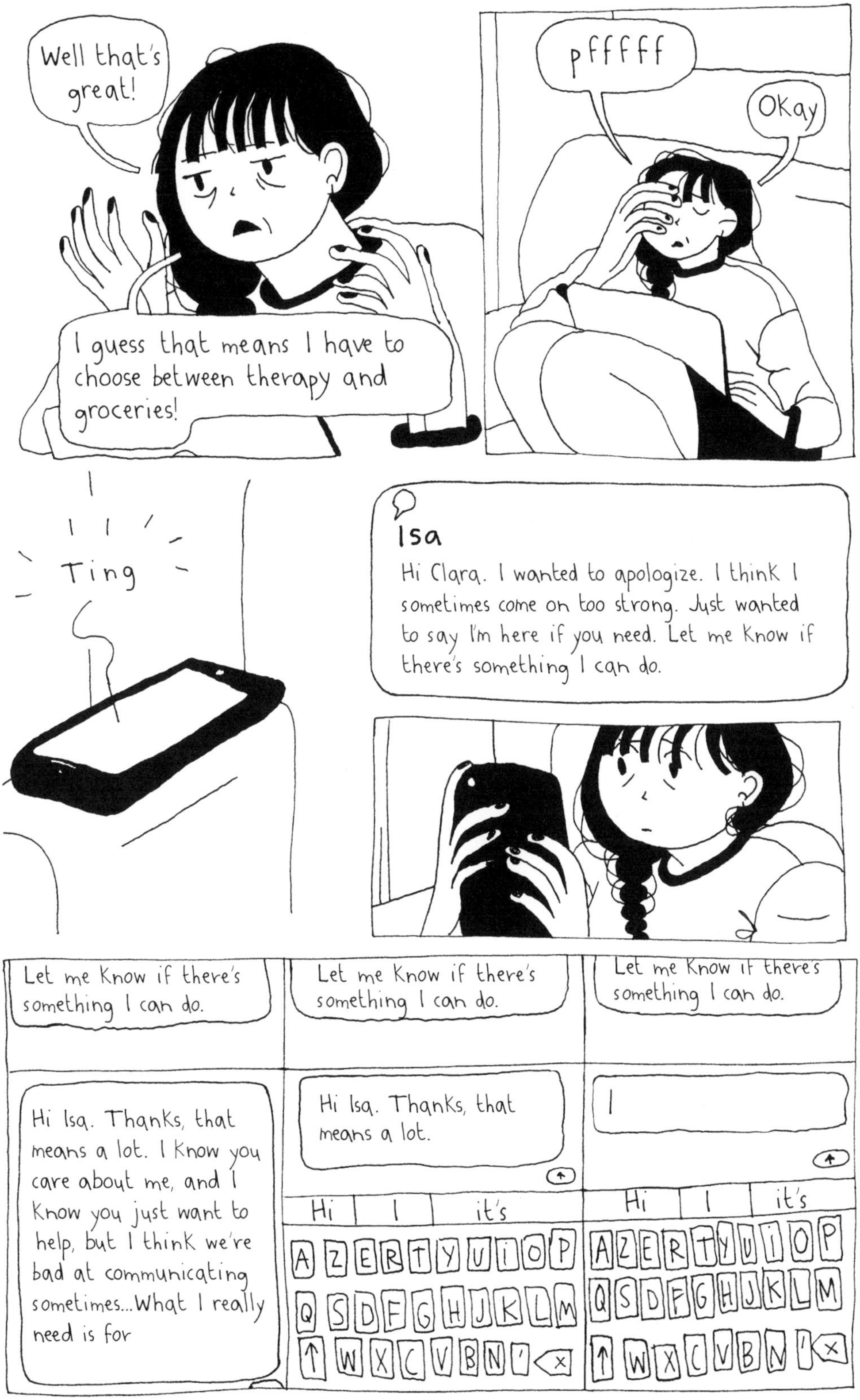
Well that's great!
I guess that means I have to choose between therapy and groceries!
pfffff
Okay
Ting
Isa
Hi Clara. I wanted to apologize. I think I sometimes come on too strong. Just wanted to say I'm here if you need. Let me Know if there's something I can do.
Let me Know if there's something I can do.
Hi Isa. Thanks, that means a lot. I Know you care about me, and I Know you just want to help, but I think we're bad at communicating sometimes...What I really need is for
Let me Know if there's something I can do.
Hi Isa. Thanks, that means a lot.
Hi
I
it's
Let me Know if there's something I can do.
I
Hi
I
it's

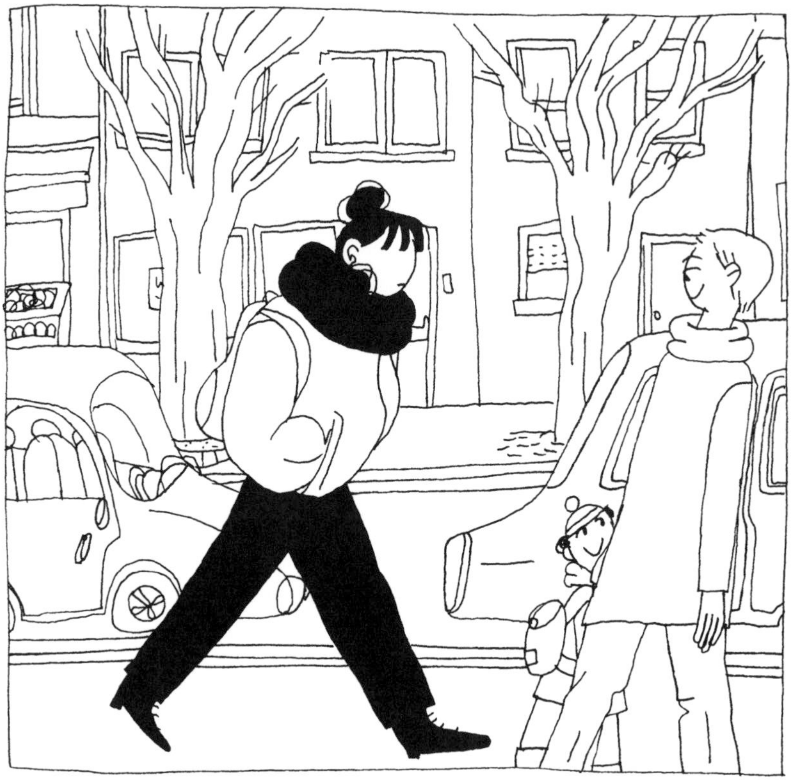

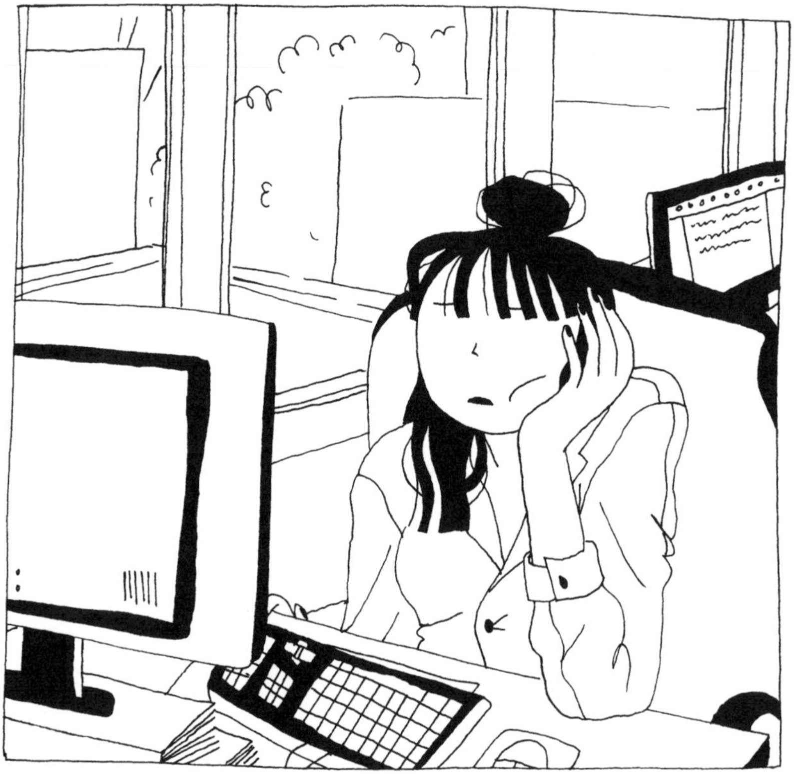

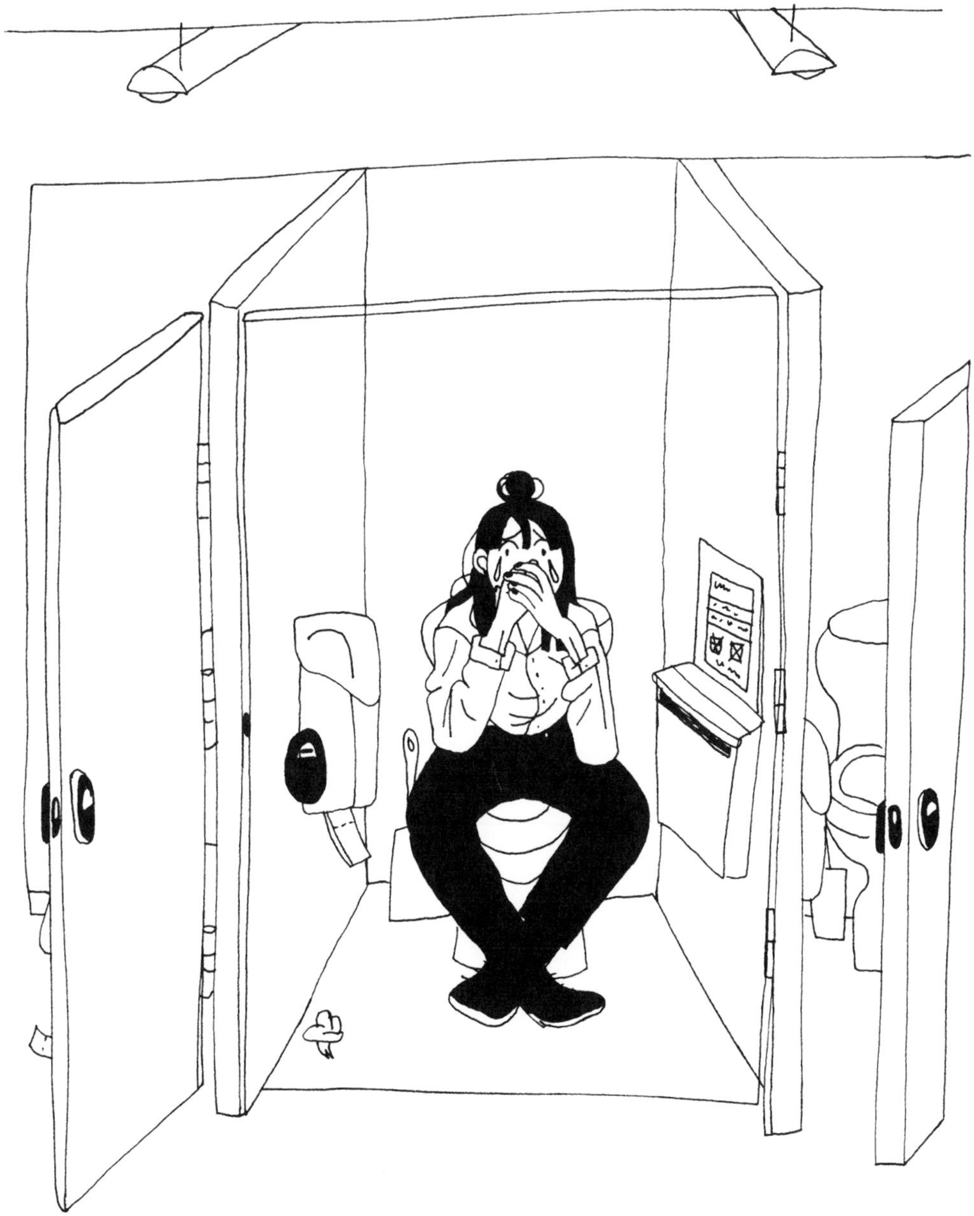

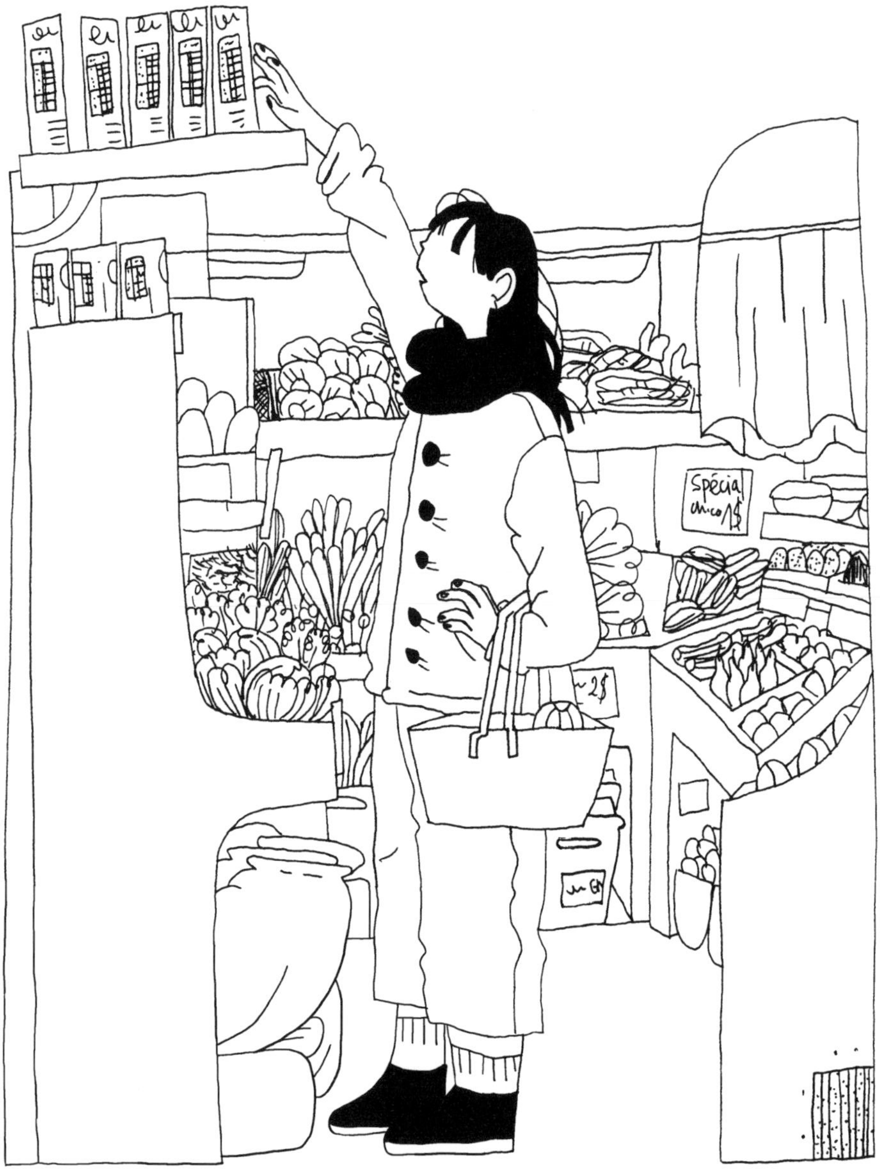
Spécial
1$
2$

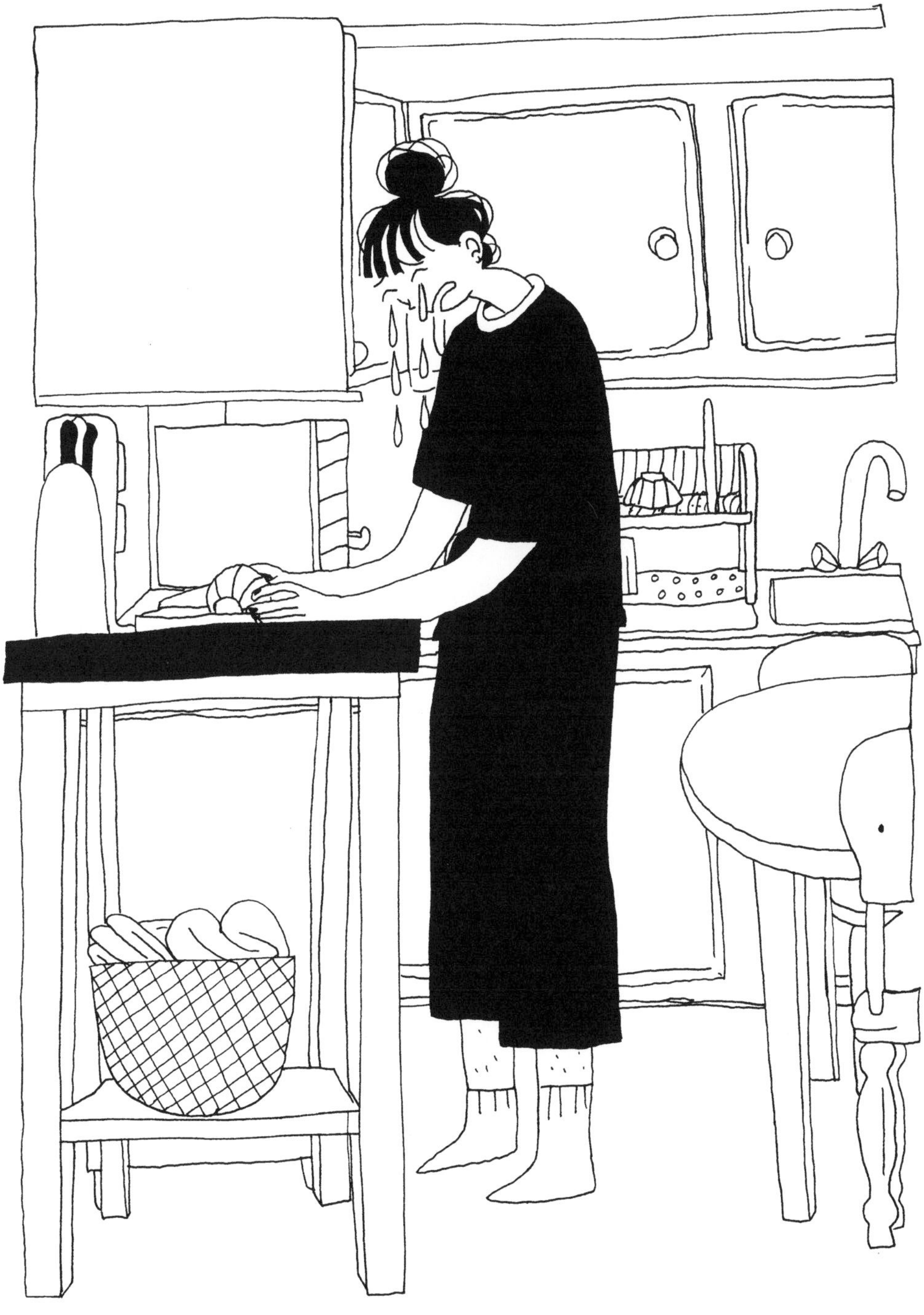

CS

from : St. Joseph Psychotherapy Center

▾ show details

date : October 18, 2019

subject : Registration for psychotherapy services

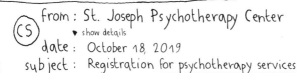

Dear Ms. Lusignant,

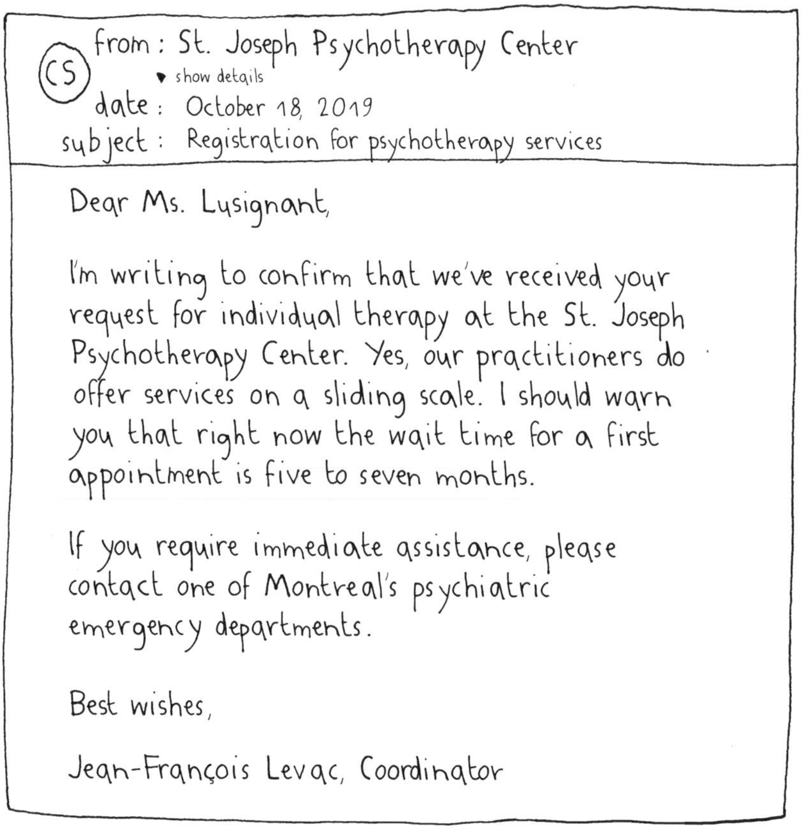

I'm writing to confirm that we've received your request for individual therapy at the St. Joseph Psychotherapy Center. Yes, our practitioners do offer services on a sliding scale. I should warn you that right now the wait time for a first appointment is five to seven months.

If you require immediate assistance, please contact one of Montreal's psychiatric emergency departments.

Best wishes,

Jean-François Levac, Coordinator

one month
later
(around mid-november)

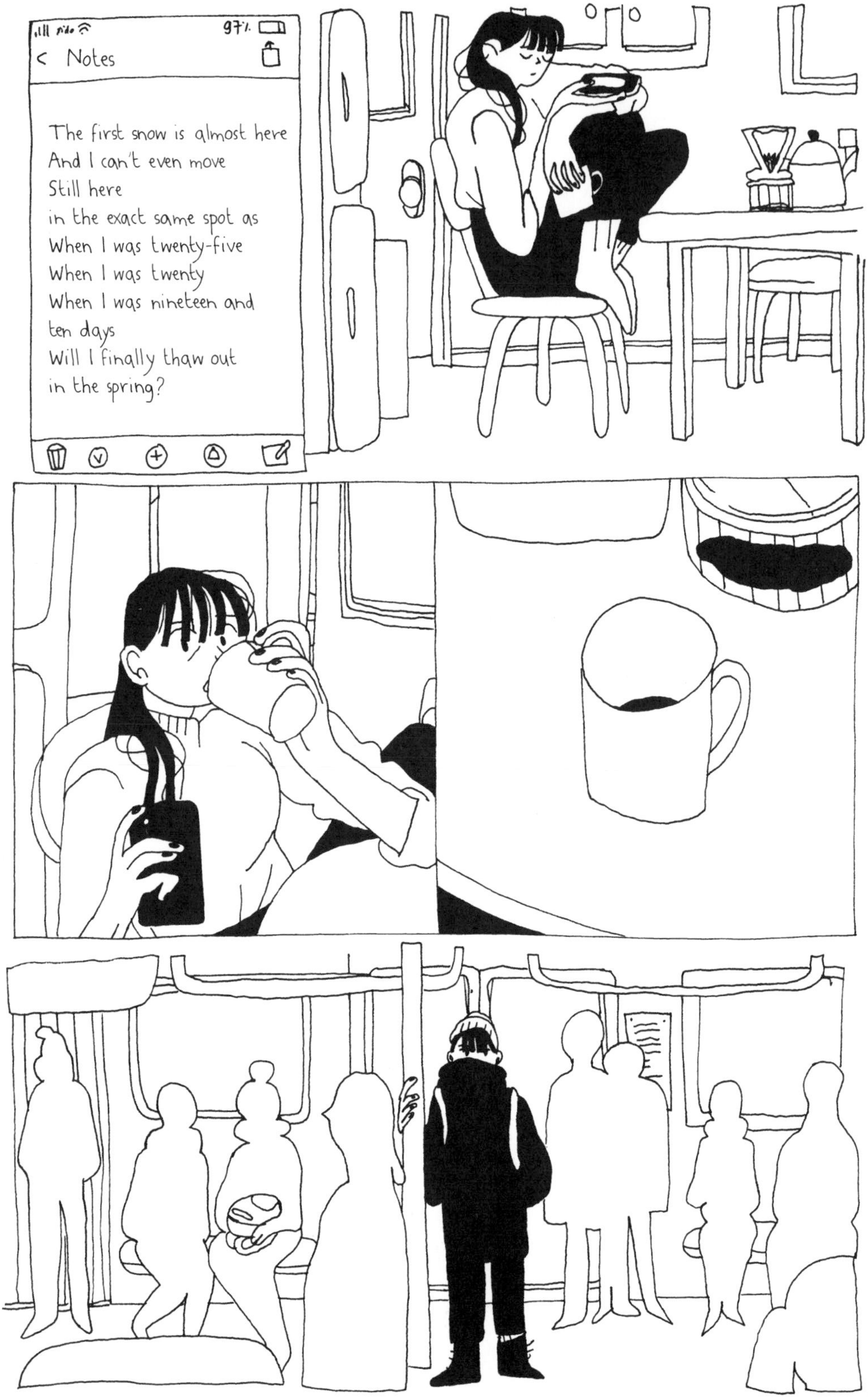

97%
< Notes
The first snow is almost here
And I can't even move
Still here
in the exact same spot as
When I was twenty-five
When I was twenty
When I was nineteen and
ten days
Will I finally thaw out
in the spring?

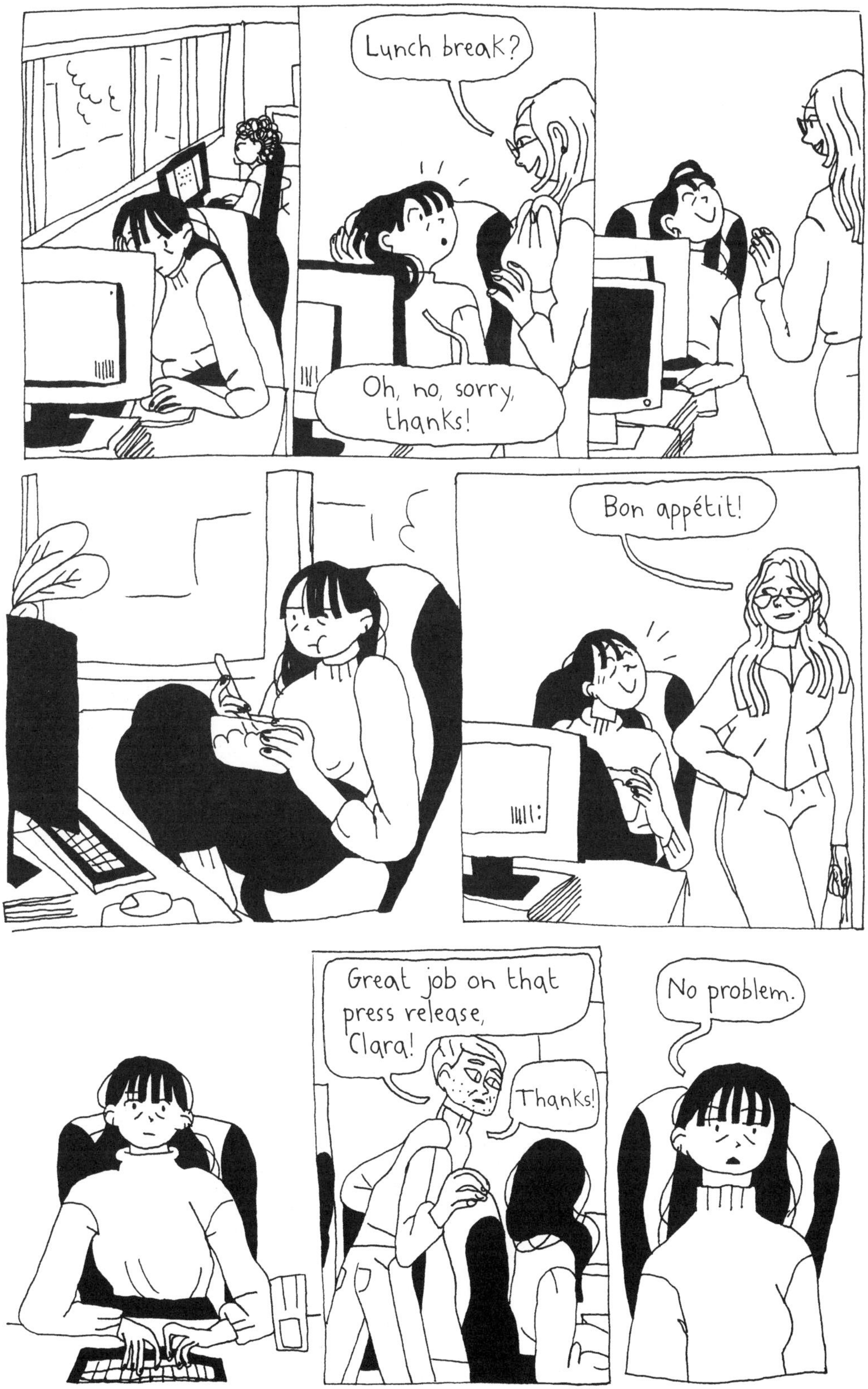

Lunch break?
Oh, no, sorry, thanks!
Bon appétit!
Great job on that press release, Clara!
Thanks!
No problem.

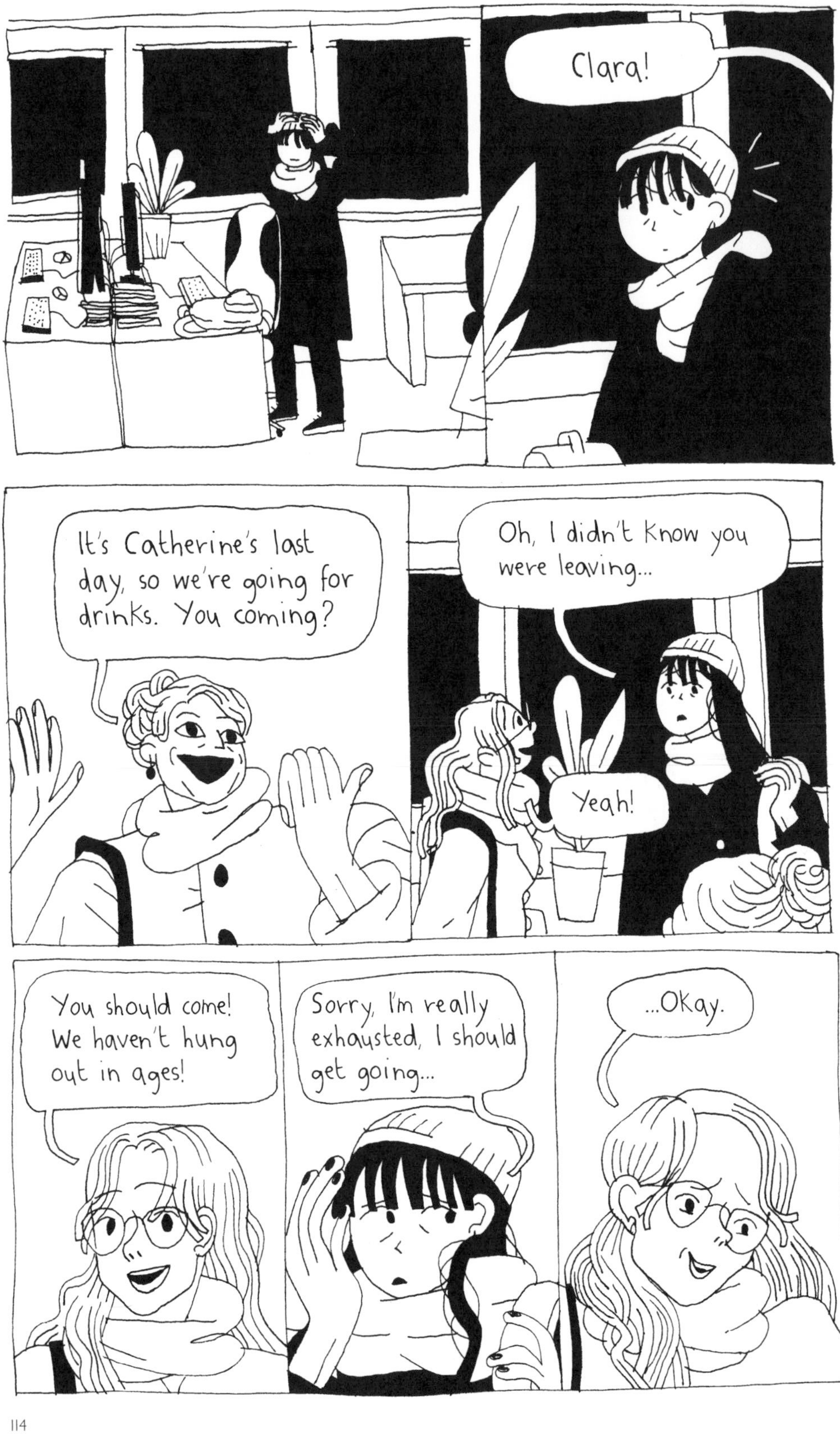
Clara!
It's Catherine's last day, so we're going for drinks. You coming?
Oh, I didn't know you were leaving...
Yeah!
You should come! We haven't hung out in ages!
Sorry, I'm really exhausted, I should get going...
...Okay.

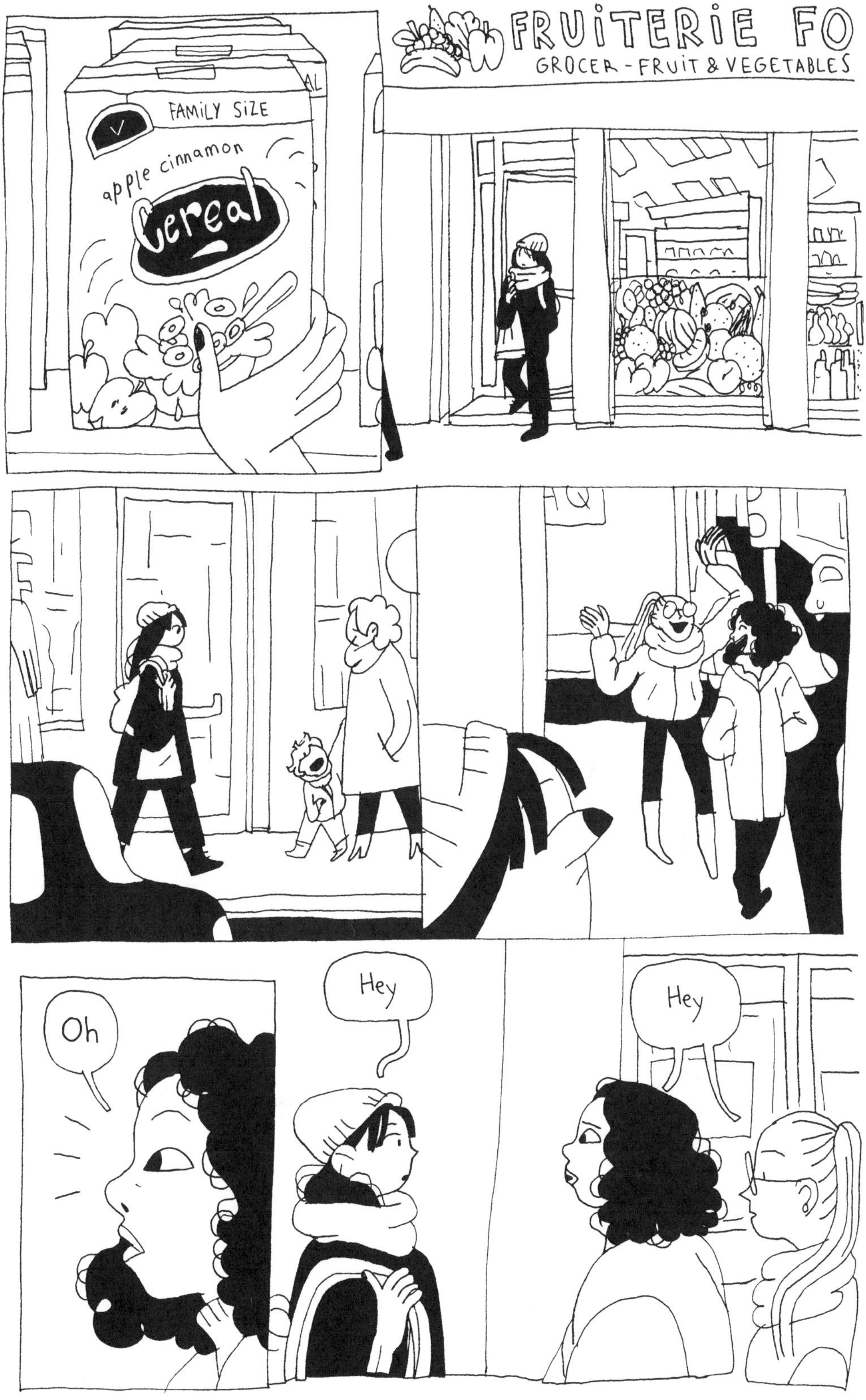
FAMILY SIZE
apple cinnamon
Cereal
FRUITERIE FO
GROCER - FRUIT & VEGETABLES
Oh
Hey
Hey

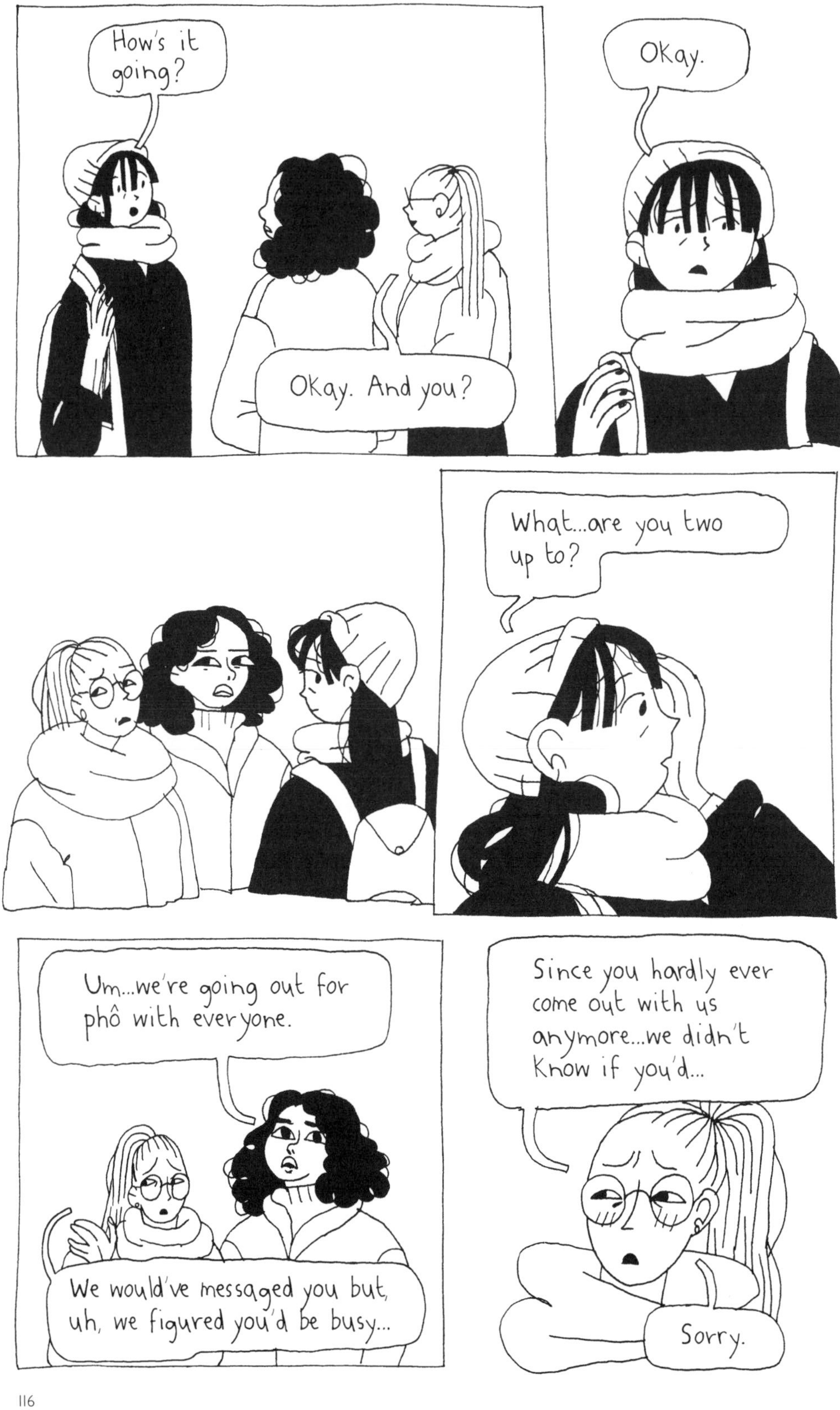
How's it going?
Okay. And you?
Okay.
What...are you two up to?
Um...we're going out for phô with everyone.
We would've messaged you but, uh, we figured you'd be busy...
Since you hardly ever come out with us anymore...we didn't know if you'd...
Sorry.

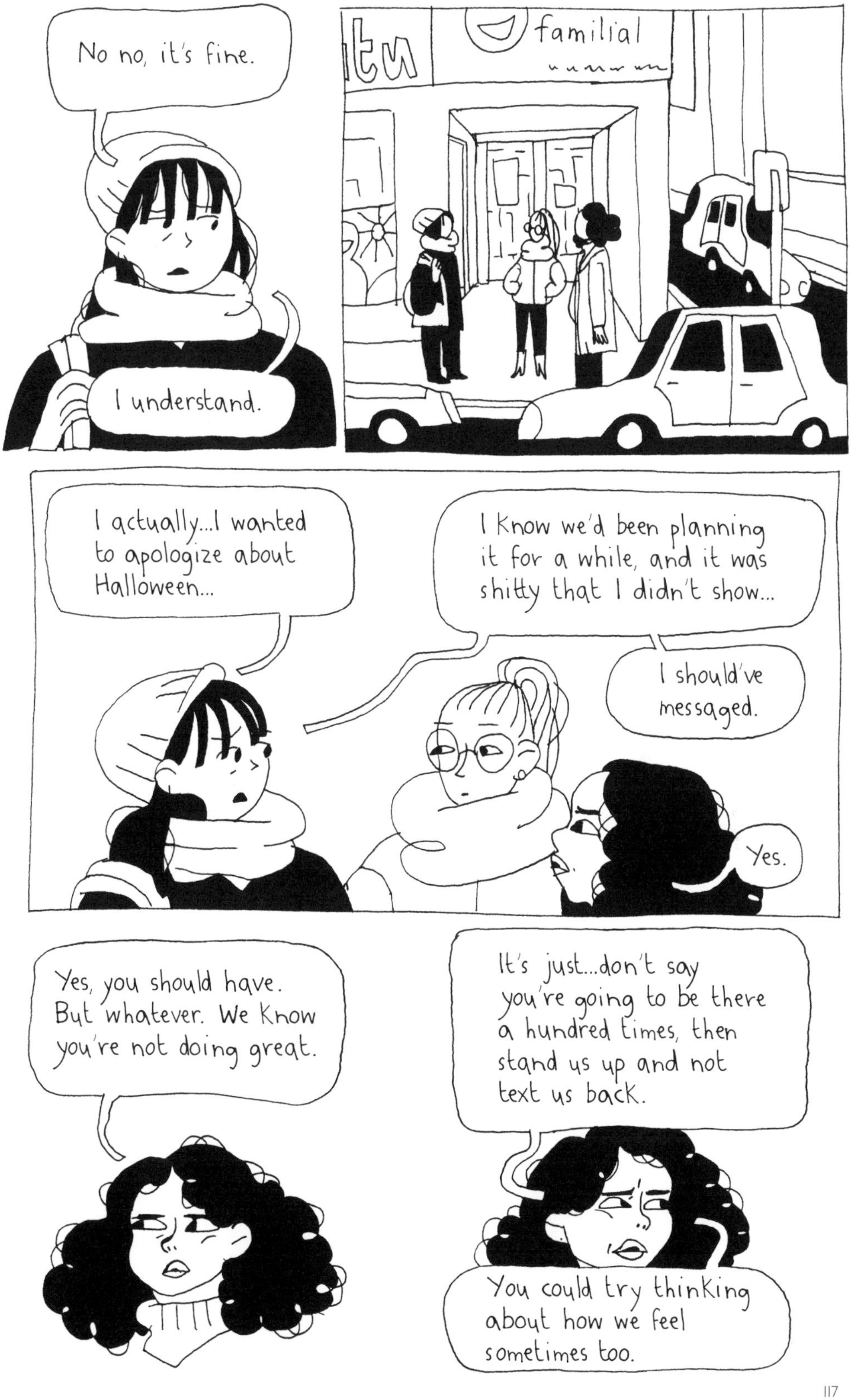
No no, it's fine.
I understand.
familial
I actually...I wanted to apologize about Halloween...
I know we'd been planning it for a while, and it was shitty that I didn't show...
I should've messaged.
Yes.
Yes, you should have. But whatever. We know you're not doing great.
It's just...don't say you're going to be there a hundred times, then stand us up and not text us back.
You could try thinking about how we feel sometimes too.

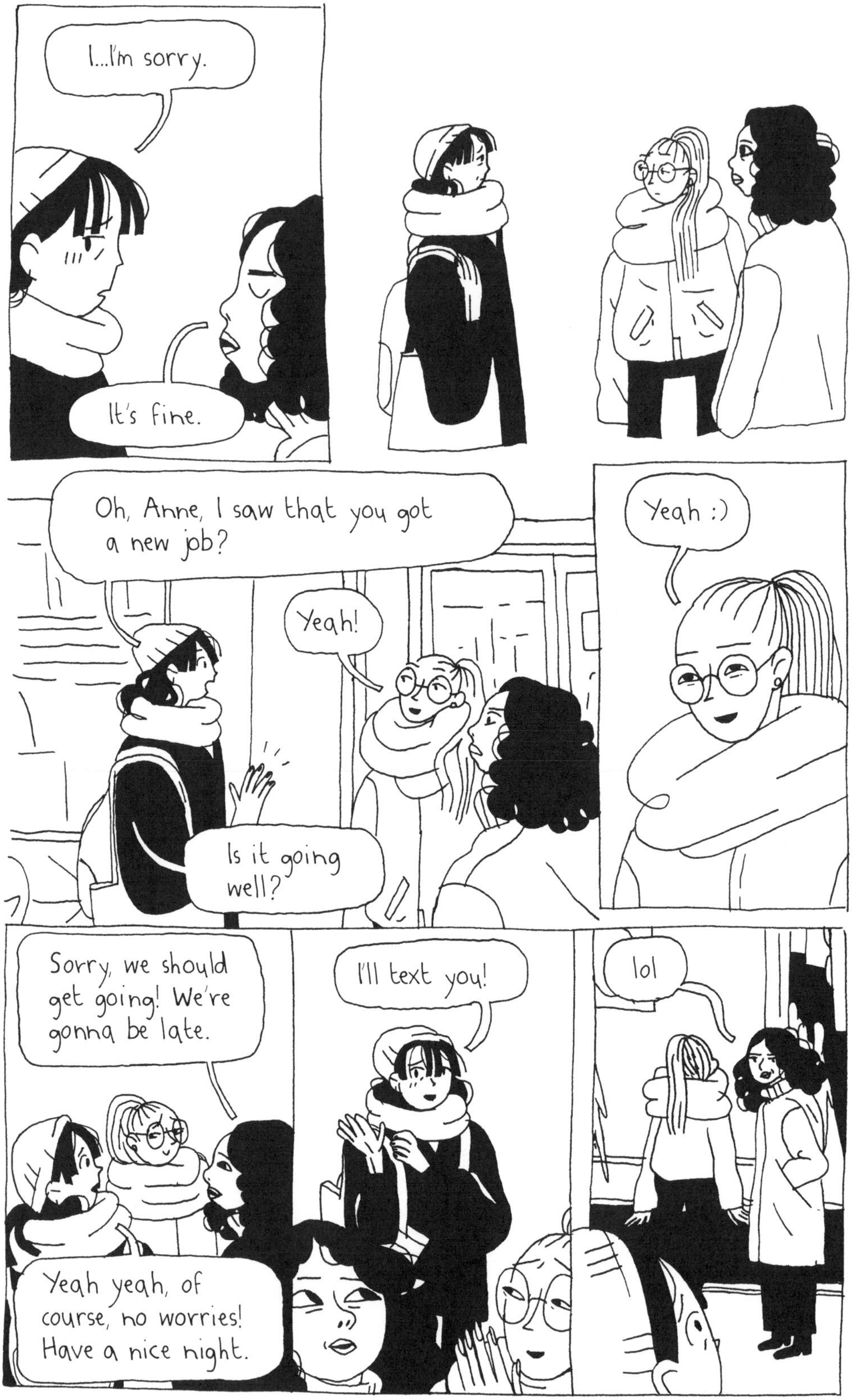
I...I'm sorry.
It's fine.
Oh, Anne, I saw that you got a new job?
Yeah!
Is it going well?
Yeah :)
Sorry, we should get going! We're gonna be late.
Yeah yeah, of course, no worries! Have a nice night.
I'll text you!
lol

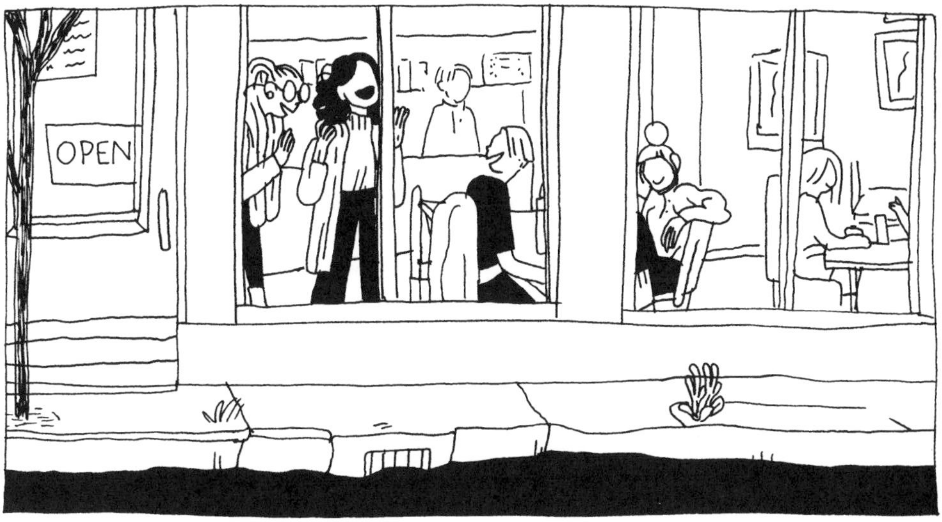
OPEN

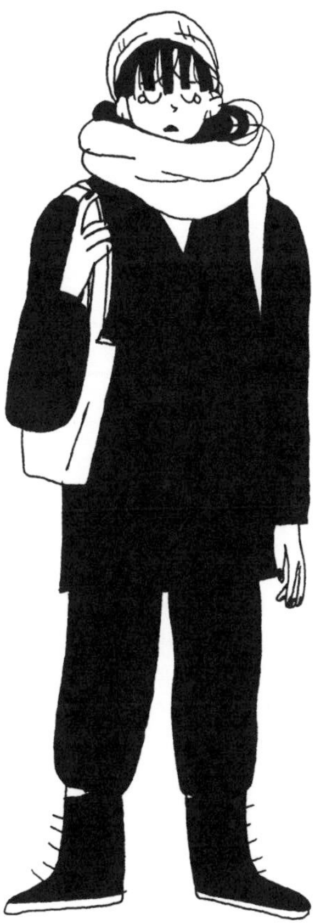

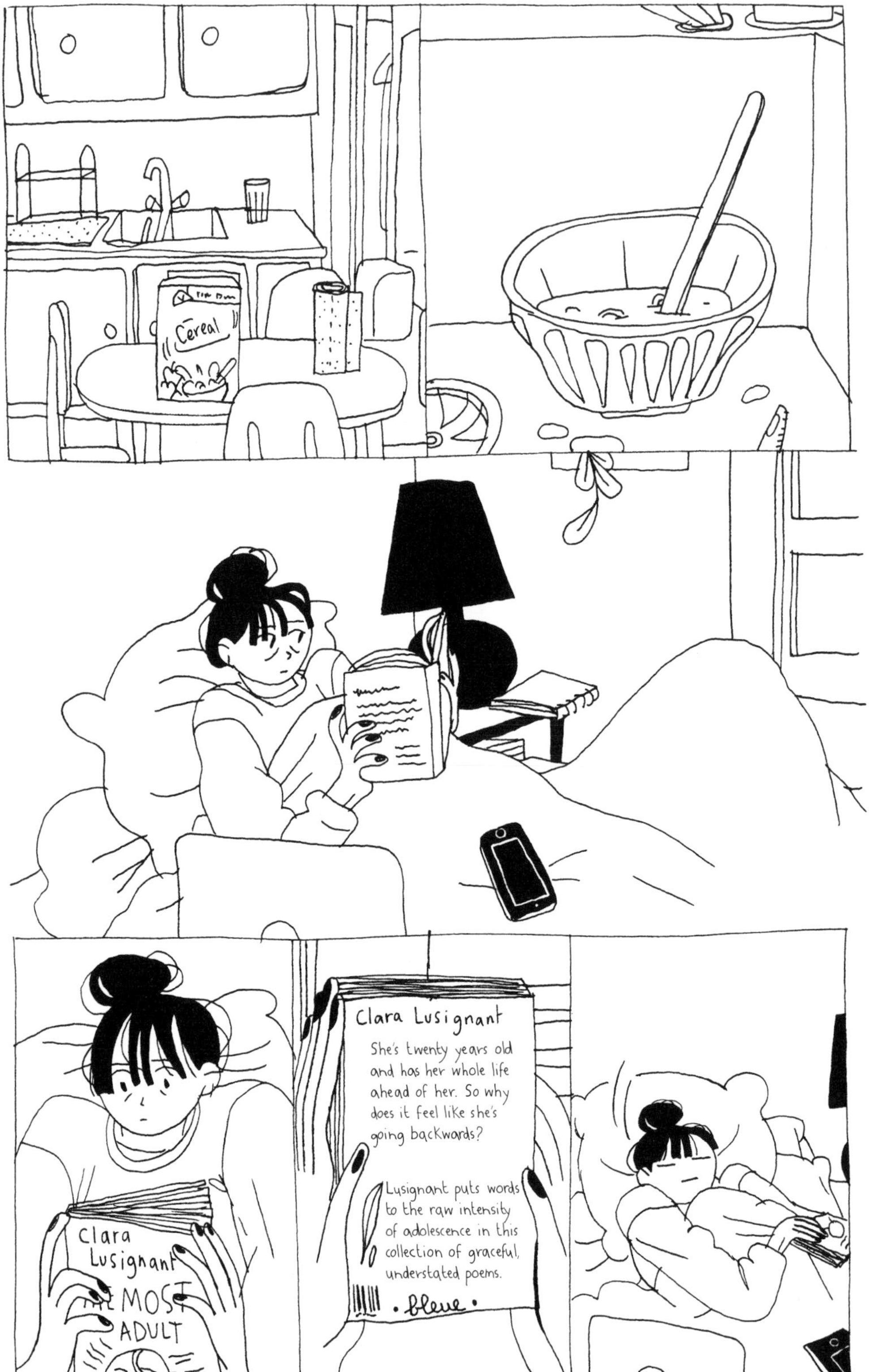

Cereal
Clara Lusignant
She's twenty years old and has her whole life ahead of her. So why does it feel like she's going backwards?
Lusignant puts words to the raw intensity of adolescence in this collection of graceful, understated poems.
bleue
Clara Lusignant
THE MOST ADULT

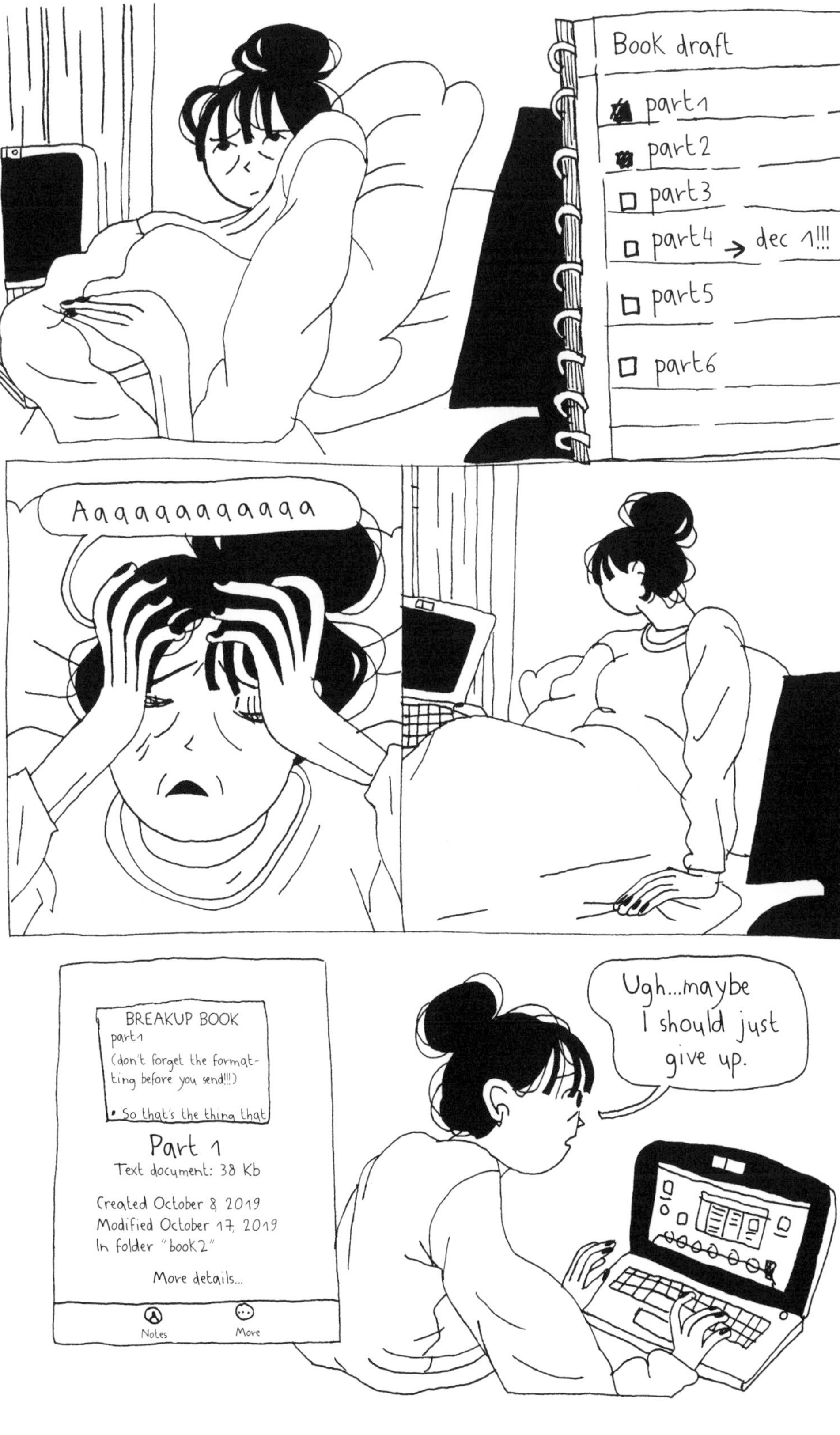
Book draft
part1
part2
part3
part4 → dec 1!!!
part5
part6
Aaaaaaaaaaaa
BREAKUP BOOK
part1
(don't forget the formatting before you send!!!)
• So that's the thing that
Part 1
Text document: 38 Kb
Created October 8, 2019
Modified October 17, 2019
In folder "book2"
More details...
Notes
More
Ugh...maybe I should just give up.

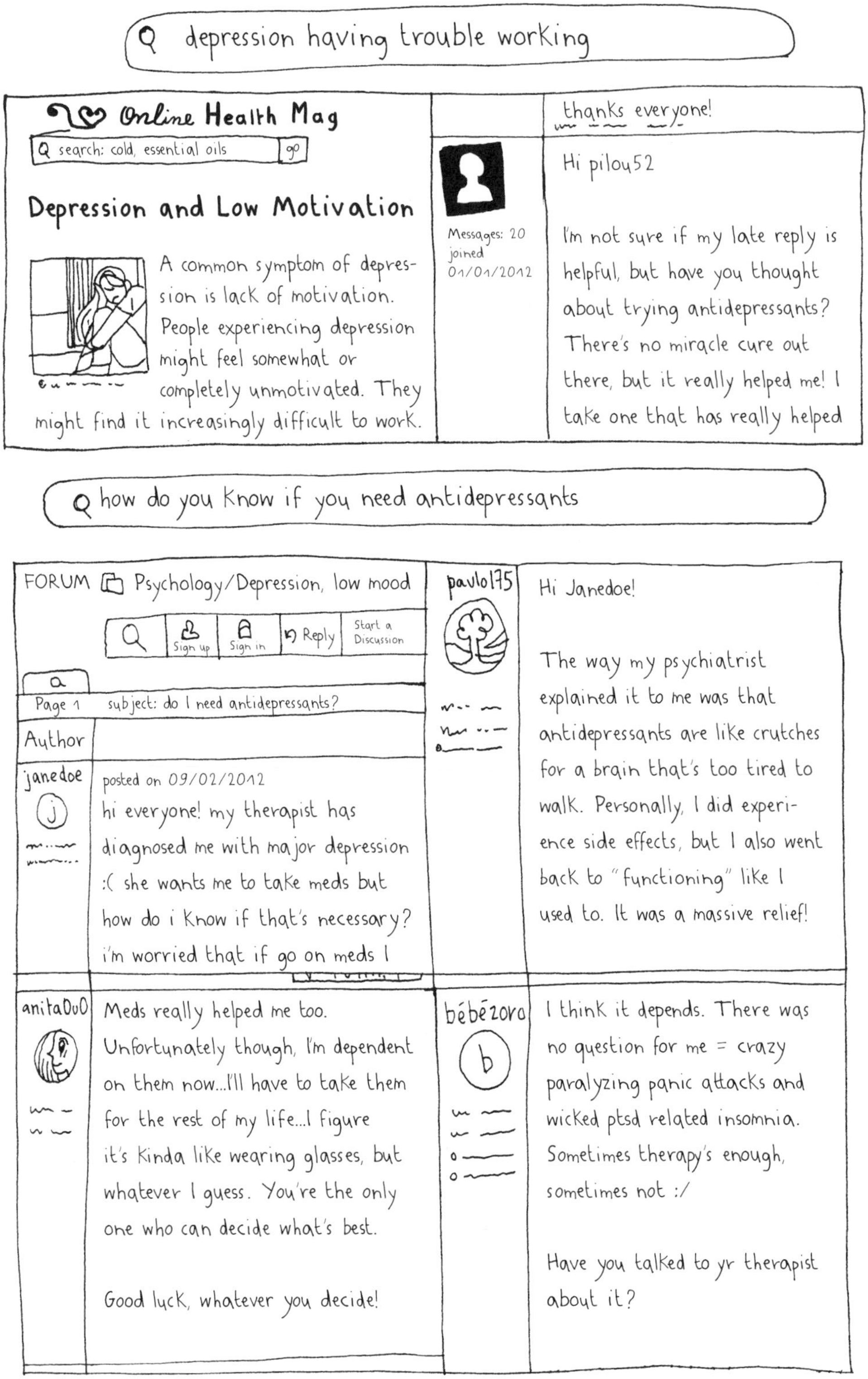
depression having trouble working
Online Health Mag
search: cold, essential oils
go
Depression and Low Motivation
A common symptom of depression is lack of motivation. People experiencing depression might feel somewhat or completely unmotivated. They might find it increasingly difficult to work.
thanks everyone!
Messages: 20
joined 01/01/2012
Hi pilou52
I'm not sure if my late reply is helpful, but have you thought about trying antidepressants? There's no miracle cure out there, but it really helped me! I take one that has really helped
how do you know if you need antidepressants
FORUM Psychology/Depression, low mood
Sign up
Sign in
Reply
Start a Discussion
Page 1
subject: do I need antidepressants?
Author
janedoe
posted on 09/02/2012
hi everyone! my therapist has diagnosed me with major depression :(she wants me to take meds but how do i know if that's necessary? i'm worried that if go on meds I
paulo175
Hi Janedoe!
The way my psychiatrist explained it to me was that antidepressants are like crutches for a brain that's too tired to walk. Personally, I did experience side effects, but I also went back to "functioning" like I used to. It was a massive relief!
anitaOuO
Meds really helped me too. Unfortunately though, I'm dependent on them now...I'll have to take them for the rest of my life...I figure it's kinda like wearing glasses, but whatever I guess. You're the only one who can decide what's best.
Good luck, whatever you decide!
bébézoro
I think it depends. There was no question for me = crazy paralyzing panic attacks and wicked ptsd related insomnia. Sometimes therapy's enough, sometimes not :/
Have you talked to yr therapist about it?

Q antidepressants side effects

☑ By **forestfairy** » 05.08.08 10:07

my meds made me gain weight and the first two months i felt a bit nauseous, but then it leveled out pretty quick. it helped a lot (I'm in therapy too, and that's what helped the most). before I couldn't even leave the house!

Forestfairy
Messages 71
Joined
Feb 11 08

Home / Psychology / Depression / Side effec

TOPICS

Is it the blues or is it depres sion?

- Depressed
- Depressio
- Recogniz
- Causes of depression
- Warning signs
- Cures an coping m
- Medicati
- Side-effe
- Counsellin
- Therapy

Antidepressants and Weight Gain

Ⓕ Ⓥ

see also - Symptoms and diagnosis
-Say no to fatigue!

One of the side effects people fear most when starting antidepressants is weight gain. In fact, it's been observed that only a small percen-

→ reply   ⦸ report

By **rita76** 🗓 01/31/17
at 12:32 a.m.

WHATEVER YOU DO, DON'T TAKE THIS SHIT!

I gained 45 pounds, despite tons of exercise and dieting. The worst is that I was invaded with all these dark thoughts all of a sudden, it's

DrKogal replied
on 03/04/2019 - 9:50 p.m.

You shouldn't demonize antidepres-sants. It's medication, not magic. But it's definitely not poison. It can help, especially when paired with therapy. I've been taking mine for 5 years and it's really helped, even though some-times I go through periods where it is less effective, and it took a while to

gerald04
9

Wow it really saddens me to read all of your posts and comments when the solution's staring you in the face! My advice: get out of the house and away from your screens... Go for a walk in the forest! Take a deep breath, look up at the blue sky, and you'll see that your "depression" will go away!

Ah yes, thanks Gérald, a walk in the forest. Why didn't I think of that?

123

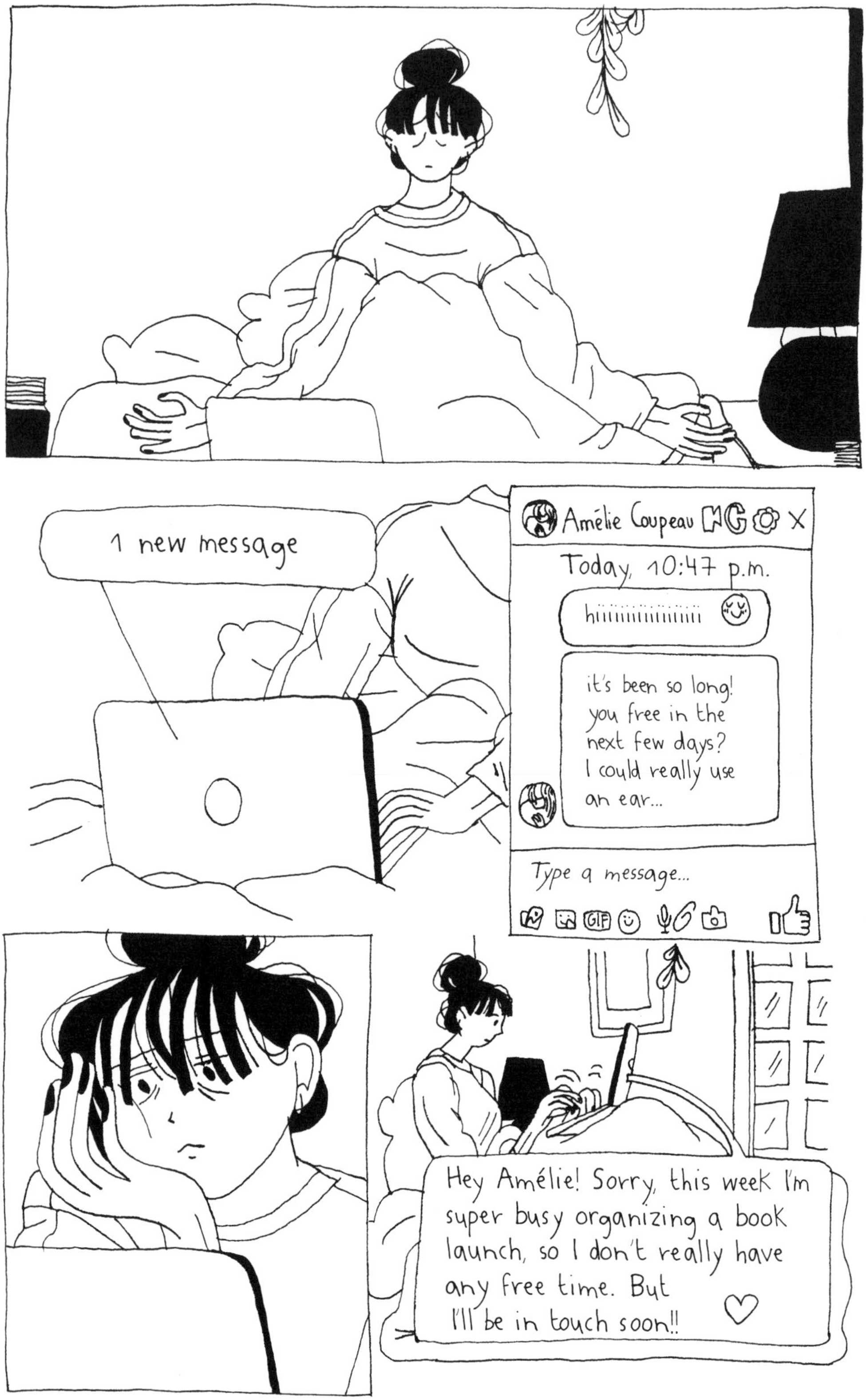
1 new message
Amélie Coupeau
Today, 10:47 p.m.
hiiiiiiiiiiiiiiiii
it's been so long! you free in the next few days? I could really use an ear...
Type a message...
GIF
Hey Amélie! Sorry, this week I'm super busy organizing a book launch, so I don't really have any free time. But I'll be in touch soon!!

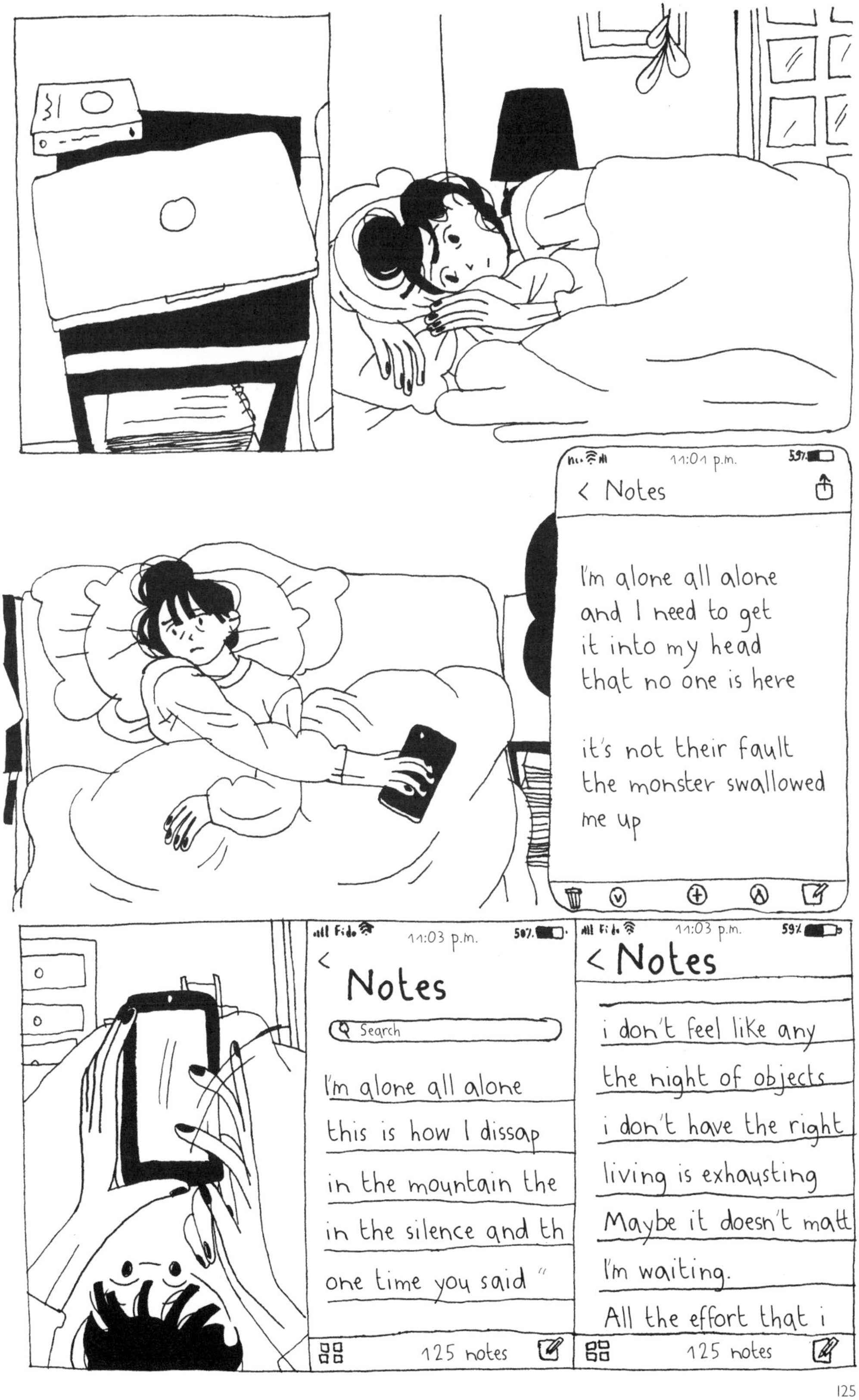
11:01 p.m.
59%
< Notes
I'm alone all alone
and I need to get
it into my head
that no one is here
it's not their fault
the monster swallowed
me up
Fido
11:03 p.m.
50%
< Notes
Search
I'm alone all alone
this is how I dissap
in the mountain the
in the silence and th
one time you said "
125 notes
Fido
11:03 p.m.
59%
< Notes
i don't feel like any
the night of objects
i don't have the right
living is exhausting
Maybe it doesn't matt
I'm waiting.
All the effort that i
125 notes

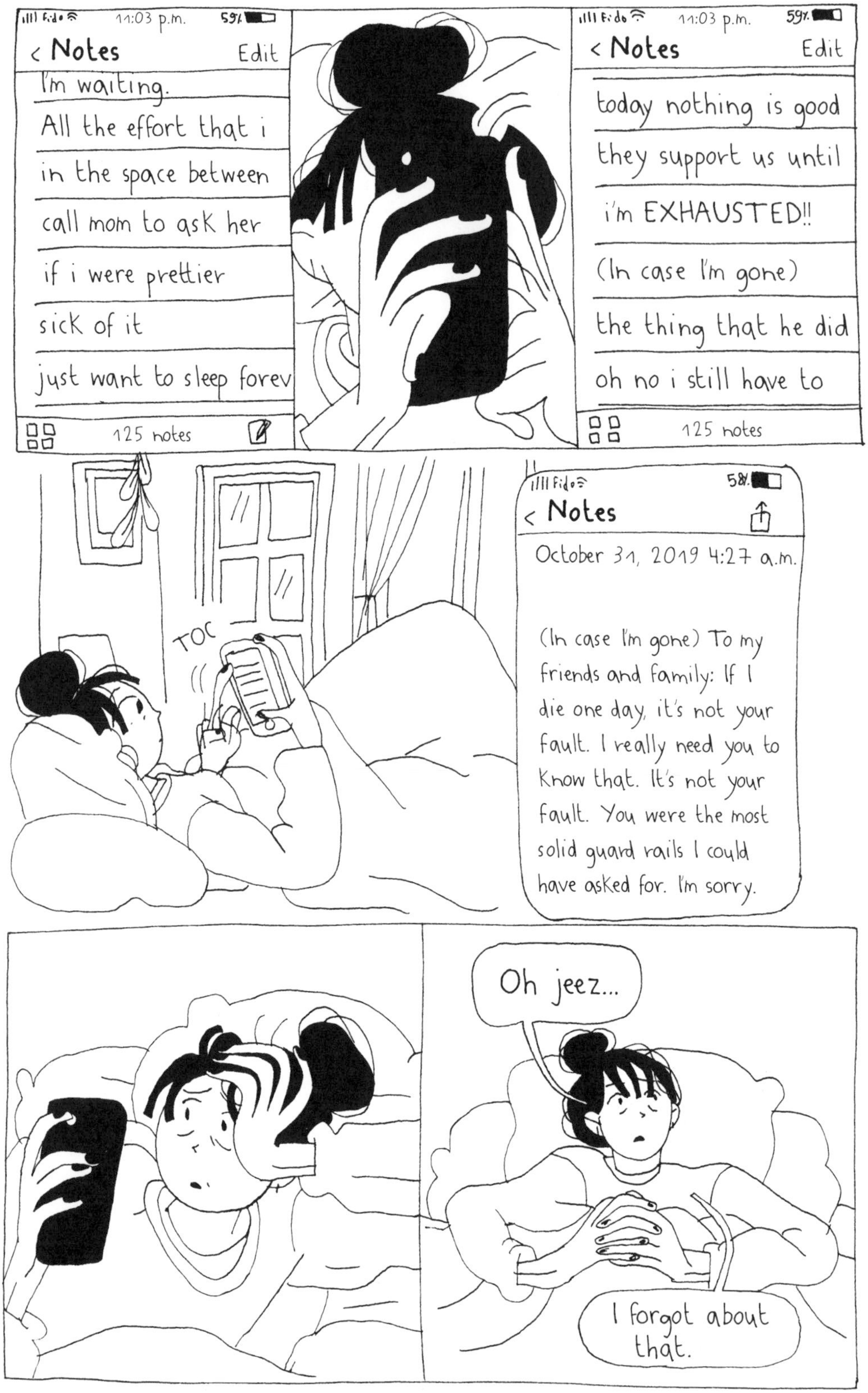
11:03 p.m.
59%
Notes
Edit
I'm waiting.
All the effort that i
in the space between
call mom to ask her
if i were prettier
sick of it
just want to sleep forev
125 notes
11:03 p.m.
59%
Notes
Edit
today nothing is good
they support us until
i'm EXHAUSTED!!
(In case I'm gone)
the thing that he did
oh no i still have to
125 notes
TOC
58%
Notes
October 31, 2019 4:27 a.m.
(In case I'm gone) To my friends and family: If I die one day, it's not your fault. I really need you to know that. It's not your fault. You were the most solid guard rails I could have asked for. I'm sorry.
Oh jeez...
I forgot about that.

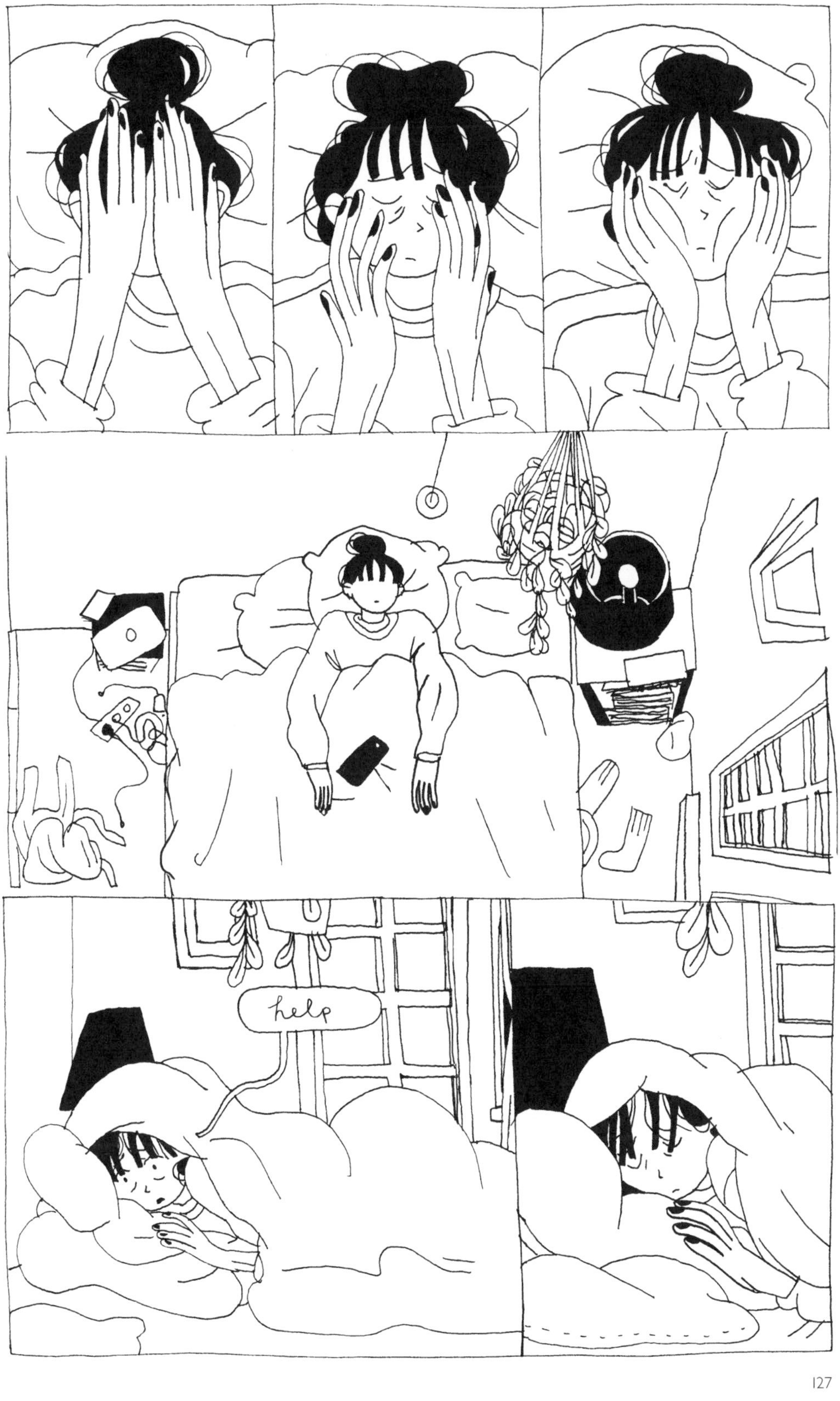
help

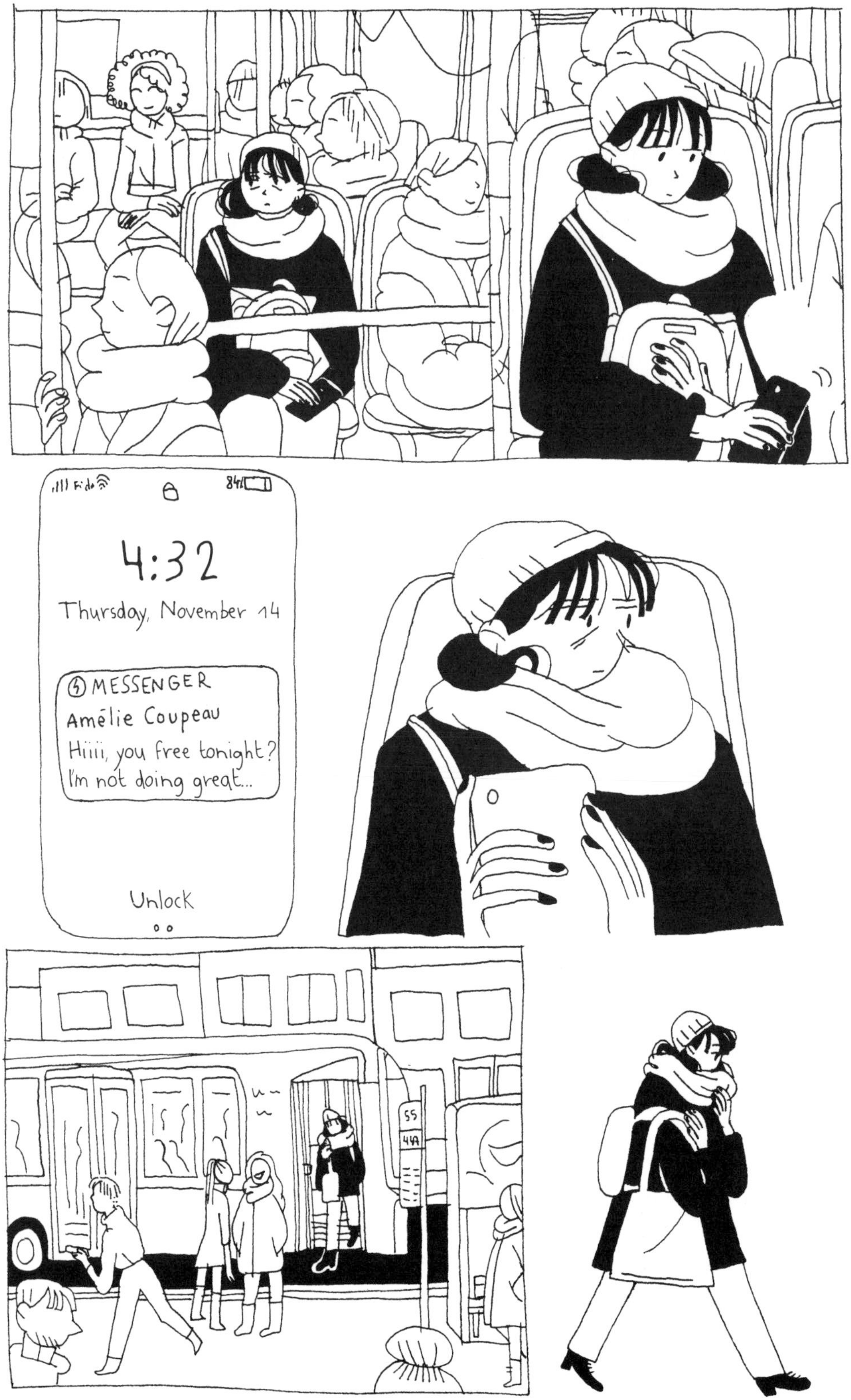
4:32
Thursday, November 14
MESSENGER
Amélie Coupeau
Hiiii, you free tonight?
I'm not doing great...
Unlock

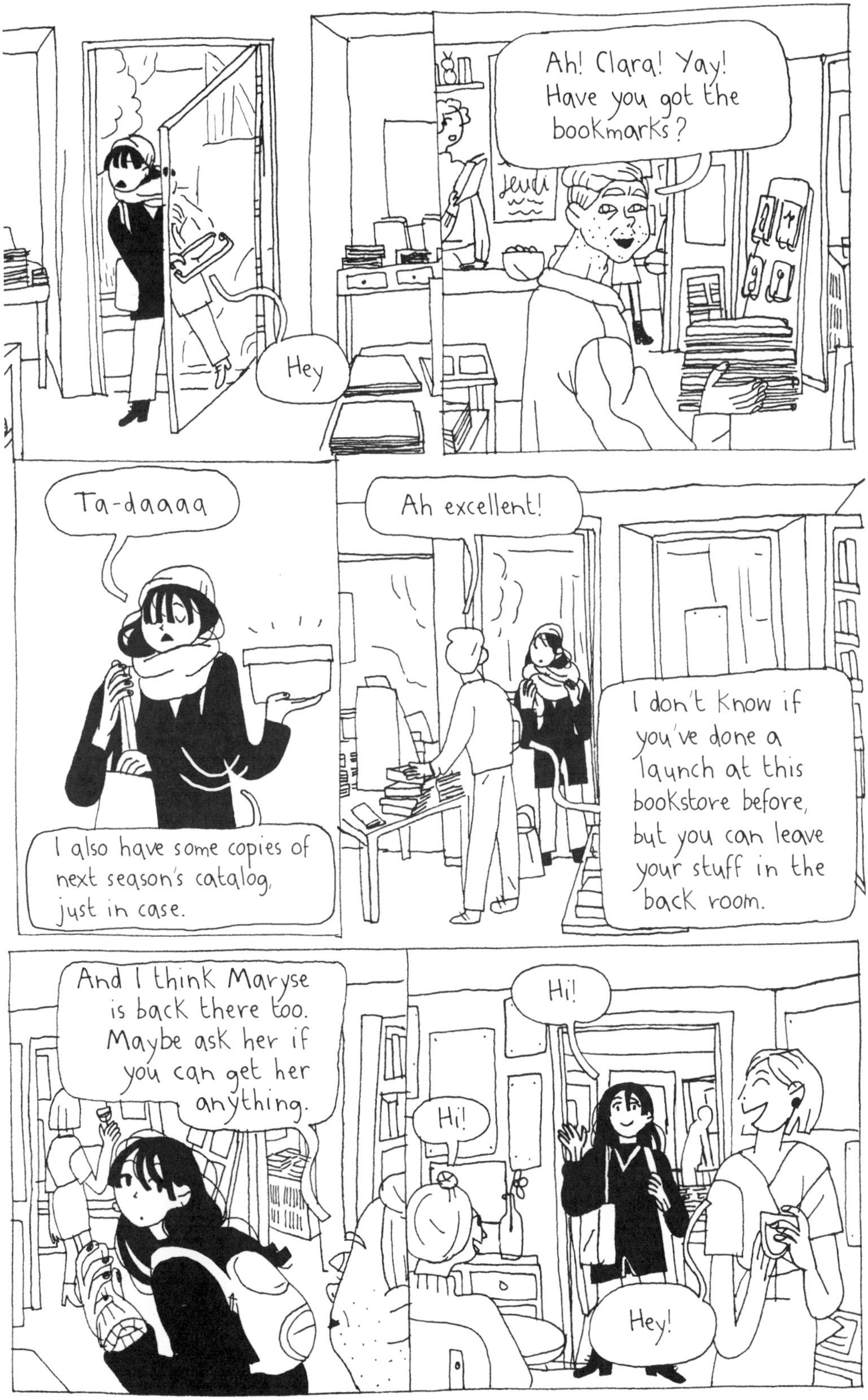
Hey
Ah! Clara! Yay! Have you got the bookmarks?
Jeudi
Ta-daaaa
I also have some copies of next season's catalog, just in case.
Ah excellent!
I don't know if you've done a launch at this bookstore before, but you can leave your stuff in the back room.
And I think Maryse is back there too. Maybe ask her if you can get her anything.
Hi!
Hi!
Hey!

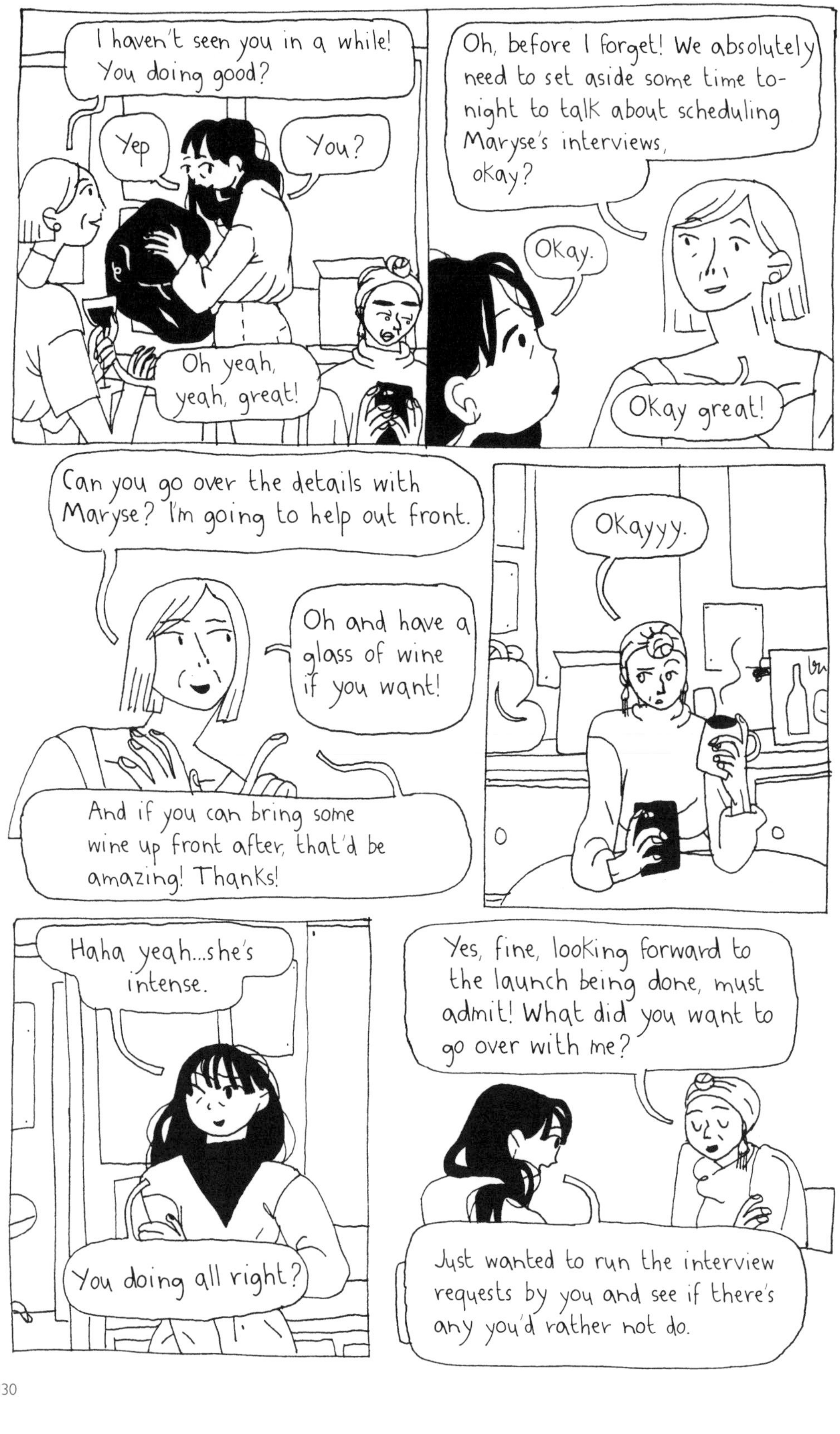
I haven't seen you in a while! You doing good?
Yep
You?
Oh yeah, yeah, great!
Oh, before I forget! We absolutely need to set aside some time tonight to talk about scheduling Maryse's interviews, okay?
Okay.
Okay great!
Can you go over the details with Maryse? I'm going to help out front.
Oh and have a glass of wine if you want!
And if you can bring some wine up front after, that'd be amazing! Thanks!
Okayyy.
Haha yeah...she's intense.
You doing all right?
Yes, fine, looking forward to the launch being done, must admit! What did you want to go over with me?
Just wanted to run the interview requests by you and see if there's any you'd rather not do.

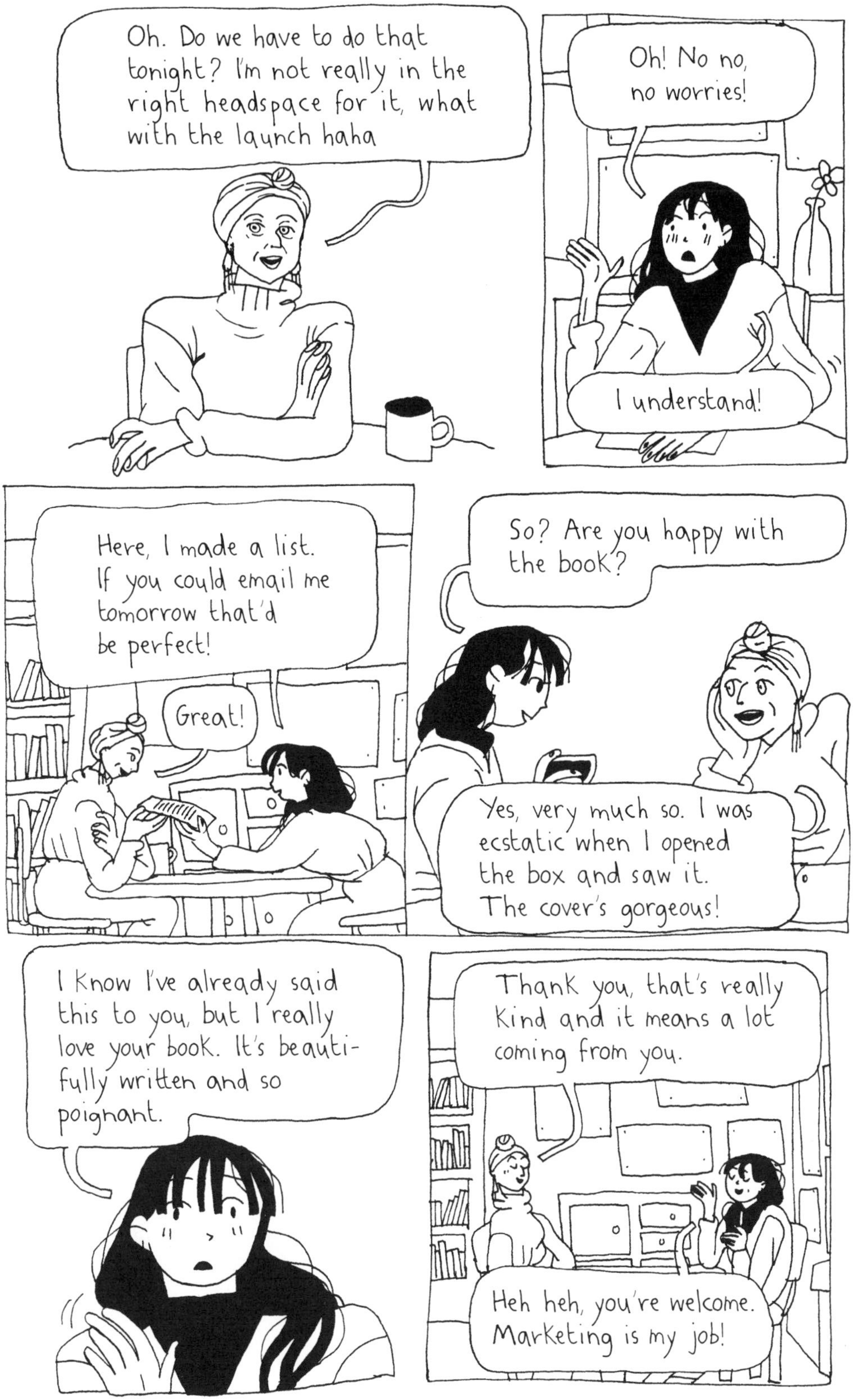
Oh. Do we have to do that tonight? I'm not really in the right headspace for it, what with the launch haha
Oh! No no, no worries!
I understand!
Here, I made a list. If you could email me tomorrow that'd be perfect!
Great!
So? Are you happy with the book?
Yes, very much so. I was ecstatic when I opened the box and saw it. The cover's gorgeous!
I know I've already said this to you, but I really love your book. It's beautifully written and so poignant.
Thank you, that's really kind and it means a lot coming from you.
Heh heh, you're welcome. Marketing is my job!

I meant your opinion as a writer.

Oh.

thanks

Looks like people are starting to arrive.

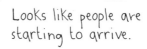

I think it's going to be a full house.

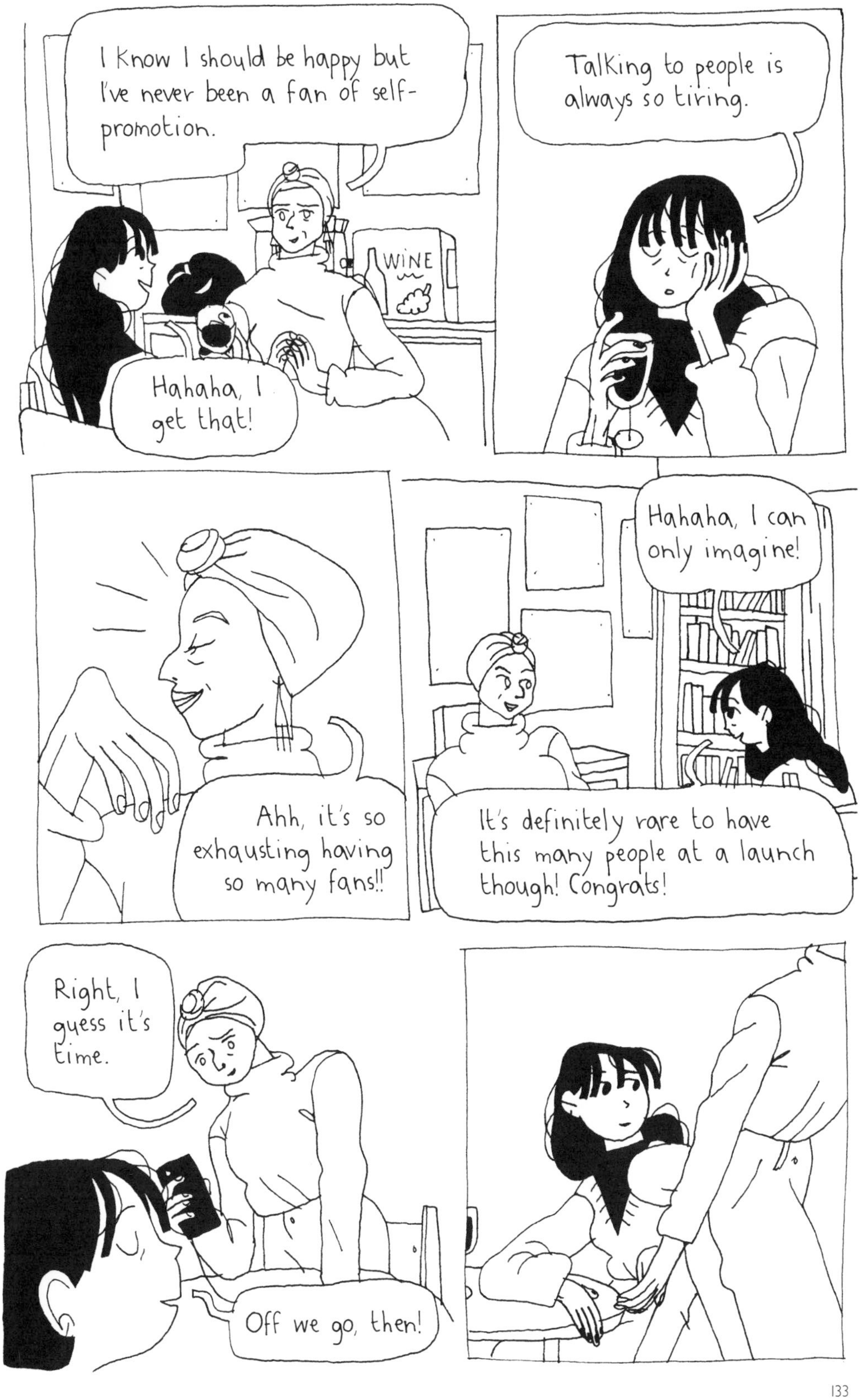
I know I should be happy but I've never been a fan of self-promotion.
Hahaha, I get that!
Talking to people is always so tiring.
WINE
Ahh, it's so exhausting having so many fans!!
Hahaha, I can only imagine!
It's definitely rare to have this many people at a launch though! Congrats!
Right, I guess it's time.
Off we go, then!

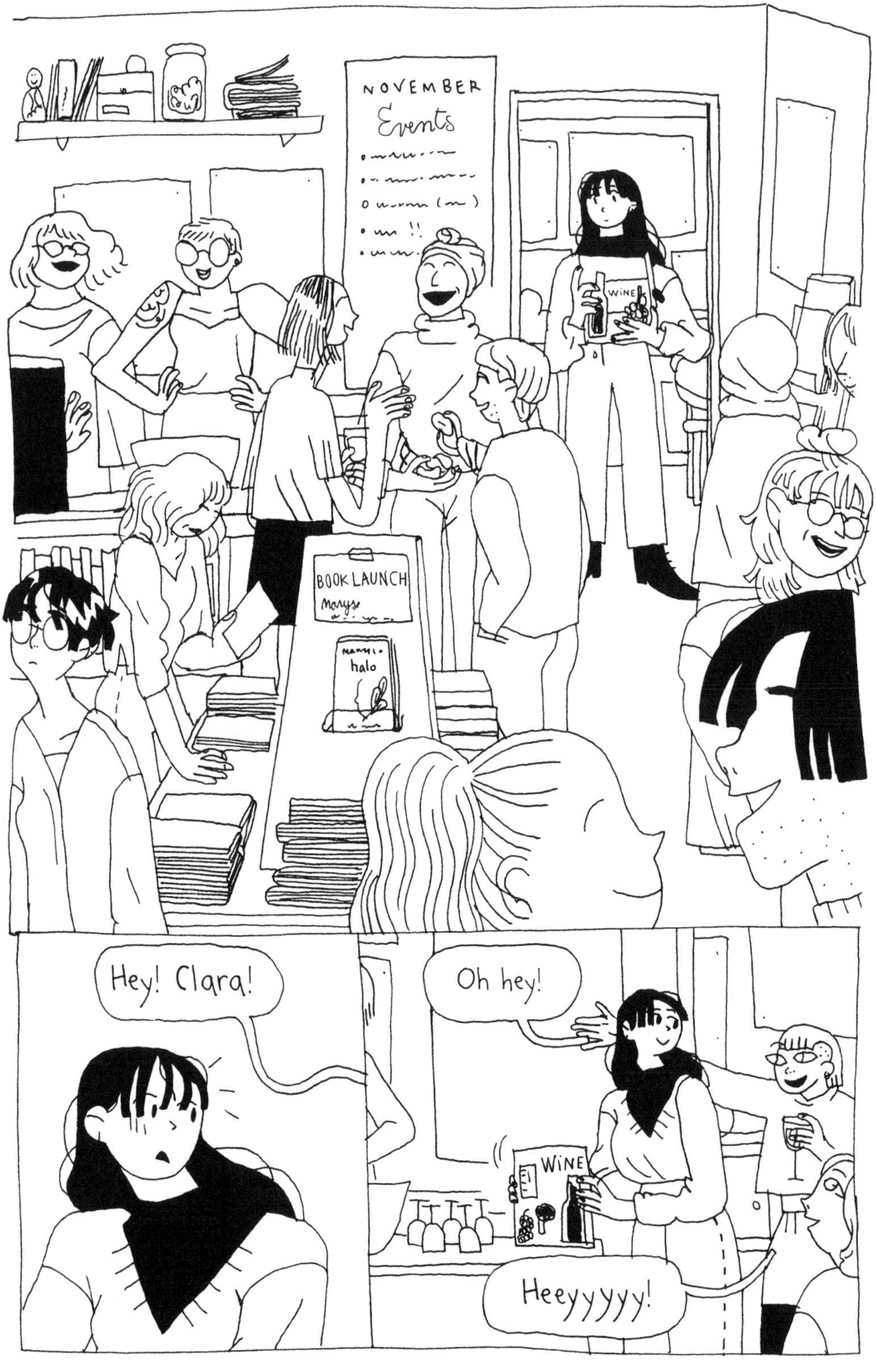
NOVEMBER
Events
WINE
BOOK LAUNCH
halo
Hey! Clara!
Oh hey!
WINE
Heeyyyyy!

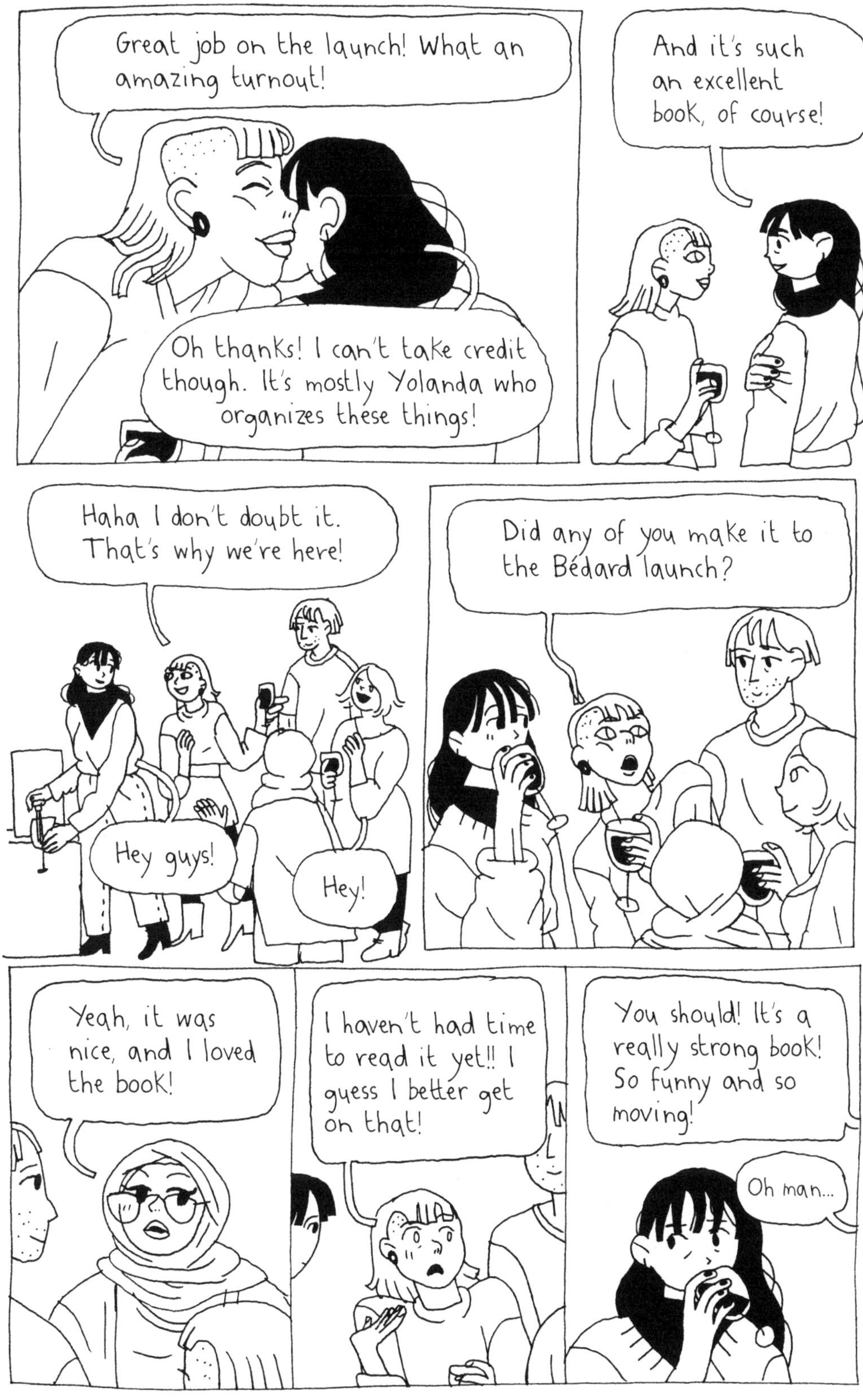
Great job on the launch! What an amazing turnout!
Oh thanks! I can't take credit though. It's mostly Yolanda who organizes these things!
And it's such an excellent book, of course!
Haha I don't doubt it. That's why we're here!
Hey guys!
Hey!
Did any of you make it to the Bédard launch?
Yeah, it was nice, and I loved the book!
I haven't had time to read it yet!! I guess I better get on that!
You should! It's a really strong book! So funny and so moving!
Oh man...

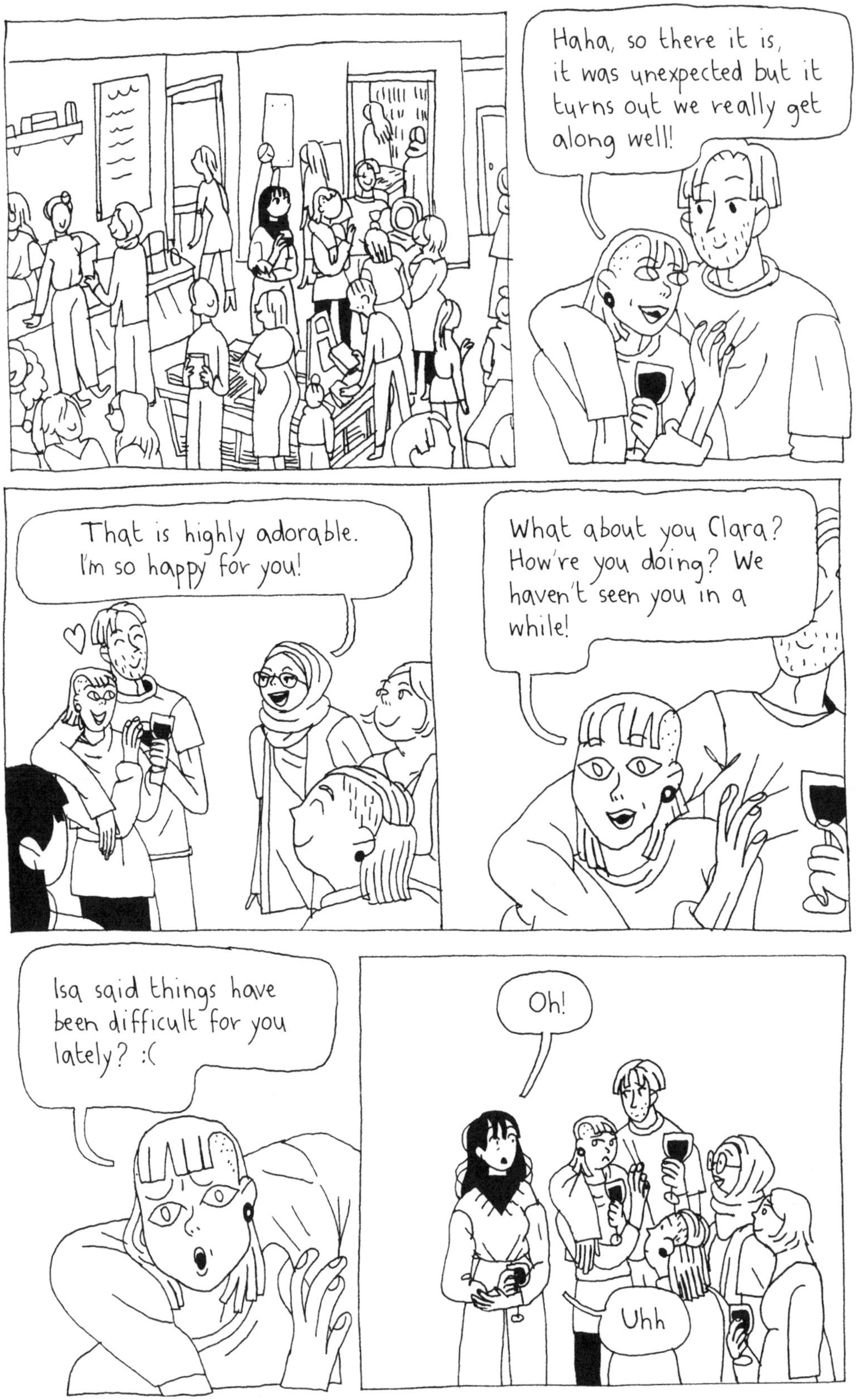
Haha, so there it is, it was unexpected but it turns out we really get along well!
That is highly adorable. I'm so happy for you!
What about you Clara? How're you doing? We haven't seen you in a while!
Isa said things have been difficult for you lately? :(
Oh!
Uhh

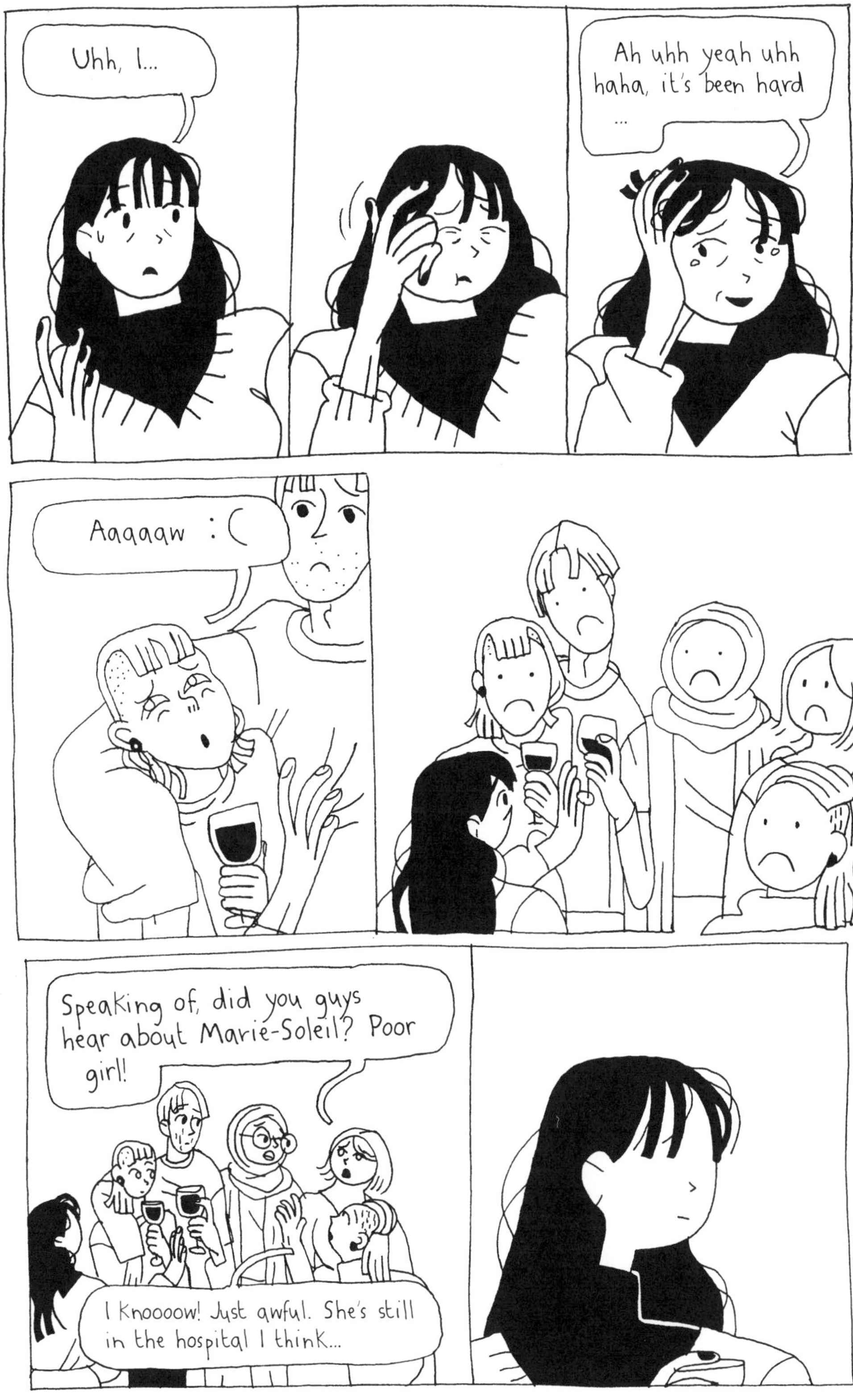
Uhh, I...
Ah uhh yeah uhh haha, it's been hard ...
Aaaaaw :(
Speaking of, did you guys hear about Marie-Soleil? Poor girl!
I Knoooow! Just awful. She's still in the hospital I think...

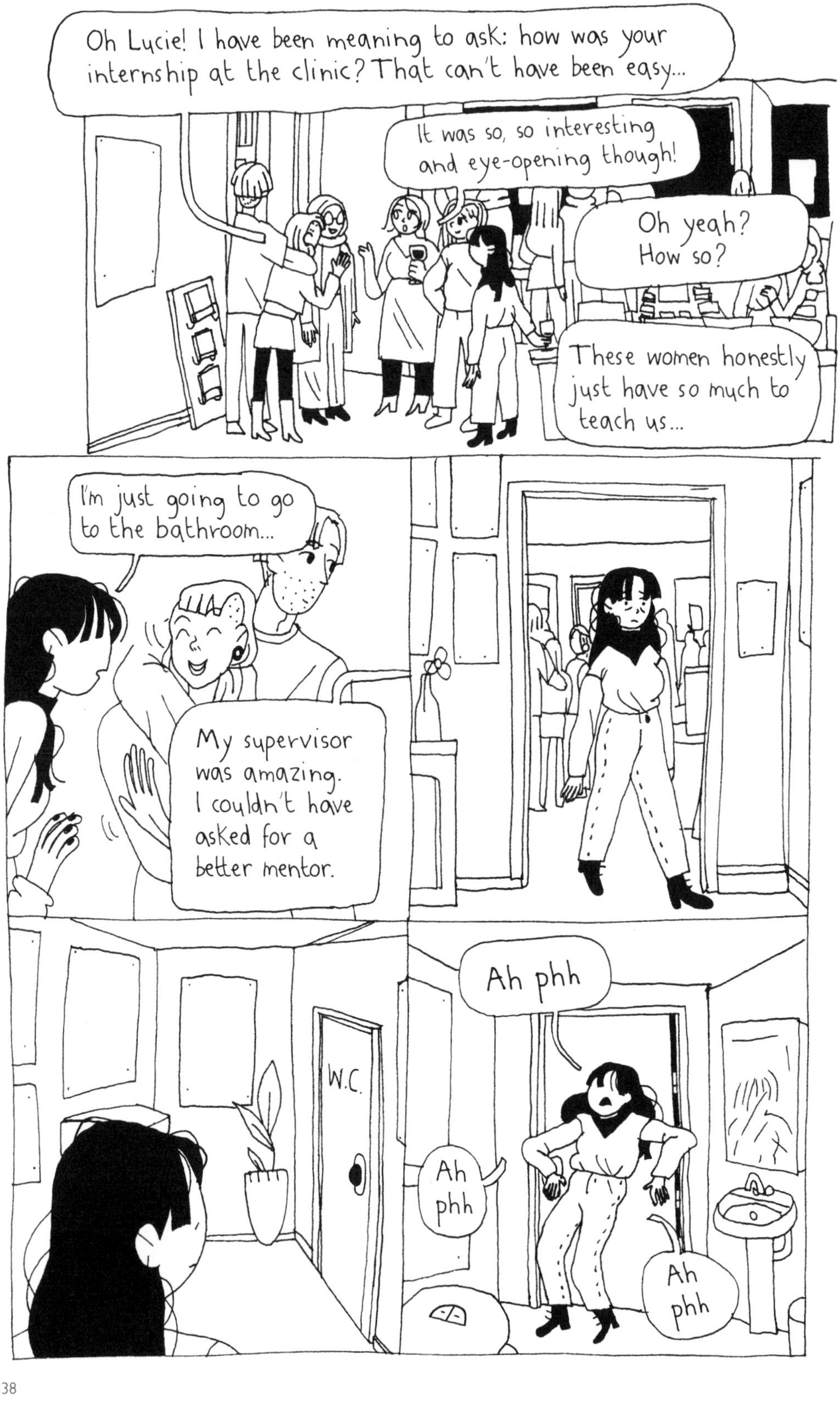
Oh Lucie! I have been meaning to ask: how was your internship at the clinic? That can't have been easy...
It was so, so interesting and eye-opening though!
Oh yeah? How so?
These women honestly just have so much to teach us...
I'm just going to go to the bathroom...
My supervisor was amazing. I couldn't have asked for a better mentor.
W.C.
Ah phh
Ah phh
Ah phh

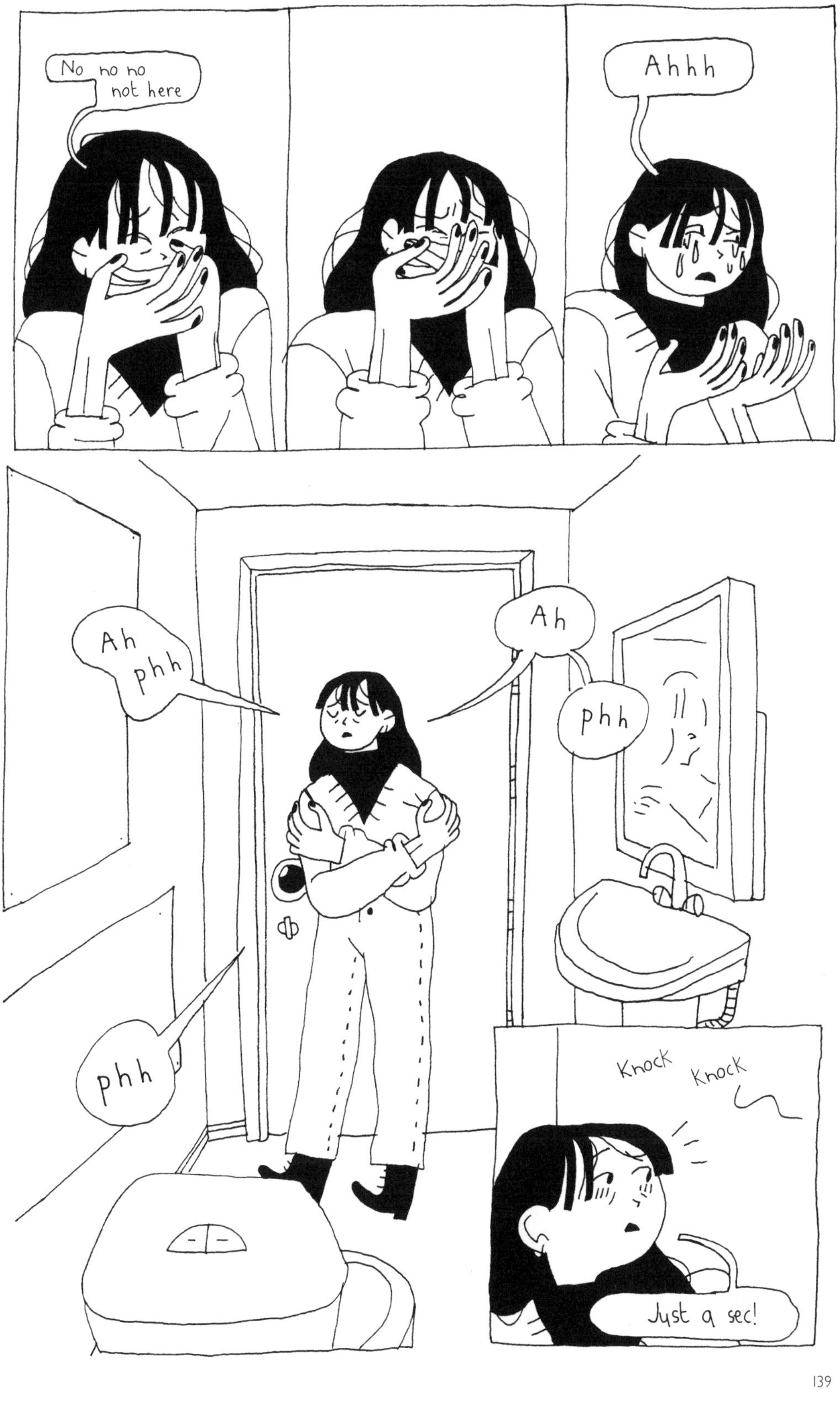
No no no
not here
Ahhh
Ah
phh
Ah
phh
phh
Knock
Knock
Just a sec!

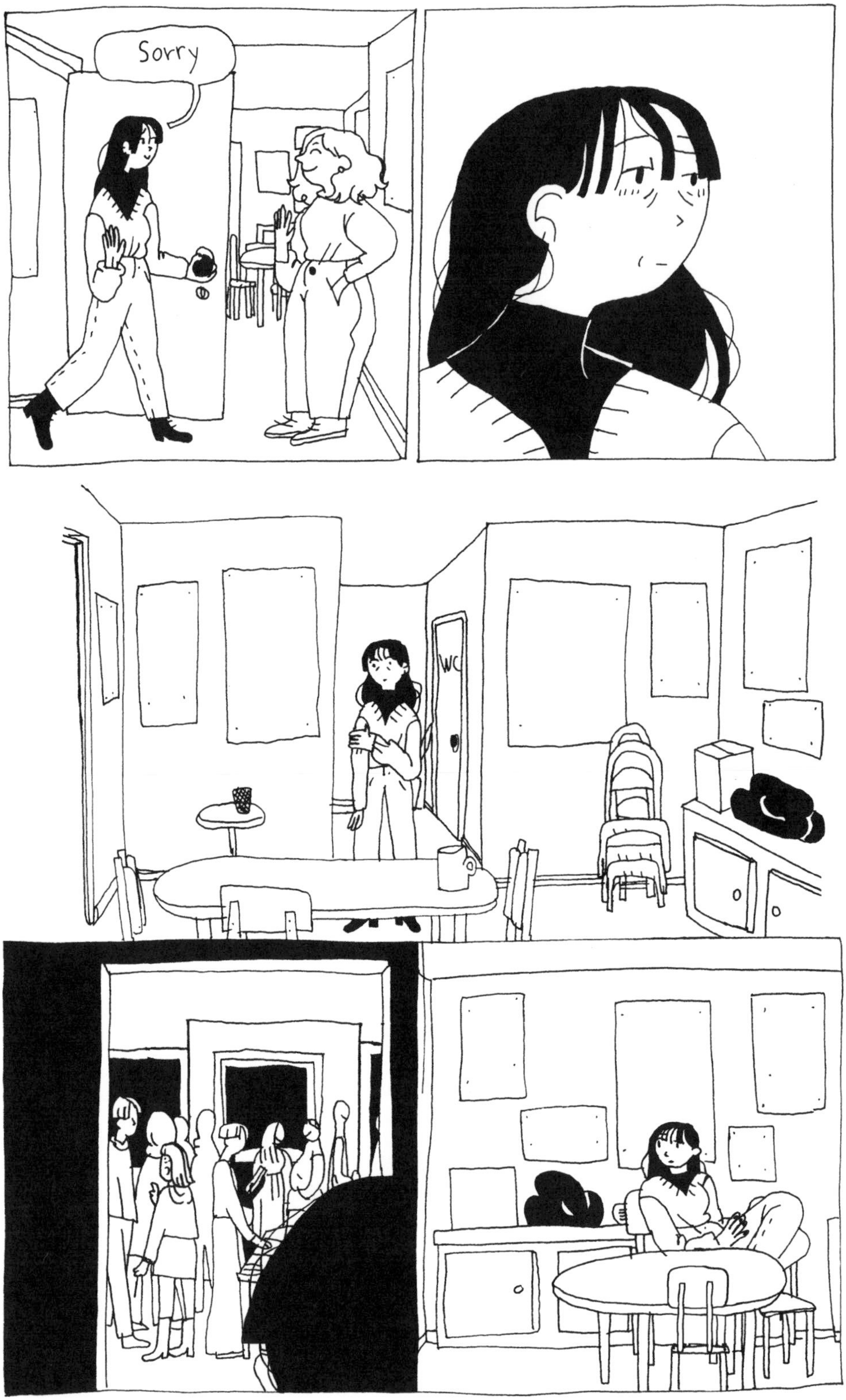
Sorry

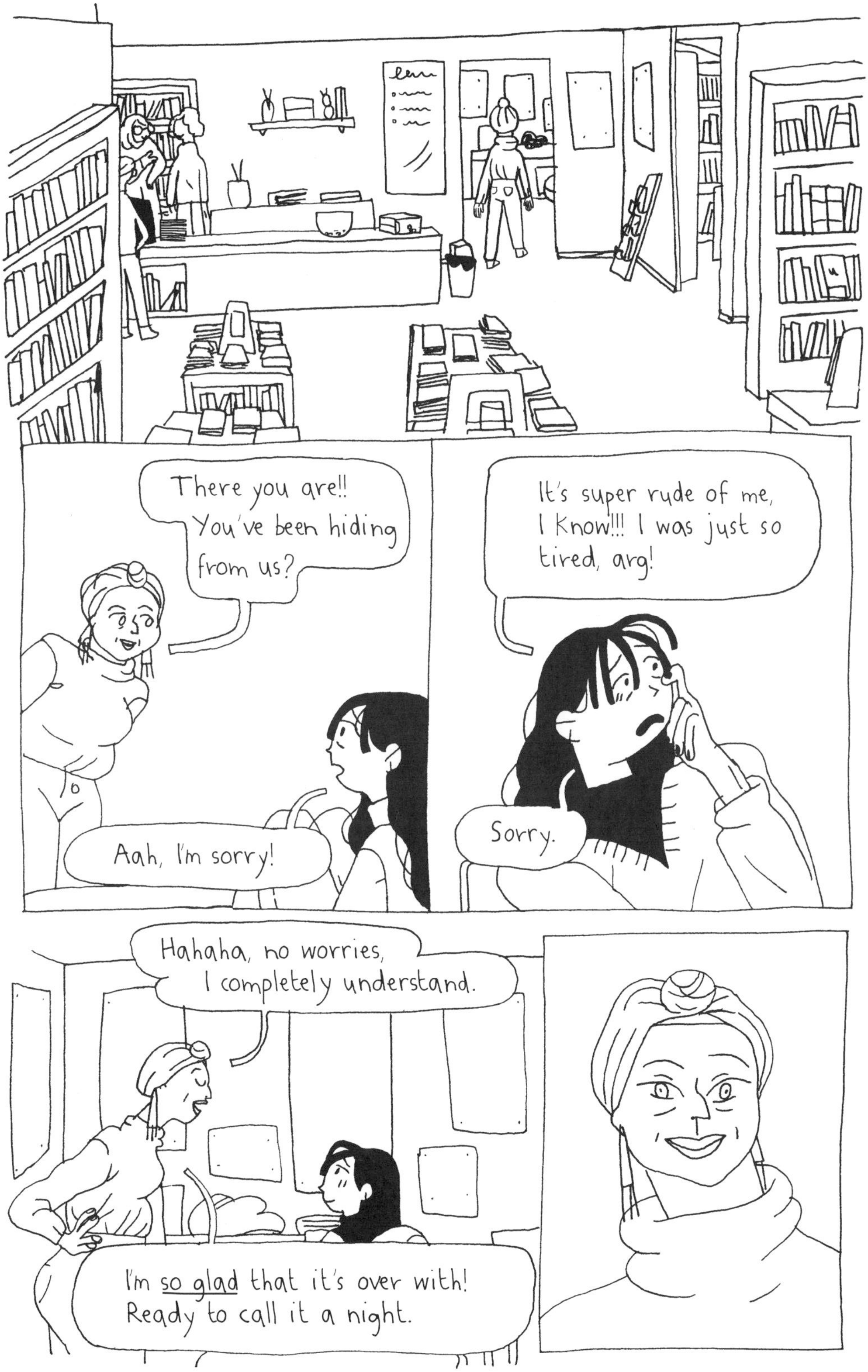
There you are!! You've been hiding from us?
Aah, I'm sorry!
It's super rude of me, I Know!!! I was just so tired, arg!
Sorry.
Hahaha, no worries, I completely understand.
I'm so glad that it's over with! Ready to call it a night.

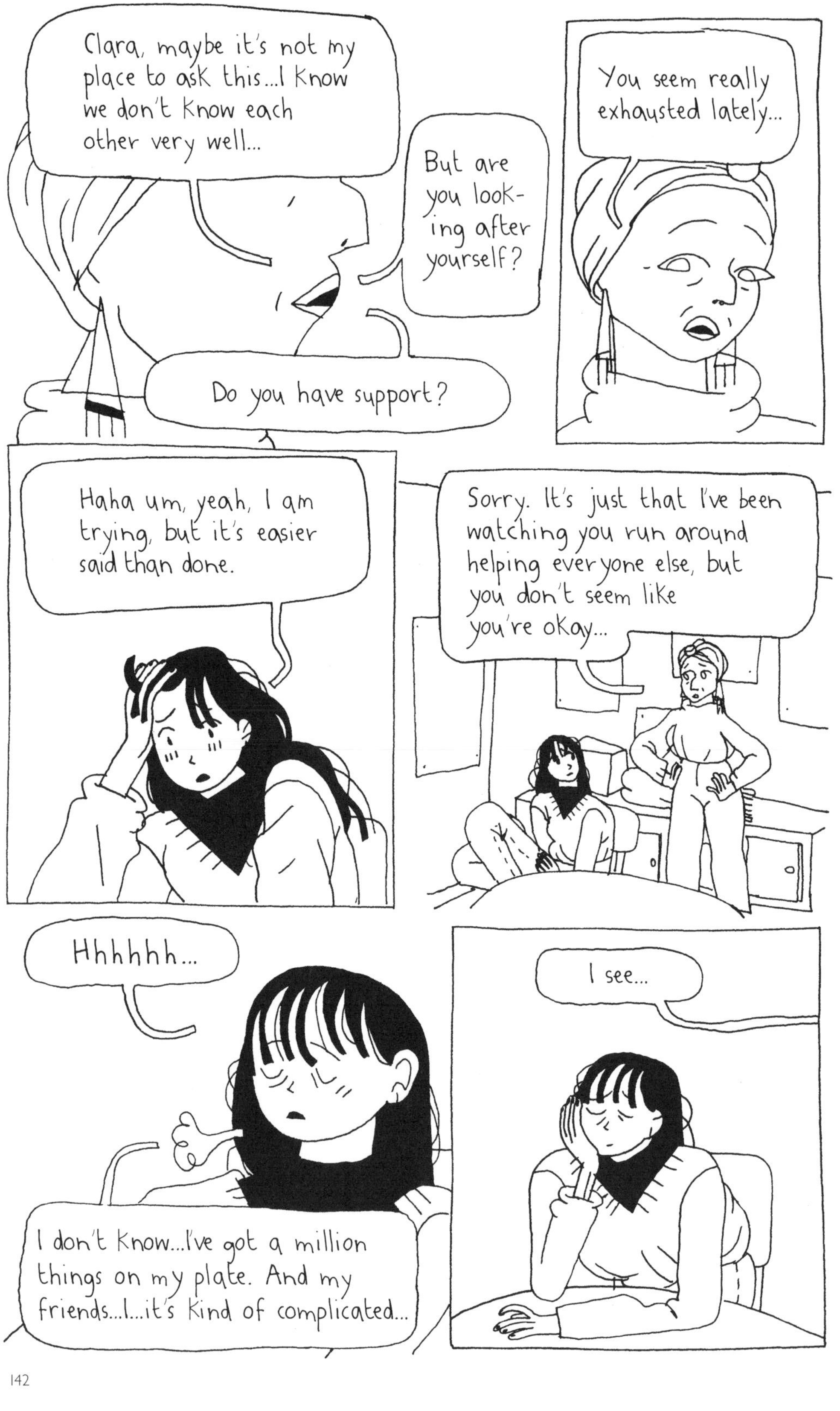
Clara, maybe it's not my place to ask this...I know we don't know each other very well...
But are you look-ing after yourself?
Do you have support?
You seem really exhausted lately...
Haha um, yeah, I am trying, but it's easier said than done.
Sorry. It's just that I've been watching you run around helping everyone else, but you don't seem like you're okay...
Hhhhhh...
I don't know...I've got a million things on my plate. And my friends...I...it's kind of complicated...
I see...

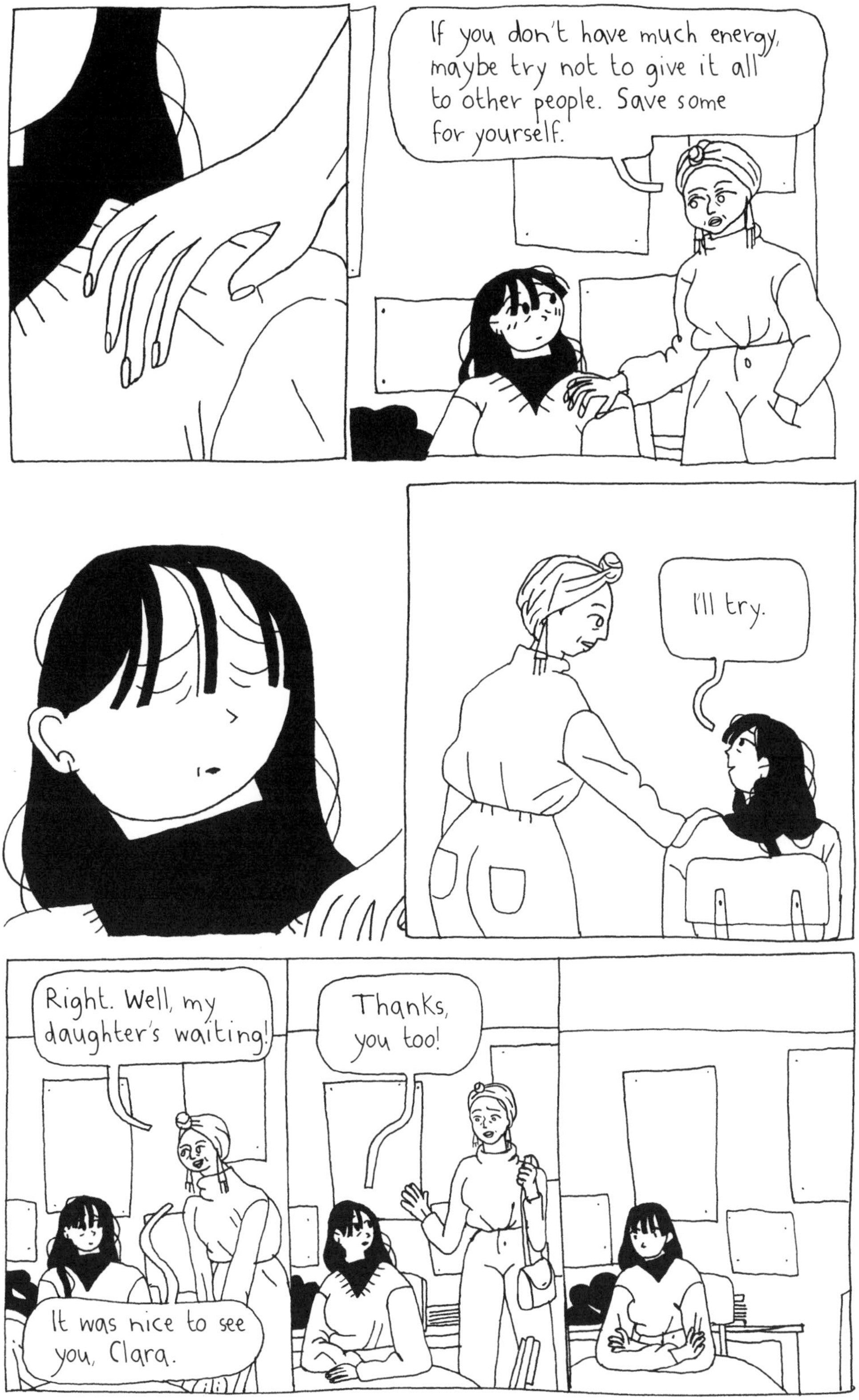
If you don't have much energy, maybe try not to give it all to other people. Save some for yourself.
I'll try.
Right. Well, my daughter's waiting!
It was nice to see you, Clara.
Thanks, you too!

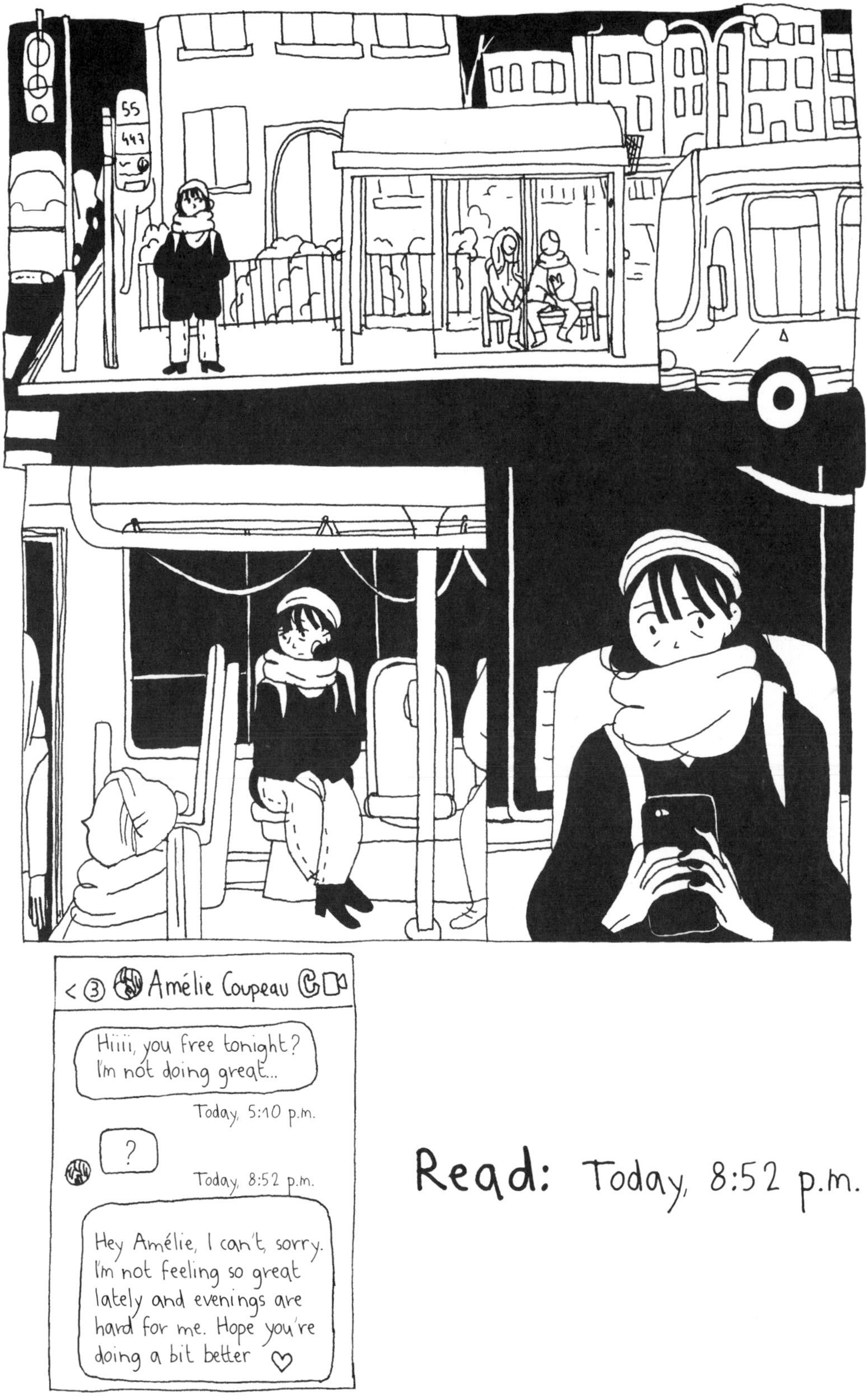
55
447
< 3 Amélie Coupeau
Hiiii, you free tonight? I'm not doing great...
Today, 5:10 p.m.
?
Today, 8:52 p.m.
Hey Amélie, I can't, sorry. I'm not feeling so great lately and evenings are hard for me. Hope you're doing a bit better ♡
Read: Today, 8:52 p.m.

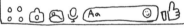

I've already left
my body my head

My eyes half closed for good
I cry like a river
Water can't help but keep running

I'm a small, hard shell
softly cracking
hollowed out,
disappearing

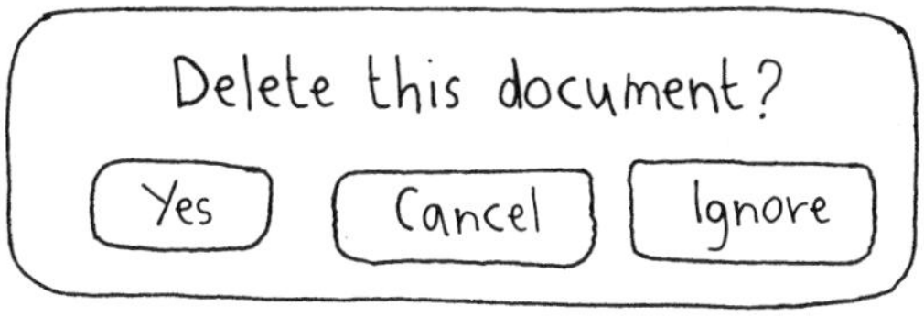
Delete this document?
Yes
Cancel
Ignore

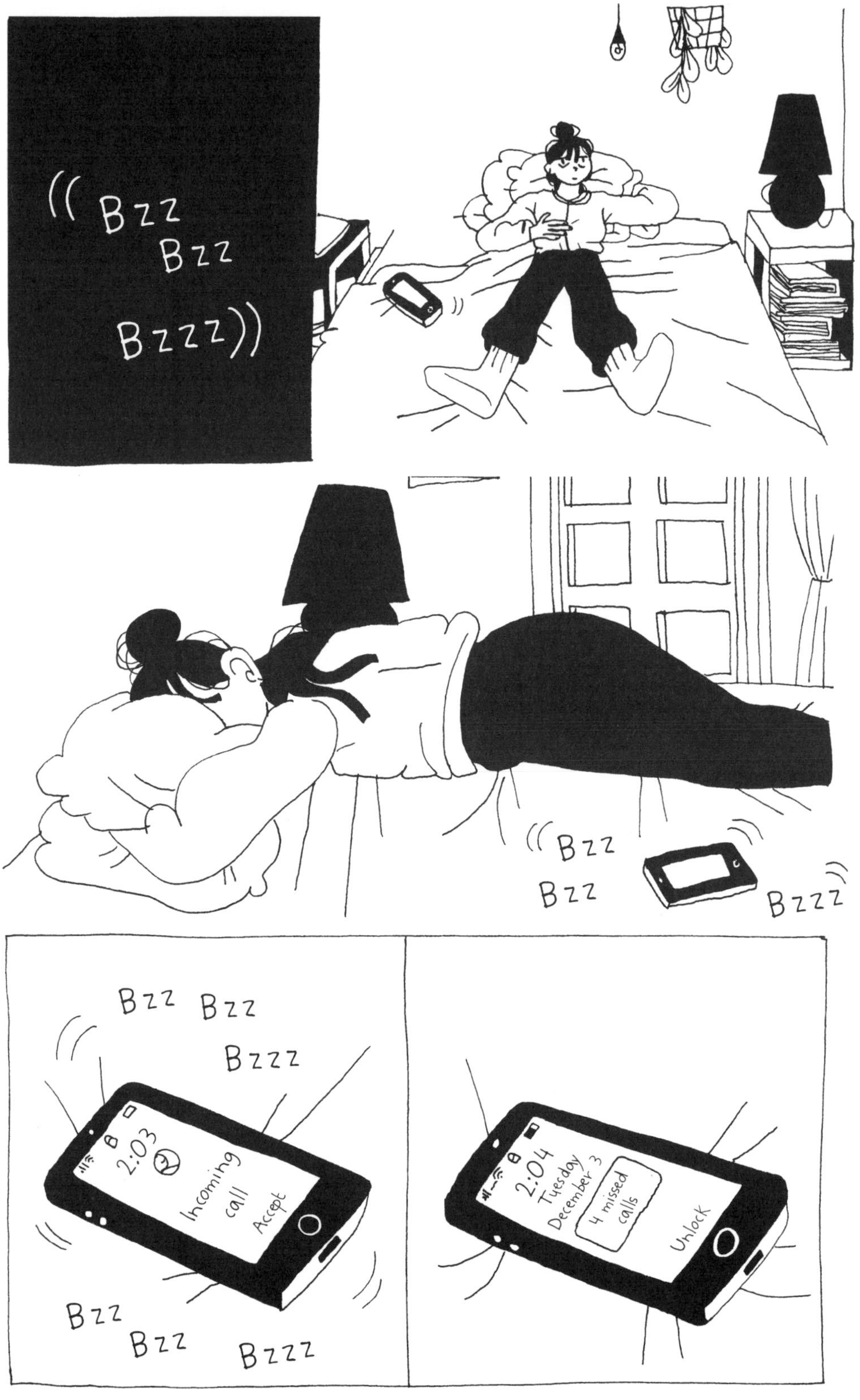
((Bzz
Bzz
Bzzz))
Bzz
Bzz
Bzzz
Bzz Bzz
Bzzz
2:03
Incoming call
Accept
Bzz
Bzz
Bzzz
2:04
Tuesday
December 3
4 missed calls
Unlock

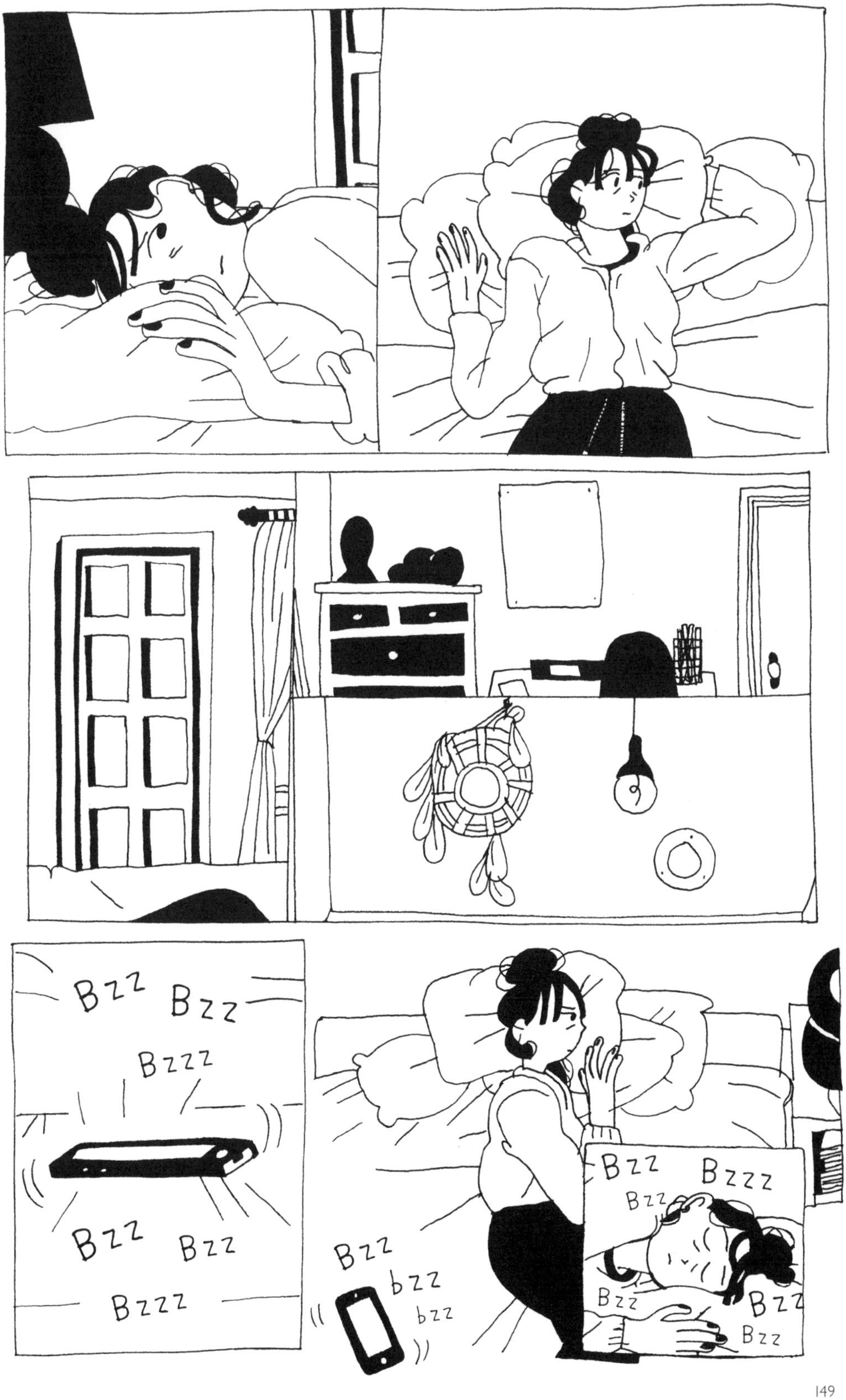
Bzz
Bzz
Bzzz
Bzz
Bzz
Bzzz
Bzz
bzz
bzz
Bzz
Bzzz
Bzz
Bzz
Bzz
Bzz

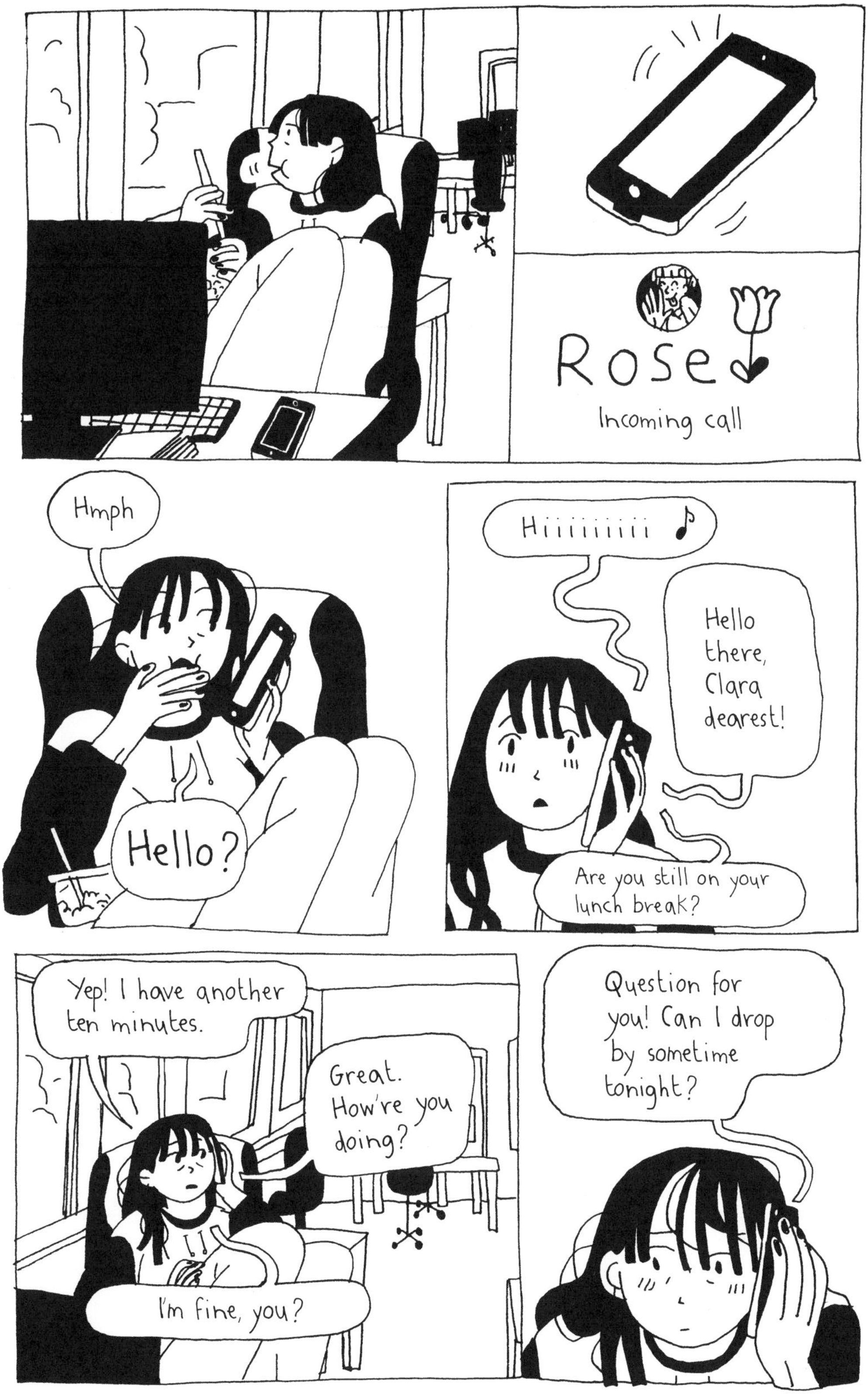
Rose
Incoming call
Hmph
Hello?
Hiiiiiiiii ♪
Hello there, Clara dearest!
Are you still on your lunch break?
Yep! I have another ten minutes.
Great. How're you doing?
I'm fine, you?
Question for you! Can I drop by sometime tonight?

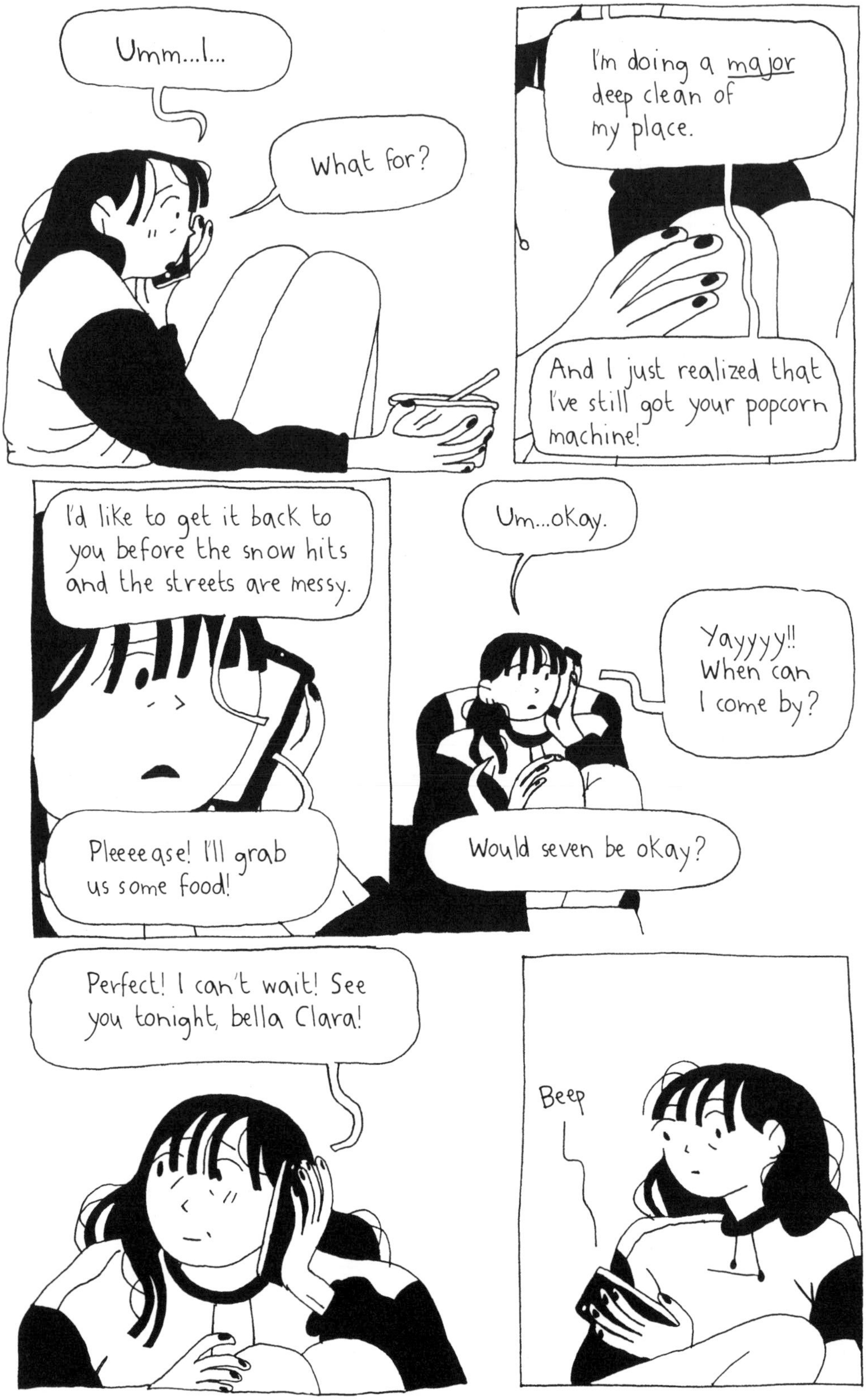
Umm...I...
What for?
I'm doing a major deep clean of my place.
And I just realized that I've still got your popcorn machine!
I'd like to get it back to you before the snow hits and the streets are messy.
Pleeeease! I'll grab us some food!
Um...okay.
Yayyyy!! When can I come by?
Would seven be okay?
Perfect! I can't wait! See you tonight, bella Clara!
Beep

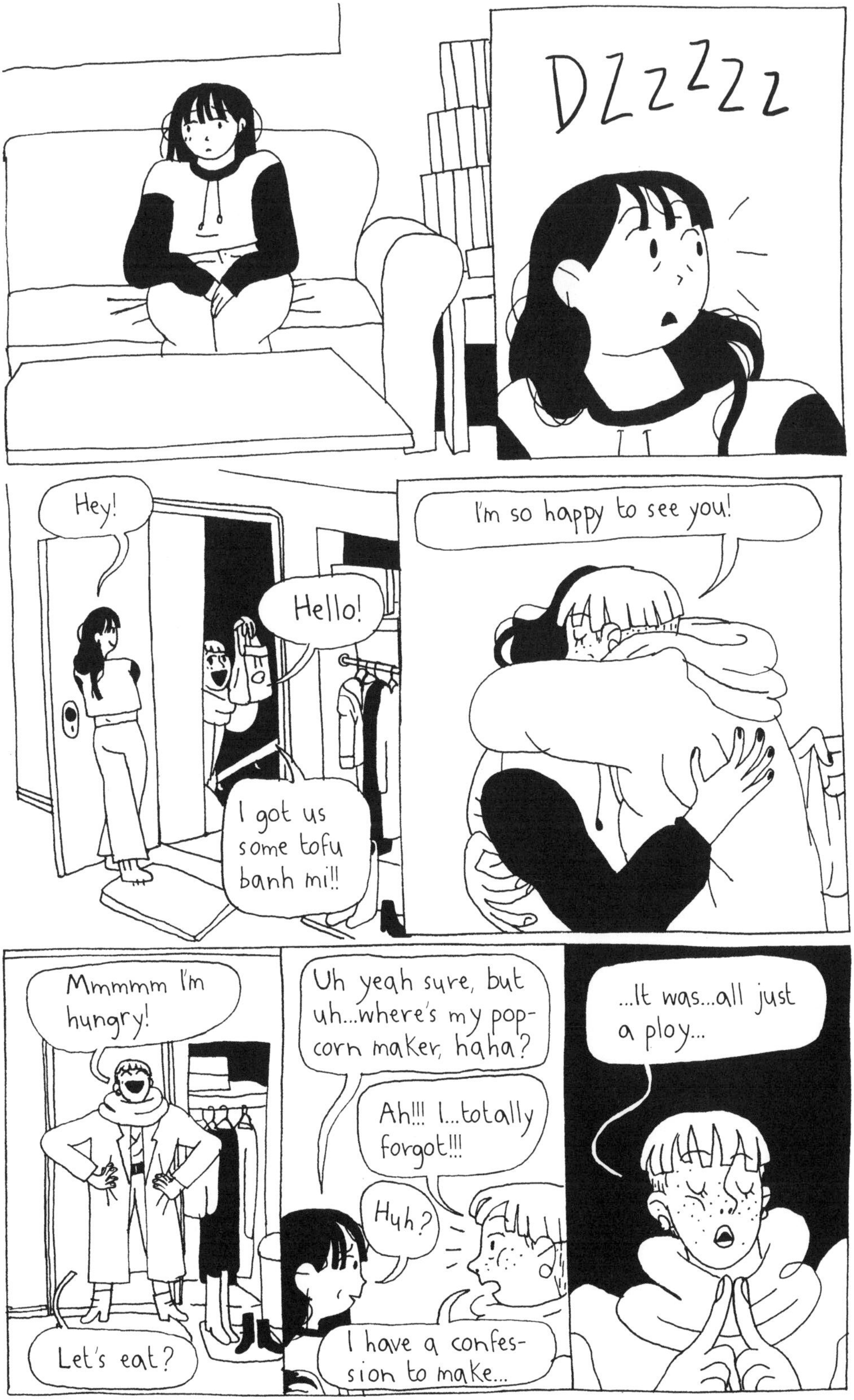
DZzZzz
Hey!
Hello!
I got us some tofu banh mi!!
I'm so happy to see you!
Mmmmm I'm hungry!
Let's eat?
Uh yeah sure, but uh...where's my pop-corn maker, haha?
Ah!!! I...totally forgot!!!
Huh?
I have a confes-sion to make...
...It was...all just a ploy...

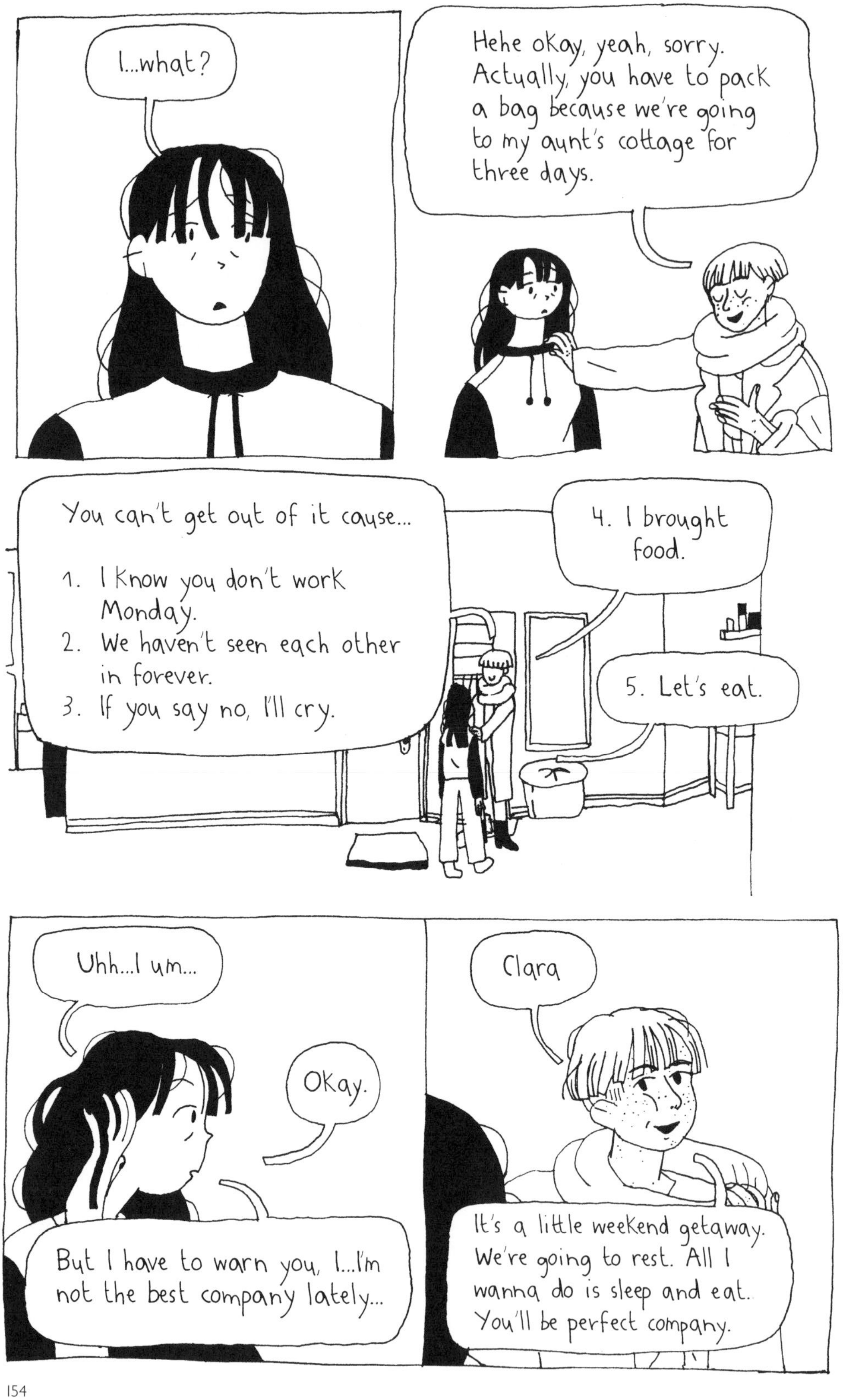
I...what?
Hehe okay, yeah, sorry. Actually, you have to pack a bag because we're going to my aunt's cottage for three days.
You can't get out of it cause...
1. I know you don't work Monday.
2. We haven't seen each other in forever.
3. If you say no, I'll cry.
4. I brought food.
5. Let's eat.
Uhh...I um...
Okay.
But I have to warn you, I...I'm not the best company lately...
Clara
It's a little weekend getaway. We're going to rest. All I wanna do is sleep and eat. You'll be perfect company.

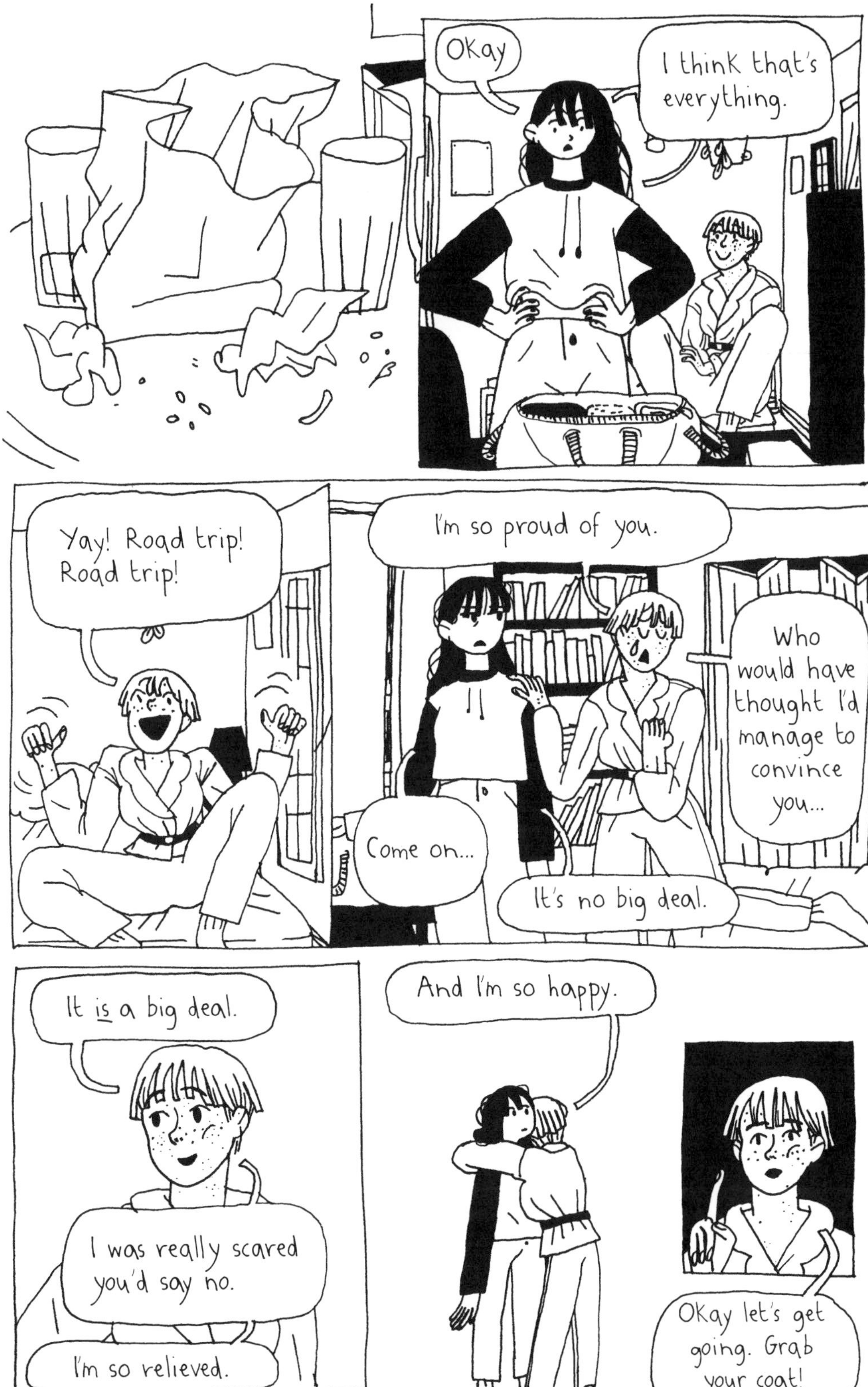
Okay
I think that's everything.
Yay! Road trip! Road trip!
I'm so proud of you.
Who would have thought I'd manage to convince you...
Come on...
It's no big deal.
It is a big deal.
I was really scared you'd say no.
I'm so relieved.
And I'm so happy.
Okay let's get going. Grab your coat!

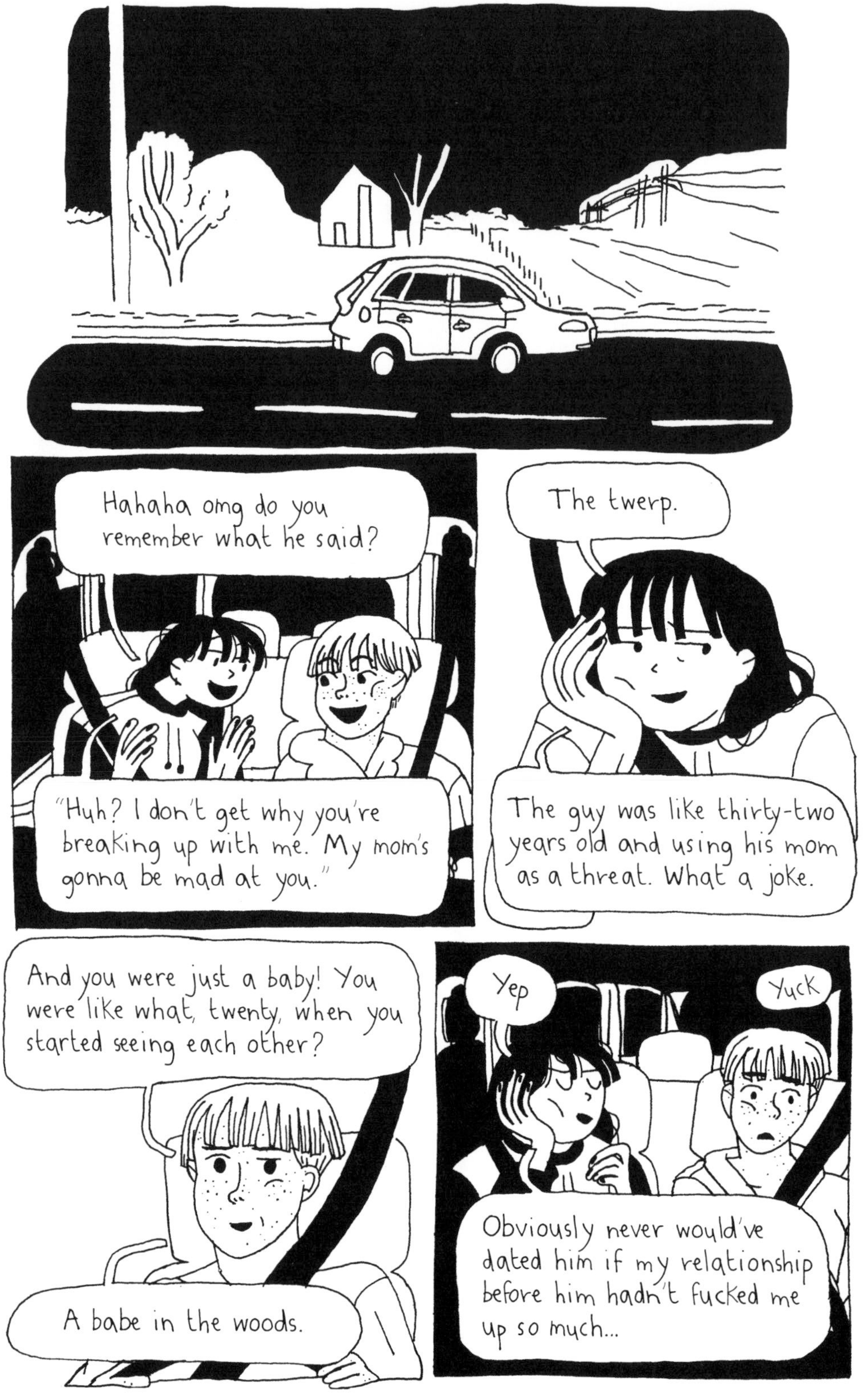
Hahaha omg do you remember what he said?
"Huh? I don't get why you're breaking up with me. My mom's gonna be mad at you."
The twerp.
The guy was like thirty-two years old and using his mom as a threat. What a joke.
And you were just a baby! You were like what, twenty, when you started seeing each other?
A babe in the woods.
Yep
Yuck
Obviously never would've dated him if my relationship before him hadn't fucked me up so much...

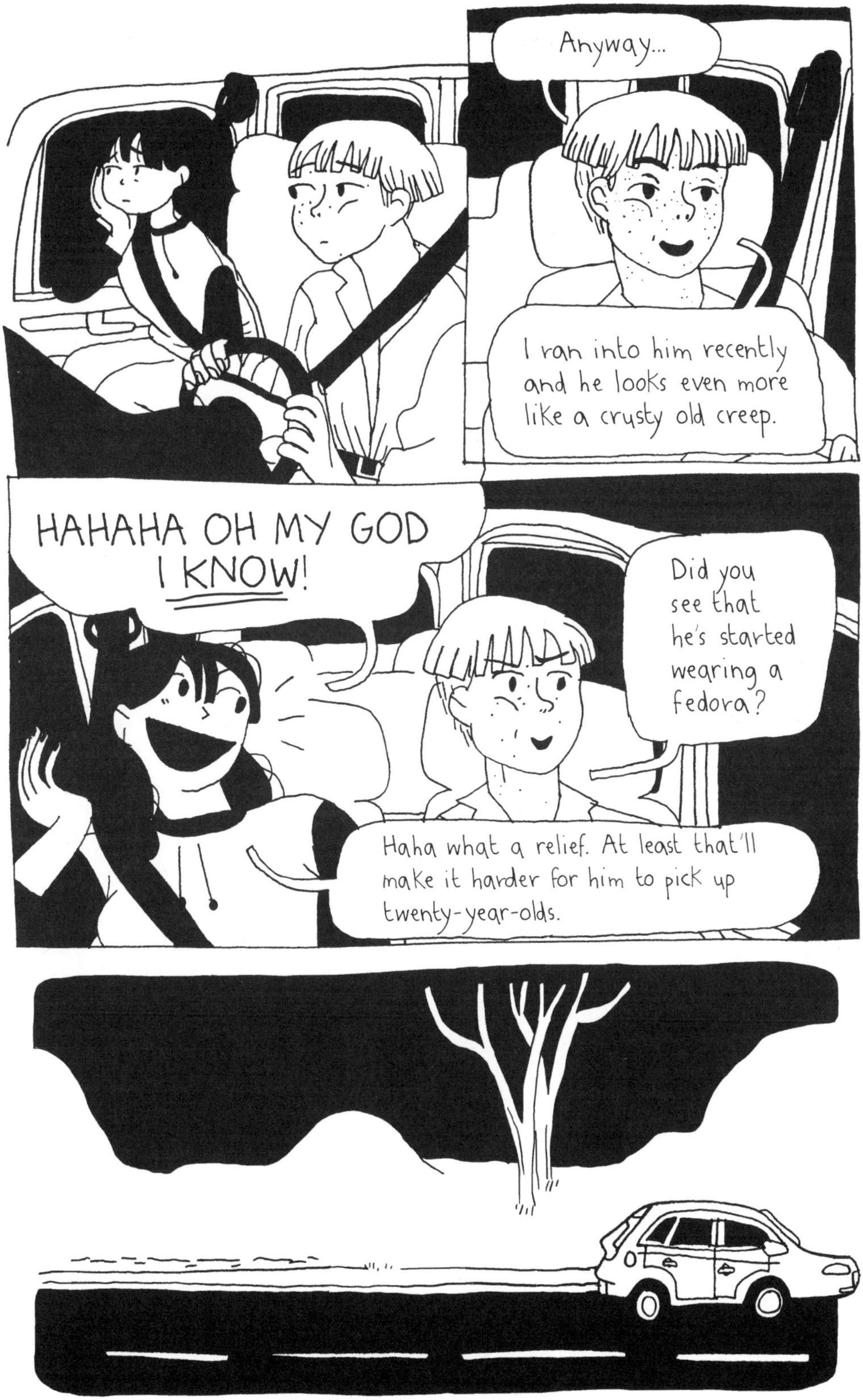
Anyway...
I ran into him recently and he looks even more like a crusty old creep.
HAHAHA OH MY GOD I KNOW!
Did you see that he's started wearing a fedora?
Haha what a relief. At least that'll make it harder for him to pick up twenty-year-olds.

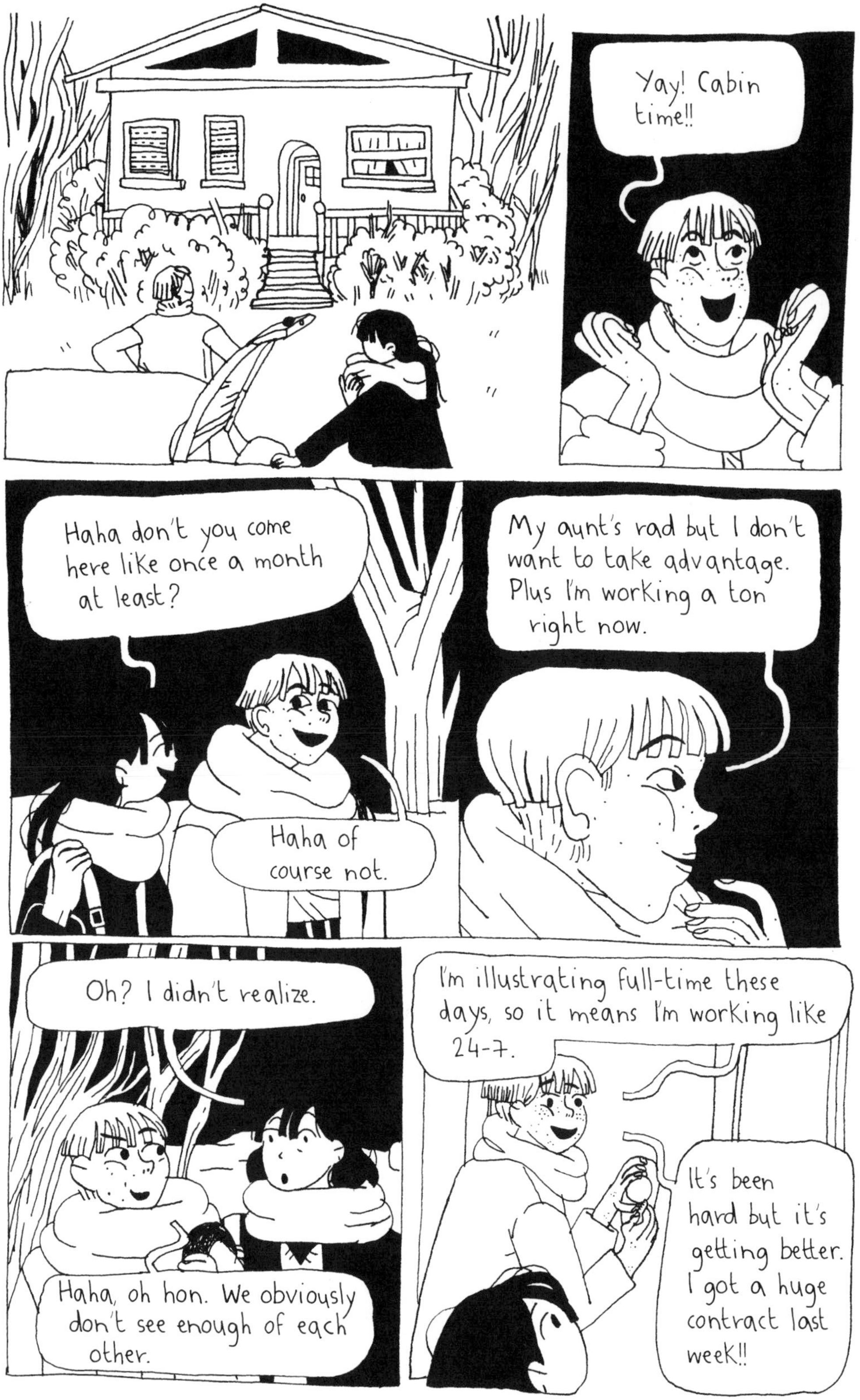
Yay! Cabin time!!
Haha don't you come here like once a month at least?
Haha of course not.
My aunt's rad but I don't want to take advantage. Plus I'm working a ton right now.
Oh? I didn't realize.
Haha, oh hon. We obviously don't see enough of each other.
I'm illustrating full-time these days, so it means I'm working like 24-7.
It's been hard but it's getting better. I got a huge contract last week!!

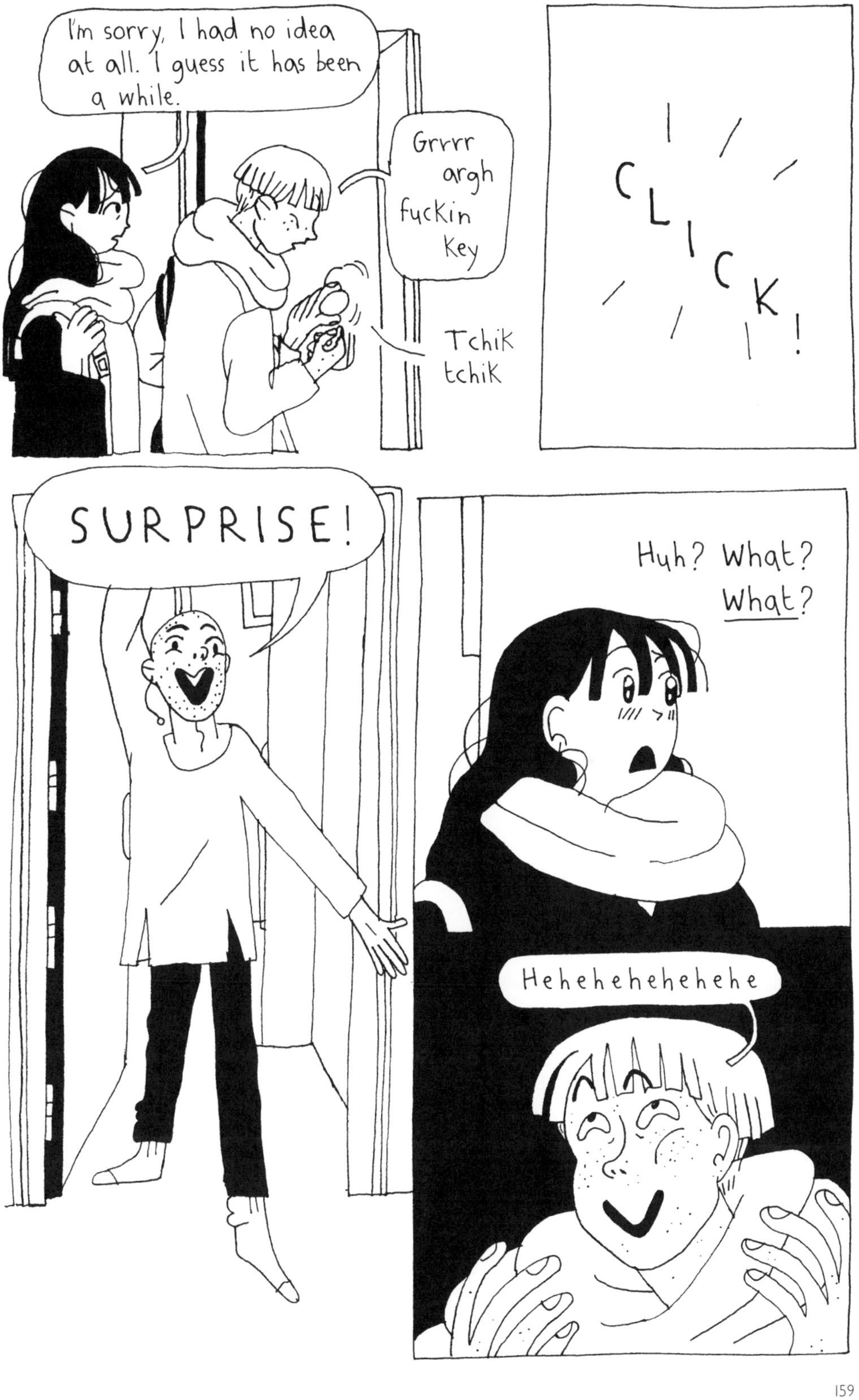
I'm sorry, I had no idea at all. I guess it has been a while.
Grrrr argh fuckin key
Tchik tchik
CLICK!
SURPRISE!
Huh? What? What?
Hehehehehehehe

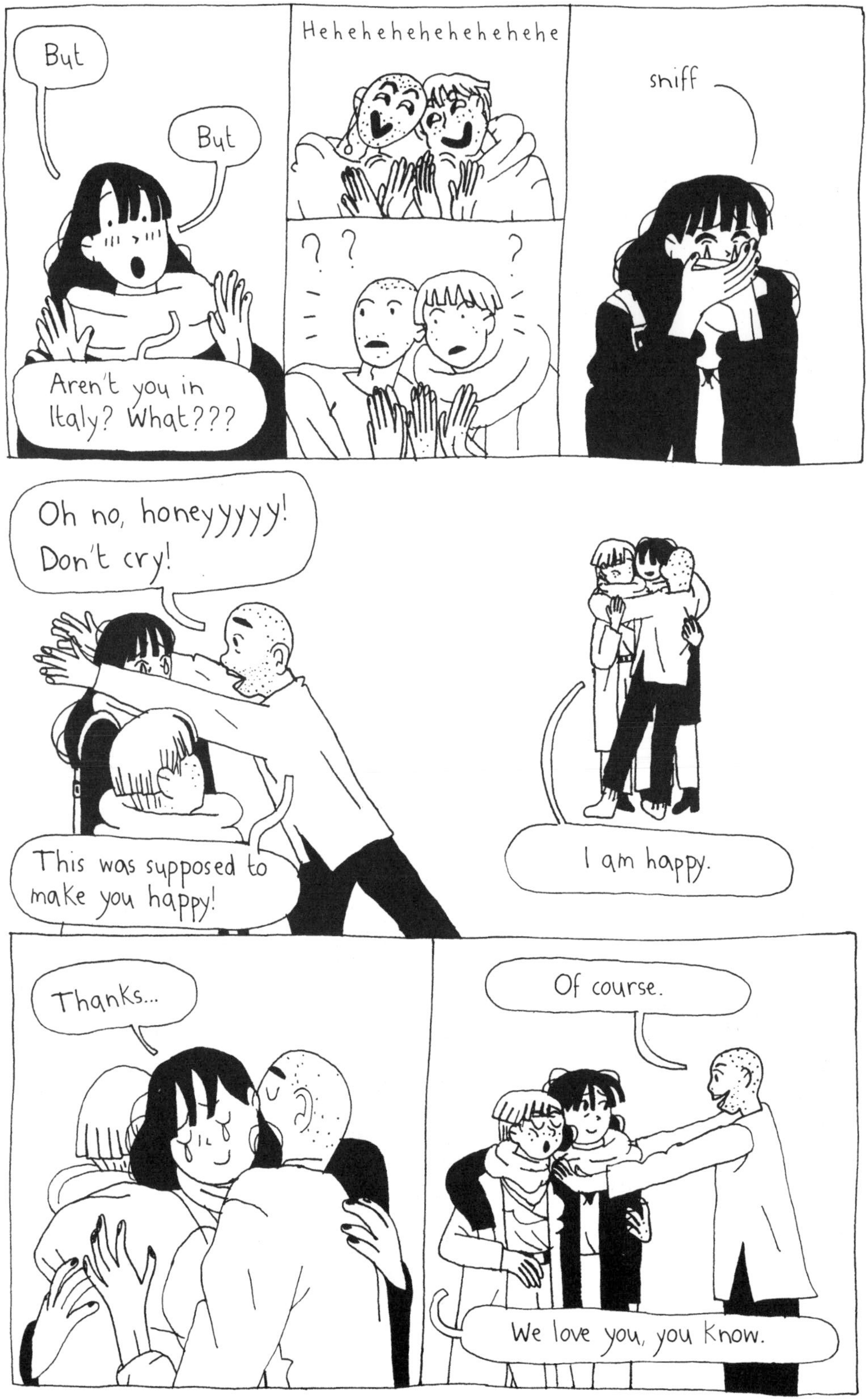
But
But
Aren't you in Italy? What???
Hehehehehehehehehe
? ? ?
sniff
Oh no, honeyyyyy! Don't cry!
This was supposed to make you happy!
I am happy.
Thanks...
Of course.
We love you, you know.

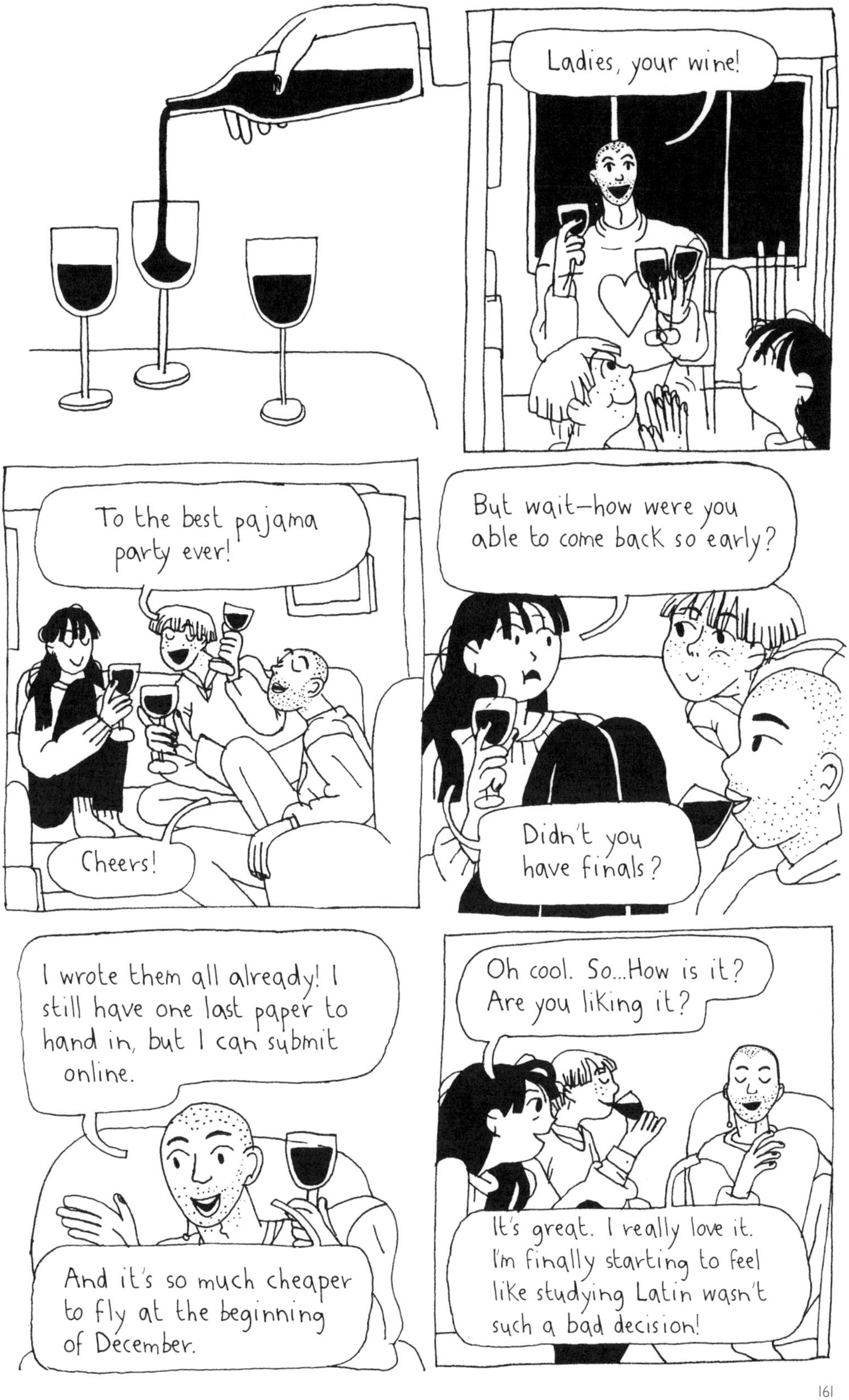
Ladies, your wine!
To the best pajama party ever!
Cheers!
But wait—how were you able to come back so early?
Didn't you have finals?
I wrote them all already! I still have one last paper to hand in, but I can submit online.
And it's so much cheaper to fly at the beginning of December.
Oh cool. So...How is it? Are you liking it?
It's great. I really love it. I'm finally starting to feel like studying Latin wasn't such a bad decision!

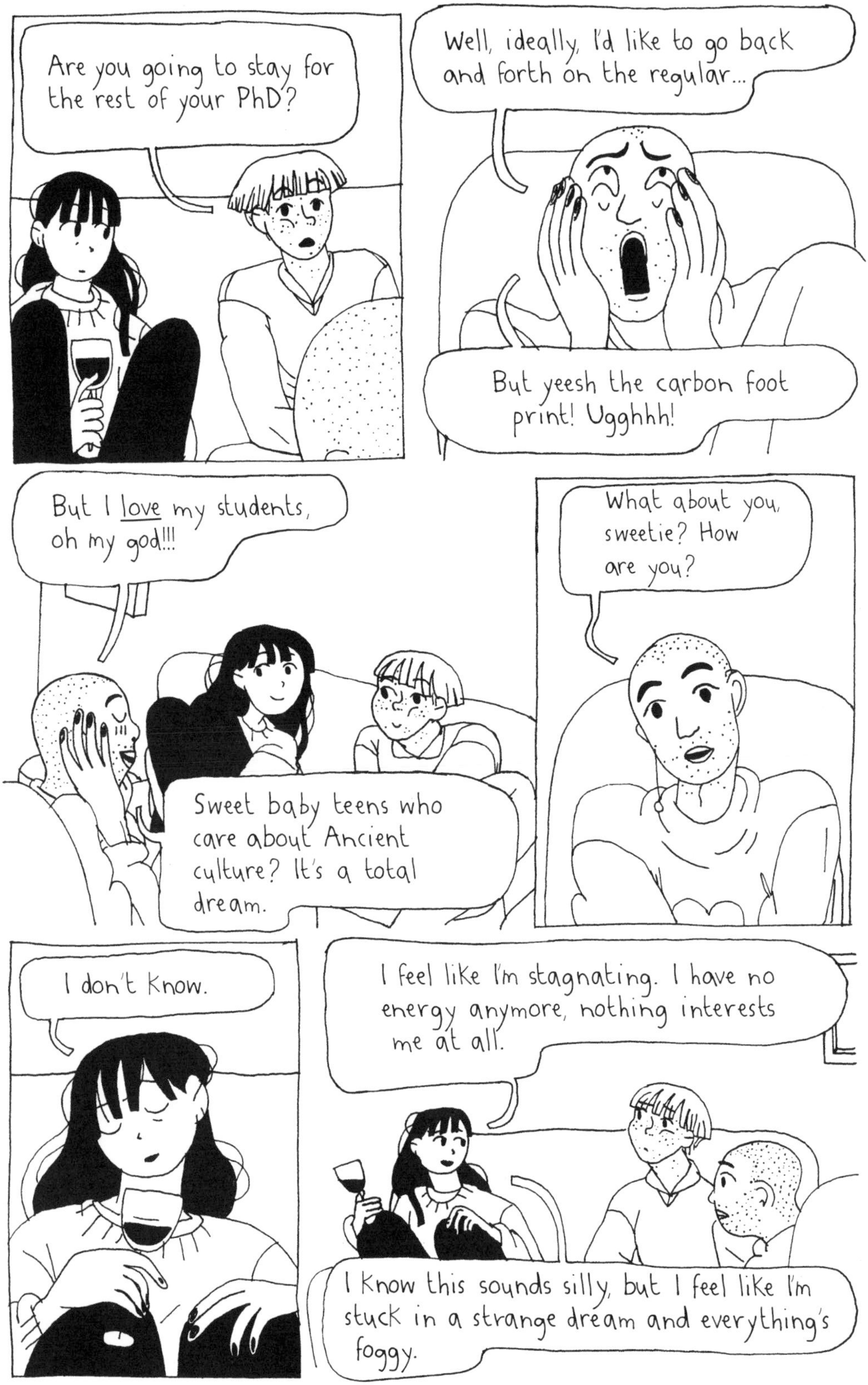
Are you going to stay for the rest of your PhD?
Well, ideally, I'd like to go back and forth on the regular...
But yeesh the carbon foot print! Ugghhh!
But I love my students, oh my god!!!
Sweet baby teens who care about Ancient culture? It's a total dream.
What about you, sweetie? How are you?
I don't Know.
I feel like I'm stagnating. I have no energy anymore, nothing interests me at all.
I Know this sounds silly, but I feel like I'm stuck in a strange dream and everything's foggy.

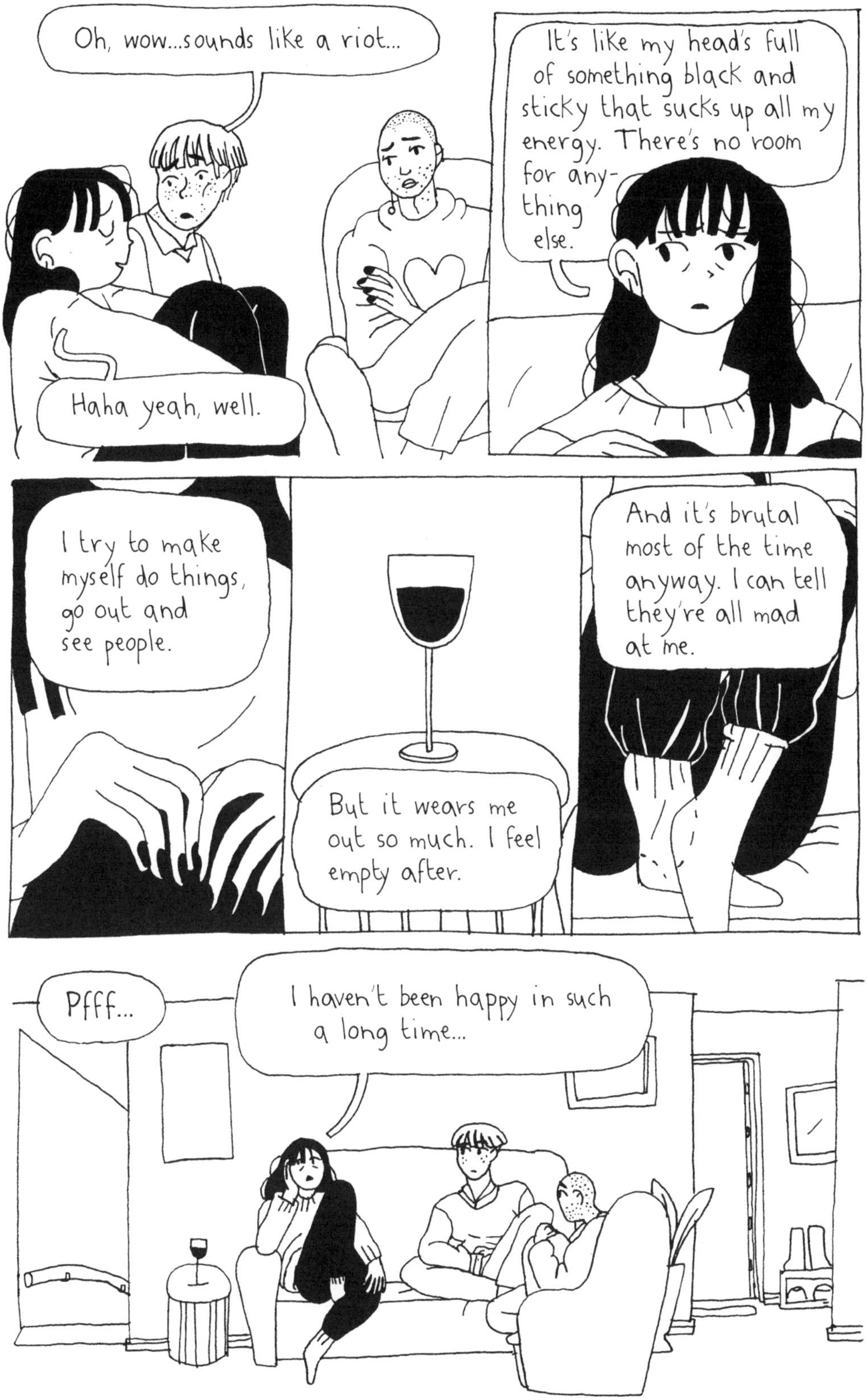

Oh, wow...sounds like a riot...
Haha yeah, well.
It's like my head's full of something black and sticky that sucks up all my energy. There's no room for any-thing else.
I try to make myself do things, go out and see people.
But it wears me out so much. I feel empty after.
And it's brutal most of the time anyway. I can tell they're all mad at me.
Pfff...
I haven't been happy in such a long time...

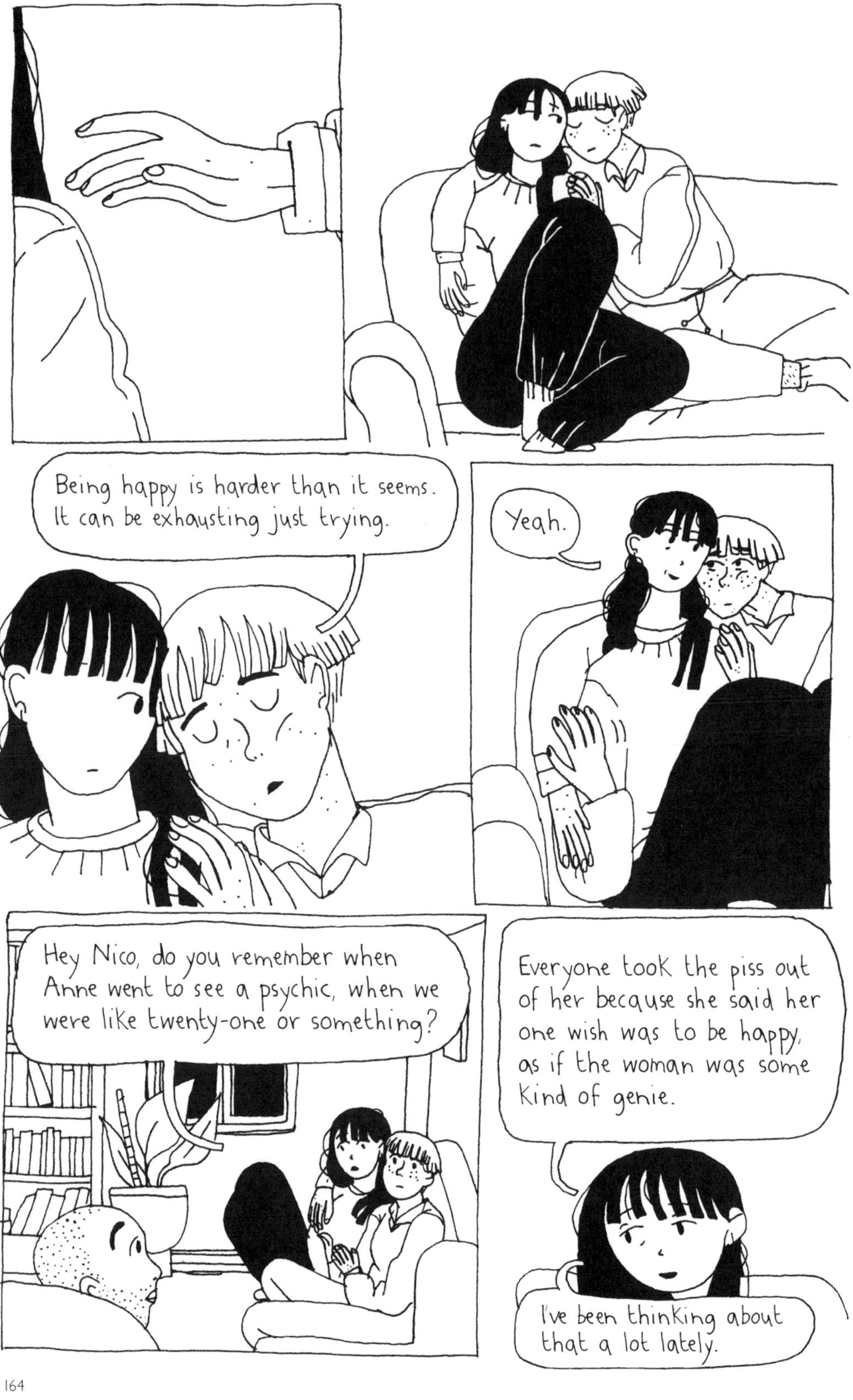
Being happy is harder than it seems. It can be exhausting just trying.
Yeah.
Hey Nico, do you remember when Anne went to see a psychic, when we were like twenty-one or something?
Everyone took the piss out of her because she said her one wish was to be happy, as if the woman was some kind of genie.
I've been thinking about that a lot lately.

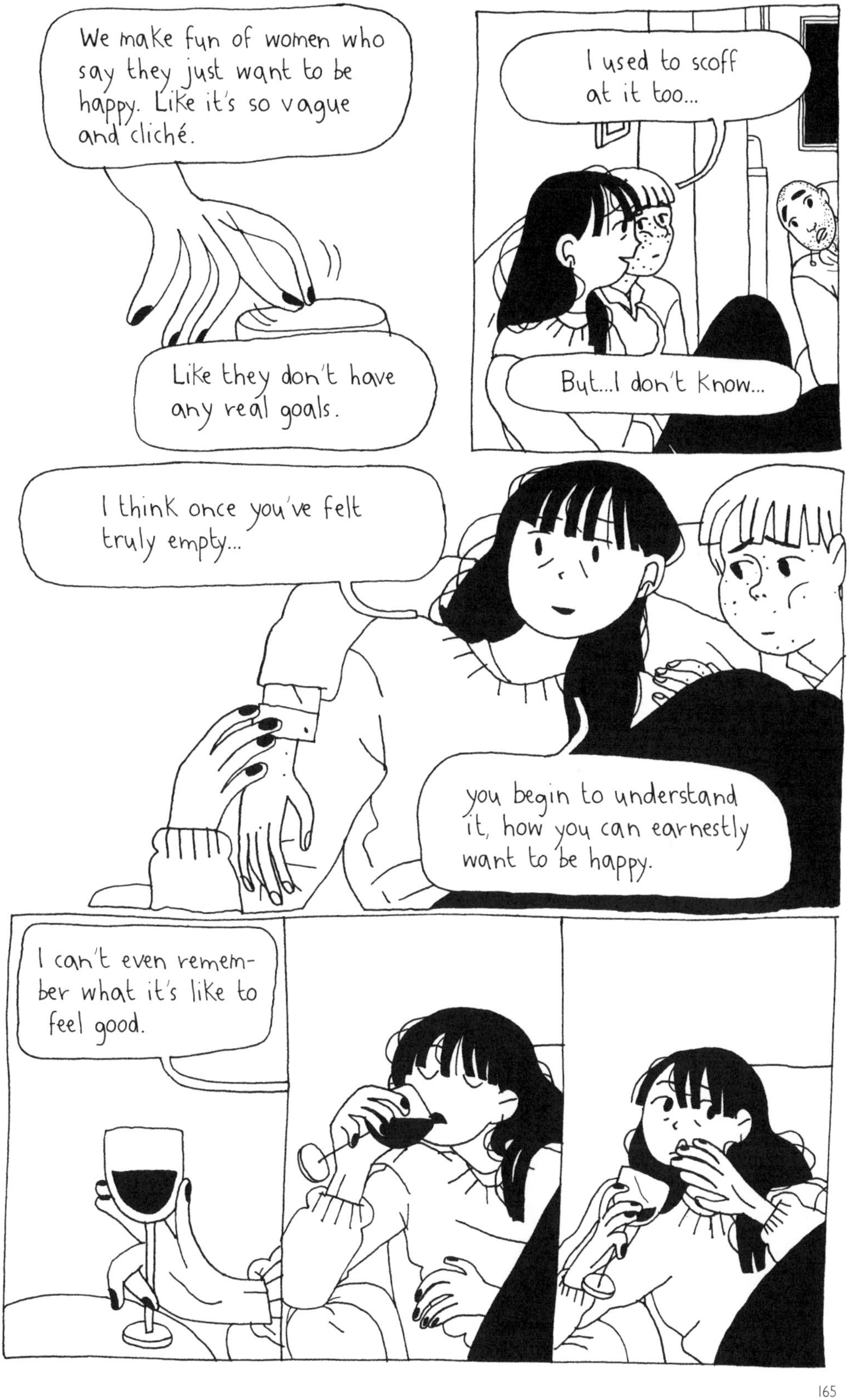
We make fun of women who say they just want to be happy. Like it's so vague and cliché.
Like they don't have any real goals.
I used to scoff at it too...
But...I don't know...
I think once you've felt truly empty...
you begin to understand it, how you can earnestly want to be happy.
I can't even remember what it's like to feel good.

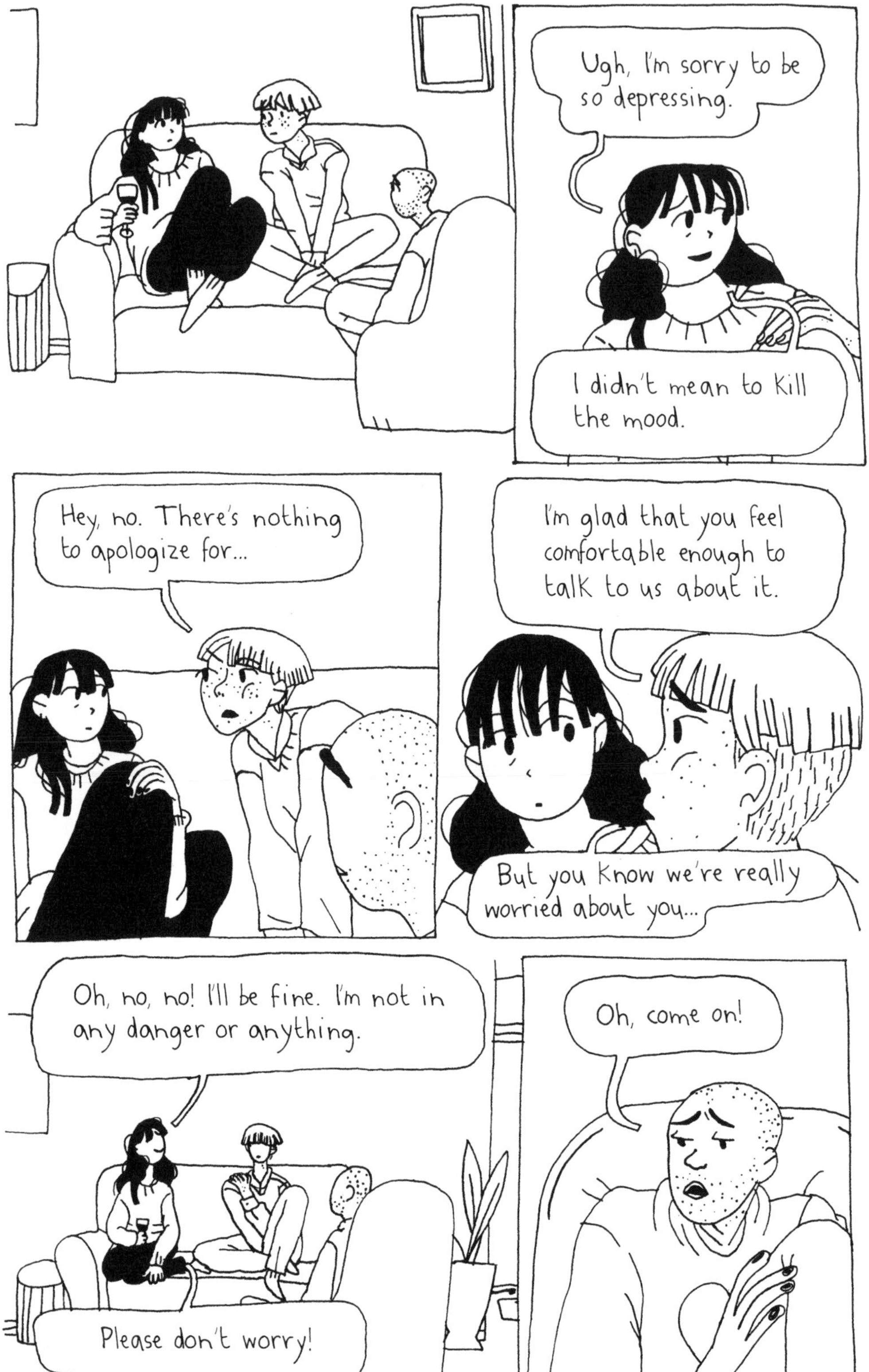
Ugh, I'm sorry to be so depressing.
I didn't mean to kill the mood.
Hey, no. There's nothing to apologize for...
I'm glad that you feel comfortable enough to talk to us about it.
But you know we're really worried about you...
Oh, no, no! I'll be fine. I'm not in any danger or anything.
Please don't worry!
Oh, come on!

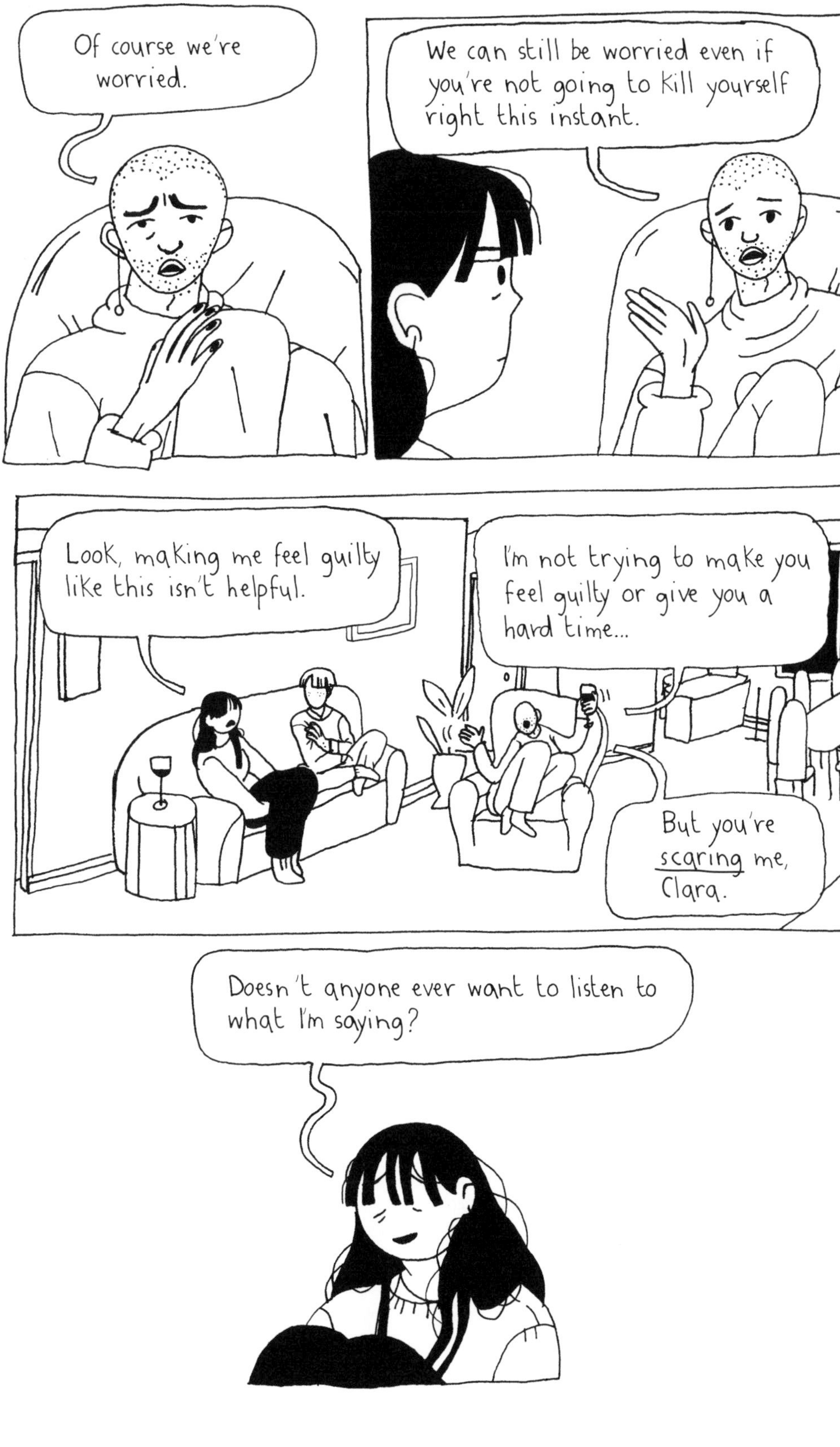
Of course we're worried.
We can still be worried even if you're not going to kill yourself right this instant.
Look, making me feel guilty like this isn't helpful.
I'm not trying to make you feel guilty or give you a hard time...
But you're scaring me, Clara.
Doesn't anyone ever want to listen to what I'm saying?

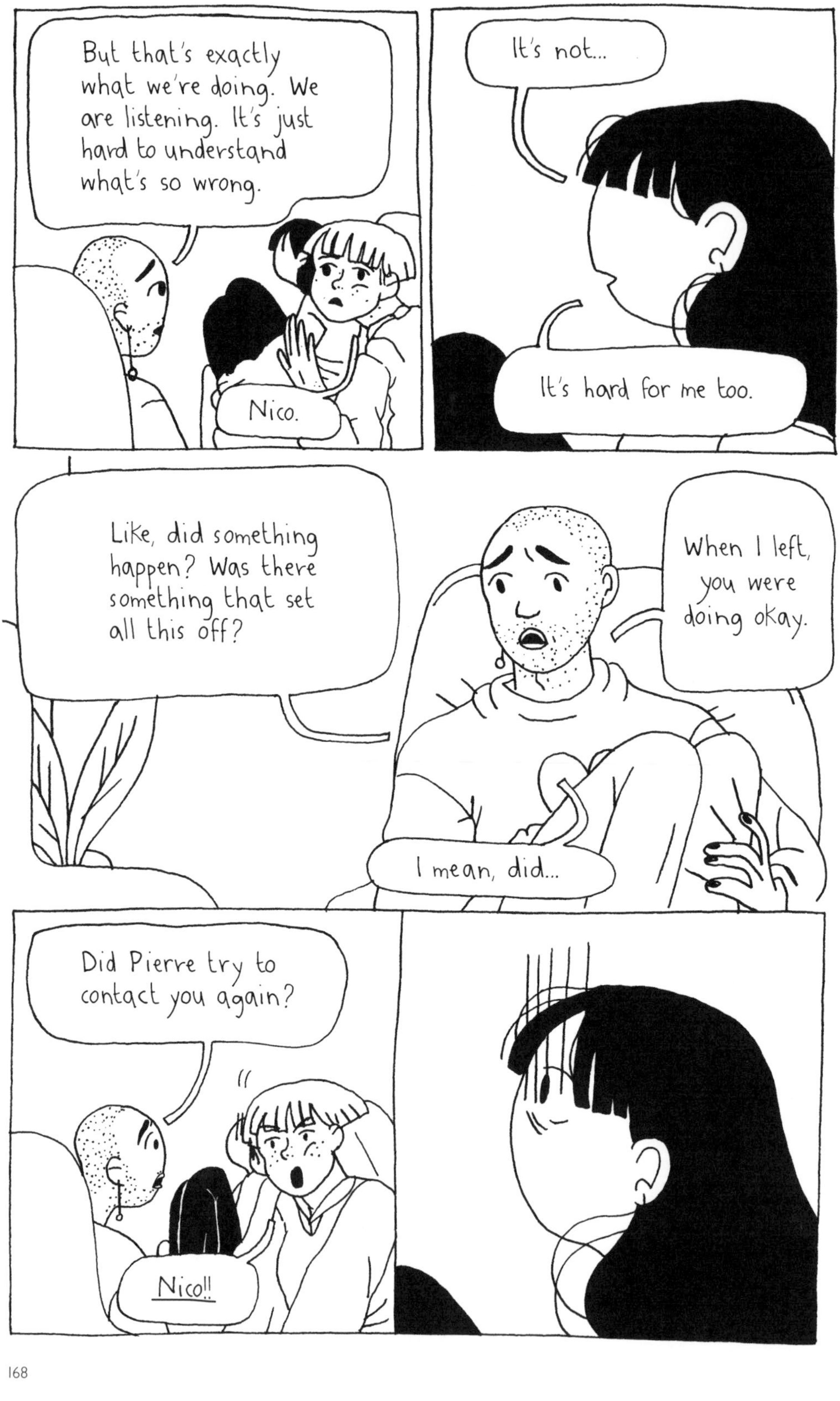

But that's exactly what we're doing. We are listening. It's just hard to understand what's so wrong.
Nico.
It's not...
It's hard for me too.
Like, did something happen? Was there something that set all this off?
When I left, you were doing okay.
I mean, did...
Did Pierre try to contact you again?
Nico!!

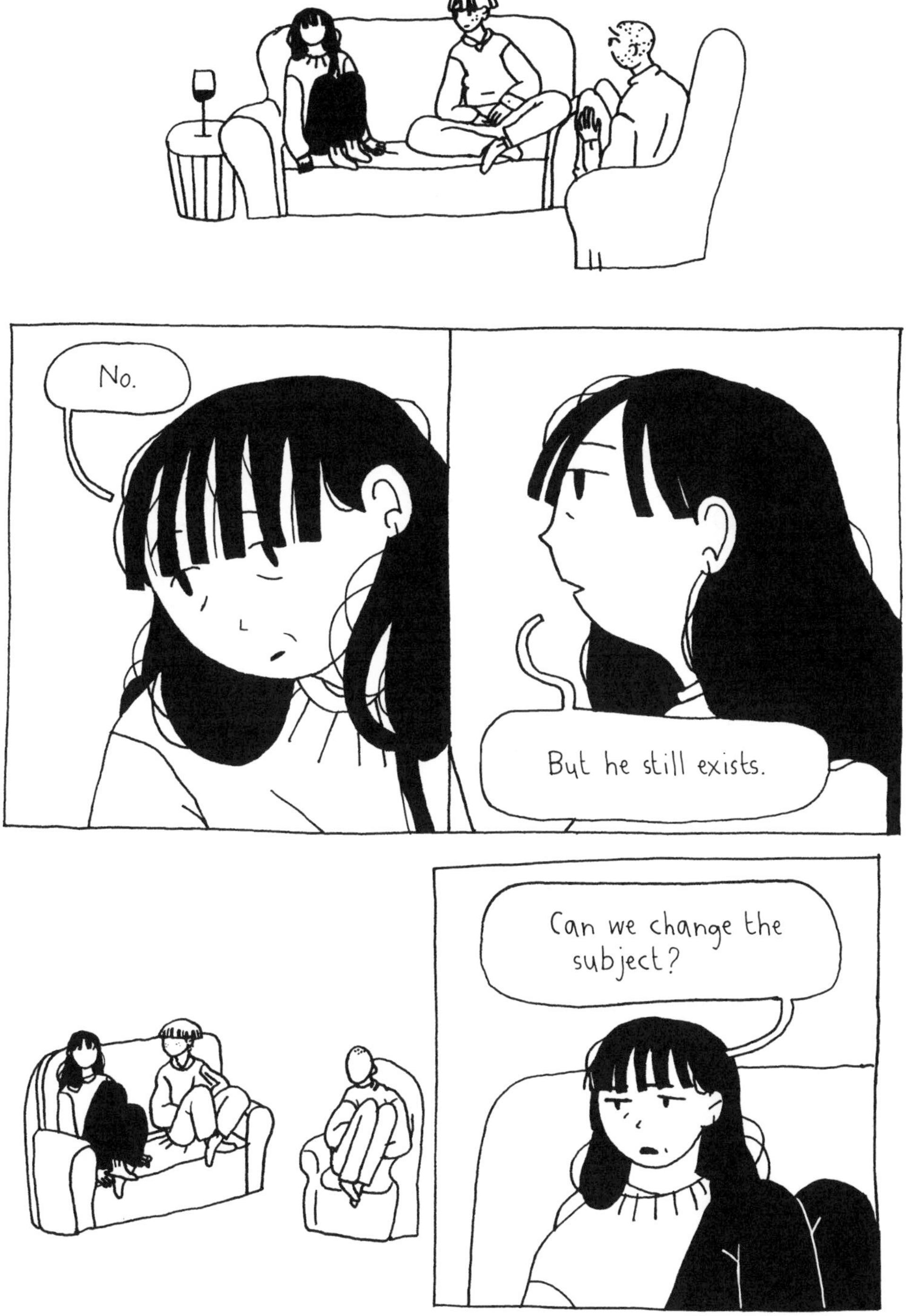
No.
But he still exists.
Can we change the subject?

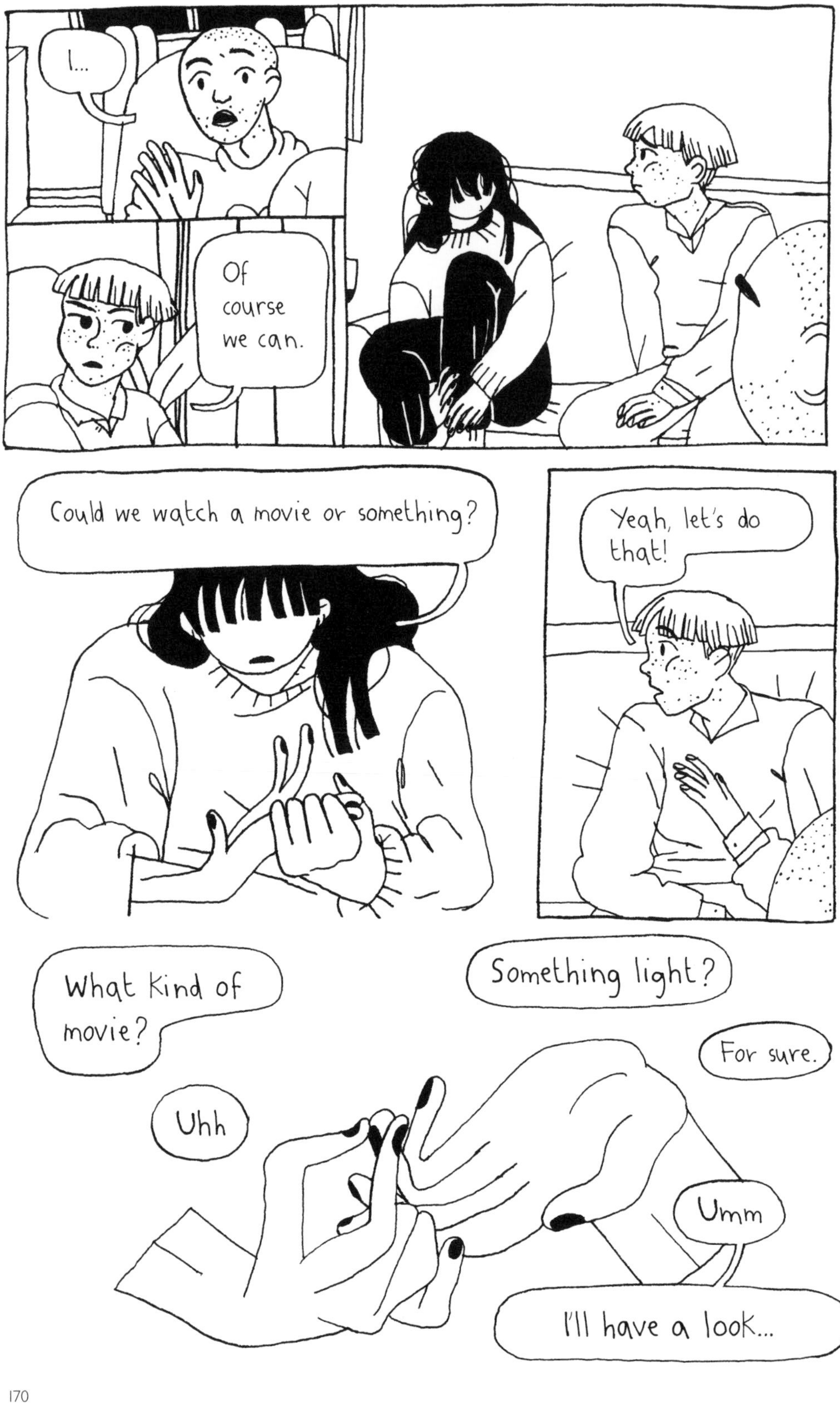
I...
Of course we can.
Could we watch a movie or something?
Yeah, let's do that!
What kind of movie?
Something light?
For sure.
Uhh
Umm
I'll have a look...

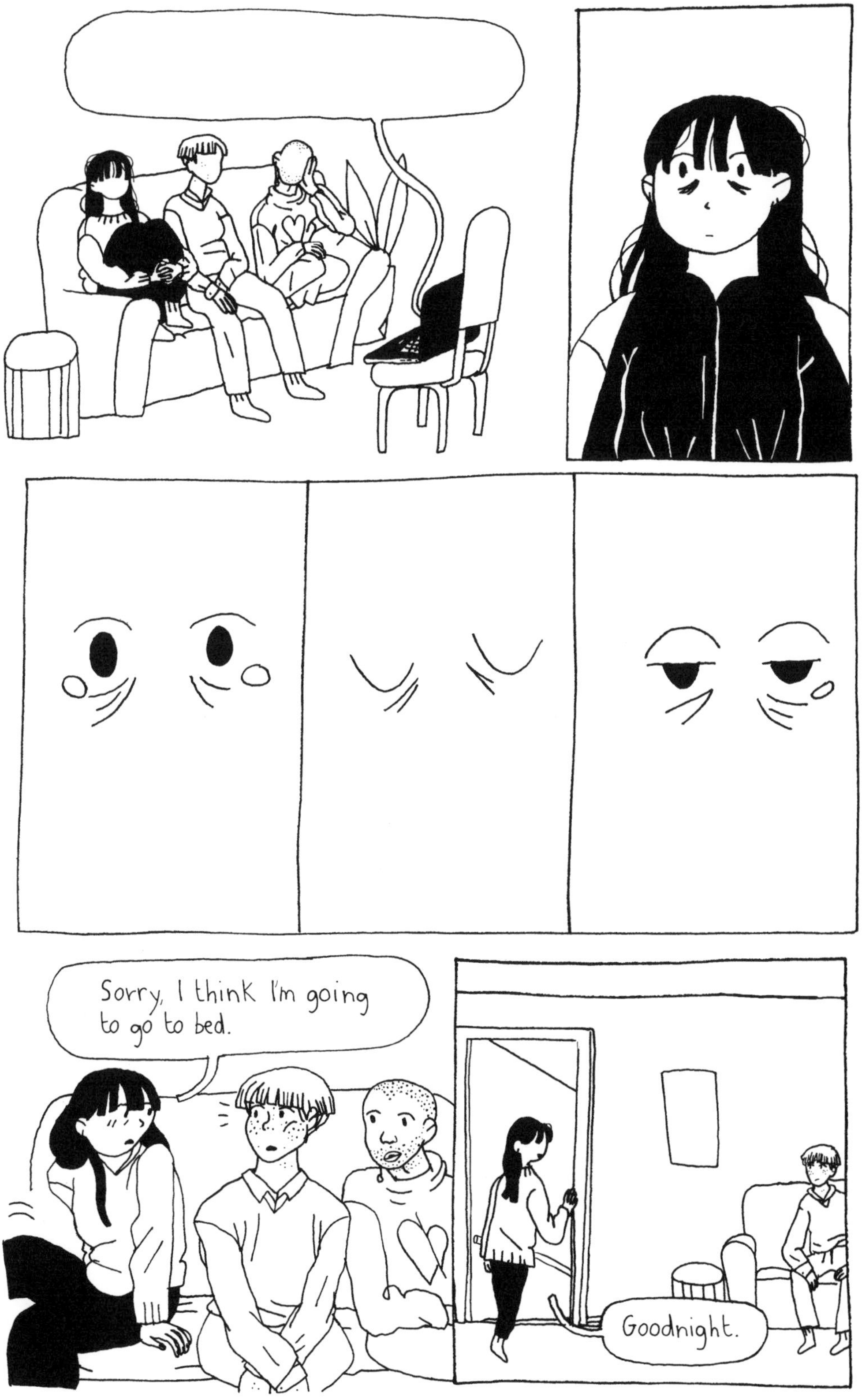
Sorry, I think I'm going to go to bed.
Goodnight.

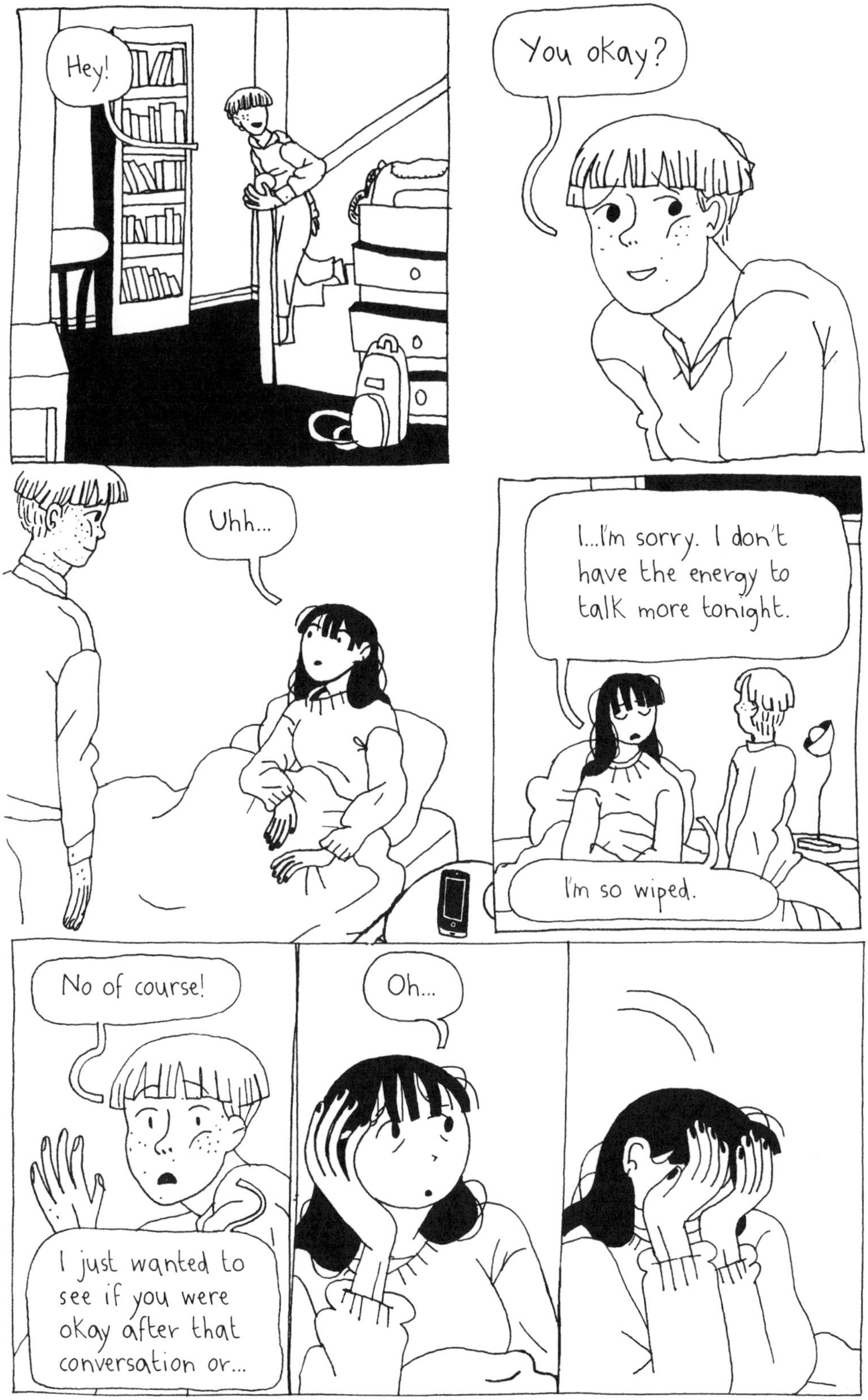

Hey!
You okay?
Uhh...
I...I'm sorry. I don't have the energy to talk more tonight.
I'm so wiped.
No of course!
I just wanted to see if you were okay after that conversation or...
Oh...

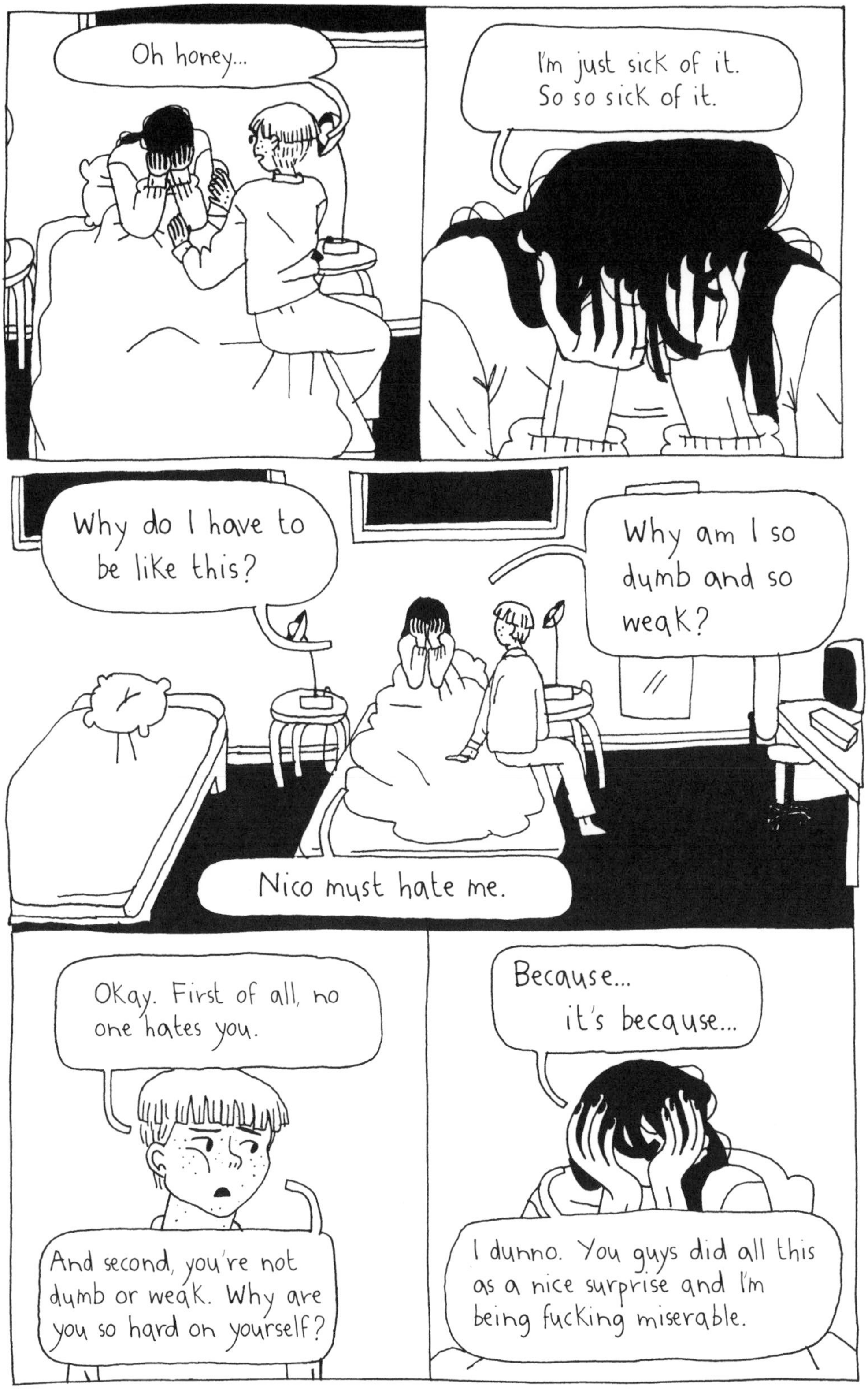
Oh honey...
I'm just sick of it. So so sick of it.
Why do I have to be like this?
Why am I so dumb and so weak?
Nico must hate me.
Okay. First of all, no one hates you.
And second, you're not dumb or weak. Why are you so hard on yourself?
Because... it's because...
I dunno. You guys did all this as a nice surprise and I'm being fucking miserable.

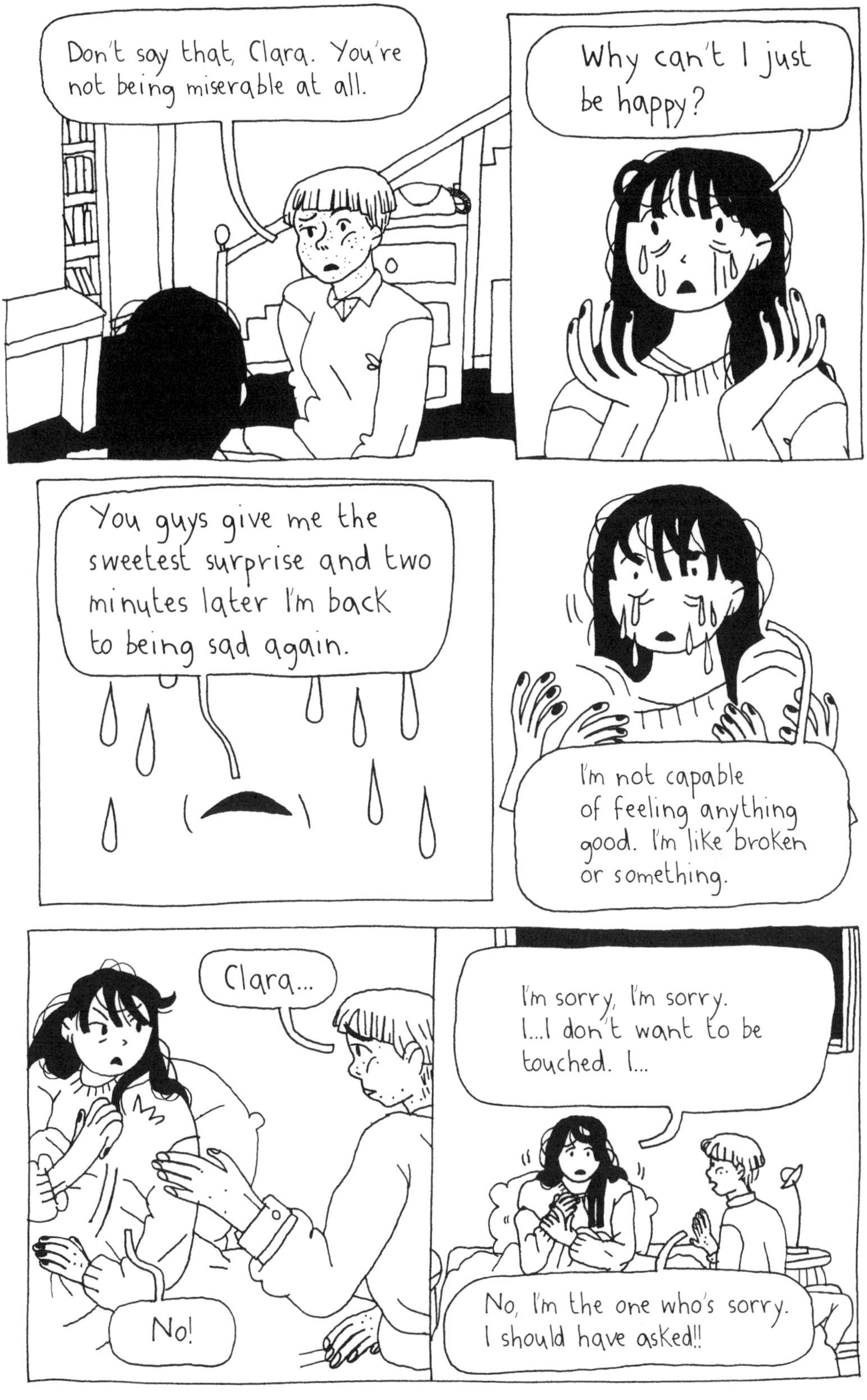

Don't say that, Clara. You're not being miserable at all.
Why can't I just be happy?
You guys give me the sweetest surprise and two minutes later I'm back to being sad again.
I'm not capable of feeling anything good. I'm like broken or something.
Clara...
No!
I'm sorry, I'm sorry. I...I don't want to be touched. I...
No, I'm the one who's sorry. I should have asked!!

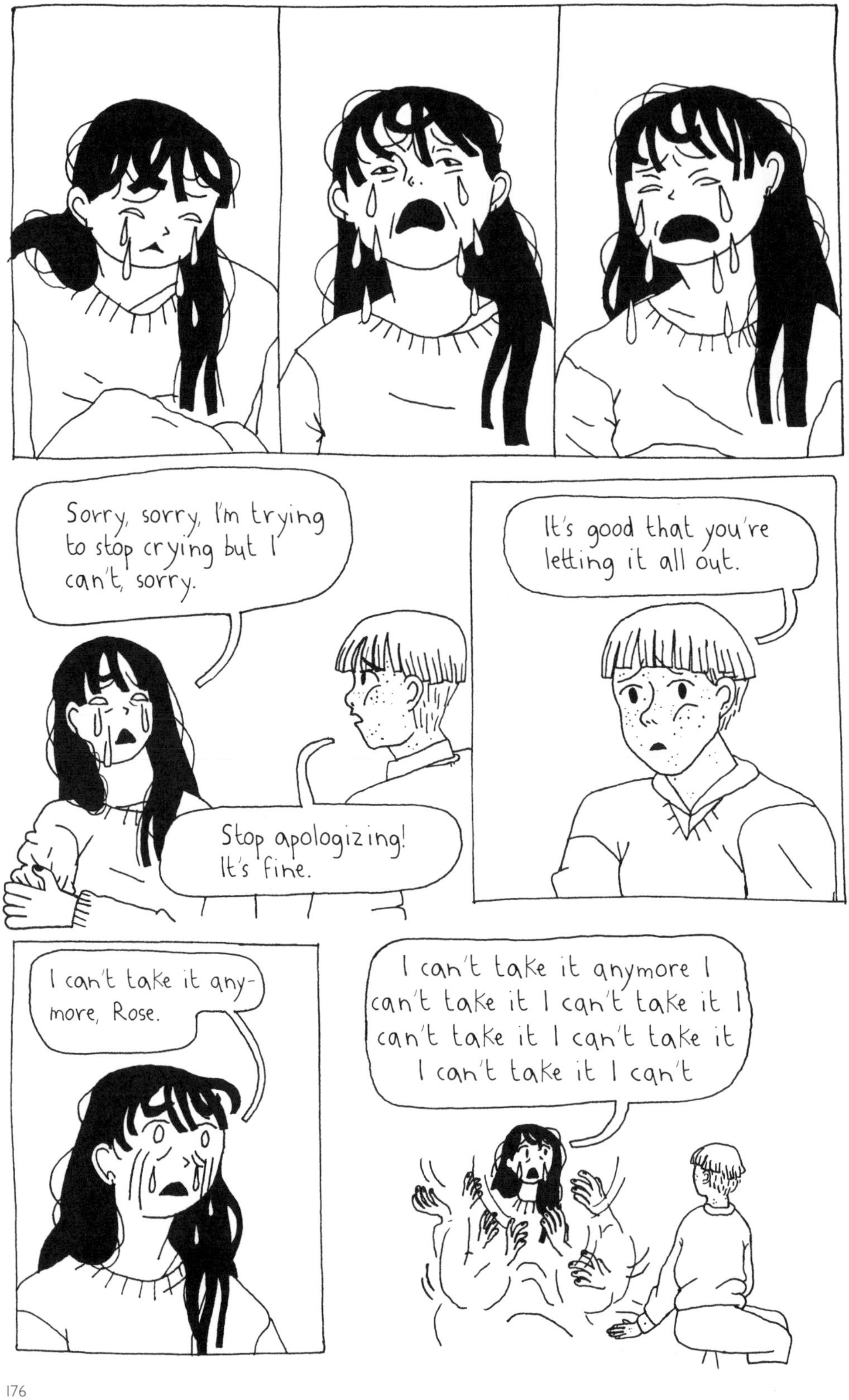
Sorry, sorry, I'm trying to stop crying but I can't, sorry.
Stop apologizing! It's fine.
It's good that you're letting it all out.
I can't take it any-more, Rose.
I can't take it anymore I can't take it I can't take it I can't take it I can't take it I can't take it I can't

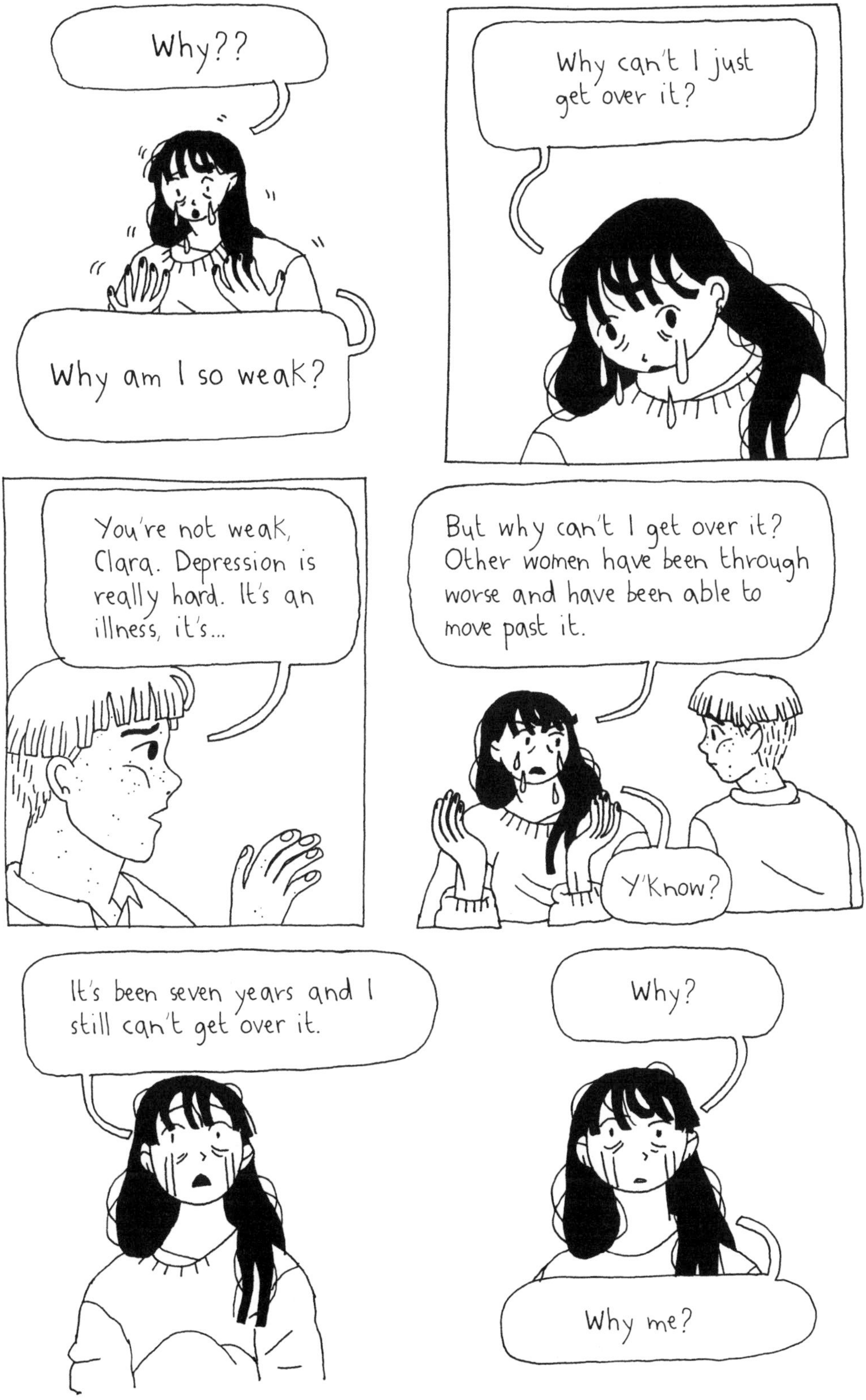
Why??
Why am I so weak?
Why can't I just get over it?
You're not weak, Clara. Depression is really hard. It's an illness, it's...
But why can't I get over it? Other women have been through worse and have been able to move past it.
Y'Know?
It's been seven years and I still can't get over it.
Why?
Why me?

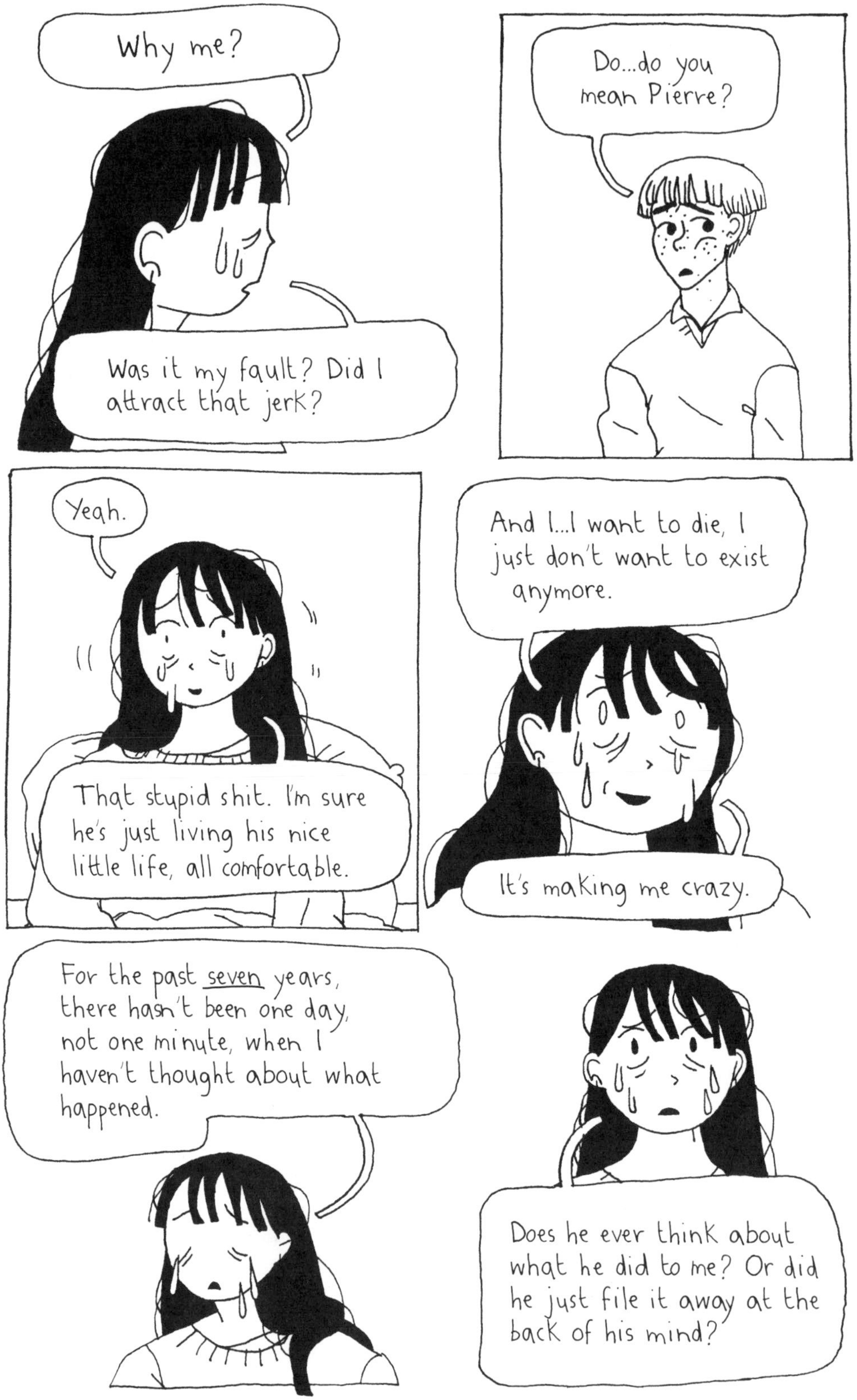
Why me?
Was it my fault? Did I attract that jerk?
Do...do you mean Pierre?
Yeah.
That stupid shit. I'm sure he's just living his nice little life, all comfortable.
And I...I want to die, I just don't want to exist anymore.
It's making me crazy.
For the past seven years, there hasn't been one day, not one minute, when I haven't thought about what happened.
Does he ever think about what he did to me? Or did he just file it away at the back of his mind?

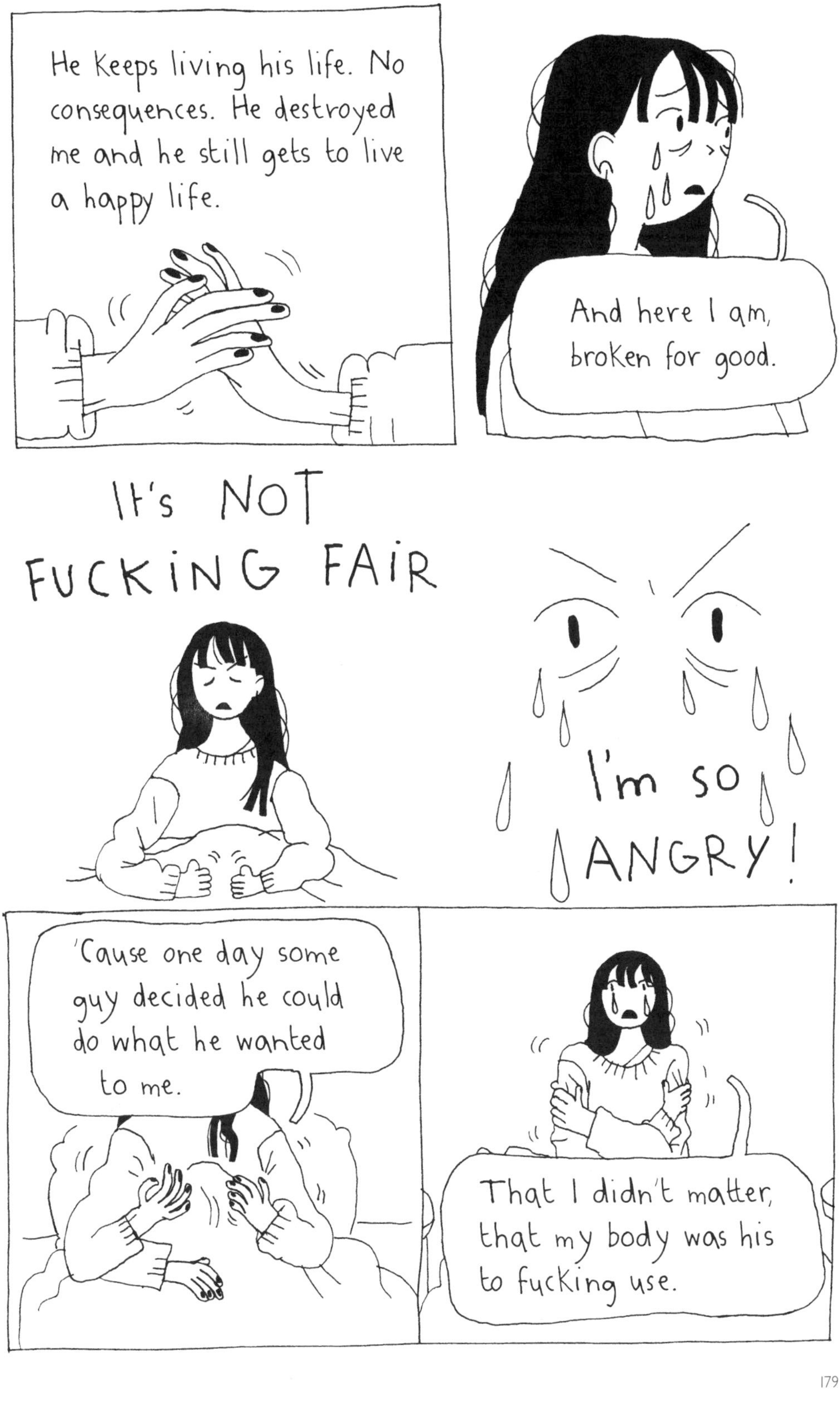
He Keeps living his life. No consequences. He destroyed me and he still gets to live a happy life.
And here I am, broken for good.
It's NOT FUCKING FAIR
I'm so ANGRY!
'Cause one day some guy decided he could do what he wanted to me.
That I didn't matter, that my body was his to fucking use.

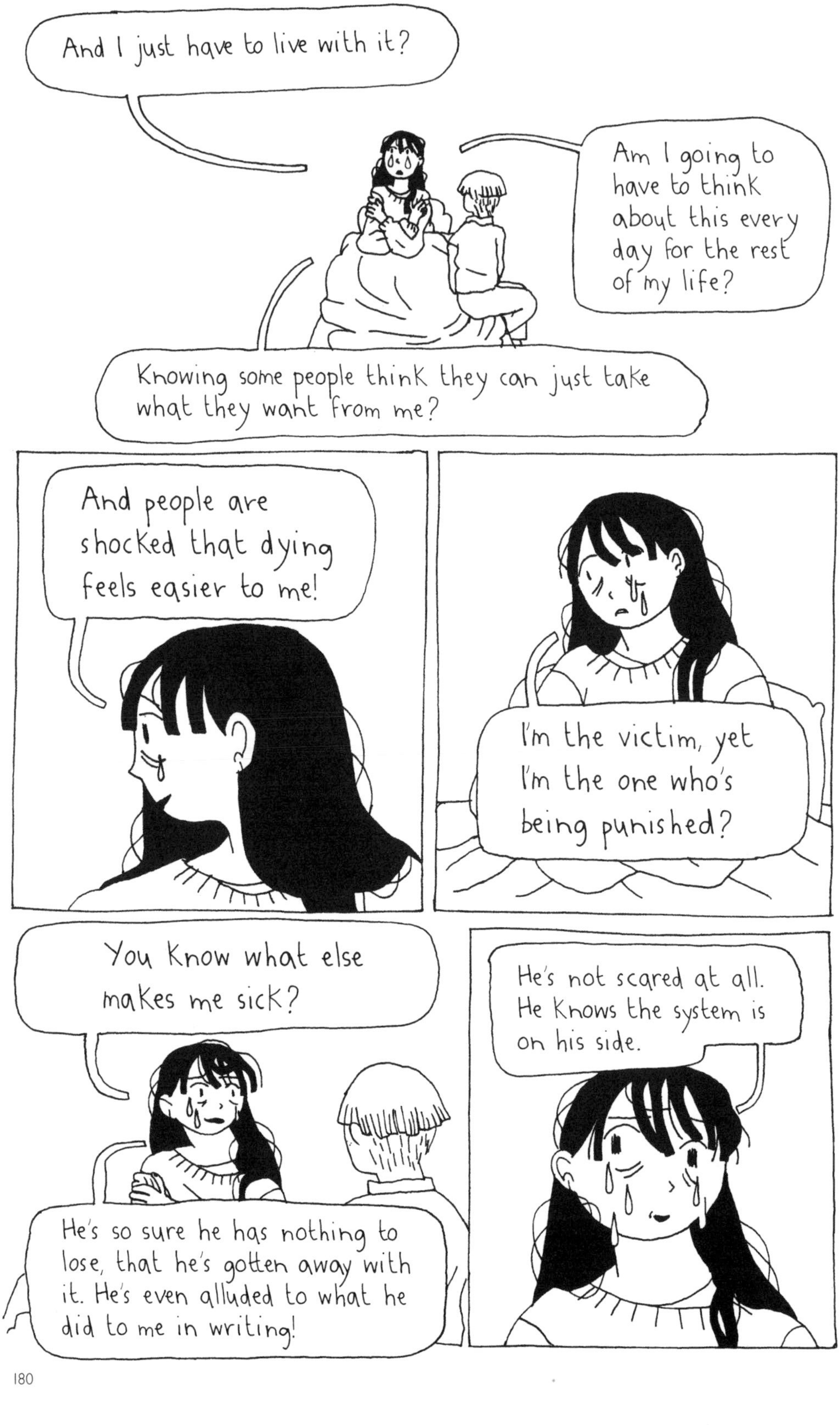

And I just have to live with it?
Am I going to have to think about this every day for the rest of my life?
Knowing some people think they can just take what they want from me?
And people are shocked that dying feels easier to me!
I'm the victim, yet I'm the one who's being punished?
You know what else makes me sick?
He's so sure he has nothing to lose, that he's gotten away with it. He's even alluded to what he did to me in writing!
He's not scared at all. He knows the system is on his side.

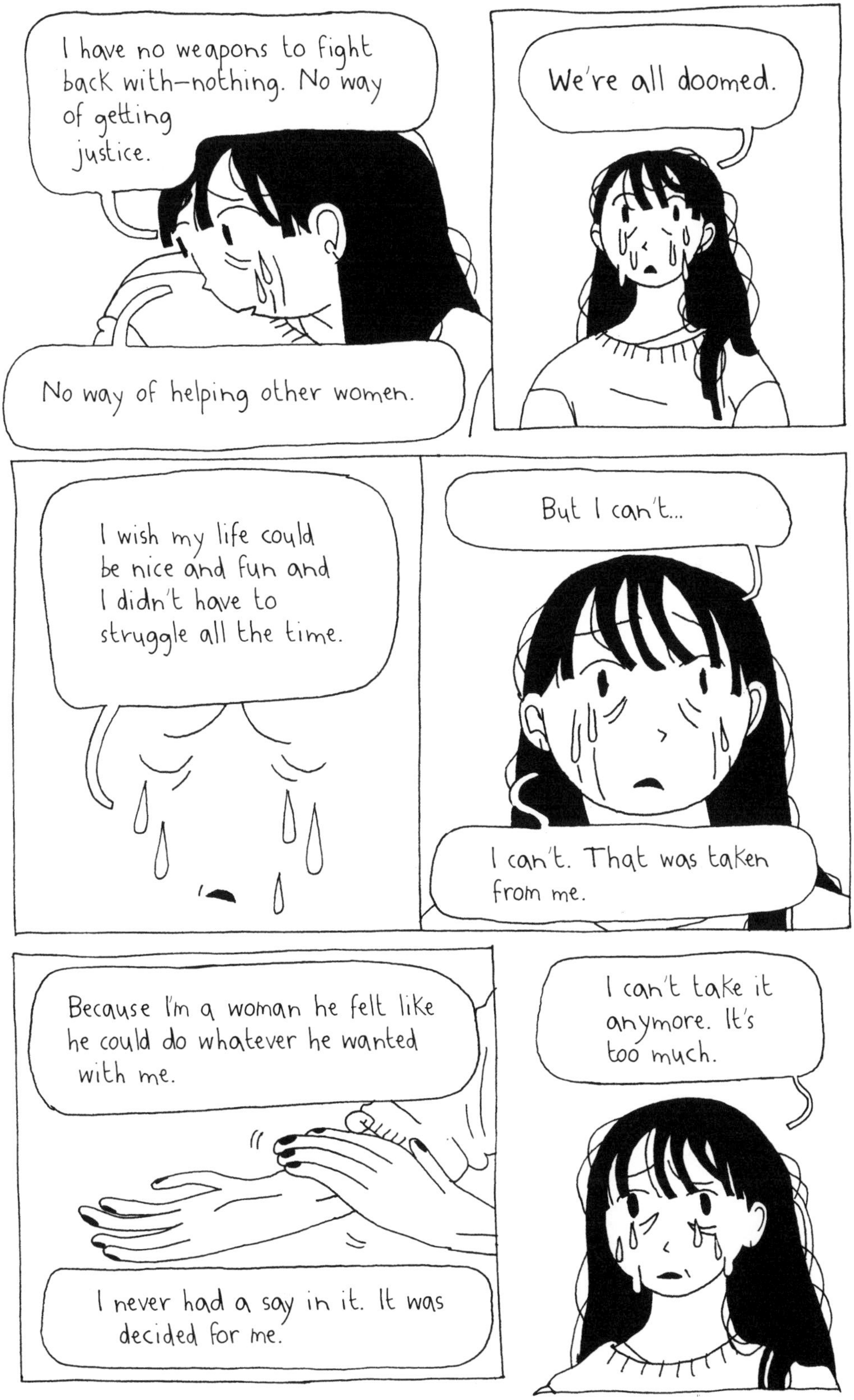
I have no weapons to fight back with—nothing. No way of getting justice.
No way of helping other women.
We're all doomed.
I wish my life could be nice and fun and I didn't have to struggle all the time.
But I can't...
I can't. That was taken from me.
Because I'm a woman he felt like he could do whatever he wanted with me.
I never had a say in it. It was decided for me.
I can't take it anymore. It's too much.

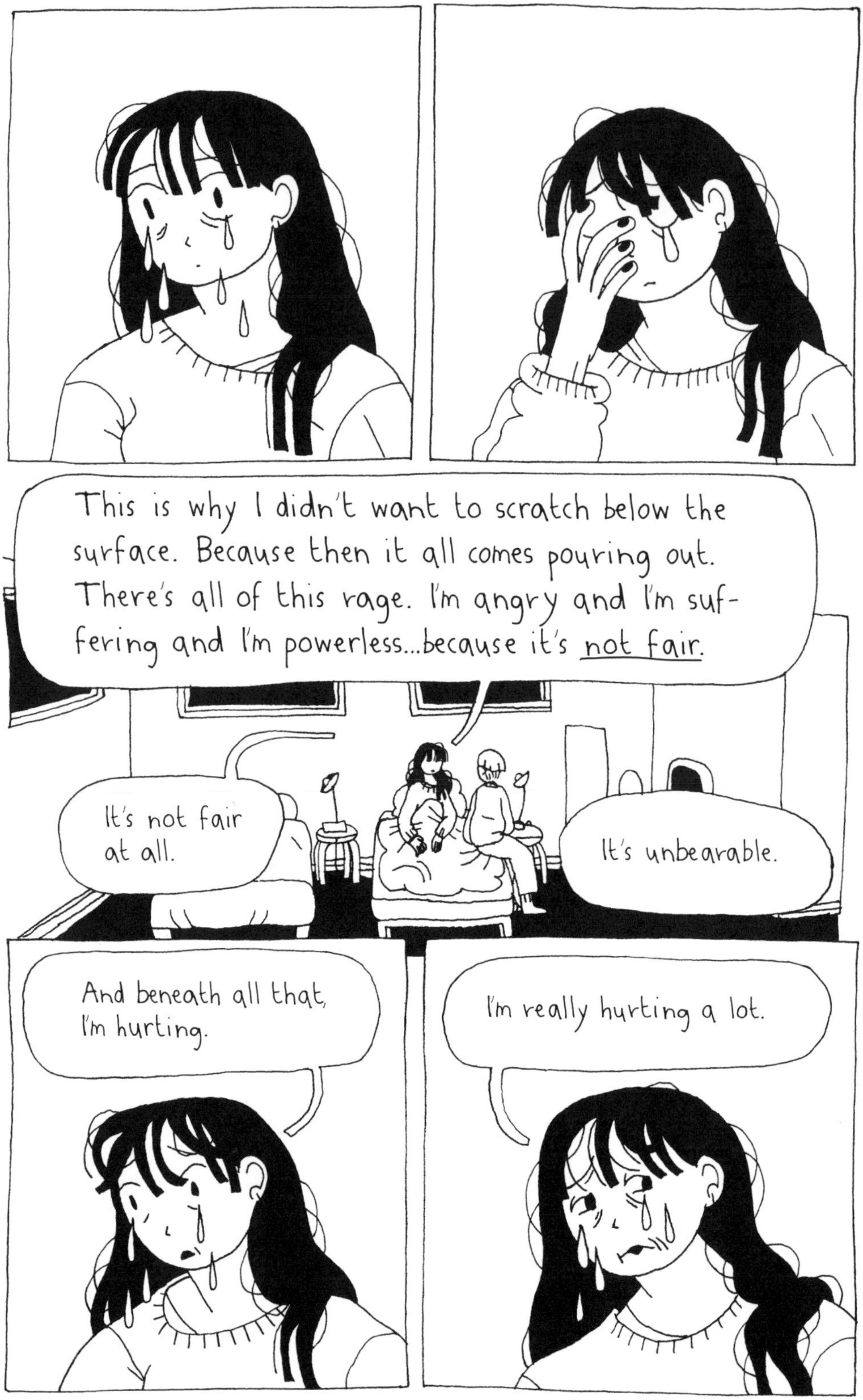
This is why I didn't want to scratch below the surface. Because then it all comes pouring out. There's all of this rage. I'm angry and I'm suffering and I'm powerless...because it's not fair.
It's not fair at all.
It's unbearable.
And beneath all that, I'm hurting.
I'm really hurting a lot.

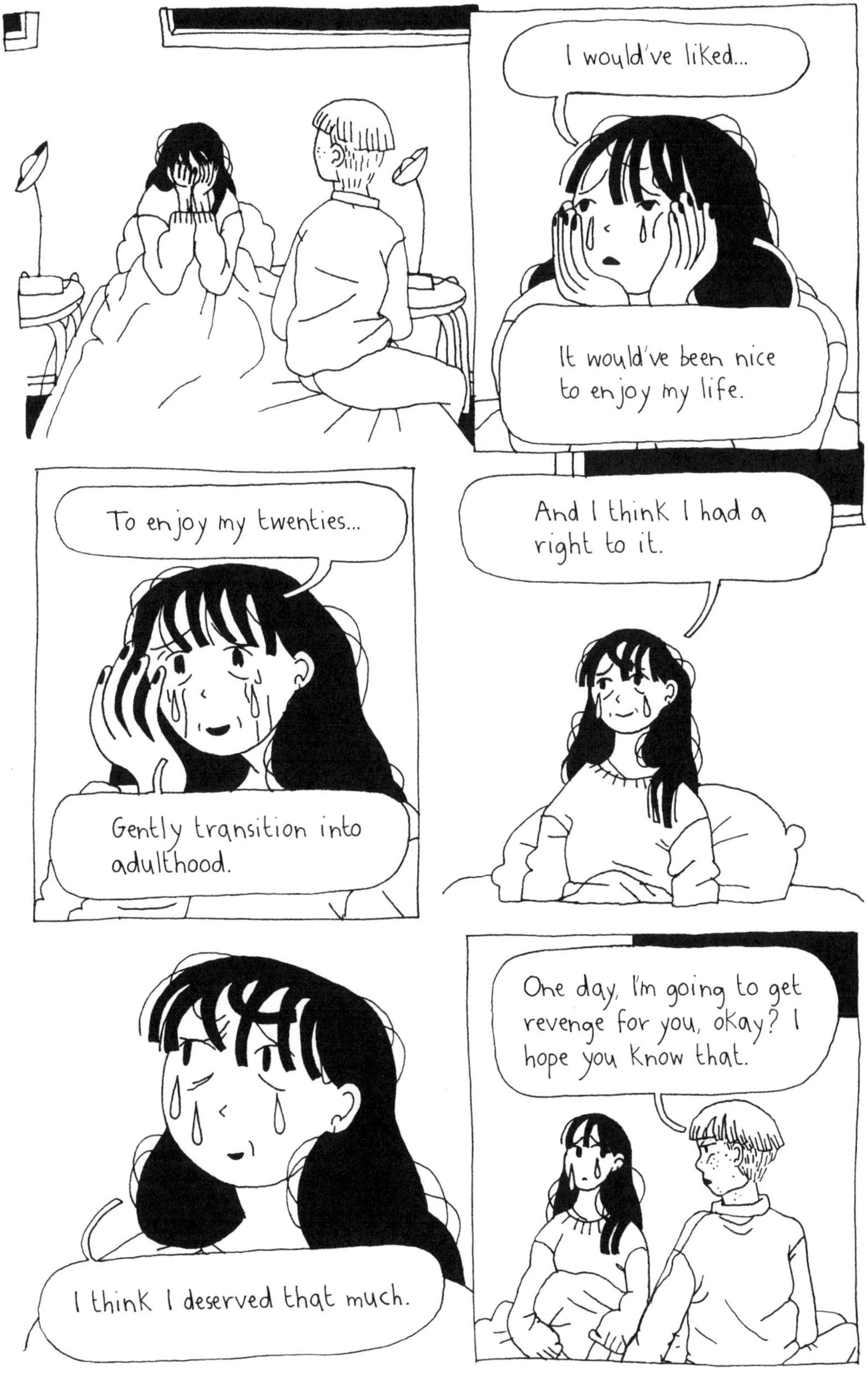
I would've liked...
It would've been nice to enjoy my life.
To enjoy my twenties...
Gently transition into adulthood.
And I think I had a right to it.
I think I deserved that much.
One day, I'm going to get revenge for you, okay? I hope you know that.

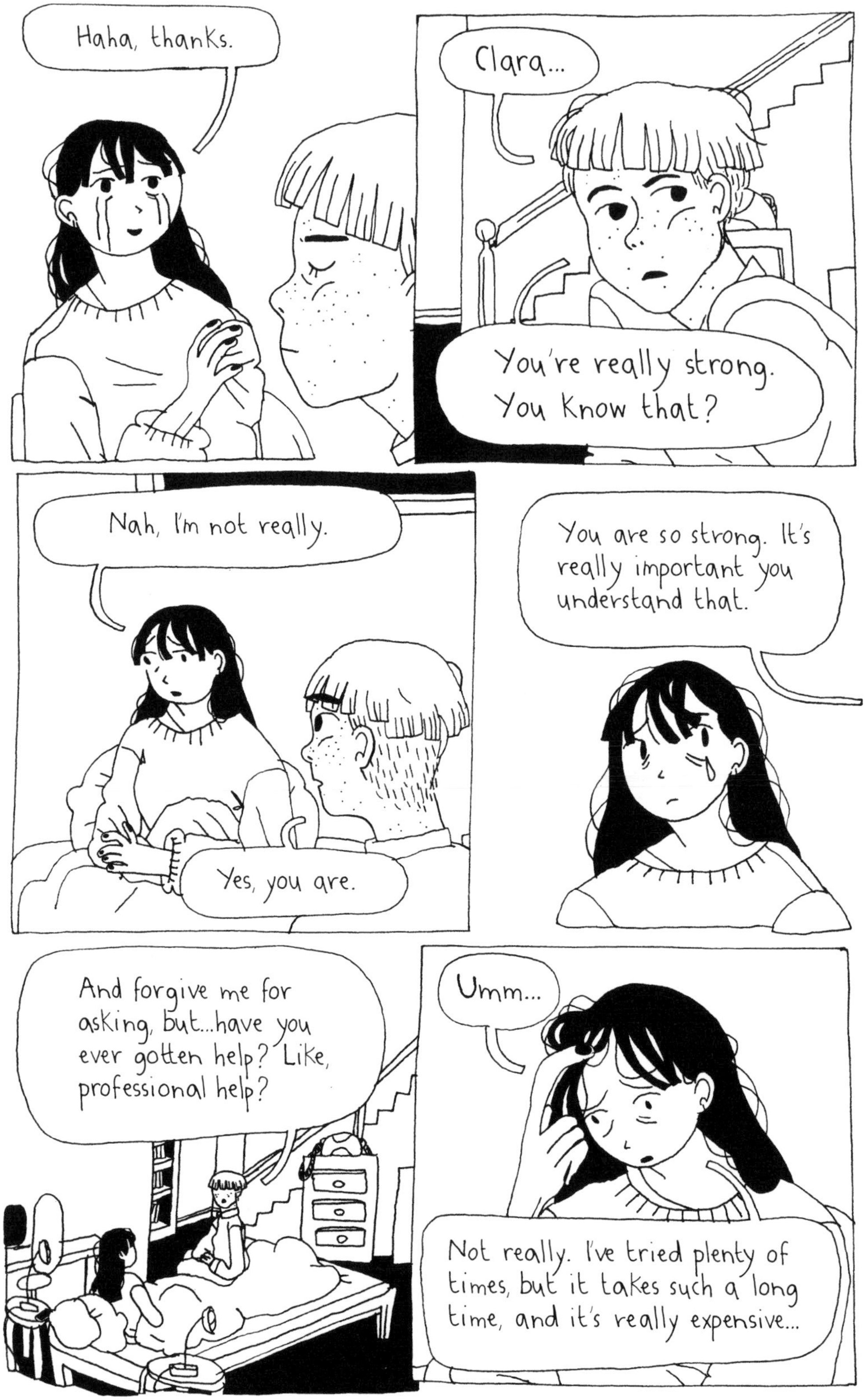

Haha, thanks.
Clara...
You're really strong. You know that?
Nah, I'm not really.
Yes, you are.
You are so strong. It's really important you understand that.
And forgive me for asking, but...have you ever gotten help? Like, professional help?
Umm...
Not really. I've tried plenty of times, but it takes such a long time, and it's really expensive...

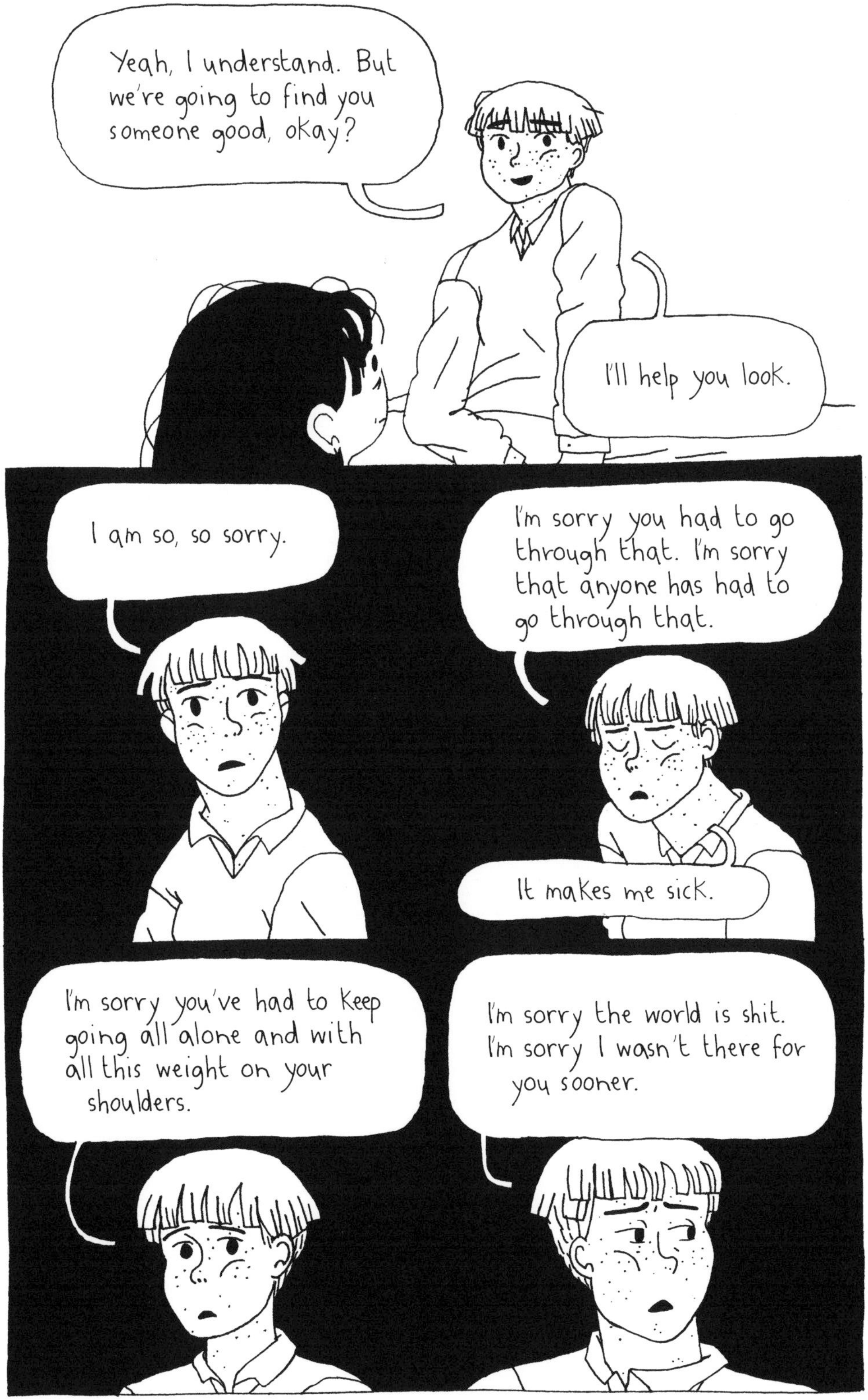
Yeah, I understand. But we're going to find you someone good, okay?
I'll help you look.
I am so, so sorry.
I'm sorry you had to go through that. I'm sorry that anyone has had to go through that.
It makes me sick.
I'm sorry you've had to keep going all alone and with all this weight on your shoulders.
I'm sorry the world is shit. I'm sorry I wasn't there for you sooner.

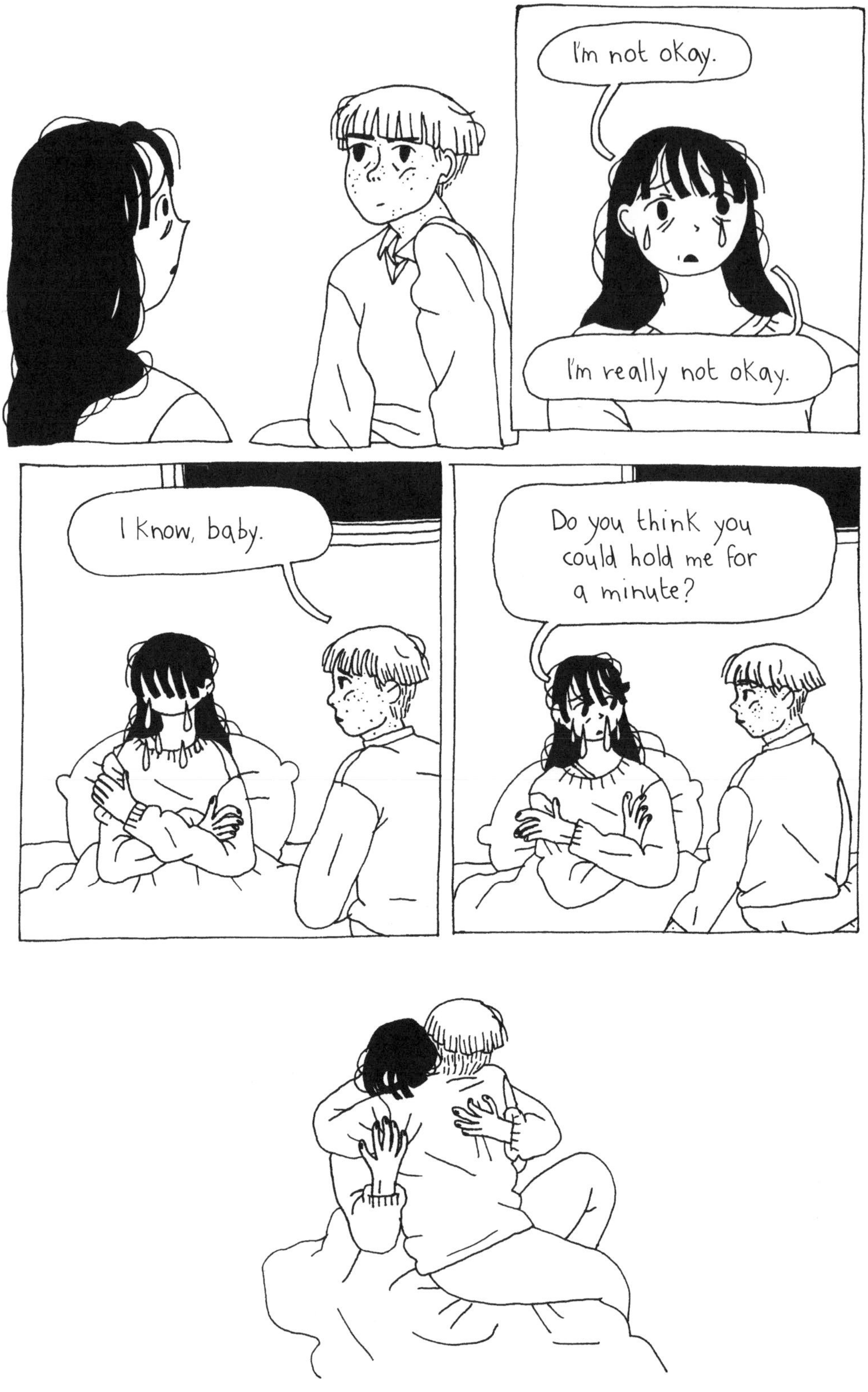
I'm not okay.
I'm really not okay.
I know, baby.
Do you think you could hold me for a minute?

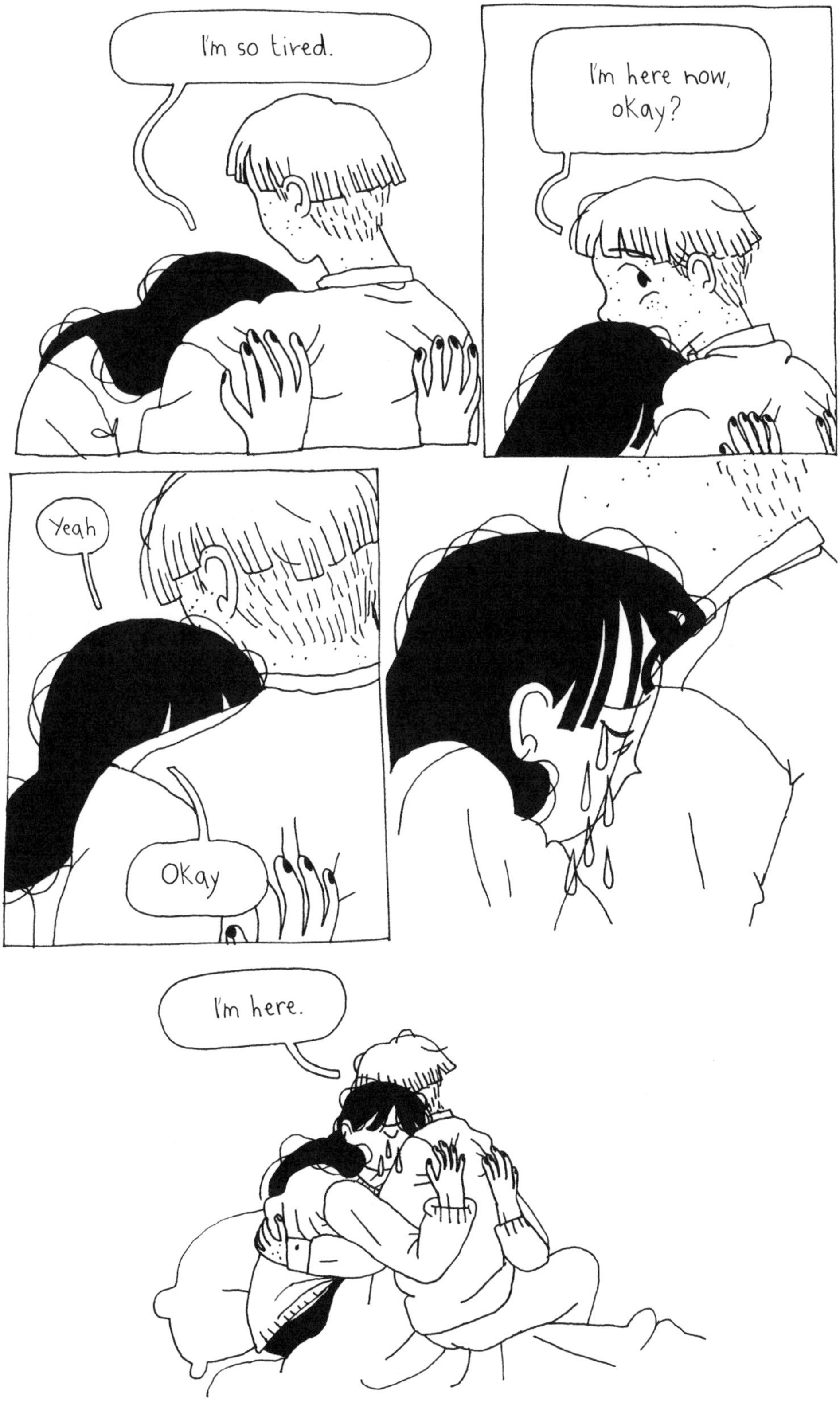
I'm so tired.
I'm here now, okay?
Yeah
Okay
I'm here.

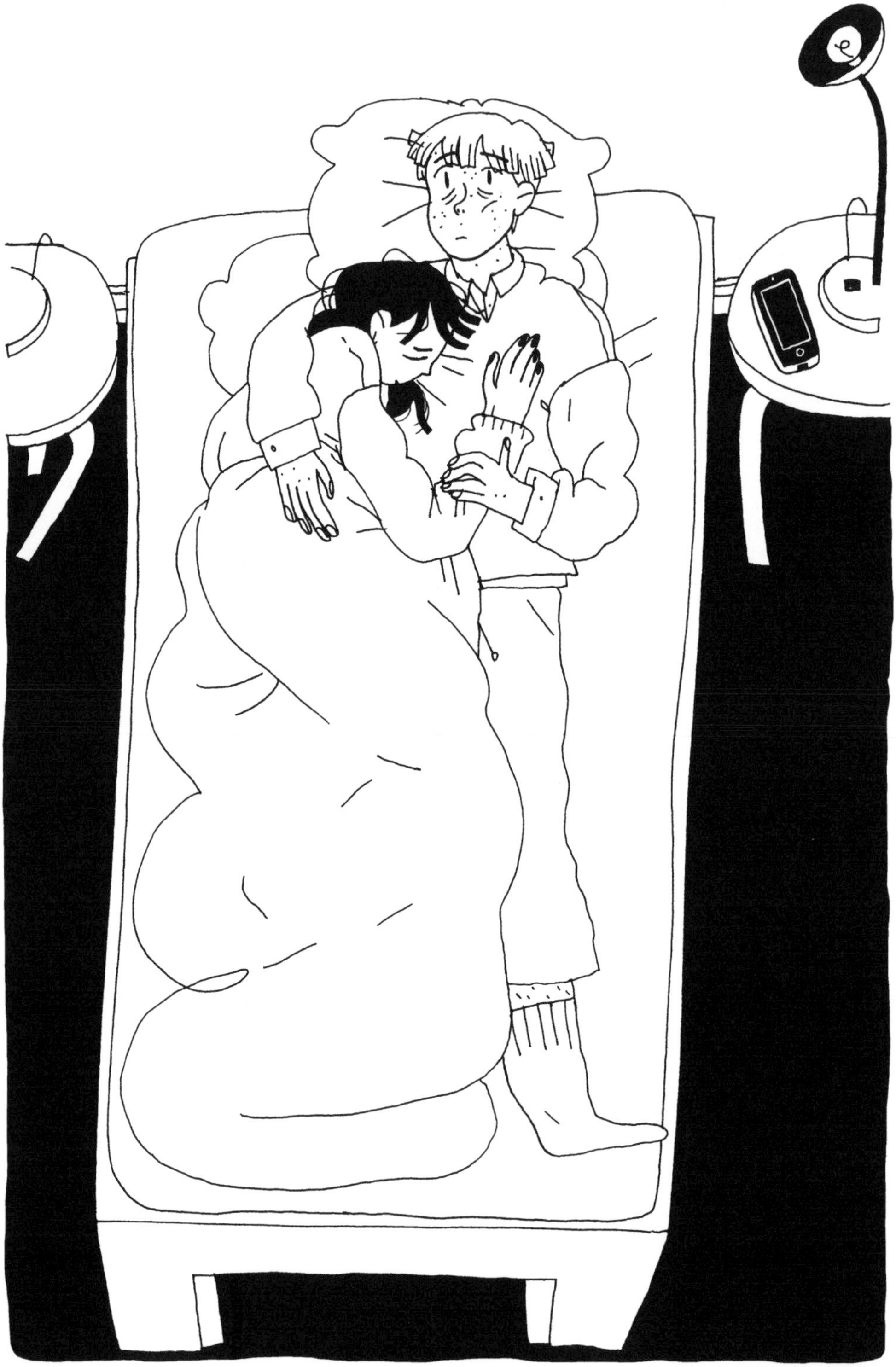

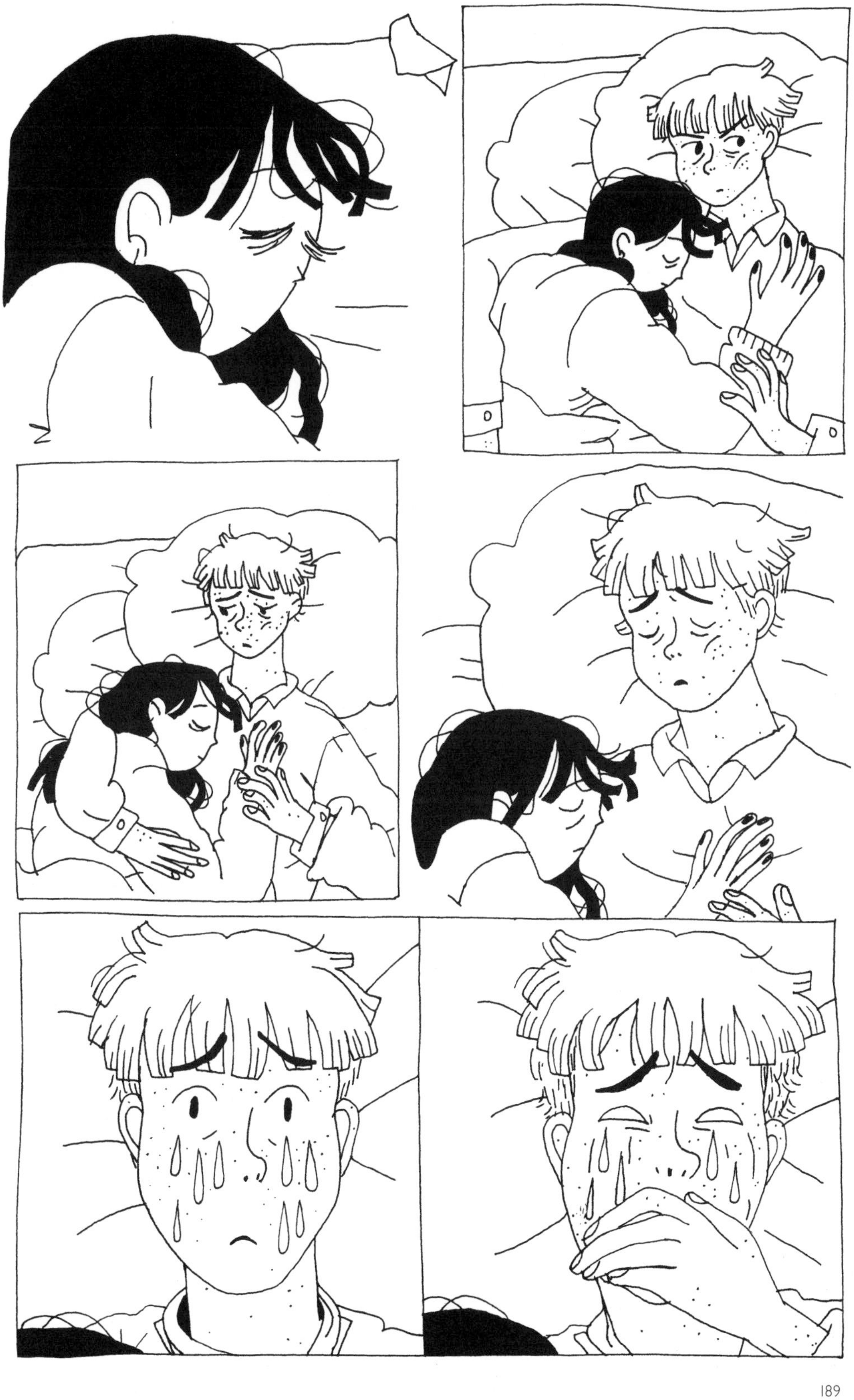

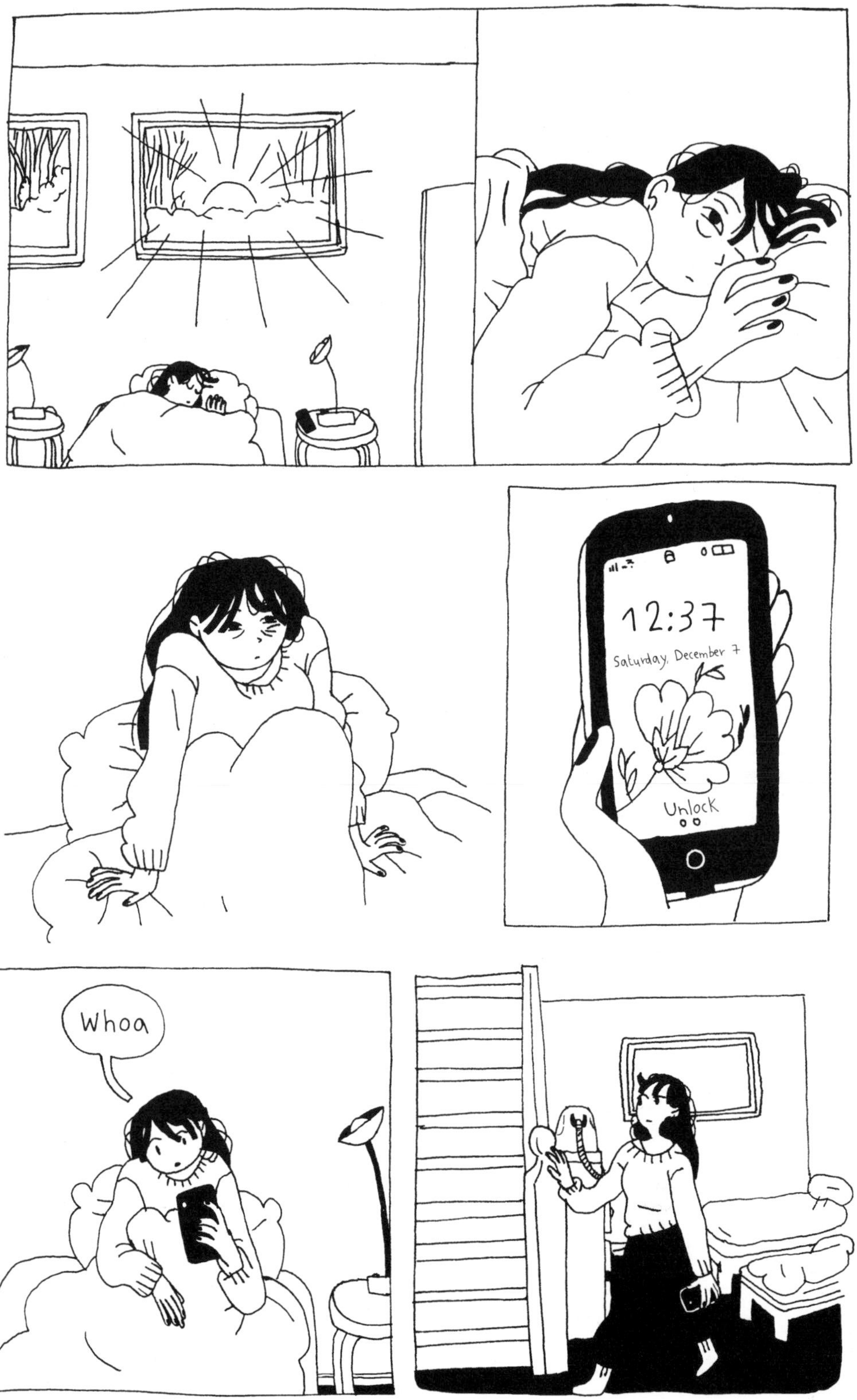
12:37
Saturday, December 7
Unlock
Whoa

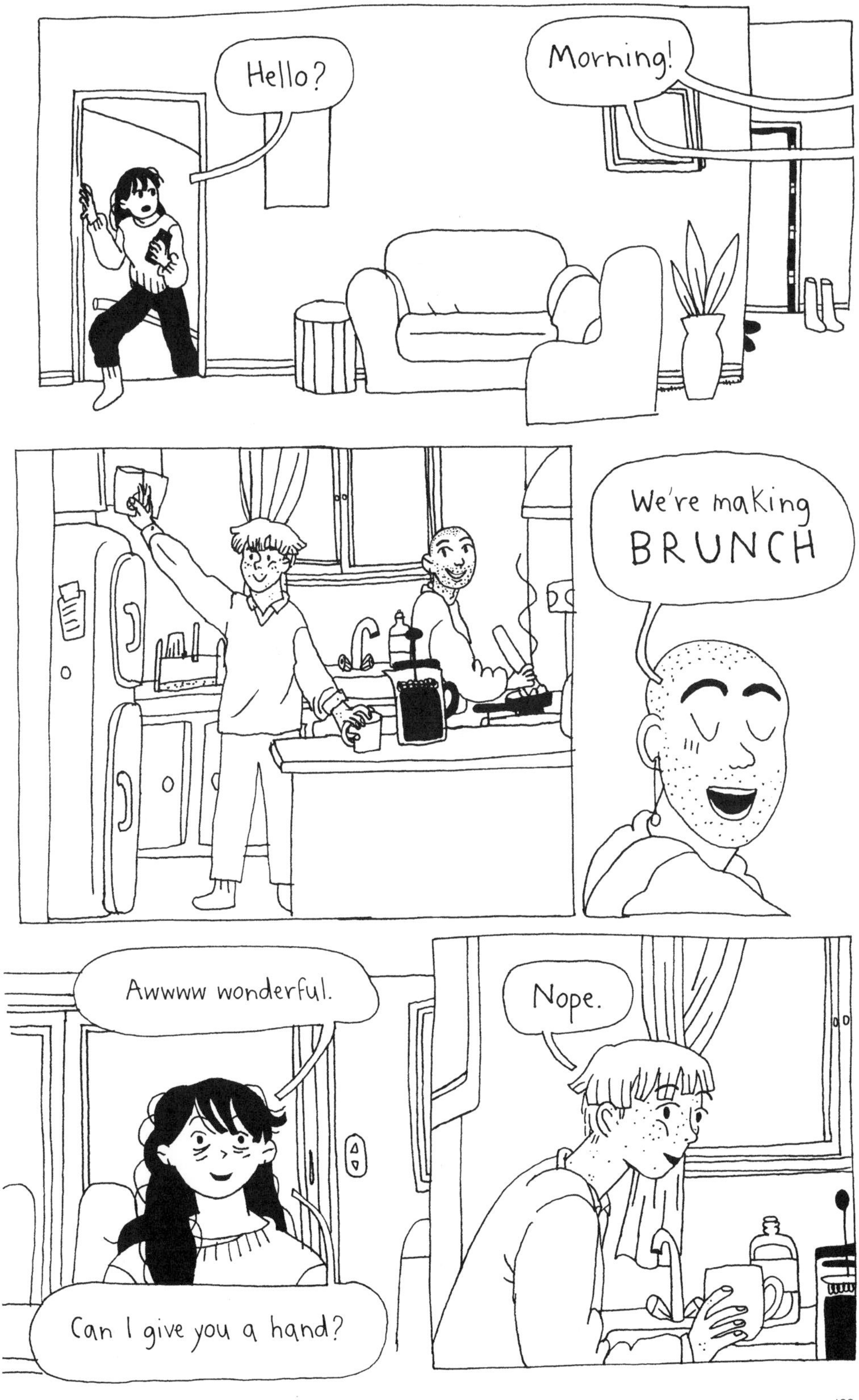
Hello?
Morning!
We're making
BRUNCH
Awwww wonderful.
Can I give you a hand?
Nope.

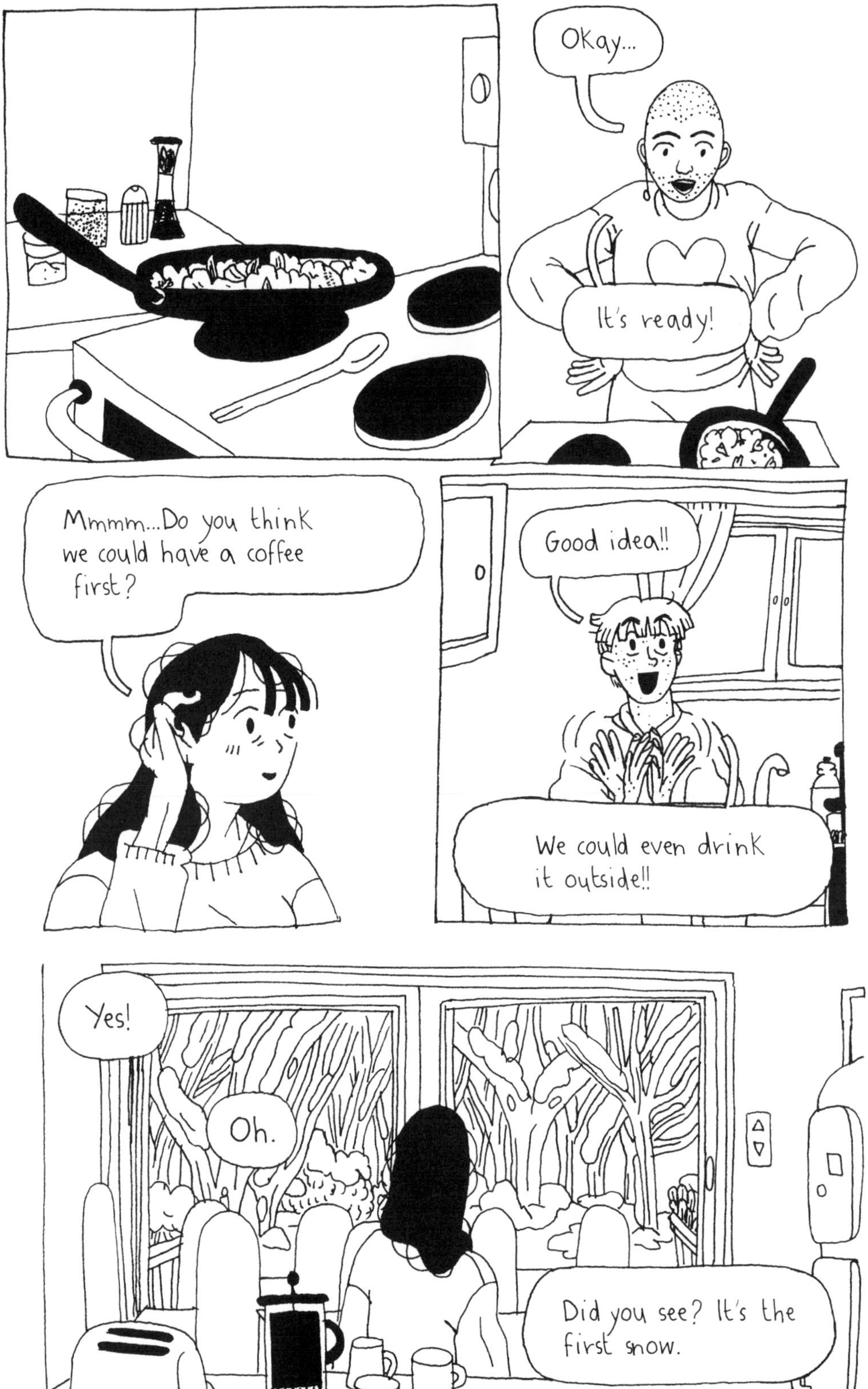
Okay...
It's ready!
Mmmm...Do you think we could have a coffee first?
Good idea!!
We could even drink it outside!!
Yes!
Oh.
Did you see? It's the first snow.

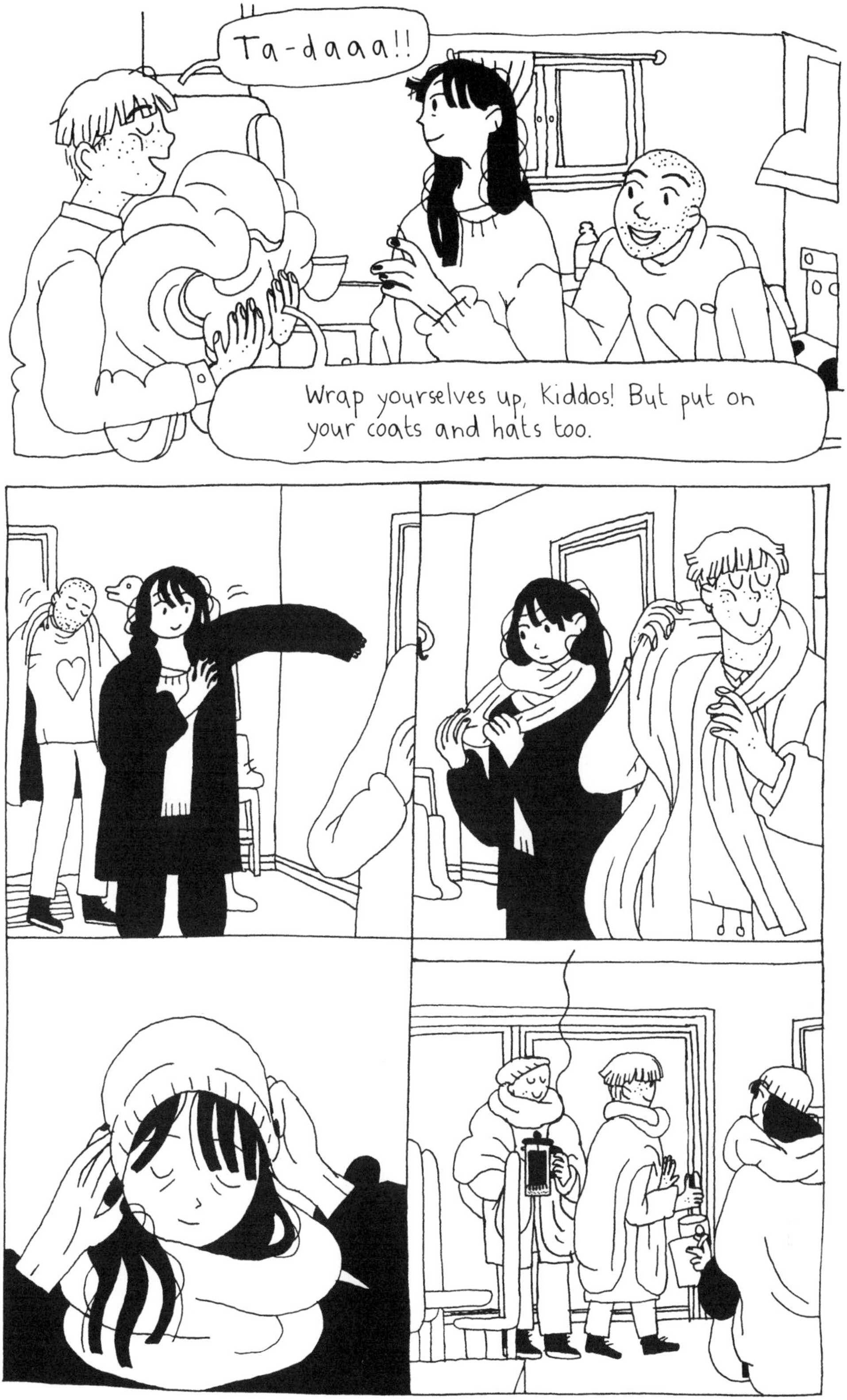

Ta-daaa!!
Wrap yourselves up, Kiddos! But put on your coats and hats too.

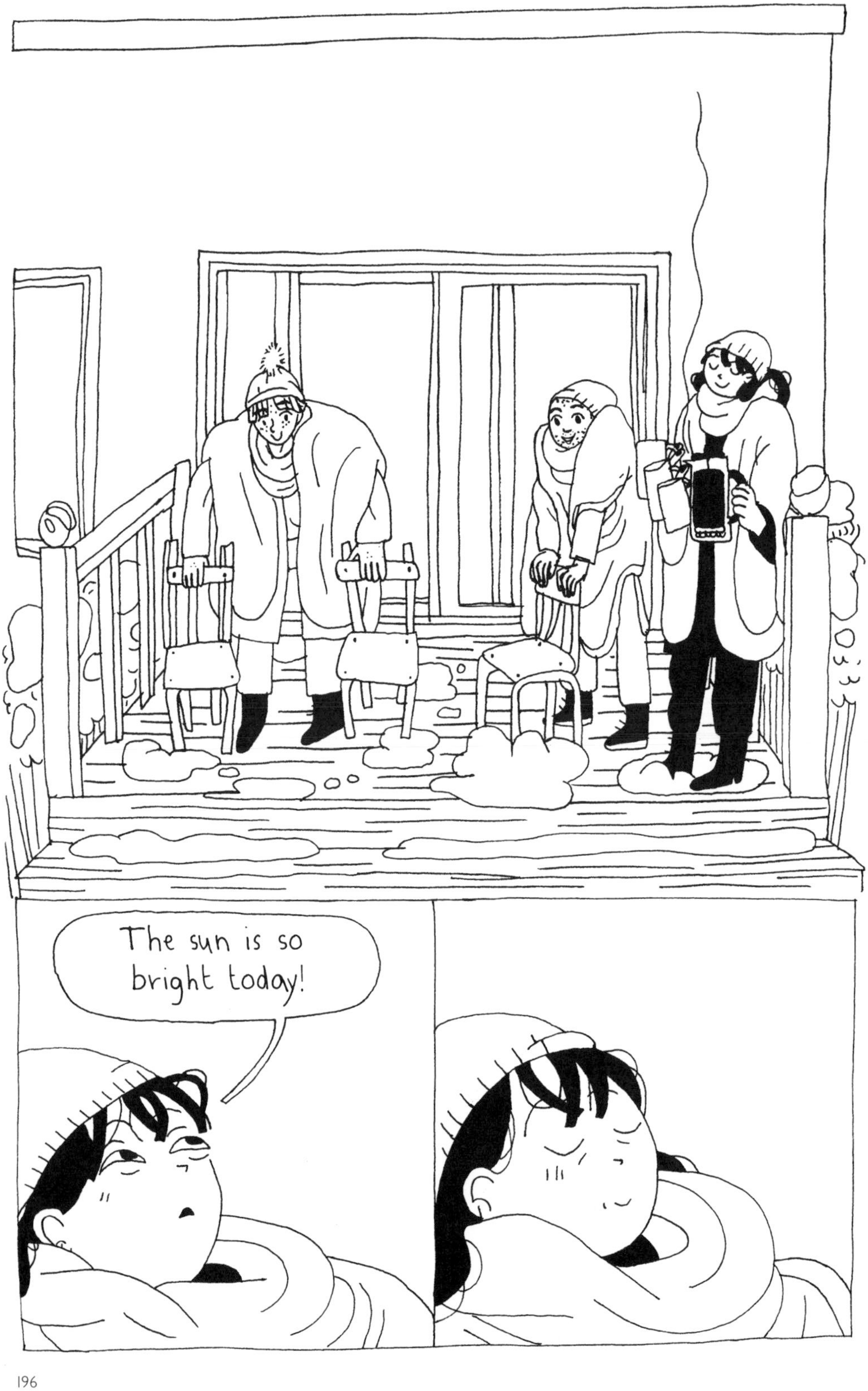
The sun is so bright today!

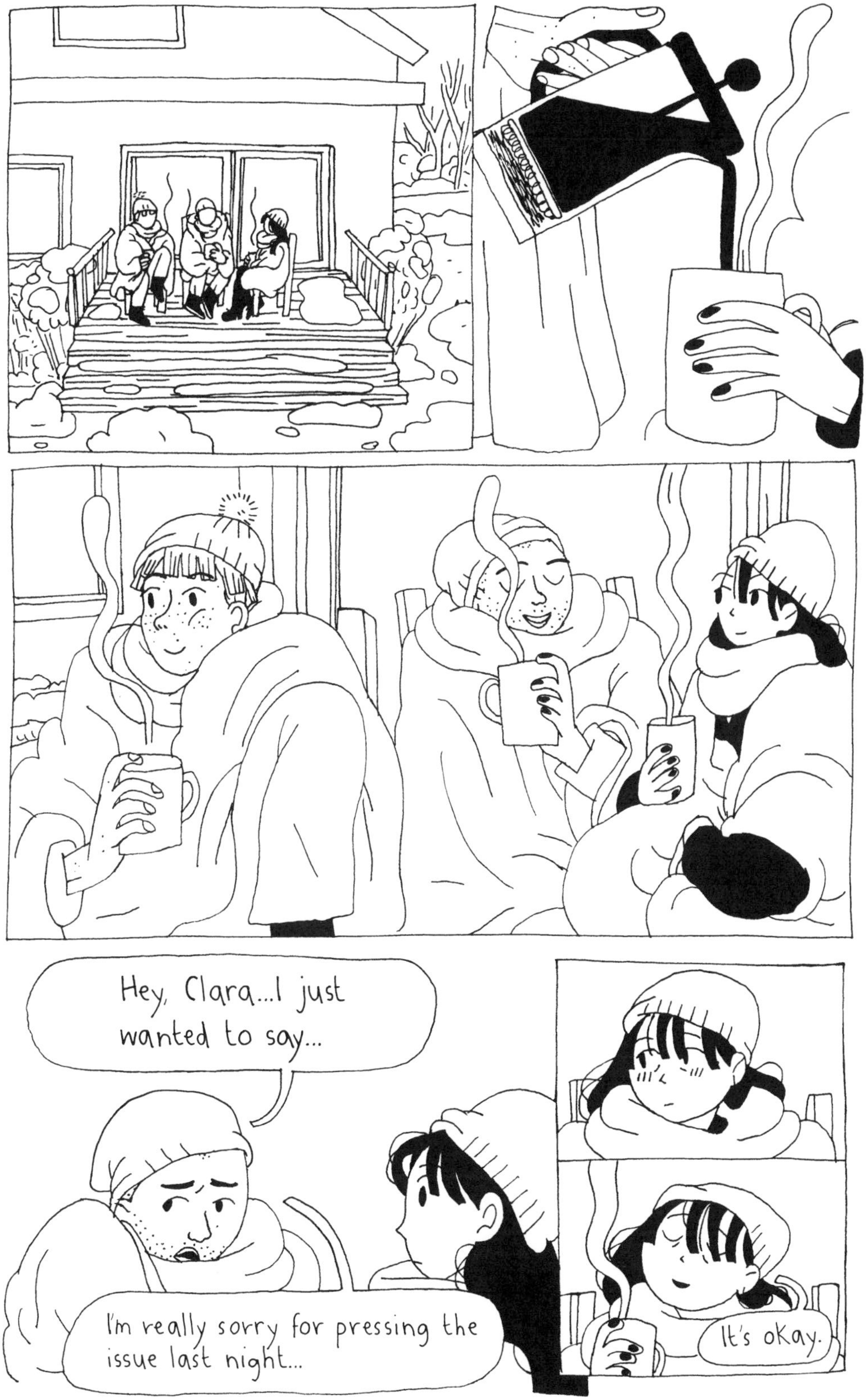
Hey, Clara...I just wanted to say...
I'm really sorry for pressing the issue last night...
It's okay.

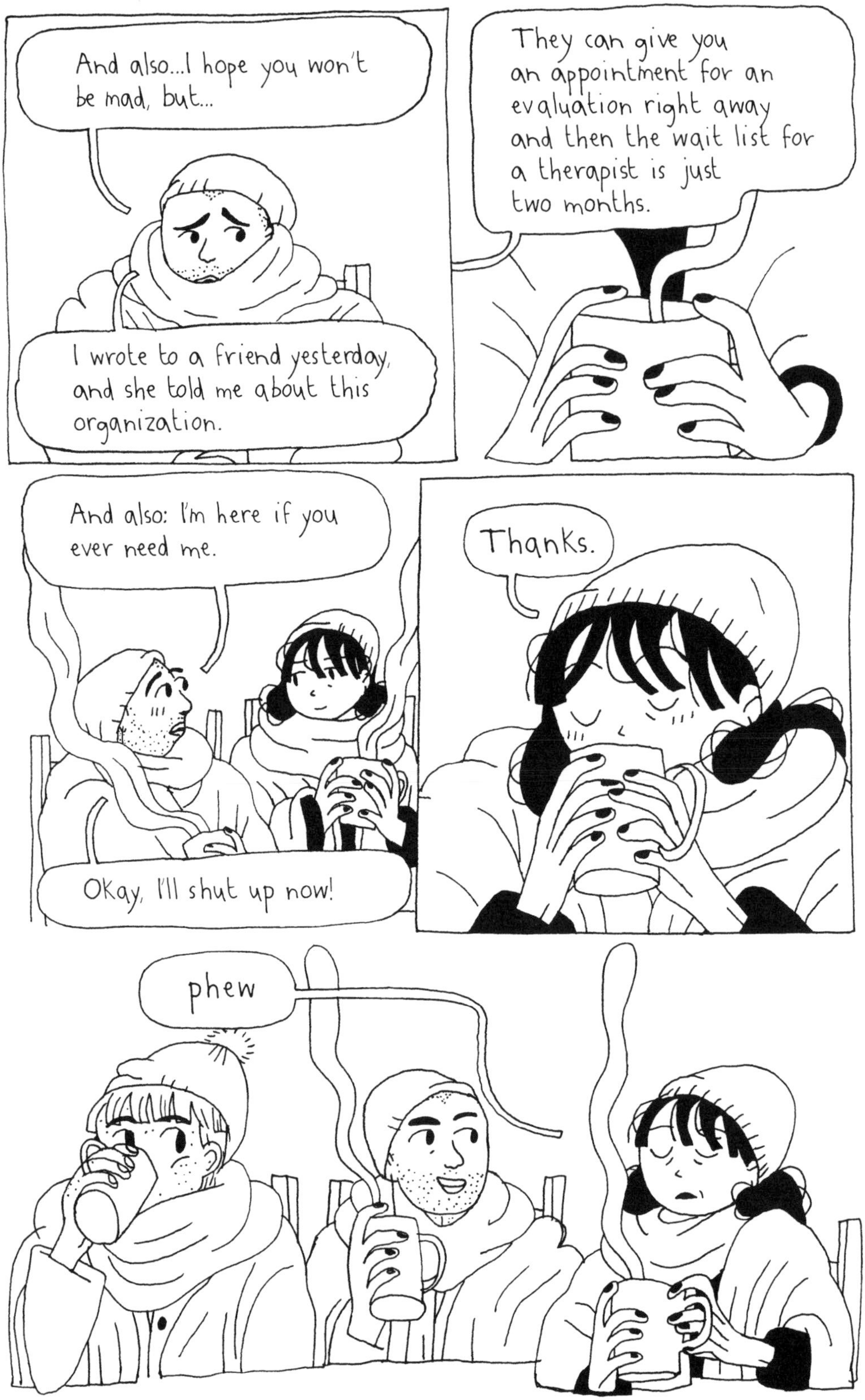

And also...I hope you won't be mad, but...
I wrote to a friend yesterday, and she told me about this organization.
They can give you an appointment for an evaluation right away and then the wait list for a therapist is just two months.
And also: I'm here if you ever need me.
Okay, I'll shut up now!
Thanks.
phew

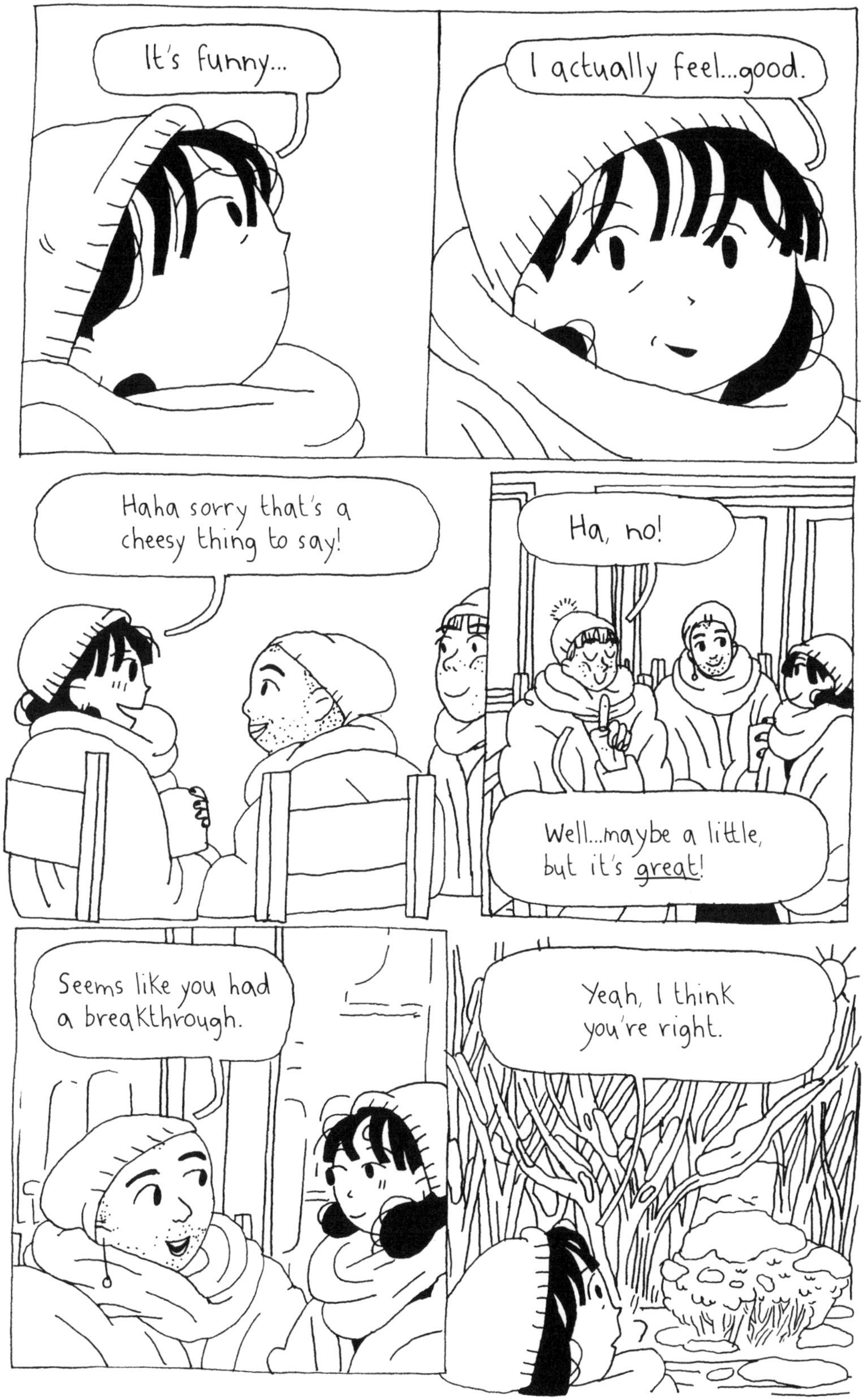
It's funny...
I actually feel...good.
Haha sorry that's a cheesy thing to say!
Ha, no!
Well...maybe a little, but it's great!
Seems like you had a breakthrough.
Yeah, I think you're right.

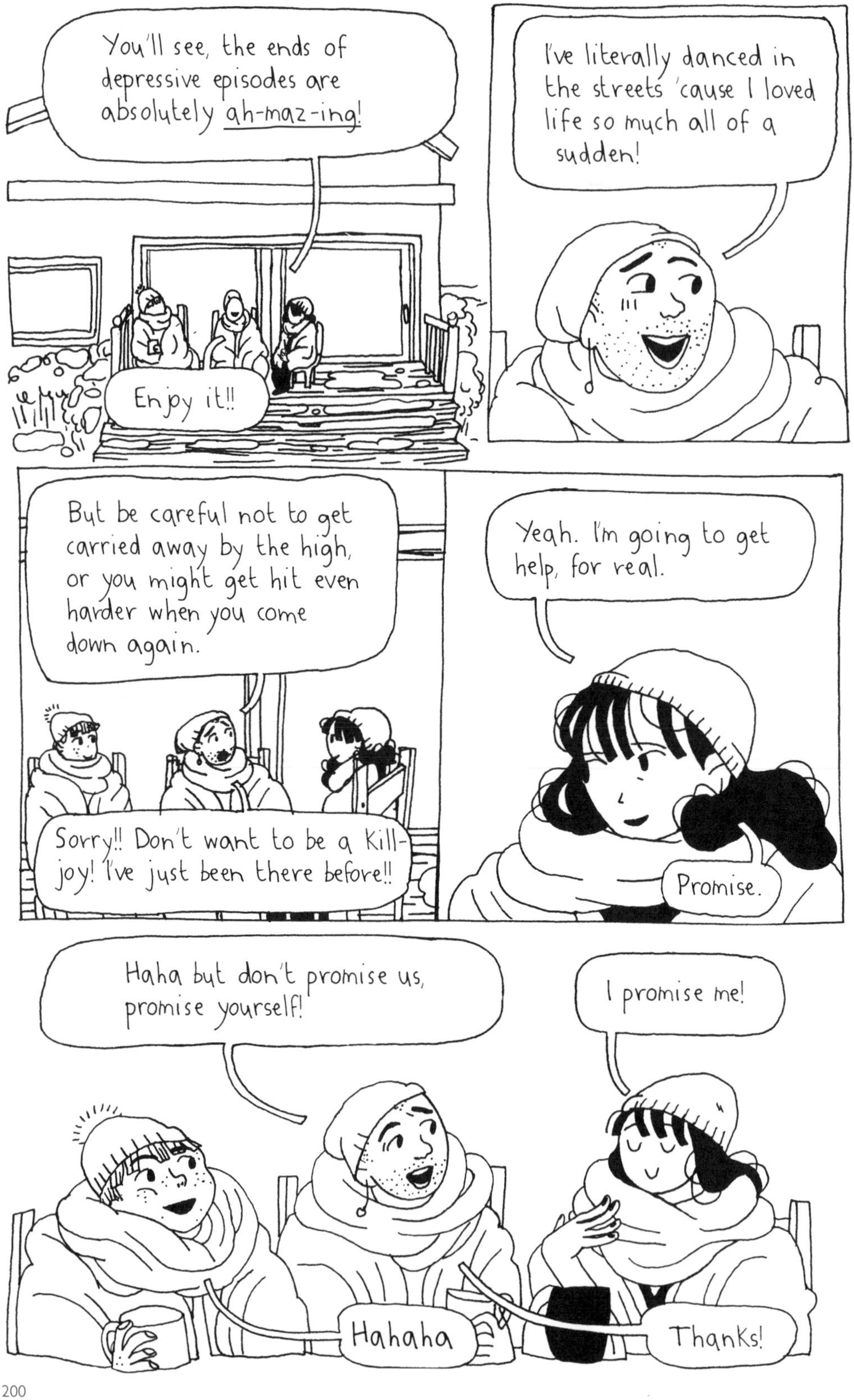
You'll see, the ends of depressive episodes are absolutely ah-maz-ing!
Enjoy it!!
I've literally danced in the streets 'cause I loved life so much all of a sudden!
But be careful not to get carried away by the high, or you might get hit even harder when you come down again.
Sorry!! Don't want to be a Kill-joy! I've just been there before!!
Yeah. I'm going to get help, for real.
Promise.
Haha but don't promise us, promise yourself!
I promise me!
Hahaha
Thanks!

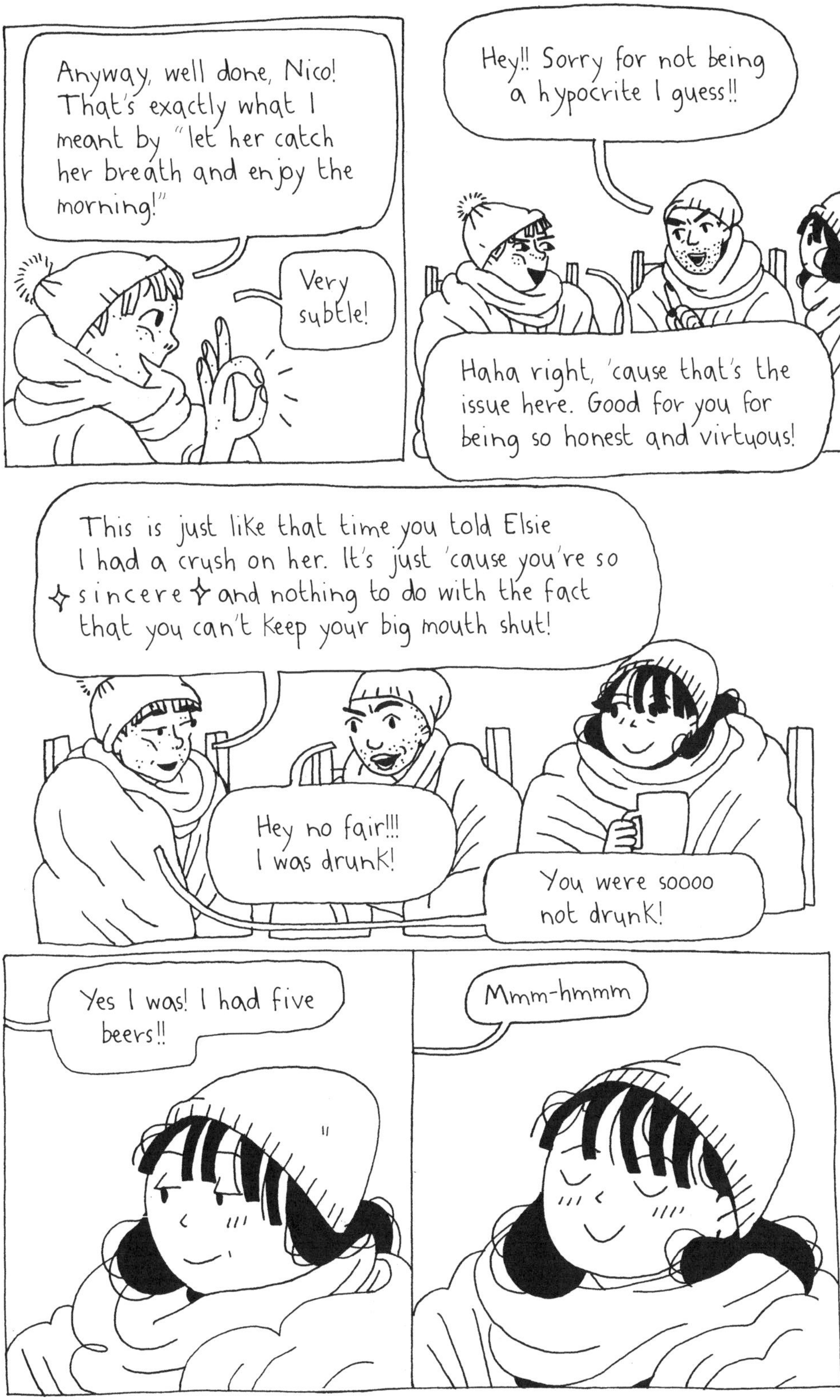
Anyway, well done, Nico! That's exactly what I meant by "let her catch her breath and enjoy the morning!"
Very subtle!
Hey!! Sorry for not being a hypocrite I guess!!
Haha right, 'cause that's the issue here. Good for you for being so honest and virtuous!
This is just like that time you told Elsie I had a crush on her. It's just 'cause you're so ✧sincere✧ and nothing to do with the fact that you can't keep your big mouth shut!
Hey no fair!!! I was drunk!
You were soooo not drunk!
Yes I was! I had five beers!!
Mmm-hmmm

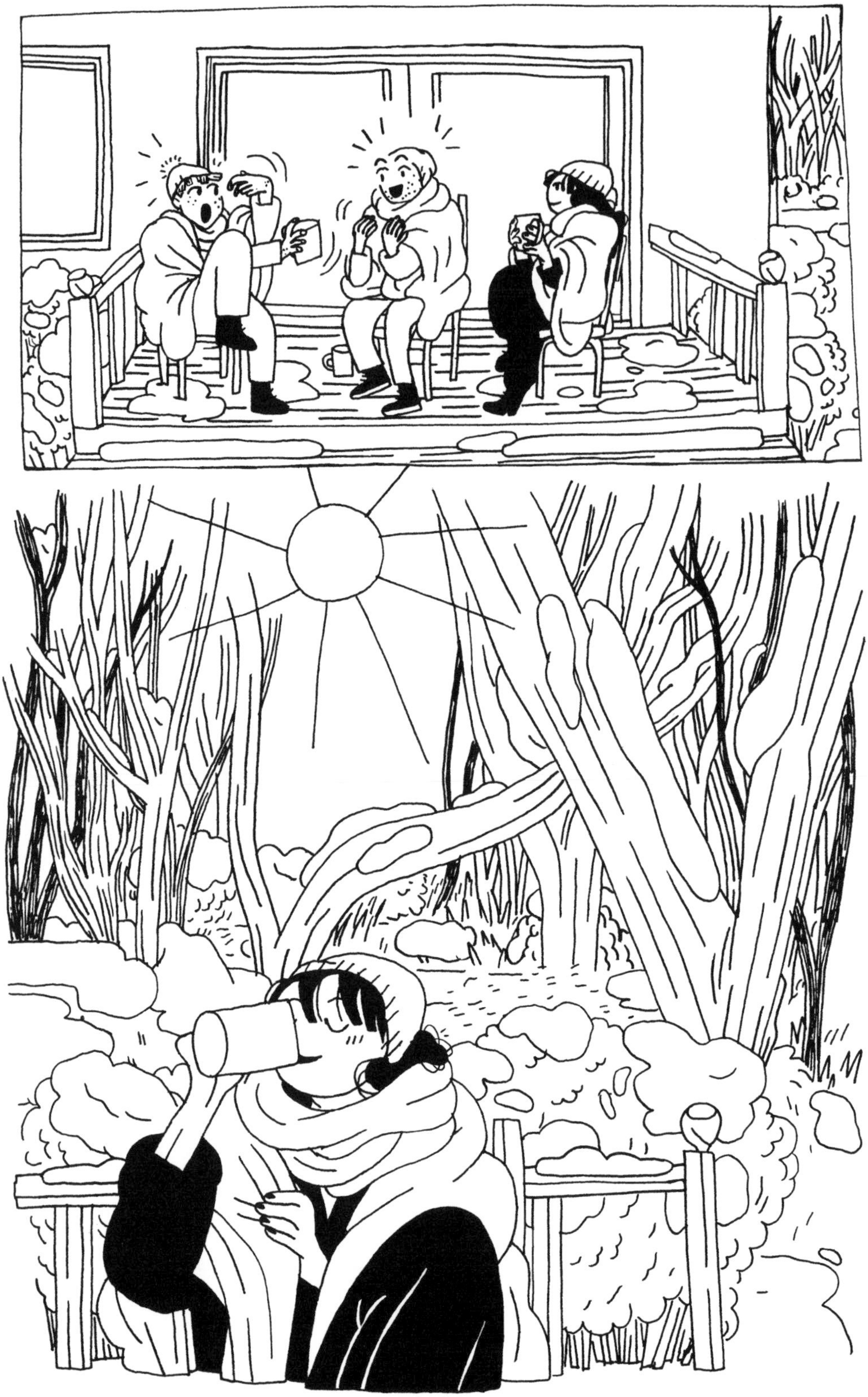

Acknowledgments

A big thank-you to Aleshia, Bronwyn, and everyone at Drawn & Quarterly for the work on the translation of this book and the English edition, and thank you so much to Pénélope, Julie, and Sophie for their words on the back.

A huge thank-you to Sophie for always having a solution when I was stuck or facing a dilemma, for reading my work many times over, and for her constant reassurance. Thank you to Juliette, Exaheva, and Sébastien for their readings, support, and opinions.

Thank you to Sorany and Jolène, Laurine, Marie, Alexa, Elosterv, Tarmasz, Julie (again!), Alice, Catherine, Evlyn, Roxane, Sorya, Poline, and Iliana for being there for me throughout this chaotic year.

Thank you, thank you, thank you to Lilian and Lulu: as always, you're my favourites. I love you and I wouldn't be much without you, so thank you sweet baby jesus for putting us in the same family. Thank you to my dearest little Mom and itsy-bitsiest Dad, I love you very much.

Thank you to CALACS Trêve pour Elles sexual violence support center and to the women in the summer 2019 Thursday night group.

Last but not least, thank you to everyone who gave this book a chance and to everyone who reads my stories.

Notes

References to other works are scattered throughout the book:

On page 42 Clara is watching episode 8, season 1 of *Sweet/Vicious*, "Back to Black" (ViacomCBS Domestic Media Networks, 2016).

The dialogue in the last panel on page 71 and the first panel of page 72 originally came from Sophie Bédard's *Les petits garçons* (Pow Pow, 2019), but has been adapted in the English.

The song that's playing on page 73 is Mitski's "Nobody" (*Be the Cowboy*, Secretly Group, 2018).

On page 80 at karaoke, Anne is singing MIKA's "Grace Kelly" (*Life in Cartoon Motion*, Universal Music Group, 2007).

On Page 84–85 Clara sings Mitski's "Last Words of a Shooting Star" (*Bury Me at Makeout Creek*, Double Double Whammy, 2014).

On page 102 Clara is watching *Shrek* (DreamWorks Pictures, 2001).

On Clara's living room wall, you can spot the US poster for Agnès Varda's
One Sings, the Other Doesn't.

The title of this book comes from My Chemical Romance's "This is How I Disappear"
(*The Black Parade*, Warner Music Group, 2006).

While writing and drawing this story, I listened to a lot of My Chemical Romance and France Gall, Mitski and Mademoiselle K, Clara Luciani's *Sainte-Victoire*, Marika Hackman's *Any Human Friend* and *I'm Not Your Man*, Miya Folick's *Premonitions*, the original *Émilie Jolie*, the *Desmoiselles de Rochefort* soundtrack by Michel Legrand and Jacques Demy, and Panic! At the Disco's *A Fever You Can't Sweat Out*.

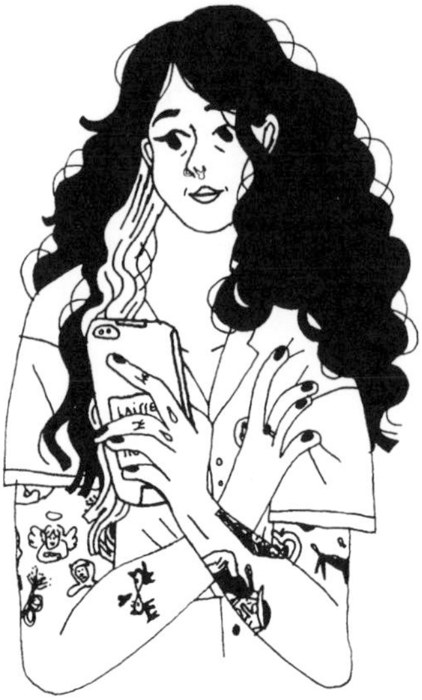
LAISSE

Mirion Malle is a French cartoonist and illustrator who lives in Montreal. She studied comics at the École Superieure des Arts Saint-Luc in Brussels before pursuing a Masters degree in Sociology specializing in Gender and Feminist studies, via Paris Diderot and the Université du Québec à Montréal. Malle has published three books. *The League of Super Feminists* is her first book to be translated into English. The French edition was nominated for the 2020 Prix Jeunesse at the Angoulême International Comics Festival.

Aleshia Jensen is a former bookseller who translates novels, non-fiction, and comics from French to English. Her translations and co-translations include graphic novels by Julie Delporte, Catherine Ocelot, Axelle Lenoir, Mirion Malle, and Pascal Girard.

Bronwyn Haslam is a translator and former bike-seller who has made Montreal her home. Her translations of poetry can be found in *Asymptote*, *Aufgabe*, and *The Capilano Review*.